W0205998

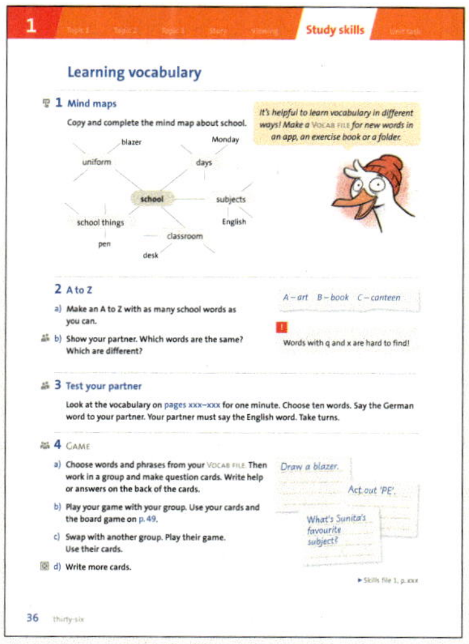

Learning vocabulary

1 Mind maps

Copy and complete the mind map about school.

It's helpful to learn vocabulary in different ways! Make a Vocab file for new words in an app, an exercise book or a folder.

2 A to Z

a) Make an A to Z with as many school words as you can.

b) Show your partner. Which words are the same? Which are different?

3 Test your partner

4 Game

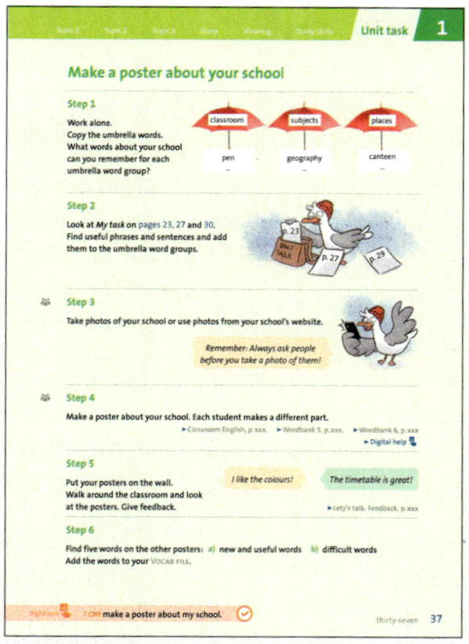

Make a poster about your school

Step 1

Step 2

Step 3

Take photos of your school or use photos from your school's website.

Step 4

Make a poster about your school. Each student makes a different part.

Step 5

Step 6

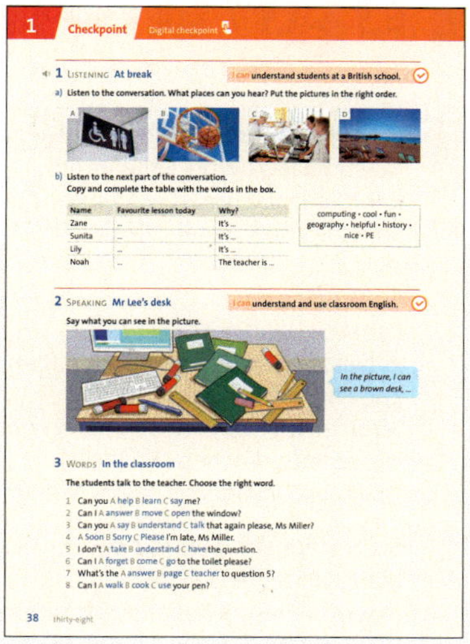

Checkpoint

1 Listening At break

2 Speaking Mr Lee's desk

3 Words In the classroom

Lern- und Arbeitstechniken

Auf der *Study skills*-Seite übst du wichtige Lern- und Arbeitstechniken, z. B. wie du neue Wörter am besten lernst.

Eine Aufgabe am Unit-Ende

In der *Unit task* erstellst du ein größeres Produkt, z. B. eine Präsentation. Dabei wendest du das Gelernte aus der Unit an.

Im *Checkpoint* wiederholst du

Hier überprüfst du, wie gut du die Lernziele der Unit schon erreicht hast.

Im Anschluss findest du ein *Text file* mit interessanten Texten zum Thema der Unit.

Diese Verweise führen dich in die *Diff bank* am Ende der Unit

▶ More help

Hilfen zu den Aufgaben

▶ Parallel exercise

einfachere Variante einer Übung

▶ More practice

weitere Übungen

▶ Challenge

weitere Übungen mit höherem Schwierigkeitsgrad

Diese Lernangebote findest du im hinteren Teil des Buches

▶ Skills file

eine Übersicht über die Lern- und Arbeitstechniken

▶ Language file

die wichtigsten Sprachregeln

▶ Wordbank

zusätzliche Wörter zu bestimmten Themen

Let's talk

Redewendungen nach wichtigen Themen und Situationen geordnet

Vocabulary

eine Liste der neuen Vokabeln einer Unit mit hilfreichen Tipps

Dictionary

alphabetische Wörterlisten zum Nachschlagen (Englisch – Deutsch, Deutsch – Englisch)

ADVANCED lighthouse 1

Im Auftrag des Verlages herausgegeben von
Martin Bastkowski, Schellerten;
Berit Schaarschmidt, Aschaffenburg sowie
Sonja Mahne, Basel; Ulrike Rath, Aachen

Erarbeitet von
Rebecca Kaplan, Mauer;
Rebecca Robb Benne, Kopenhagen;
Zoe Thorne, Royston sowie
Jennifer O'Hagan, Bristol *(Checkpoints)*;
Ulrike Rath, Aachen *(Skills file)*;
Dr. Philip Devlin und Ralph Williams *(Unit 6)*

In Zusammenarbeit mit der Englischredaktion
Klaus Unger (Projektleitung), Jutta Seuren (koordinierende Redakteurin), Katrin Heinecke, Lisa Ahmadi, Doreen Arnold, Michael Dunkel, Franziska Gräbe, Karin Wedepohl sowie
Ingrid Raspe, Düsseldorf *(Vocabulary, Dictionary E-D)*

Beratende Mitwirkung
Nikolas Grote, Hannover; Christina McCrum, Köln; Sandra Mercatoris, Ilvesheim; Stefanie Kelly, Villingen-Schwenningen; Annette Kramer, Kassel; Lara-Sophie Räuschel, Hamburg; Christina Sieber, Schorndorf; Andriana Zaroti, Krefeld sowie
Vertr.-Prof. Dr. Christian Ludwig, Berlin;
Prof. Dr. Bernd Rüschoff, Essen;
Prof. Dr. Michaela Sambanis, Berlin

Medienmanagement
Silke Kirchhoff

Illustrationen
Harald Ardeias, Schelklingen; Irina Zinner, Hamburg

Fotos
Anja Poehlmann, Brighton
Für die freundliche Unterstützung danken wir der *Varndean School, Brighton.*

Umschlaggestaltung
Rosendahl, Berlin

Layoutkonzept
Klein & Halm, Berlin

Designberatung
Ungermeyer, Berlin

Layout und technische Umsetzung
Straive

Druck
Mohn Media Mohndruck, Gütersloh

PEFC
PEFC/04-31-1033

PEFC zertifiziert
Dieses Produkt stammt aus nachhaltig bewirtschafteten Wäldern und kontrollierten Quellen.

www.pefc.de

www.cornelsen.de

Soweit in diesem Lehrwerk Personen fotografisch abgebildet sind und ihnen von der Redaktion fiktive Namen, Berufe, Dialoge und Ähnliches zugeordnet oder diese Personen in bestimmte Kontexte gesetzt werden, dienen diese Zuordnungen und Darstellungen ausschließlich der Veranschaulichung und dem besseren Verständnis des Buchinhaltes.

Dieses Werk berücksichtigt die Regeln der reformierten Rechtschreibung und Zeichensetzung.

Die Webseiten Dritter, deren Internetadressen in diesem Lehrwerk angegeben sind, wurden vor Drucklegung sorgfältig geprüft. Der Verlag übernimmt keine Gewähr für die Aktualität und den Inhalt dieser Seiten oder solcher, die mit ihnen verlinkt sind.

Die *Cornelsen Lernen App* ist eine fakultative Ergänzung zu *Lighthouse Advanced*, die die inhaltliche Arbeit begleitet und unterstützt. Als solche unterliegt sie nicht der Genehmigungspflicht.

© 2023 Cornelsen Verlag GmbH, Berlin

Das Werk und seine Teile sind urheberrechtlich geschützt. Jede Nutzung in anderen als den gesetzlich zugelassenen Fällen bedarf der vorherigen schriftlichen Einwilligung des Verlages.

Hinweis zu §§ 60 a, 60 b UrhG: Weder das Werk noch seine Teile dürfen ohne eine solche Einwilligung an Schulen oder in Unterrichts- und Lehrmedien (§ 60 b Abs. 3 UrhG) vervielfältigt, insbesondere kopiert oder eingescannt, verbreitet oder in ein Netzwerk eingestellt oder sonst öffentlich zugänglich gemacht oder wiedergegeben werden.
Dies gilt auch für Intranets von Schulen.

Alle Drucke dieser Auflage sind inhaltlich unverändert und können im Unterricht nebeneinander verwendet werden.

1. Auflage, 1. Druck 2023
ISBN 9783060362646 broschiert

1. Auflage, 1. Druck 2023
ISBN 9783060358373 gebunden

ISBN 9783060345847 E-Book

ADVANCED lighthouse 1

Cornelsen

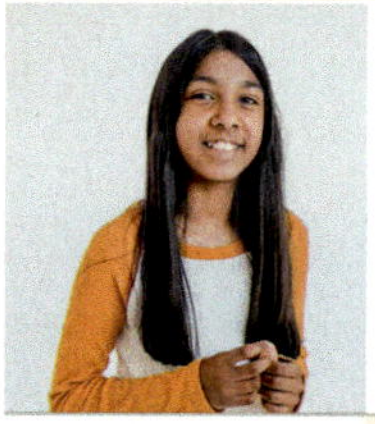

L Listening · R Reading · S Speaking · W Writing · M Mediation · V Viewing · IC Intercultural competence · MK Medienkompetenz · LS Life skills · Voc Vocabulary · G Grammar

Unit 2
My family and home

Inhalt

Unit 4 Where I live

L Listening · R Reading · S Speaking · W Writing · M Mediation · V Viewing · IC Intercultural competence · MK Medienkompetenz · LS Life skills · Voc Vocabulary · G Grammar

Inhalt

Unit 5 Enjoy!

L Listening · R Reading · S Speaking · W Writing · M Mediation · V Viewing · IC Intercultural competence · MK Medienkompetenz · LS Life skills · Voc Vocabulary · G Grammar

Anhang

Die Angebote des Schulbuchs sind nicht obligatorisch zu bearbeiten. Die Auswahl der Übungen und Übungsteile richtet sich nach den Schwerpunkten des schulinternen Curriculums.

Hello!

Nice to meet you

1 Hello, Scout

Look at pictures 1–6. Right or wrong?

1 Scout is a seagull.
2 Scout is white and green.
3 Scout is hungry.
4 Scout is 7 years old.
5 Scout is from Hove.
6 Scout is clever.

Right!

Wrong!

2 What about you?

a) **Look at picture 4. Listen and repeat.**

b) **Now ask and answer about you.**

► Numbers, p. 307 ► Wordbank 1, p. 214

3 Hello, class

WALK AROUND Find out about other students.

1 *Hello! I'm ... What's your name?*

2 *Hi! I'm ... I'm ... (years old). How old are you?*

3 *I'm ... (years old). I'm from ... Where are you from?*

4 *I'm from ... (too). I like ... What about you?*

5 *I like ... Nice to meet you!*

6 *Nice to meet you too. Bye!*

Digital quiz I can **say hello.**

Goodbye, holidays!

1 In the picture

a) Look at the picture. Listen, find and point.

b) Find, point and say.

▸ Wordbank 2, p. 214

Scout the seagull • Leo's mum • Ben's dad • two numbers • three animals • four colours • three drinks • two things to eat • three other things

Here's Scout.
And here's Leo's mum.
I can see a dog / ...

c) Look at the picture for 30 seconds again. Close your books. What can you remember?

I remember Scout and a dog.

I remember Scout.

I remember Scout and a dog and a ...

2 Song Scout's song

a) Listen and act out the song. Then listen again, act and sing.

Hi, hello, nice to meet you today.
How are you? I'm fine, I'm OK.
I live here in Brighton, right by the sea.
It's a nice day to meet
And to find something to eat.
Ooh, what's that?
(Look out! It's Scout!)
Wheeeeeeee!

I'm a seagull, I'm Scout the seagull,
Just look how high
in the sky I can fly.
That's where I like to be.
I'm a seagull, I'm Scout the seagull,
Just look how high in the sky I can fly
Over the sea.

b) Ask and answer.

A: *Ali, how are you?* B: ☺ *I'm fine / OK. Mia, how are you?* C: ☹ *I'm not so good. Ole, how …*

► Workbook, p. 8

Digital quiz I can talk about a picture.

About me

1 My favourite animal

a) What animals can you see? Match the words to the pictures.

In picture 1, I can see ...

In picture 2, there is ...

1

2

3

4

a cat • a dog •
an elephant • a horse •
a lion • a monkey •
a parrot • a snake

5

6

7

8

b) Listen. Write six animals from a).

c) Mime, draw or make an animal noise. Your partner says the animal.

It's a dog!

d) GAME Stand in a circle. One student says their favourite animal. Students with the same favourite animal change places.

► Wordbank 3, p. 215

My favourite animal is a fish.

► Workbook, p. 9

2 My hobbies and sports

a) Look at the code.
Write Scout's hobbies and sports.

a	e	i	o	u
♋	♏	♓	☐	◆

f☐☐tb♋ll

l♓st♏n♓ng t☐ m◆s♓c

dr♋w♓ng

d♋nc♓ng

sw♓mm♓ng

t♋k♓ng ph☐t☐s

b) DOUBLE CIRCLE Think about your free time. Talk to a partner.
One circle moves to find a new partner.

My favourite hobby / sport is ...
What about you?

🙂 😍 *I like / I love ... too.*

☹️ *I don't like ...*
My favourite hobby / sport is ...

▸ Wordbank 4, p. 216

3 My favourite things

a) Listen and point.

b) Look at the picture again.
Read 1–8 and say what it is.

1 My favourite thing is small, new and black.
2 It's big and blue.
3 This thing is small and gold.
4 I love it – it's big and silver.
5 I can play music with it.
6 It's cool and white.
7 This thing is small and old. I read it.
8 It's red and I put things in it.

▸ Workbook, pages 9–10

4 Song My favourites

a) Listen. Then listen again and sing.

b) Make a new song or poem with your favourite animals, colours, numbers, things and hobbies.

▶ Wordbanks 1–4, pages 214–216
▶ Wordbanks 8–9, p. 220

What's your favourite animal?
My favourite animal is a kangaroo.
What's your favourite colour?
My favourite colour is blue. What about you?

I like silver and I don't like gold.
Ten is my favourite number 'cause I'm ten years old.
I like my bike and I love my football,
But my scooter is my favourite thing of all.

What's your favourite hobby?
Dancing is my favourite thing to do.
What's your favourite sport?
I like swimming too. What about you?

5 Scout's top six

Write the correct words.

animal • colour • film • hobby • sport • thing

My favourite ... is a fish.
My favourite ... is orange.
My favourite ... is swimming.
My favourite ... is my hat.
My favourite ... is *Finding Nemo*.
My favourite ... is singing.

6 My top six

a) Write your top six.

b) Walk around Ask and answer the six questions. Who has the same favourite things?

What's your favourite film / ... ?

My favourite film ... is ...

🙂 *I like that too.*

☹ *Sorry, I don't like that. My favourite film / ... is ...*

Im Dossier kannst du deine wichtigen und schönen Arbeiten sammeln.

c) Put your top six in your Dossier.

▶ Workbook, p. 10

Digital quiz I can talk about what I like.

Ready for school

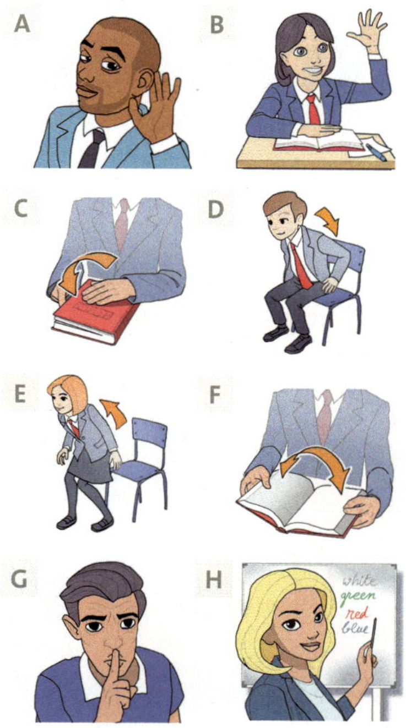

1 Listen, please!

a) Listen. Point to the correct pictures.

b) Match the speech bubbles to the pictures.

1 Quiet, please. *2 Listen.* *3 Stand up.*

4 Sit down. *5 Look at the board.* *6 Open your books.*

7 Put your hand up. *8 Close your books.*

c) Listen. Do the actions.

d) Now you're the teacher: Read a speech bubble and the students do the actions.

2 Song The school song

a) Listen.
Then listen again and sing.

b) Complete the song.

Ready, steady, 1, 2, 3.
(1) ... and repeat after me.
First (2) ... down and then stand up.
Don't forget, (3) ... your hand up.
(4) ... your book at page four.
(5) ... at me, look at the board.
(6) ..., please, don't make a sound.
(7) ... the question, write it down.
Quick, put all your (8) ... away.
Now it's break, it's time to (9) ...

3 My new English book

Find these pictures of Scout. What part of the book is she in?

A B C D E F G

► Workbook, p. 11

Digital quiz I can understand classroom English.

Unit 1
My new school

Name	Sunita Chandra
How old?	A 10 B 11 C 12
Hobby	A coding B drawing C reading
Sport	A badminton B dancing C yoga

Name	Noah Williams
How old?	A 10 B 11 C 12
Hobby	A listening to music B reading C taking photos
Sport	A basketball B football C walking

1 LISTENING **Four students at Varndean School**

a) BEFORE YOU LISTEN **Complete Scout's sentences. Then tell a partner about you.**

Hello, I'm ... I'm ... years old. I like ...
My favourite hobby is ... My favourite sport is ...
What about you?

b) **Look at the pictures of Sunita, Noah, Zane and Lily from Brighton and read about them. Then listen. Write A, B or C for the answers.**

Nach dieser Unit kann ich …

- ◯ mich im Klassenzimmer auf Englisch verständigen
- ◯ meinen Stundenplan schreiben
- ◯ meine Schule beschreiben
- ◯ Vokabeln auf verschiedene Arten üben

Unit task

- ◯ ein Poster über meine Schule anfertigen

3

Name	Zane Adebayo
How old?	A 10 B 11 C 12
Hobby	A coding B cooking C listening to music
Sport	A basketball B football C swimming

4

Name	Lily Hall
How old?	A 10 B 11 C 12
Hobby	A drawing B reading C listening to music
Sport	A dancing B parkour C yoga

c) **Choose Sunita, Noah, Zane or Lily. What's the same or different to you?**

Sunita is … years old. I'm … too. / But I'm …
I like … too. / I don't like …
Sunita's favourite hobby is … My favourite hobby is …
Sunita's favourite sport is … My …

► Workbook, p. 12

Digital quiz I can understand students at a British school.

Time for school

1 Listening At school

a) Before you listen **Look at the photo. Point and say the names of the students:**
This girl is Sunita. This boy is ...

b) **Listen to two conversations. Write the correct names.**

1 ... and ... are friends.
2 ... is busy and tired.
3 ... is happy about the school tie.
4 ... is scared of the school.
5 ... and ... like the uniform.
6 ... and ... are in the same class.

Good to know

British schools have a school uniform, often with a blazer and a tie.

► Background file, p. 31

2 Speaking School uniform

Say your opinion of the school uniform.

I like / I don't like the uniform.
The uniform is nice / cool / great / horrible.
I like / I don't like the colour.

► Workbook, p. 13

3 WORDS Sunita's desk

a) Look at the picture of Sunita's desk, listen and point.

b) Listen to the words and repeat.

4 LOOKING AT LANGUAGE *a/an*

Complete the list of Sunita's things with *a* or *an*. Find the rule.

a	*an*
... rubber	... art folder
...	...

art folder • English book • exercise book • glue stick • orange • pencil sharpener • rubber • ruler

► More practice 1+2, p. 44 ► Language file 1+2, pages 202–203

5 I can remember

Close your books.
What things from 3a) can you remember?

I can remember a pink ...

I can remember an orange ...

► Workbook, pages 13–14

6 SPEAKING Different desks

Partner A: Look at Sunita's desk on p. 21.
Partner B: Look at Noah's desk on p. 44.
What nine things are different?

a / one pencil

two pencils

In my picture, I can see an orange.

In my picture, I can't see an orange.

▶ More practice 3, p. 45
▶ Language file 3, p. 203

7 READING Hello, class 7C!

a) **Read and find the students in the picture.**

Mr Lee Hello, class 7C! I'm Mr Lee, your class teacher and English teacher.
Emma Sorry I'm late, Mr Lee.
Mr Lee OK, please sit down. Don't be late again.
Ravi Can I open the window, please?
Mr Lee Yes, you can.
Layla Can I go to the toilet?
Mr Lee Yes, you can.
Now please take your pencil case and your exercise book.
Mel Can you say that again, Mr Lee?
Mr Lee Yes. Please take your pencil case and your exercise book. Don't talk!
Now – let's start!

b) **Act out the conversation in a).**

Good to know

In England the first year of secondary school is year 7.

▶ More practice 4, p. 45 ▶ Challenge 1, p. 45
▶ Workbook, p. 14

8 SPEAKING In class

a) Match what Noah says on the left to Sunita's answers on the right.

1 What page is it?
2 I don't understand exercise 1.
3 Can you help me with question 2?
4 What's the answer to question 3?
5 Can I use your book?
6 Thanks.

a Yes, here you are.
b The answer is b.
c It's page 9.
d You're welcome.
e Let's ask Mr Lee.
f Yes, I can.

b) Listen and check.

c) Listen to the questions in a). Say the answers.

d) WALK AROUND Practise the questions and answers in a) with different partners.

My task

9 My classroom questions and answers

a) Write new questions and answers: Change the parts in blue in 8a). Practise with your partner.

b) Present your questions and answers to another pair.

► Workbook, p. 15

Digital quiz I can understand and use classroom English.

My timetable

1 The English lessons

a) Read the conversation.

Mr Lee 7C, please look at your timetable. Can you see the English lessons? They're in room 2.
Lily Mr Lee, look at Tim. He's asleep. I think he's tired.
Mr Lee You're right, Lily. And Emma - she's tired too. Emma and Tim, I know you're tired, you're at a new school. We're all tired! But it's time for break soon. It's in five minutes.
Tim I'm sorry, Mr Lee.

b) Write the things or people.

1 They're in room 2.
2 He's asleep.
3 She's tired.
4 It's in five minutes.
5 "I'm the teacher."

2 People and things in class

a) Who or what can you see in the pictures? *I can see ...*

b) Match the people and things to the correct words in the box.

he • she • it • they (2x)

1 

2 

3 

4 

5 

▶ Digital help ▶ More practice 5, p. 46 ▶ Language file 4, p. 204

3 Looking at language *to be*

Erklär-film

Read the conversation in 1 again. Copy and complete the table.

long form	short form	long form	short form
I am	...	we are	...
you are	...	you are	...
he is	...		
she is	...	they are	...
it is	...		

▶ Language file 6, p. 205
▶ Workbook, pages 15–16

4 Messages

▶ Parallel exercise, p. 46

a) Complete the messages from Noah and his mum. Use short forms.

Hi, Mum! I like the classroom. (1) ... big. I like Mr Lee, my teacher, too. (2) ... cool. And I like my new friends. (3) ... nice. ☺

Great! (4) ... lucky, Noah! Varndean School is big, but (5) ... a good school. Sorry, (6) ... busy now. See you! ☺

▶ More practice 6, p. 46 ▶ More practice 7, p. 47

b) Write a note about you and your day to your English teacher. The sentences in the boxes can help you. Give the note to your teacher.

Dear Mr / Ms ...

English is fun.
I like the classroom.
I'm eleven.
You're nice.
We listen to music in the break.
My day is busy / great.
My favourite hobby is cooking.
I'm from ...
I'm tired / happy.
I have a new friend. She's / He's great.

Yours
(name)

5 Song Days of the week

a) Words Look at the days. Listen to the song and put them in the correct order.

Thursday
Tuesday
Sunday
Friday
Monday
Wednesday
Saturday

1 Monday 2 ...

b) Now sing the song.

c) Complete the sentence:

My favourite day of the week is ...

▶ Workbook, p. 16

6 Words School subjects

Good to know

At registration teachers check: Are all the students at school?

a) Look at the timetable for 7C. Which words can you understand? German and other languages can help you.

Lesson	Time	Monday	Tuesday	Wednesday	Thursday	Friday
	8:45 – 9:05	registration and assembly				
1	9:05 – 9:55	English	art	French	computing	
2	9:55 – 10:45	English	maths	French	computing	
	10:45 – 11:05	break				
3	11:05 – 11:55	history	English	science	geography	
4	11:55 – 12:45	geography	music	science	history	
	12:45 – 13:25	lunch				
5	13:25 – 14:15	maths	science	design and technology	physical education (PE)	
6	14:15 – 15:05	maths	science	computing	PE	

b) Match the pictures to the subjects in the timetable. Then listen and check.

1

2

3
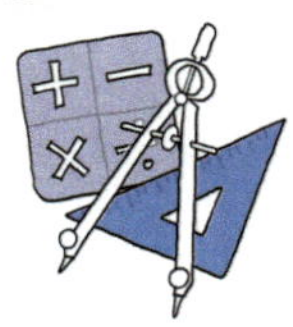
4

5

6

7

8

9

10

11

c) Listening Listen to Lily (7C) and Zane (7B). Complete Lily's timetable for Friday in your exercise book.

Lesson 1: ... Lesson 2: ... ...

▶ More practice 8, p. 47

▶ Workbook, p. 17

7 Song The timetable song

a) Listen. Stand up when you hear a school subject, then sit down again.

b) Listen again. Write the correct subject (a–f) for 1–6.

On Monday morning I have (1) ...
The next lesson is (2) ...
After lunch we have (3) ...
And then at three, go home to play.

On Tuesdays I study (4) ... at ten.
After break (5) ... with Mr Wren.
Finally it's time for (6) ... and then
We do it all again another day.

a biology
b French
c geography
d history
e maths
f PE

8 Speaking My subjects

a) Speed Dating Make two lines: line A and line B. Talk about your favourite subjects with your partner. Say three sentences.

Say why:
... because it's cool / hard / fun ...
... because I like / I don't like ...
... because Mr / Ms ... is nice / ...

b) Line A: Move to the next partner.

My task

9 My timetable

Write your timetable in English for an English friend. Put your timetable in your Dossier.
Write about your timetable for your friend:

English is on ... and on ...
German lessons are in lesson ... on ... *They're in room 310 / the science lab / ...*

► Digital help ► Wordbank 5+6, pages 217+218

► Workbook, pages 17–18

Digital quiz I can write my timetable in English.

It's a big school!

1 Words Places at school

a) Look at the pictures. Read the conversation and complete the rooms with a, e, i, o, u.

1 
the c■rr■d■r

2 
the c■nt■■n

3 
the c■mp■t■r r■■m

Zane Hi, Lily! I'm not alone in 7B. Our friends are in my class.
Lily Hi, Zane. That's great! This is Sunita and this is Noah. They're in 7C with me.
Sunita Nice to meet you, Zane.
Noah I'm hungry. My sandwich isn't in my bag. Where's the canteen?
Sunita Maybe it's down this corridor ... No, this room isn't the canteen, it's the art room.
Zane This is the computer room. And the toilets are here.
Lily Look at this map! We're in building 1. The canteen and the sports hall aren't in this building. They're in building 2. It's a big school!
Noah Yes, and we aren't near the canteen. I'm really hungry.
Lily Oh, Noah isn't happy!
Sunita You're lucky, Noah! I'm not hungry. Maybe I have two sandwiches. You can have one.
Noah You aren't hungry? Thanks, Sunita. I'm always hungry!
Sunita You're welcome.

4 
the sp■rts h■ll

5 
the ■rt r■■m

b) Listen and repeat the places.

► More practice 9, p. 47

2 At the new school

Complete the sentences with the words from the box.

I'm • I'm not • is • isn't • we aren't • we're • you aren't • you're

1 Zane: "... alone in 7B."
2 Noah: "... hungry."
3 The computer room ... in building 1.
4 The canteen ... in building 1.
5 Lily: "... in building 1."
6 Noah: "... near the canteen."
7 Sunita: "... lucky, Noah."
8 Noah: "... hungry, Sunita."

► Workbook, p. 18

Erklär-
film

3 LOOKING AT LANGUAGE *to be* (negative)

Look at exercises 1 and 2 on p. 28. Copy and complete the table.

I'*m not*	we...	I *am not*	we ...
you ...	you *aren't*	you ...	you *are not*
he ...		he ...	they ...
she *isn't*	they ...	she *is not*	
it ...		it ...	

▸ Language file 7, p. 205

4 The new school

are • aren't • I'm • is (2x) • isn't

Write the missing words.

1 The new school ... big.

2 We ... scared.

3 The teachers ... nice.

4 The food ... bad.

5 ... happy at my school.

6 My new school ... cool.

▸ More practice 10, p. 48

5 MEDIATION Today at Varndean

Was ist heute anders? Sieh dir das Poster rechts an und beantworte die Fragen eines deutschen Austauschschülers auf Deutsch.

1. Was findet in Raum 216 statt?
2. Wo kann man eine Schuluniform kaufen?
3. Was wird im Flur gezeigt?
4. Wo wird Varndeans neue Website gezeigt?
5. Was findet in der Kantine statt?
6. In welchem Klassenraum wird in der Pause heute Sport gemacht?

activity	place
assembly	canteen
get new school uniforms	sports hall
student art show	corridor
Ms Smith's maths lessons	classroom 216
see Varndean's new website	computer room
lunch break yoga	classroom 102

▸ Workbook, p. 19

6 Where are they?

a) **Match sentences 1–6 to the places in pictures A–F. Complete the sentences. The timetable on** **p. 26** **can help you.**

1 In the break, Lily, Sunita and Noah *are in the playground*.
2 At lunch, the students ...
3 In lesson 1 on Tuesday, Lily ...
4 After school on Tuesday, Zane ... with the band.
5 In English class on Monday, 7C ...
6 In lesson 6 on Wednesday, class 7C ...

library

playground

computer room

art room

theatre

canteen

b) **With a partner, talk about your timetable. Partner A says a time; Partner B says where your class is. Take turns.**

It's lesson 1 on Monday.

We're in the sports hall.

c) **Complete the sentence:** *My favourite place at school is ...*

My task

7 My school

a) **Read what Lily writes to her grandparents. What two things are wrong?**

b) **Write five sentences about your school. Write two wrong things.**

c) **Read your text to your partner. Your partner must say the wrong things.**

Hi, Grandma and Grandpa!
The name of my school is Varndean School.
It's an old school and it's very big. I'm in class 7B.
My class teacher is Mr Lee.
My favourite place at school is the art room.
My favourite day is Monday because lesson 1 is music and lesson 5 is art. My school is great!
Lily xx

▸ Digital help ▸ Wordbank 5+6, pages 217+218

▸ Workbook, p. 20

Digital quiz

I can describe my school.

Background file

1 Uniforms

a) **Read the text and look at the picture.**

Students at most British schools wear uniforms with the school colours. Most uniforms have a tie for boys and girls. You can get your uniform online, in a shop or at school.

b) **Draw a picture of a cool school uniform. Tell your partner or your class about your uniform.**

My uniform has a pink blazer and green shoes. ...

2 The goat club

Varndean has a farm with five goats. Read the text and match the rules to the picture.

1 Close the gate.
2 Don't go away with the goats.
3 Don't give the goats your snacks.
4 Give food with an open hand.
5 Don't be scared: The goats are friendly.
6 Be kind.

► Workbook, p. 20

After school

1 Before you read A good friend

Describe a good friend.

A good friend is … *A good friend isn't …*

brave • careful • friendly • fun • helpful • horrible • kind • mean • nice • quiet

2 Reading Characters in the story

Read the story. Answer the questions.

1 Who is busy?
2 Who is mean?
3 Who is sad?
4 Who is helpful?
5 Who is scared, then brave?
6 Who is friendly?

► Challenge 2, p. 48

Lily Hey, Zane! Are you free after school today? It's a nice day – let's go to the beach!
Zane Sorry, I'm busy! It's time for band now and I'm the star! Bye!
Lily Zane is always busy.
Sunita He's so cool!

Kyle Move! You're too slow!
Jade He's so weird.
Noah I'm not weird!
Lily Who are they?
Sunita They aren't from Varndean. They're bullies.

Lily That's Noah from our class. He's in trouble! Those bullies are really mean.
Sunita Can we help Noah?
Lily I don't know. I'm scared of them!

Noah Hi, seagull. Those bullies aren't kind, but you're nice. You understand me. I'm sad. Some people are mean to me because they think I'm different. But I'm clever too.

5

Lily Oh no! Noah is so nice, but he's alone. We aren't good friends ...
Sunita Let's help him!

6

Jade Look! The weird boy is still here!
Kyle You're in trouble now ...
Sunita No! He's our friend. Go away!
Lily We aren't scared of you!

7

Noah That's my friend, the seagull! And her friends too – they're very helpful!
Kyle Ugh! Let's go!
Jade Those seagulls are horrible!

8

Noah Thanks. You're good friends. And you're brave.
Lily You're welcome!
Sunita That seagull is very clever! You're good with animals, Noah.

9

Noah Hi, Dad. These are my friends, Lily and Sunita. They're in my class.
Dad Hello! Nice to meet you. I'm happy that you're all friends. This is Noah's dog, Buddy. He's very friendly.
Lily He's cool!

3 READING What's wrong?

Write the correct sentences.

1 Zane is free after school.
2 Kyle and Jade are nice to Noah.
3 Sunita and Lily aren't scared of the bullies at first.
4 Lily and Sunita aren't Noah's friends.
5 The seagulls are nice to Kyle and Jade.
6 Noah's dog is mean.

4 Showtime

a) Make seagulls with paper circles or paper plates.

b) Make groups of five students:
Noah / Scout, Lily, Sunita, Kyle and Jade.
Read and practise scenes 2–8.

c) Act out the scenes for the class or another group. Use actions and feelings. Hold up the seagulls in the correct scene.

d) Give feedback to other groups. Be helpful and kind!

Act friendly / mean / scared / ….

Louder, please, Noah.

You are a very good Lily!

5 Speaking **What's your opinion?**

Talk about the characters in the story:

I like / I don't like … because …

brave • cool • clever • friendly • a good friend • good with people / animals • happy • helpful • kind • nice

I like Noah because he's nice and clever and he's good with animals. What about you?

I like Noah too. But I don't like Jade because she isn't kind to Noah.

▸ More practice 11, p. 48

6 You choose **The next day**

Do a) or b).

a) Draw a picture and write 1–2 speech bubbles about the next day in the story.
You can draw and write about

- Noah, Sunita and Lily.
- the bullies: Are they friendly or mean?
- Scout and her seagull friends.
- …

b) Write and act out a scene from the next day.

▸ Workbook, p. 21

Digital quiz I can understand a story about friends.

The Brighton dares[1]: At school

1 The two dares

BEFORE YOU WATCH **Daisy and Emir do funny[2] dares. Match the dares to the pictures.**

a Wear a funny school tie.
b Wear a beard[3].
c Don't wear shoes.
d Speak backwards[4].
e Walk backwards.
f Write words backwards.

1

2
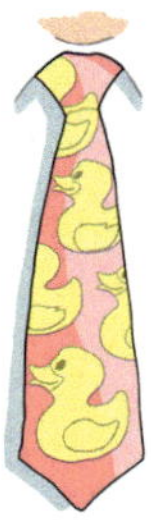

3

4

5
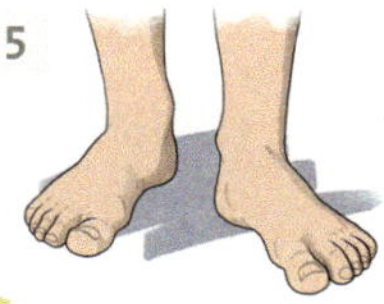

6

2 VIEWING At school

a) **Watch the video from 00:00 to 02:17. Write the correct dares from 1.**

Daisy's dare for Emir: ... Emir's dare for Daisy: ... and ...

b) **Watch the whole video. Choose the correct answer.**

1 Mr Campbell, the teacher, has a brown / black beard.
2 Mrs Collins has Emily's school bag / pencil case.
3 Emir / Mr Campbell looks for Emily.
4 Emily is in Room 12 / the school garden.
5 Mr Campbell is OK with / isn't happy about Emir's beard.
6 Mrs Collins really can't see well / can see fine.

Good to know

Dares are often funny.
You do dares because other people ask you.
Dares can show you are clever or brave.

c) **Compare your answers with a partner. Then watch the video again and check.**

3 My opinion

Copy and complete the sentences for you. Then tell a partner.

I think ...
1 the beard dare is ...
2 the backwards dare is ...
3 Mr Campbell is ...
4 Mrs Collins is ...

bad • clever • cool • friendly • funny • good • great • horrible • kind • mean • nice • OK • weird

[1] **dare** *Mutprobe* [2] **funny** *witzig* [3] **beard** *Bart* [4] **backwards** *rückwärts*

Erklär-film

Learning vocabulary

1 Mind maps

Copy and complete the mind map about school.

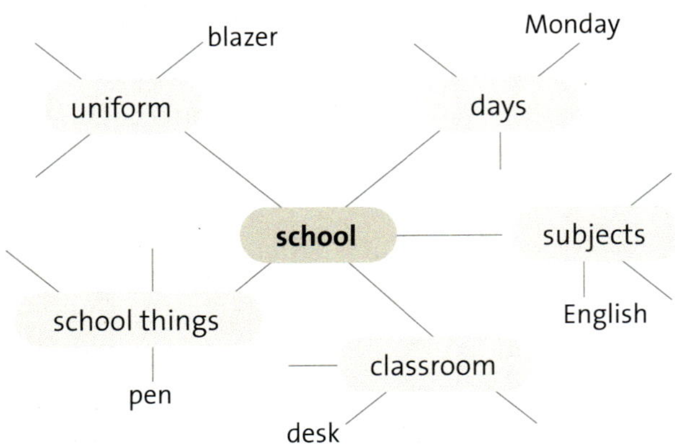

It's helpful to learn vocabulary in different ways! Make a VOCAB FILE *for new words in an app, an exercise book or a folder.*

2 A to Z

a) Make an A to Z with as many school words as you can.

b) Show your partner. Which words are the same? Which are different?

A – art   B – book   C – canteen

Words with q and x are hard to find!

3 Test your partner

Look at the Vocabulary on pages 244–245 for one minute. Choose ten words. Say the German word to your partner. Your partner must say the English word. Take turns.

4 GAME New words

a) Choose words and phrases from your VOCAB FILE. Then work in a group and make question cards. Write help or answers on the back of the cards.

b) Play your game with your group. Use your cards and the board game on p. 49.

c) Swap with another group. Play their game. Use their cards.

d) Write more cards.

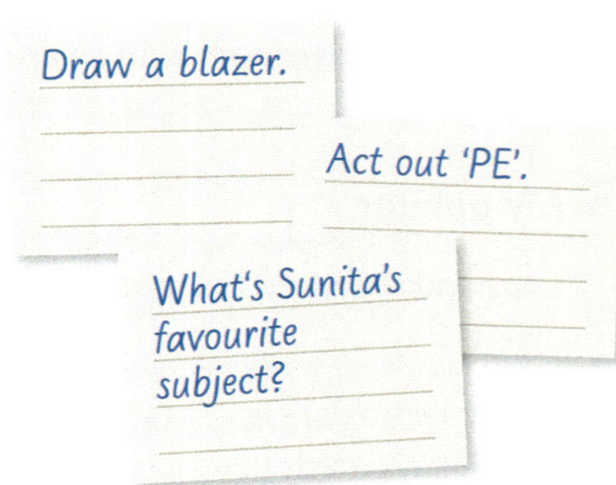

► Skills file 1, p. 191   ► Skills file 2, p. 194

Digital quiz   I can learn vocabulary in different ways.

Make a poster about your school

Step 1

Work alone.
Copy the umbrella words.
What words about your school can you remember for each umbrella word group?

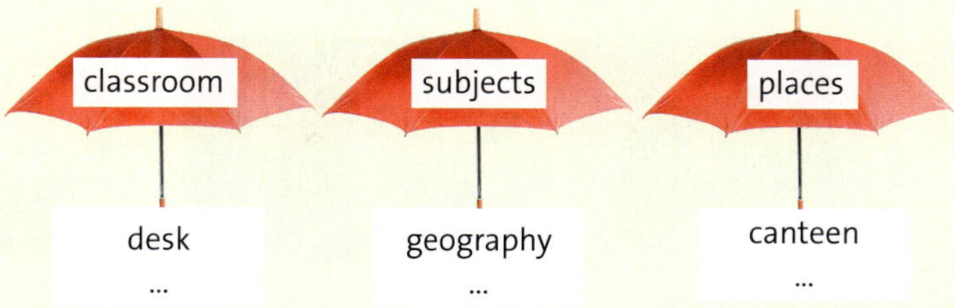

Step 2

Look at *My task* on pages 23, 27 and 30.
Find useful phrases and sentences and add them to the umbrella word groups.

Step 3

Take photos of your school or use photos from your school's website.

Remember: Always ask people before you take a photo of them!

Step 4

Make a poster about your school. Each student makes a different part.

► Classroom English, p. 232 ► Wordbank 5, p. 217 ► Wordbank 6, p. 218
► Digital help

Step 5

Put your posters on the wall.
WALK AROUND Look at the posters.
Give feedback.

I like the photos!

The timetable is great!

► Lets's talk: Feedback, p. 231

Step 6

Find five words on the other posters: a) new and useful words b) difficult words
Add the words to your VOCAB FILE.

1 Listening At break

I can understand students at a British school.

a) Listen to the conversation. Put the pictures in the correct order.

A 
B 
C 
D 

b) Listen to the next part of the conversation.
Copy and complete the table with the words in the box.

Name	Favourite lesson today	Why?
Zane	...	It's ...
Sunita	...	It's ...
Lily	...	It's ...
Noah	...	The teacher is ...

computing • cool • fun • geography • helpful • history • nice • PE

2 Speaking Mr Lee's desk

I can understand and use classroom English.

Say what you can see in the picture.

In the picture I can see a brown desk, ...

3 Words In the classroom

The students talk to the teacher. Choose the correct word.

1 Can you A help B learn C say me?
2 Can I A answer B move C open the window?
3 Can you A say B understand C talk that again please, Ms Miller?
4 A Soon B Sorry C Please I'm late, Ms Miller.
5 I don't A take B understand C have the question.
6 Can I A forget B come C go to the toilet, please?
7 What's the A answer B page C teacher to question 5?
8 Can I A walk B cook C use your pen?

Check

4 Language Sunita's email

I can write my timetable in English *(to be)*.

Sunita and her friend Jasmine are at different schools. Complete Sunita's message with *am / is / are*.

Hi, Jasmine!
How (1) ... you? I (2) ... now in class 7C at Varndean School. Lily (3) ... in 7C too: We (4) ... very happy at the new school! My timetable (5) ... great! English lessons (6) ... on Mondays, Tuesdays and Fridays. I have two music lessons. One (7) ... in lesson 4 on Tuesdays and one (8) ... in lesson 1 on Fridays. Science lessons (my favourite lessons) (9) ... on Tuesdays and Wednesdays. And PE (10) ... in lessons 5 and 6 on Thursdays.
Is your timetable OK? What's your favourite day?
See you
Sunita

5 Language Jasmine's school

I can describe my school (*to be* – negative).

Jasmine talks about her school. Look at the picture and complete Jasmine's sentences with *is / isn't / are / aren't*.

This is my school in Hove. The students (1) aren't in the building because it's break. The uniform (2) is nice – the blazer (3) ... red and the tie (4) ... blue. There (5) ... two seagulls – they (6) ... friendly. But they like our sandwiches! The canteen (7) ... very big and the food there (8) ... great. But the classrooms (9) ... in building 1 – they (10) ... near the canteen in building 2. The sports hall (11) ... great, but there (12) ... a pool.

6 Writing Seb's school

Seb is Lily's friend from Bochum. Read his notes about his school. Write his message to Lily.

Hi, Lily! My school is Schiller School. It's ...

- Schiller School
- in Bochum
- not big
- students: friendly
- old friends: not in same class
- class teacher: Ms Lang
- favourite place: sports hall

Check

7 Reading Zane's homework

I can understand a story about friends.

a) Read the story.

Mr King So, class 7B. This is your homework. Make a poster about your favourite band, with facts and photos.

Zane Erm ... Sir ... Can I ask a ...
Mr King Sorry, Zane. I'm busy. Let's talk at break.

Sunita Why are you sad, Zane? You like music! And you're in a band!
Zane I want to make a great poster. But my computer is old and slow.
Sunita Where's your computer? I can help with that.

Zane Wow. You're good with computers. Thanks, Sunita.
Sunita You're welcome!

b) Complete the sentences with the words from the box.

1 Mr King is ...
2 Sunita is ... and ...
3 Zane is ..., then ...

busy • clever • happy • helpful • sad

c) Choose the correct answer.

1 Mr King is the A maths teacher B French teacher C music teacher.
2 Mr King can talk A now B at break C at lunch.
3 Zane likes A computers B music C posters.
4 Zane's computer isn't A old B new C big.
5 Sunita is good with A problems B music C computers.

Check

8 Study skills **All about Lily**

I can learn vocabulary in different ways.

**Copy the mind map about Lily.
Complete it with the words in the box.**

drawing • elephants • friendly • happy • kind • parkour • pencil • phone • writing stories

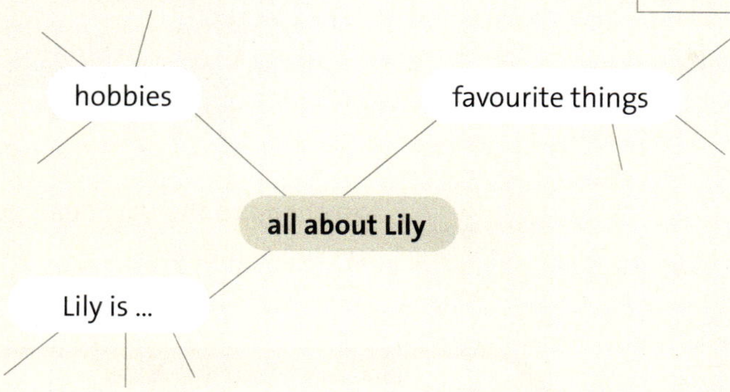

9 Reading and Words **Noah's poster**

I can make a poster about my school.

a) **Look at Noah's poster. Match the texts (1–4) to the pictures (A–D).**

Welcome to Varndean

1 This is my timetable. My favourite ... is maths.

2 This is the goat club. It's my favourite ...

3 This is my uniform. The ... is red.

4 This is Mr Lee. He's my class ... He's nice!

A

B

C

	Monday	Tuesday	Wednesday	Thursday	Friday
			registration and assembly		
1	English	art	French	computing	maths
2	English	maths	French	computing	music
			break		
3	history	English	science	geography	English
4	geography	music	science	history	French
			lunch		
5	maths	science	design and technology	physical education (PE)	art
6	maths	science	computing	PE	design and technology

D

b) **Complete the sentences in Noah's poster.**

Check

VARNDEAN Teen Zine

This month's topic: our school

Our school magazine: by students for students

Ask the students

What's your favourite place at Varndean School?

Lin, 7B: *My favourite place is the theatre because I love acting!*

Kate, 8A: *Books, books, books ... I love the library!*

Robin, 7D: *I like reading too, but my favourite place is the school farm.*

Say hello to the Varndean goats on social media!
@VarndeanGoats

Varndean Goats @varndeangoats · Dec 16
The sun is up
The sky is blue
It's beautiful[1]
And so are we![2]
#Varndean #Sunrise

Varndean Goats @varndeangoats · Jul 9
Band photo
#Goats with #Attitude

Varndean Goats @varndeangoats · Mar 11
And here's number 13 in the list of things goats can do that you can't ...
#goatskills

[1] **beautiful** *schön* [2] **So are we.** *Wir auch. / Das sind wir auch. / Das gilt auch für uns.*

Puzzle time

Find[1] the small school and the tie colour for these five Varndean students.

Varndean is one big school with five small schools.
The small school names are famous[2] people and the ties are different colours: blue, blue-green, purple, red and silver.

Varndean School

- Angelou School
- Ellis School
- Lennox School
- Russell School
- Turing School

Nia is in Turing School and Angelou School's tie is blue-green.

Jagvir

Lara isn't in Lennox School. My tie is purple.

Adam

Jagvir's tie is silver and my tie is red.

Nia

Adam is in Ellis School.

Lara

I'm in Angelou School.

Millie

Make your own[3] small school with a famous person and a tie!

---

[1] **find** *finden* [2] **famous** *berühmt* [3] **own** *eigene, eigener, eigenes*

Partner page

▸ Page 22

6 SPEAKING Different desks

Partner B: Look at Noah's desk. Talk to partner A. What nine things are different?

In my picture I can see an orange.

In my picture I can't see an orange.

Diff bank

▸ Page 21

More practice 1 This is Noah's ...

1 This is ... (Noah / blue folder).

2 This is ... (Zane / nice pencil case).

3 This is ... (Lily / cool pen).

4 This is ... (Scout / old apple).

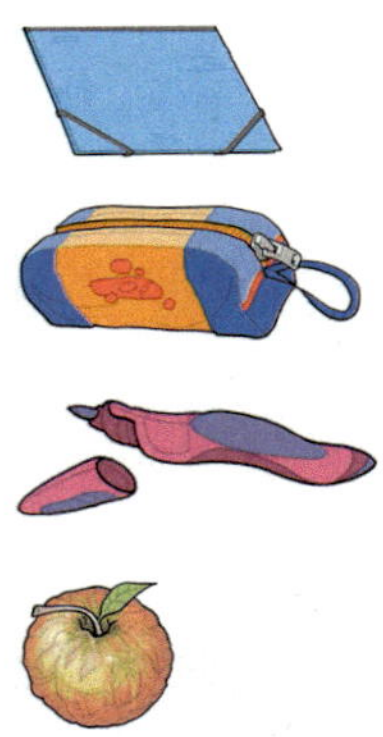

▸ Language file 1, p. 202

More practice 2 WORDS Lily's things

Write what's in Lily's rucksack.

In Lily's rucksack I can see ...

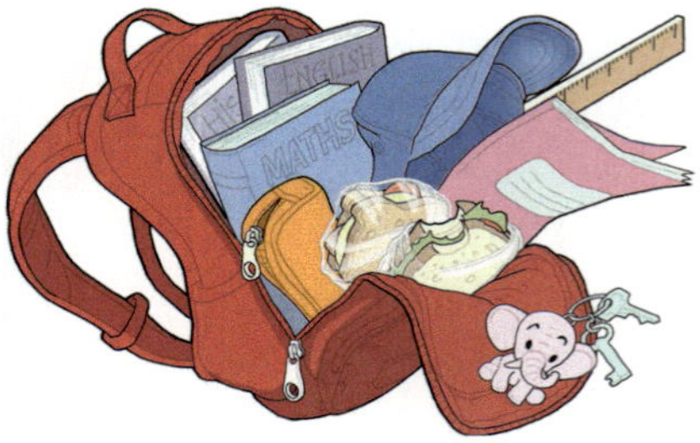

▸ Page 22

More practice 3 WORDS **Your school things**

Put your school things on your desk. Close your eyes.
Tell your partner about your school things and the colours.
Your partner checks.

I have a / an / two ...

More practice 4 **Class rules**

Complete the rules.
Use the words in the box.

be (2x) • forget • listen • put • stand up • talk • write

1 Don't ... late.
2 Don't ... your school things.
3 ... when the teacher comes into the classroom.
4 ... to the teacher.
5 Don't ... when the teacher talks.
6 ... your hand up to speak.
7 ... nice to other students.
8 Don't ... on the desks.

Challenge 1 **Open the window, please**

Write the sentences for the speech bubbles.

1 Open the window, please.
2 Don't ...

▸ Page 24

More practice 5

Scout's conversation

Complete Scout's sentences with the words in the box.

I • you • ~~he~~ • she • it • we • you • they

1 Zane is a busy boy. *He* is always tired.
2 Noah and Sunita are good students. ... are clever.
3 Lily is nice. ... is always happy.
4 The kids and I are from Brighton. ... are friends.
5 ... are new here, Blue Bird. Welcome to Brighton!
6 Brighton is a nice place. ... is by the sea.
7 ... am hungry.
8 Blue Bird and Black Bird, I think ... are hungry too. Let's find lunch!

▸ Page 25

☒ Parallel exercise

4 Messages

Complete the messages from Noah and his mum. Choose the correct short form.

Hi, Mum! I like the classroom. (1) It's / They're big.
I like Mr Lee, my teacher, too. (2) She's / He's cool.
And I like my new friends. (3) They're / We're nice. ✓

Great! (4) It's / You're lucky, Noah! Varndean School is big, but (5) she's / it's a good school.
Sorry, (6) you're / I'm busy now. See you! ☺ ✓

More practice 6

Zane's message

a) **Complete Zane's message to a friend in London. Use *am* / *is* / *are*.**

Hi Zara
How *are* you? Brighton (1) ... great. The beach (2) ... my favourite place.
I (3) ... at my new school now. My new school friends (4) ... nice. Noah (5) ... cool and Sunita (6) ... friendly. Noah and Sunita (7) ... in a different class. My friend Lily (8) ... in their class too.
I must go. I (9) ... very busy! Please come to Brighton soon! Zane ☺

☒ b) **Write a message to Zane. Use his message to help you.**

More practice 7 Scout's day

a) **Write the correct short forms.**

1 I... tired!
2 Remember my friend Black Bird? He... tired too.
3 And my new friend Blue Bird? She... tired too.
4 We... all tired!
5 Today is a nice day. But it... busy.

b) **Write about you and your day.**

Me: ... tired / happy / hungry / ...
My day: ... nice / busy / horrible / ...

▸ Page 26

More practice 8 WORDS I like English

a) **Copy the table. Then listen and write the subjects.**

	♥	☺	☹
Sunita			
Lily			
Noah			
Zane			

b) **Listen again and check.**

c) **Make notes why the students like their favourite subjects.**

Sunita ♥ science: fun

▸ Page 28

More practice 9 WORDS Places in school

a) **Write the correct place.**

1 You can use computers in this room.
2 You can draw pictures here.
3 You can go to different rooms from here.
4 You can do sport in this place.
5 You can eat lunch and snacks here.
6 You have lessons in this room.

b) **Complete the sentence.**
My favourite place in school is ...

▸ Page 29

☒ More practice 10 **Big or small?**

a) **Describe the students, things and animals. Write two sentences for each picture.**

1 The dog is big. It isn't small. *2 Lily and Noah are ...*

1

big / small

2

nice / horrible

3

old / new

4

good / bad

5

grey / black

6

hungry / tired

b) **Write two sentences about students or things in your class.**

▸ Page 32

Challenge 2 **Characters in the story**

Describe the characters in the story.
Use the words from the box and *is* or *are*.
There are four extra words in the box.

brave • careful • busy • friendly • helpful • hungry • mean • old • sad • scared • tired

1 Zane ...
2 Jade and Kyle ...
3 Noah ...
4 Scout ...
5 Lily and Sunita ..., then ...
6 Buddy ...

▸ Page 34

More practice 11 LIFE SKILLS **Your best friend**

YOU CHOOSE **Do 1 or 2.**

1 **Write about your best friend. Look at Noah's description.**

My dog, Buddy, is clever and friendly. He isn't mean.
He's my best friend because he's very helpful when I'm sad.

2 **Write a nice note to a friend in your class.**

You are my friend because you are ...

▸ Page 36

4 GAME

Start at reception. Take a card and answer the question or do the task. If you're correct, move to the next room. If you're wrong, stay in the room.

Unit 2
My family and home

1 Words Sunita's family

Listen to Sunita and Lily and look at the photos. Complete the sentences with the words in the box.

A is Meera, Sunita's ...
B is Nish, Sunita's ...
C is Ben, Meera's ...
D is Willow, Ben's ...
E is Priya, Sunita's ...
F is Rahi, Sunita's ...
G and H are Jay and Anika, Sunita's ...
I is Sunita's ...
J is Sunita's ...

aunt • brother • cousins • daughter • grandma • grandpa • mum • partner • uncle

▸ More practice 1, p. 79

Nach dieser Unit kann ich ...

- ○ über meine Familie und unsere Haustiere sprechen
- ○ mein Zuhause und mein Zimmer beschreiben
- ○ Wörter buchstabieren

Unit task

- ○ mein Traumzimmer präsentieren

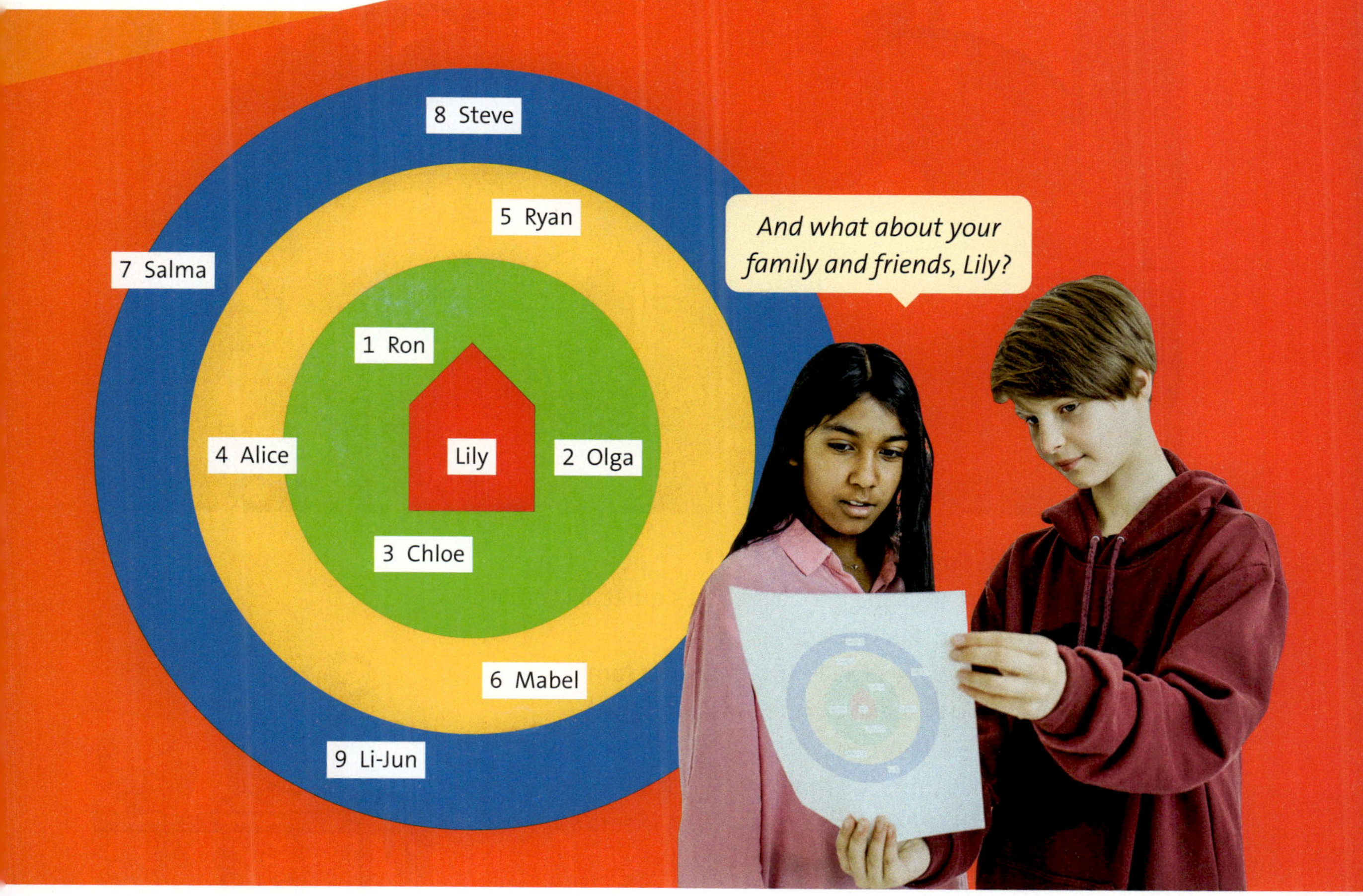

2 LISTENING A circle of family, friends and neighbours

a) Look at Lily's circle. Listen and make nine sentences.

1 Ron is Lily's ...   2 Olga is ...

b) Draw your circle of important people and tell your partner about them.

Gabriela is my stepmum. She's married to my dad. She's very kind.

▶ Wordbank 7, p. 219

Put your circle of important people in your DOSSIER.

▶ Workbook, p. 27

Digital quiz

I can talk about my family. ✓

My pets

1 Reading A lot of animals!

a) Before you read **One animal in the box isn't in the picture. Find the animal.**

a cat • a fish • a horse • a parrot • a rabbit • a snake • two hamsters

Scout	Hello, I'm Scout. Are you lost?
George	No, I'm not. I'm here because it's quiet. Nice to meet you, I'm George.
Scout	You're George. Oh, is Sunita in your family?
George	Yes, she is. Are you and Sunita friends?
Scout	Yes, we are. Are you angry?
George	Yes, I am. Sunita's mum is a vet. It's the weekend, so we have a lot of animals from Meera's work in our house.
Scout	Oh, is that good?
George	No, it isn't!
Scout	Oh, are they too loud?
George	Yes, they are! And the house is so messy! Am I happy there? No, I'm not! Not today!

b) **Read the conversation and complete the sentences.**

George is ... *He isn't ... because ...*

2 Words A cat, a fish ...

Listen and repeat the words in 1a). Point to the animals.

► Workbook, p. 28

3 Looking at language Questions and short answers

Erklär-film

a) Read the conversation on p. 52 again. Find the matching questions. What's different?

1 You are lost. → Are you lost?
2 Sunita is in your family. → Is ...?
3 You are angry. → ...?
4 That is good. → ...?
5 They are too loud. → ...?
6 I am happy. → ...?

b) Match the questions and answers.

1 Is George happy?
2 Are the animals in Sunita's house loud?
3 Is Sunita's house messy?
4 Is George Sunita's pet?
5 Are the hamsters quiet?
6 Is Sunita a vet?

A Yes, it is.
B No, they aren't.
C Yes, he is.
D No, she isn't.
E No, he isn't.
F Yes, they are.

It's not polite to answer only *Yes* or *No*. Use short answers:
Are you lost? **– Yes, I am.**
– No, I'm not.

► Language file 8, p. 206

4 Scout's questions

a) Scout has some questions for you. Write the questions in the correct order.

1 you / good with animals / are / ?

2 friendly / is / your favourite animal / ?

3 in your house / loud / it / is / ?

4 your favourite animals / are / monkeys / ?

5 are / scared of snakes / you / ?

6 cat fans / you and your family / are / ?

b) Ask your partner the questions in a). Answer your partner's questions with short answers.

c) Think of one more question. Ask your partner.

► More practice 2+3, p. 79
► Challenge 1, p. 79
► Workbook, p. 29

5 Listening Is that your pet?

a) Before you listen **What animals can you see?**

I can see ...

A

B

C

D

E

b) **Listen to the conversation about pets. Which picture (A–E) is correct for:**

1 Noah 2 Zane 3 Zane's aunt 4 Lily?

c) **Listen again and write the answers.**

▸ Parallel exercise, p. 80

1 Are you OK, Sunita? – *No, I'm not.*
2 Is it hard to do your homework? – ...
3 Is your dog Buddy loud? – ...
4 Are you too busy for pets? – ...
5 Are they your pets? – ...

6 Speaking A missing pet

a) **Noah and Zane see some *Missing Pet* posters, but they have rain on them.**

Partner B: Look at p. 78.
Partner A: Copy the poster.
Read the first three sentences to partner B. Your partner completes the missing words in his or her poster.
Then listen to your partner and complete your missing words.

b) **Read the completed poster.**
Which pet is missing?
Tell your partner.

I think the missing pet is ...

MISSING

Our friendly parrot is missing. He's blue and orange and he's ten years old. He likes talking and flying and he's very nice.
He ... scared of people and ... . He isn't ... when it's ... .

... call **07700 900426** if you find him.

7 Reading *FindAPet*

Lily wants a new pet.

a) Before you read **Look at the photos of the three pets. Guess what they're like. Use the words in the box.**

active • big • cute • fast • friendly • hungry • interesting • loud • mean • old • quiet • slow • small • special

I think Rex is … *He isn't …*

b) **Now read the profiles from *FindAPet* and match the words from a) to the three pets.**

Rex: *big, …*
Axel: …
Maude: …

Rex is big, but he isn't mean. He's a very friendly and active dog. But he's always hungry and he's very loud!

Axel is a special pet – he's a small, green lizard. He's very quiet, but he's interesting. And he isn't slow!

Maude is quite old, but still very fast. She's cute, but be careful – she isn't friendly!

c) **Read about Lily's dream pet. Which pet from *FindAPet* is right for Lily?**

I think … is right for Lily (because …).

My dream pet is different and interesting. It isn't too big or loud and it's nice.

d) **Which of the three pets is your favourite and why?**

My favourite pet is … because he's / she's … and he / she isn't …

► Challenge 2, p. 80

My task

8 My pet or dream pet

a) **Make notes about your pet or dream pet: animal, colour, size, other things.**

► Digital help ► Wordbank 8, p. 220

b) **Interview your partner about his or her pet or dream pet.**

I have a … / My dream pet is a …   *Is it cute / active / …?*   *Yes, it is. / No, it isn't.*

► Workbook, p. 30

Digital quiz   I can talk about pets.

Different homes

1 Listening Four homes

a) Before you listen **Talk about the homes in the photos.**

The home in photo A/B/... is a house/flat.

The flat is on the ground/top floor.

It's old/new/big/small.

It has a garden/a balcony/a garage.

b) **Listen. What's the correct photo for Zane, Sunita, Noah and Lily?**

c) **Listen again and check.**

2 Looking at language There is ... / There are ...

Complete the sentences about the four homes. Put the things and people in the correct list.

There is/There's ...	*There are ...*
...	...

a nice balcony • friendly neighbours • a garage • a lot of flats • a big garden • some trees

► Language file 9, p. 206

3 A special house

a) **Zane's friend has a special house. Write *there is* or *there are* in Zane's sentences.**

1 ... eleven floors. The building is white and red.
2 ... one room on each floor.
3 ... eleven rooms. The top two floors are red.
4 On the top floors ... big balconies.
5 ... a red lamp at the top of the building.
6 ... no garden.

b) **Draw the house with a partner. Then compare with the photo on p. 78.**

► More practice 4, p. 80 ► Challenge 3, p. 81

4 Viewing A tour of Sunita's home

a) Before you watch What can you remember about Sunita's family, pet and home? In your group, collect information and make notes. Then compare with another group.

Sunita's mum is Meera. – Yes, and Meera's partner is ...

b) Watch the tour of Sunita's house. Write the people and animals that Sunita talks about.

5 Words Rooms

a) Look at the picture of Sunita's house. Write the rooms. There's one extra room.

1 Meera's bedroom 2 ...

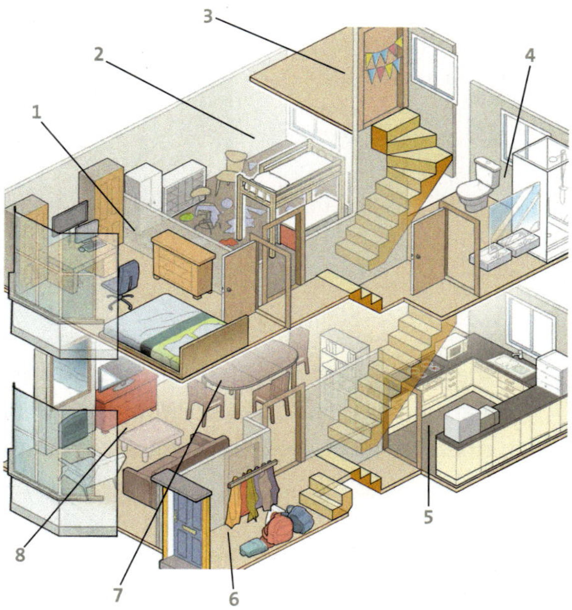

bathroom • dining room • hall • kitchen • living room • ~~Meera's bedroom~~ • Nish's bedroom • office • Sunita's bedroom

b) Watch and check your answers in a).

c) Watch the video again. Write what's in these rooms: hall, kitchen, living room, Meera's bedroom.

hall: shoes and ...

6 Listening Animals in Sunita's house

a) Before you listen Where are the pets in your home?

My hamster is in my room.

There are no pets in my home.

The fish are in the office.

b) There are a lot of animals in Sunita's house today. What rooms are they in? Listen and match the pets (1–5) to the rooms (a–f). There's one extra room. Write the answers in your exercise book.

1 hamster
2 cat
3 dog
4 snake
5 parrot

a toilet • b dining room • c kitchen • d hall • e bathroom • f living room

c) Listen again and check your answers from b).

► Workbook, p. 31

7 LISTENING Dream homes

a) Listen. What's the correct photo for Zane's, Sunita's, Noah's and Lily's dream rooms?

b) Listen again and check.

A

B

C

D

E

8 MEDIATION Holiday flat

Deine Familie fährt nach England. Lies die drei Anzeigen für Ferienwohnungen. Ihr braucht zwei Schlafzimmer, eine Küche, ein Wohnzimmer und ein eigenes Badezimmer. Schreib deiner Mutter in einer Nachricht, welches Angebot passt und warum, und welche nicht.

1
Flat in Hove
Sunny, modern flat. Kitchen, living room, two bedrooms. Bathroom for two flats in the hall. Ground floor.

2
Brighton: Holiday house
Big house on a quiet street near the beach. Living room, kitchen, six bedrooms, three bathrooms.

3
New flat in Brighton
Cool flat for your family! Big kitchen, balcony, living room. One small bedroom, one big bedroom, one bathroom.

My task

9 My home

a) What's in Lily's message to a new friend?

a the rooms in her home
b her family
c how big her home is
d how old her home is
e what floor her home is on
f other places (garden or balcony)

I live with my mum and dad.
We live in a flat in Brighton.
It's a small flat and it's very nice.
There's a kitchen, a bathroom and three other rooms: a living room and two bedrooms. There's a big balcony too.
Tell me about your home!

b) Write about your home or dream home for a new friend. Change the words in blue. You can add other things.

► Digital help ► More help, p. 81

Digital quiz I can describe my home or dream home.

Background file

1 Homes in Britain

a) Look at the photos and read the text.
Most people in Britain live in homes like in the photos.

block of flats

terraced homes

detached home

semi-detached homes

b) Look at p. 56 again. What types of homes do Sunita, Noah, Zane and Lily live in?

c) What type of home do you live in?

2 Talking about homes

a) Read the text and look at the pictures.

Some people in Britain give their homes names. The names often describe the house or things the people like. Lots of people use the word *cottage* in house names: A cottage is a small house.

b) YOU CHOOSE Do 1 or 2.

1 Make a sign for a house. It can be your house, a house from 1a) or a house from p. 56.
Why is the name good for the house?

A

B

C

D

2 Which type of home in 1 do you like and why? Write 1–2 sentences. *I like ... because ...*

► Workbook, p. 32

In my room

1 Speaking Sunita's room

a) **Look at the picture. What can you see?**

I can see ...

There's a ...
There are two/three/some ...

b) **Right or wrong? Correct the wrong sentences.**

1 There are three red cushions on the bed.
2 There's a bag under the bed.
3 There's a big table with a yellow lamp.
4 There's a chair in front of the desk.
5 The computer is behind a robot.
6 There's a computer and a book on the desk.
7 There are a lot of books on the shelves.
8 There's a mirror next to the desk.
9 The chocolate is between the sofa and the bed.
10 There's a lamp over the sofa.

2 Words Things in my room

a) **Listen and repeat the words.**

b) **Make mind maps for things in your room.**

► Skills file 2, p. 194

... ... things in and on my wardrobe ... ...

... ... things on, under and next to my bed ... ...

... ... things on and next to my desk ... ...

► Workbook, p. 33

3 Where is it?

a) Look at the picture of Sunita's room and answer the questions.

1 What's different to the room on p. 60? *The room in this picture is ...*
2 Who is in the room? *I can see ...*

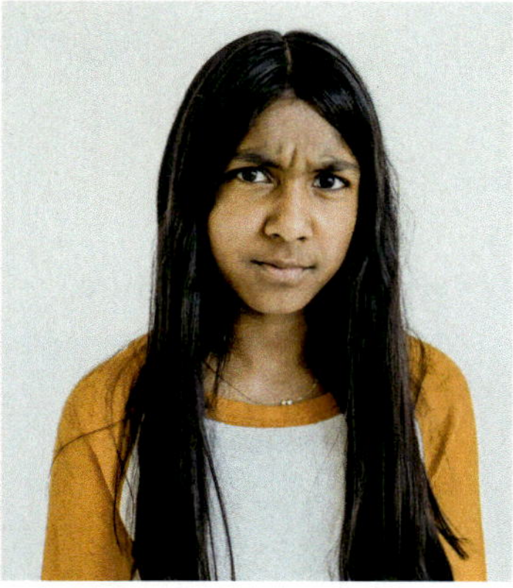

Oh no! Look at my room! It's so messy!
Who is in here? George, I can see you.
And who is that under the bed? Is it Scout the seagull?
Where's my lamp? Where are the cushions?
What's on the floor?
And where's Robbie the robot?
Are you OK, Robbie?
My chocolate isn't on my desk. I know where that is!
Chocolate is Nish's favourite thing!
Hey Nish, where's my chocolate?

b) Read what Sunita says. Look at Sunita's room and answer the questions.

1 Who is behind the door? – *George* is behind the door.
2 Who is under the bed? Scout is ...
3 Where's the lamp?
4 Where are the cushions?
5 What's on the floor next to the lamp?
6 Who is Robbie?
7 What's in Nish's room?

c) OPINION LINE **Is your room messy or tidy? Stand in a line. Then count the students.**

very messy – quite messy – OK – quite tidy – very tidy

Seven students have very messy rooms. Five students ...

► Workbook, p. 33

4 Where's Scout?

a) Choose a picture. Tell your partner where Scout is.
Use the words in the box. Your partner says the picture.
Take turns.

behind • in • in front of • next to • on • under

Partner A: *Scout is ...*
Partner B: *That's picture 1/2/...*

1

2

3

4

5

6

b) WALK AROUND **Draw another picture with Scout in a house.**
Walk around and show your picture to different partners.
Your partner says where Scout is. You say where Scout is in your partner's picture.

► More practice 5, p. 82

5 Question words

a) **Look at the picture and answer the questions.**

WHO is George? – George is a ...
WHERE is George? – George is on ...
WHAT is George's favourite food? – George's favourite food is ...

b) **What are the three question words in German?**

6 Questions for you

a) **Your teacher has a questionnaire for you. Write the correct question word: *who, what* or *where*.**

b) **Ask and answer the questions with a partner.**

1 ... is your home?
2 ... is your favourite person?
3 ... is your favourite room in your home?
4 ... is your room in your home?
5 ... is your favourite thing in your room?
6 ... are your neighbours?

► Workbook, p. 34

7 Where are my things?

a) **Sunita can't find her things. Complete Sunita's questions with the correct question word.**

1	... are my sandwiches?	Nish:	Ask George. He is a sandwich fan.
2	... has my blazer?	Mum:	Not me! Maybe it's in the hall.
3	... has my sweets?	Nish:	Not me! I like chocolate.
4	... is my black shoe?	Nish:	Maybe with the other black shoe!
5	... animals are in the house today?	Mum:	A dog, a cat and a snake.
6	... is the snake?	Mum:	It's in its terrarium.

b) **Look at the pictures. Which answer isn't correct?**

► More practice 6, p. 82 ► Challenge 4, p. 82

My task

8 My room

a) SPEAKING **Ask your partner questions about his / her room. Make notes.**

► Digital help ► More help, p. 83 ► Wordbank 9, p. 220

Is it your own room?
Or is it your sister's / brother's room too?
Is your room big or small?
Where's your room?
What's in your room?
Are there pets in your room?
What colour are the walls?
What's on the walls?
Is it loud or quiet in your room?

b) **Use your notes. Draw your partner's room.**

c) **Swap pictures with your partner. Is the picture of your room correct?**

► Workbook, pages 34–35

Digital quiz I can describe my room.

At home with Sunita

1 Song Ben's song

a) Listen to the song about Ben and Willow's flat. Put the lines in the correct order: *1f, 2c, 3 …*

b) Listen again and check on p. 78.

c) Describe the flat in one sentence.

It's …

My little flat

a *And the living room is always very messy*
b *There are two small bedrooms, there aren't three*
c *And it isn't new or modern at all*
d *There aren't expensive pictures on the wall*
e *But my little flat is perfect for me*
f *People ask, 'Is your flat big?' No, it's small*
g *There's my family, that's enough*
h *My little flat is perfect for me*
i *Because there's music, there's love*

2 Reading Sunita's problem

a) Before you read Talk about how the people in the pictures feel.

b) Read the story. What's Sunita's problem? Is there a happy ending?

Hi, Lily. Are you at home?

Hi, Sunita. Yes, I am. I'm alone and it's very quiet 🙂. My parents are at work, of course.

It isn't quiet here! My mum is at work, but my brother is in his room. Willow is at her mum's house, but Ben is here.

Ben is nice, right?

Yes, he is. He's funny and he's a great cook! But he's always in the living room with his guitar. And his music is horrible!

Tell him!

But he's so nice. And Mum is a big fan of his music.

Sorry, Sunita. It's time for parkour. Speak later! Remember: Talk to Ben!

Later in the dining room ...

Sunita Thanks for dinner, Ben. You're a really good cook!
Meera Yes, thanks, love.
Ben Let me play my new song.
Nish Erm, I have a lot of homework ...
Sunita Me too.
Meera Nish, Sunita ... don't be rude. You can listen.

Later in the living room ...

Ben ♬ ♬ ♬ My little flat is perfect for me ...
Nish Erm ... look, Ben, I like you, but I don't like your music. It's really bad! You can play your music in your flat. This isn't your house!
Sunita And your music is too loud, Ben. I can't do my homework or code.
Meera Nish and Sunita, this isn't Ben's home, but he's part of our family. We can talk about problems – but be polite!
Nish Erm ... sorry, Ben.
Ben That's OK. It's an electric guitar. I can use headphones.
Sunita Thanks, Ben. ... And Nish, you can use headphones too!
Ben Sunita, I can play different music. Maybe I can help you with the music for your video game?
Sunita Erm ... Great, thanks!

Hi, Sunita. I'm home. ✓

Hi, Lily! Are you tired? ✓

Yes, parkour is hard! Is there still a problem with Ben's music? ✓

No, it's OK now. And not all Ben's music is bad. Listen to this ♬ – it's for my video game. ✓

That's great! ... Oh, Mum is back at home now – time for dinner! 🙂 See you! ✓

Bye, Lily. See you at school! ✓

3 Reading The story

a) Read the story again. Are the sentences right or wrong? Correct the wrong sentences.

1 Sunita is on her phone with Lily: She isn't happy about the noise at home.
2 Sunita, Nish, Meera and Ben eat dinner.
3 Nish is polite about Ben's new song.
4 Meera isn't happy with Nish and Sunita.
5 Nish isn't sorry.
6 Ben has an idea about the noise.
7 Ben has an idea to help Sunita.
8 Sunita and Lily think Ben's music for the video game is really bad.

b) Check with a partner.

► More practice 7, p. 83

4 Showtime & Life skills Talk about problems

a) Speaking Do the role-plays. Use the ideas in the box or a different idea. Take turns to be A and B.

A I have a problem when you ...
B I'm sorry. I can ...
A That's a good idea. Thanks.
B You're welcome.

problems
play loud music
be in the bathroom a long time
make the kitchen messy
put shoes on the floor in the hall

solutions
be tidy
put my shoes away
be fast
be quiet

b) Act out one role-play for the class or for another pair. Partner B acts out the problem. Partner A acts out a reaction and then starts the dialogue.

c) Give feedback to one or more other pairs.

Speak louder, please.

I like the solution.

I have the same problem with my sister.

► Workbook, p. 36

Digital quiz — I can understand a problem and talk about it.

The Brighton dares: Family

1 What are the dares?

BEFORE YOU WATCH **Look at the pictures and complete the sentences.**

1

2

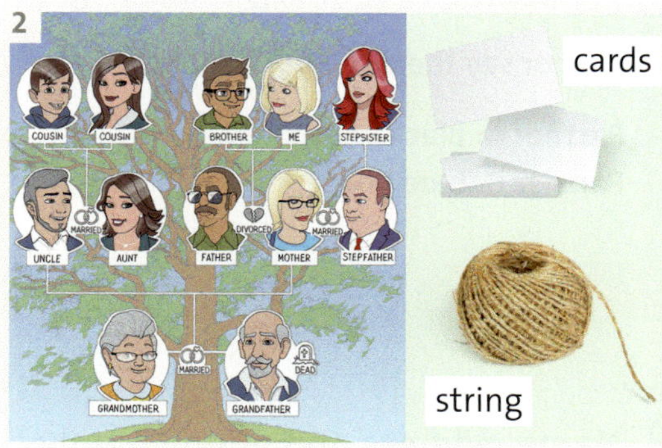

1 One dare is to ... a ... for ... hours[1].
2 The other dare is to make a 3D family ... with ... and ... in public[2].

2 VIEWING Two families

a) **Watch the video from 00:00 to 01:30 and check your answers from 1. Complete the sentences. Then check with a partner.**

Daisy isn't happy about her dare because the postbox is ... Luke's house.
Mrs Arinze's homework for Daisy and Emir is ...

b) **Watch the whole video. True (T) or false (F)?**

1 Mr Campbell and Mrs Collins have letters[3] for the postbox.
2 Mrs Collins wants to find her father.
3 Mrs Collins has tea and biscuits[4] for Daisy after her dare.
4 Emir and Gloria do his dare on the beach.
5 Mrs Collins and Robert Collins speak on the phone.

c) **Compare your answers with a partner. Take turns. Then watch the video again and check.**

Is sentence 1 true or false?

I think it's true. / I think it's false.

3 Emir's family tree

Stop the video at 10:00. What do you think of Emir's tree?

I think Emir's tree is ...

[1] **hour** *Stunde* [2] **in public** *in der Öffentlichkeit* [3] **letter** *Brief* [4] **tea and biscuits** *Tee und Kekse*

Spelling

1 Song The alphabet

a) Look at the alphabet song in the box and listen. Then listen again and sing.

b) Sing or say the alphabet in pairs.

Partner A: black lines.
Partner B: blue lines.

The alphabet
A B C D E
F G H I J
K L M N O
P Q R S T
U V W
X Y Z
That's the alphabet!

2 Name, address and phone number

a) Sunita is on the phone about a coding course. Copy the form. Then listen and complete it.

First name	*Sunita*
Family name	...
Address	...
Phone number	...

Say phone numbers in English like this: 07700 912638

oh–seven–seven–oh–oh
nine–one–two–six–three–eight

b) **Partner A:** Copy the form in a) again. Ask partner B the yellow questions and complete the form. Use the green questions to check.
Partner B: Answer the questions: *It's ...*

What's your first / family name?

What's your address?

What's your phone number?

Is that right?

Can you say that again, please?

Can you spell that, please?

3 Spell, write and say

a) Write three long words from this unit. Don't show your partner! *bathroom, ...*

B-A-T-H-R-O-O-M.

b) **Partner A:** Spell a word for partner B.
Partner B: Write the word.
Then say it and check the spelling. Take turns.

B or P?

It's "bathroom". B-A- ...

Can you say that again, please?

► Skills file 3, p. 196

Digital quiz I can spell words correctly.

Present your dream room

Step 1

a) Collect words and phrases for your dream room. Use a mind map. ► Digital help

- my dream room
  - things in the room: blue bed, red walls
  - where?: under, on
  - the room is ...: modern, big
  - pets

b) Check the spelling in the English-German Dictionary (pages 283–296). ► Skills file 2, p. 194

Step 2

Think about your dream room. Draw it, find photos or make it on the computer.

When you use pictures from the internet, write the name of the photographer or the website.

Step 3

a) Write about your dream room (at least five sentences). ► Digital help ► More help, p. 83 ► Wordbank 8, p. 220

There's a big red sofa. There are a lot of posters. It's quiet. ...

b) Read your partner's sentences and check the spelling.

c) Practise with your partner: Read your sentences and show your picture.
Look at ... *This is my ...* ► Challenge 5, p. 83

Step 4

a) Present your room to your group. Read your description and show your picture.

b) Answer three questions from your group.

Is your dream room in a house?

Yes, it is. It's in a house with a garden. / No, it isn't. It's in a flat.

c) Give other students feedback on their dream room. ► Let's talk: Feedback, p. 231

Your dream room is cool / great / very nice / ...

Digital quiz I can present my dream room.

1 WORDS Jay's favourite picture

I can talk about my family.

Look at Jay's picture and complete the sentences.

This is my favourite photo. It's my (1) f... in my flat. That's my (2) m..., Priya, and my (3) d..., Rahi, behind the sofa. Next to me is my (4) s..., Anika. She's nice!
Then there's my (5) a..., Meera, with her (6) d..., Sunita. Sunita is my (7) c...
Behind Sunita is her (8) b..., Nish. My (9) g... is on the sofa too. He's my mum's dad.

2 READING Priya's pictures

What's the correct picture? Write A or B.

1 That's me and Rahi. He's my partner.
2 And that's Anika. She's our daughter.
3 These are Anika's cousins, Sunita and Nish.
4 Here you can see my sister – she's Anika's aunt.
5 That's Anika's brother Jay. He's 11.
6 That's George, the parrot. The animals are very loud!

A

B

3 On the phone with FindAPet

I can talk about pets (questions and short answers).

a) LANGUAGE **Lily is on the phone with Ms Taylor from *FindAPet*. Complete Ms Taylor's questions and Lily's answers.**

1 ... you good with animals? – Yes, I ...
2 ... your home big? – No, it ...
3 ... your home quiet? – Yes, it ...
4 ... you and your family cat fans? – No, we ...
5 ... your neighbours dog fans? – No, they ...
6 ... you scared of lizards? – No, I ...

b) SPEAKING **Ask your partner four questions from a). Answer the questions for you. Take turns.**

Check

4 WRITING Amira's message to Jay

I can describe my home or dream home.

Look at Amira's mind map about her home. Write her email to her new British friend.

my home
- *a small house near Bremen*
- *a modern house, always tidy*
- *a kitchen, a living room, two bedrooms, a bathroom, a big garden*
- *friendly neighbours*
- *my parents and my brother*

Start your sentences like this:

Hi, Jay
I live with ...
We live in ...
It's ...
There's / There are ...
Our neighbours are ...
Bye
Amira

5 LISTENING Noah's room

I can describe my room.

a) **Listen to Noah. What's in his room? Write the words.**

A
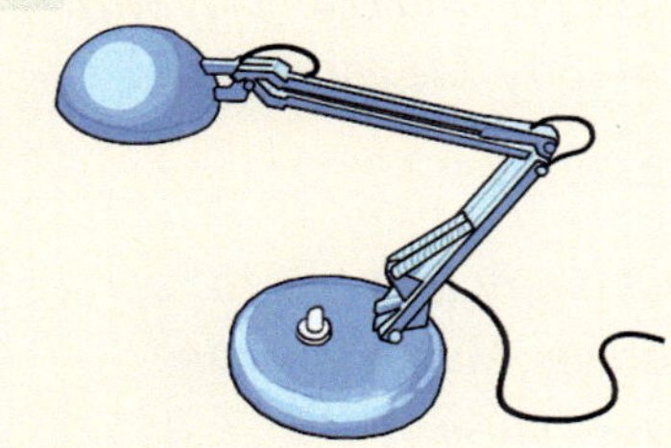

B

C

D

E

F

b) **Listen again. Choose the correct answer. Write A, B or C.**

1 Is Noah's room tidy?
A No, it isn't tidy. B Yes, it's quite tidy. C Yes, it's very tidy.

2 Where's Noah's desk?
A It's in front of the shelves. B It's behind the shelves. C It's next to the shelves.

3 Where's Buddy?
A He's next to the bed. B He's under the bed. C He's behind the bed.

4 Is Noah's room quiet?
A No, it isn't quiet. B Yes, it's often quiet. C Yes, it's always quiet.

Check

6 Reading Lily wants a new pet

I can understand a problem and talk about it.

a) Read the messages. Then put the pictures in the correct order.

Friday, 16.00

NOAH
Hi, Lily. Buddy says "hello"! That's his favourite ball.

LILY
Hi, Noah, hi, Buddy! You're so lucky. My pets are cute, but they don't play with me.

Saturday, 11.00

NOAH
We're near your flat. Are you at home?

LILY
That's great! Yes, I'm at home. You and Buddy can meet my two fish. And we can play with Buddy.

Saturday, 13.00

LILY
I'm very sorry, Mum. Noah and Buddy are in our flat and now it's very messy. You're right, the flat is too small for a dog.

MUM
Buddy is in our flat?!

LILY
Mum, I REALLY like animals! I'm often alone in the flat and I can play with Buddy. I'm sorry. Are you angry?

MUM
No, I'm not angry. Let's talk to Noah's parents. Maybe you can go to Noah's house.

Sunday, 10.30

LILY
Hi, Mum. This is me and Buddy in Noah's garden. He's so friendly! See you!

A

B

C

D

E

b) Right or wrong? Correct the wrong sentences.

1 Lily often plays with her pets.
2 Noah, Buddy and Lily meet at Lily's flat.
3 Lily's mum is angry because Buddy is in the flat.
4 Lily can't go to Noah's house.
5 Lily is often alone and wants to play with a pet.
6 Lily is at Noah's house on Sunday.

Check

7 Study skills Sunita's messages

I can spell words correctly.

One word is wrong in each message. Write the correct word.

1 Ben's music is too luod – again! ☹
2 Hi, Lily! The art homwork is hard – can you help me?
3 Coding isn't easy to lern, but it's fun!
4 Nish, 😋 thank you for the chocolade!
5 Have a nic weekend, Anika. 🙂
6 Mum, what's for dinnre? I'm really hungry.
7 Hello, Zane. What's your addres, please?
8 Hi, Mum. I'm bak at home now. See you.

8 Listening At the vet

There are two new animals at the vet. Copy the forms. Listen and complete them.

1

Pet's name: ...
Animal: ...
Family name: ...
Phone number: ...

2

Pet's name: ...
Animal: ...
Family name: ...
Phone number: ...

9 Speaking Zane's dream room

I can present my dream room.

Look at Zane's picture of his dream room. Say at least five sentences about it. You can use the words in the boxes.

big • cool • great • messy • modern • nice • small • yellow

bag • bed • cat • computer • desk • football posters • guitar • sofa • walls

This is Zane's dream room.
It's ... and ...
The ... is / are ...
There's / There are ...
The ... is on the ...

Check

VARNDEAN Teen Zine

This month's topics: pets, homes and families

Our school magazine: by students for students

Lucy's poems

I love writing poems! Here are three poems about pets.
You can write a pet poem too and send it to Teen Zine!

I have a mouse
In my room in our house
She has a little cap
And she's really good at rap!

I have a dog
She has a blog
She's always fine
When she's online!

I have a snake
His name is Jake
He's white and green
And very mean!

My pet by Max

I have a bearded dragon[1] or a 'beardie'. Here's a photo of him – isn't he cute? His name is Drago and he's grey and yellow.

Beardies can swim and run[2] fast. Beardies can live for 10–12 years. Drago is four. He's active in the day and he's very funny.

Drago has a big terrarium with a lamp. It's nice and warm under the lamp. Bearded dragons eat insects, fruit[3] and vegetables[4].

I think a bearded dragon is a fantastic pet!

We think Max has a great pet! What about you?
Do you have a great pet? Write to us and send a photo!

[1] **bearded dragon** *Bartagame (Echsenart)* [2] **run** *rennen, laufen* [3] **fruit** *Obst* [4] **vegetable** *Gemüse*

Puzzle time

What am I?

Can you say the animals?

I have four legs[1], but I'm not a dog
I can run fast, but I'm not a lion
I like carrots, but I'm not a rabbit
You can ride me, but I'm not a camel
What am I?

I'm small, but I'm not a mouse
I'm gold, brown or white, but not often black
I'm very active, but not in the day
You can play with me, but I like being alone
What am I?

Where do they live?

Emma, Zendaya, Leon and Danny all live in the same street. What are their house numbers?

1 Emma's house number isn't 2 or 6.
2 Zendaya's neighbours are Emma and Leon.
3 Leon's house is next to Danny's house.

Make a paper family

You need:

- a piece of paper (DIN A4)
- a pencil
- scissors[2]
- coloured pens

1

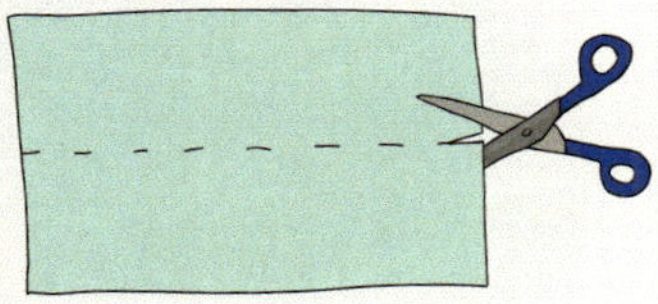

Fold[3] an A4 piece of paper in half. Cut[4] it in two.

2

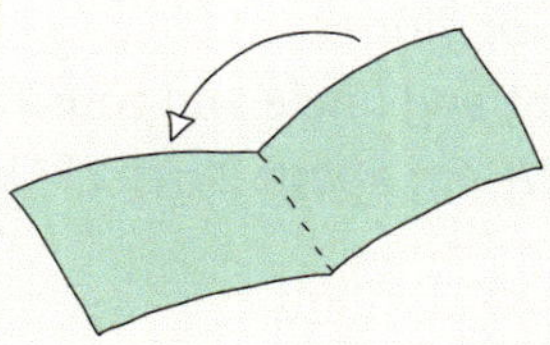

Take one piece. Fold it in half.

3

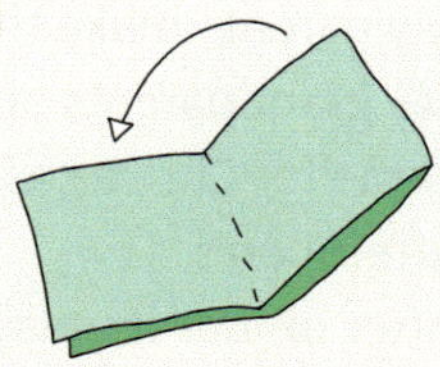

Fold it in half again.

4

Draw a person on one side of the folded paper.

5

Cut out the person.

6

Open the paper. Draw faces[5] and clothes on the people.

[1] **leg** *Bein* [2] **scissors** *Schere* [3] **fold** *falten* [4] **cut** *schneiden* [5] **face** *Gesicht*

Teen Zine Special: Festivals

Christmas

I'm Lyle and this is my sister Astra. This is how we celebrate[1] Christmas in my family:

Before Christmas

- ★ We send e-Christmas cards to my grandparents. My parents send cards and messages on social media to friends.
- ★ We decorate a Christmas tree.
- ★ My friends and I go to the neighbours' houses and sing Christmas carols[2].

We wish[3] you a merry Christmas
We wish you a merry Christmas
We wish you a merry Christmas
and a happy New Year.

Christmas Eve[4] (24th December)

- ★ We hang up[5] our stockings.
- ★ We make Christmas cookies.
- ★ We put cookies and milk under the tree for Father Christmas and a carrot for reindeer Rudolph.

Christmas Day (25th December)

- ★ We open our presents[6] in the morning. There are always some small presents in the stockings and some big presents under the tree.
- ★ My parents make the turkey for dinner.
- ★ My grandparents and my aunt and uncle and cousins come for Christmas dinner. We eat about 2 o'clock[7] in the afternoon[8].
- ★ After dinner we play a game.

What holidays do you celebrate?

What are your family's Christmas traditions?

---

[1] **celebrate** *feiern* [2] **Christmas carol** *Weihnachtslied* [3] **wish** *wünschen* [4] **Christmas Eve** *Heiligabend*
[5] **hang sth. up** *etwas aufhängen* [6] **present** *Geschenk* [7] **2 o'clock** *14 Uhr* [8] **afternoon** *Nachmittag*

Chinese New Year

I'm Vivian and my family is Chinese. There are about 400,000 Chinese people in the UK and Chinese New Year is a very important festival for us. It can be in January or February. Some British cities have big parties for the festival and Brighton is one of them!

There are 15 days of Chinese New Year celebrations[1] and we do something special each day.

Day 1 We visit[2] the oldest people in our family, eat sweets and drink tea.
Day 2 We give food to dogs in the streets because today is a special day for dogs.
Day 3 This is a quiet day: We respect the dead, stay[3] at home and go to bed early.
Day 4 We welcome the Kitchen God and make meals for the week.
Day 5 We clean[4] the house and welcome the God of Money[5].
Day 6 We throw away[6] old things.
Day 12 We get ready[7] for the Lantern[8] Festival.
Day 13 We eat simple vegetarian meals[9] to give our body a rest[10].

Kung Hei Fat Choi! Happy New Year!

Tell us about you and your family's New Year's traditions: the food you eat, the things you do ...

[1] **celebration** *Feier* [2] **visit** *besuchen* [3] **stay** *bleiben* [4] **clean** *putzen* [5] **God of Money** *Gott des Geldes*
[6] **throw away** *wegwerfen* [7] **get ready** *sich vorbereiten* [8] **lantern** *Laterne* [9] **meal** *Mahlzeit*
[10] **rest** *Ruhe, Pause, Erholung*

Partner page

▸ Page 54

6 Speaking A missing pet

a) Noah and Zane see some *Missing Pet* posters, but they have rain on them.

Partner B: Copy the poster.
Listen to partner A and complete the missing words in the first three sentences. Then read the next sentences to your partner and he / she completes the missing words in his / her poster.

b) Read the completed poster. Which pet is missing? Tell your partner.

I think the missing pet is ...

MISSING

Our friendly [illegible] is missing. He's [illegible] and orange and he's [illegible] years old. He likes [illegible] and flying and he's very [illegible].
He isn't scared of people and animals. He isn't happy when it's loud.

Please call **07700 900426** if you find him.

▸ Page 56

3 A special house

Compare your drawing with the photo.

▸ Page 64

1 Song Ben's song

My little flat

People ask, 'Is your flat big?' No, it's small
And it isn't new or modern at all
There aren't expensive pictures on the wall
There are two small bedrooms, there aren't three
And the living room is always very messy
But my little flat is perfect for me
Because there's music, there is love
There's my family, that's enough
My little flat is perfect for me

Diff bank

▸ Page 50

More practice 1 WORDS Family words

aunt • ~~brother~~ • cousin • dad • daughter • grandma • grandpa • mum • partner • sister • son • uncle

a) **Copy and complete the table. Use the words from the box.**

		or
brother	...	...
...		

b) **Read the sentences about Noah's family. Complete the sentences with words from the box in a).**

1 Mark is Noah's dad. → Noah is Mark's ...
2 Amy is Mark's sister. → Amy is Noah's ...
3 Eliana is Amy's daughter. → Eliana is Noah's ...
4 Albert is Mark's dad. → Albert is Noah's ...
5 Gladys is Noah's grandma. → Gladys is Mark's ...

▸ Page 53

More practice 2 Scout's family and friends

Read the sentences about Scout's family and friends. Make questions.

1 Sally is Scout's cousin.
Is Sally Scout's cousin?
2 Scout's parents are from Brighton.
3 Scout's brothers are loud.
4 She is very friendly.
5 We are all Scout's friends.

More practice 3 Character interview (1)

Partner A: You are Sunita's mum, Meera.
Partner B: You ask questions, partner A answers.
Use the picture and notes to help you.

1 ... you a vet?
2 ... Sunita your sister?
3 ... this your house?
4 ... you and Ben happy?
5 ... cats your favourite animals?

Challenge 1 Character interview (2)

Look at More practice 3. Choose a different character. A asks questions and B answers.

▸ Page 54

Parallel exercise

5c LISTENING Is that your pet?

c) Listen again and match the answers to the questions.

1 Are you OK, Sunita?
2 Is it hard to do your homework?
3 Is your dog Buddy loud?
4 Are you too busy for pets?
5 Are they your pets?

a No, they aren't.
b Yes, I am.
c No, I'm not.
d No, he isn't.
e Yes, it is.

▸ Page 55

Challenge 2

The right pet

What's a good pet for …?

1 a small home
2 a big home
3 a busy person
4 a quiet person
5 an old person
6 a small kid

▸ Page 56

More practice 4

Different houses

a) Partner A: Choose a picture – don't tell your partner! Talk about the home.
Partner B: Guess the picture: ***I think it's picture 1/2/…***

	a big / small / old / modern house / building.	
In this picture there is There are	a garden / a balcony / a lot of trees a big window / two windows a red / blue / … door	on the ground floor. on the top floor.

b) Partner B: Choose a different picture and talk about it. Partner A: Guess the picture.

Challenge 3 New homes

a) Zane asks his friend Alfie about his family's new house. Read their conversation.

Zane Are there kids at the neighbour's house?
Alfie No, there aren't. But there are a lot of kids in our street.
Zane Is there a garden?
Alfie There is. There isn't a really big garden, but it's nice.
Zane Is there a trampoline in the garden?
Alfie No, there isn't. But there's a swimming pool!
Zane Wow!

1 kids at the neighbour's house
2 a lot of kids in the street
3 a garden
4 a really big garden
5 a trampoline
6 a swimming pool

b) Write *yes* or *no* about the things in the list on the right.

c) Lily's friend Kinza has a new home. Complete their conversation.

Lily (1) ... a lot of floors in the building?
Kinza Yes, (2) ... There are twelve floors.
Lily (3) ... a lot of rooms in your flat?
Kinza No, (4) ... There are three rooms.
Lily (5) ... one room for you and your sister?
Kinza Yes, (6) ... It's a nice big room.
Lily (7) ... a balcony?
Kinza No, (8) ... Our flat is on the ground floor.

▸ Page 58

More help 9 MY TASK My home

b) Write about your home or dream home for a new friend.

I live with my	dad / mum / grandma / grandpa. little brother / sister. big brother / sister. two sisters and my brother.
We live in	a house / flat in ...
It's	old / new / big / small / nice / quiet / loud / ...
There's a kitchen and a bathroom and	a living room / a dining room / an office / a TV room / a toilet / three bedrooms / ...
There's	a garden / a balcony.
Our neighbours are	nice / friendly / not very friendly / ...

▸ Page 62

More practice 5 **Where is it?**

Say where the things or animals are. Your partner says the thing or animal. Take turns.

I see something brown under the desk. – It's a rabbit!

▸ Page 63

More practice 6 QUIZ **Who? What? Where?**

a) **Can you remember? Do the quiz. Write the answers.**

1 Who is Meera? She's ...
2 What room is next to the dining room in Sunita's house? The ... is next to the dining room.
3 Where is Nish's bedroom? It's ...
4 What colour are the walls in Sunita's bedroom? They're ...
5 Who is Ben? He's ...
6 Where is the snake? It's ...

b) **Now ask a partner the questions in a). Check your partner's answers. Take turns.**

Challenge 4 **Who is it?**

Write questions for the answers. Use *Who*, *Where* or *What*. Who is the student?

1 ... – The name of this student's school is Varndean.
2 ... – This student's home is in Hove.
3 ... – This student's mum is Meera.
4 ... – This person's favourite thing is chocolate.
5 ... – This student is ...

More help 8 MY TASK My room

a) SPEAKING **Answer your partner's questions.**

I have my own room. / I have a room with ...
My room is big / small.
My room is next to ...
There are / There aren't a lot of things in my room.
There are pets in my room: I have ...
There's a bed and a wardrobe / desk / ...
The walls are white / blue / ...
On my walls there are posters / photos / ...
My room is quiet / loud.

▸ Page 66

More practice 7 Who?

Write the names.

1 ... is alone at home.
2 ... is at her mum's house.
3 ... is nice and a great cook.
4 ... can't code because it's loud.
5 For ..., it's important to be polite.
6 ... and ... can use headphones.

▸ Page 69

More help UNIT TASK Present your dream room

a) Step 3 **Write about your dream room.**

There's	a big red sofa / a wardrobe for my clothes / ... a dog on the bed / a parrot / ... a guitar / a computer / a lamp / ...
There are	purple / red / ... walls. a lot of posters / photos / lamps / cushions / ... two cats / hamsters / ...
It's	big / small. quiet / loud. tidy / messy.

Challenge 5 SPEAKING A great house or room

Find a great house or room of a star you like.
Show your class a picture of it and talk about it.

Unit 3
My day

School journeys
Our students come from different places in Brighton and Hove. Some come to school by bus, by car or by train. A lot of students walk or go to school by bike. ❤️
🙂 #greenschooljourneys

1 Listening School journeys

a) Before you listen **Look at the photos. Write how the students go to school.**

1 Zane: I ... to school. 2 Sunita: I go to school by ... 3 Noah: I go ...
4 Lily: ... 5 Alice: ...

b) **Listen to the students. True (T) or false (F)? Correct the false statements.**

1. Zane's flat is near the school.
2. Sunita's bus is electric.
3. Noah's school journey is very short.
4. Lily has a long journey to school.
5. Alice is alone on her school journey.

Nach dieser Unit kann ich ...

- ○ über meinen Schulweg sprechen
- ○ meinen Alltag beschreiben
- ○ mich verabreden
- ○ neue Wörter nachschlagen und lernen

Unit task

- ○ die Höhepunkte meiner Woche vorstellen

2 SPEAKING **My school journey**

a) WALK AROUND **Tell different partners about your school journey. Make groups of students with the same transport.**

– *I go to school by bus.* – *Me too!*

Say more in your group: *I walk to school alone / with my sister / dad / friend / ... It's a short / long journey.*

b) **Say how students go to school.**

A lot of students in my class ... *Some ...*

► Workbook, p. 42

Digital quiz I can **talk about my school journey.**

A weekday

1 Words Big numbers

a) Listen and repeat the numbers.

b) Listen and stand up for the blue numbers. Sit down for the black numbers: 10, 15, 20, 25, 30, 35, 40, 45, 50, 55, 60, 65, 70, 75, 80, 85, 90, 95, 100

c) Listen to the numbers. If the number is under 50, make yourself small. If it's over 50, make yourself big.

► More practice 1, p. 111 ► Challenge 1, p. 111 ► Numbers, p. 307

2 Listening It's time for ...

8.00 = eight o'clock
8.05 = eight oh five
8.10 = eight ten
8.15 = eight fifteen

a) Before you listen Look at the box with times. Listen and clap the rhythm. Say the times from 8 o'clock to 9 o'clock.

b) Match the times.

1 It's four fifteen p.m.
2 It's three forty-five p.m.
3 It's four fifty a.m.
4 It's two thirty p.m.
5 It's three oh five a.m.

A 03.05
B 14.30
C 04.50
D 16.15
E 15.45

Good to know

The UK uses the twelve-hour clock with a.m. and p.m.
a.m. = midnight to noon
9 a.m. = nine o'clock in the morning
p.m. = noon to midnight
9 p.m. = nine o'clock in the evening

c) Listen to a school tour with a new student. Write the times.

The start of school: ...
Registration: ...
Lesson 1: ...
Break: ...
Lunchtime: ...
The end of school: ...

d) Check your answers.

The start of school is at ...

Yes, that's right.

No, it's at ...

3 Speaking The time

Partner A: Look at p. 110.
Partner B: Look at p. 111.

► More practice 2, p. 111 ► More practice 3, p. 112 ► Wordbank 10, p. 221
► Workbook, p. 43

4 READING Before and after school

a) BEFORE YOU READ **What's true (T) or false (F) about Zane? Decide with a partner.**

His hobby is parkour. I think that's false. – Yes, you're right./I think you're wrong. Let's check.

1 His hobby is parkour. (Unit 1, p. 19)
2 He's a swimmer. (Unit 1, p. 19)
3 He's always busy. (Unit 1, p. 32)
4 He has time for his friends after school. (Unit 1, p. 32)
5 He has a new computer. (Unit 1, p. 40)
6 His dream room is messy. (Unit 2, p. 73)

b) **Look at the picture, the headline and the first two paragraphs. Answer the questions.**

1 Why is Zane's family in the newspaper? *It's a letter from his ... for a competition.*
2 Why is Zane always busy on weekdays? *He helps his ... because she has a ...*

My son is the best ever!

Today's letter for our 'Best Kids Competition' is from Louise Adebayo. It's about her son Zane (11). Remember: You choose the winner, readers!

I have a bad illness and I use a wheelchair. My husband Eno has a cafe and he works long days. On weekdays my son Zane helps me.

Zane gets up at 7 o'clock, has a shower and gets dressed. His little sister Holly gets up at 7.30. Eno makes breakfast for us and we all eat breakfast. Zane takes Holly to her school at 8.15 and then he goes to his school. Then I work – I write books with special software.

Zane meets Holly at her school at 3.20 and they walk home. Zane makes a snack for us and tidies the kitchen. Then he does his homework. It takes an hour. On some days Zane helps me with dinner: He likes cooking! Or he talks with his friends or watches TV. On Fridays he goes to swimming training. He goes to bed at 9 o'clock.

Zane, you help me a lot. You're the best son ever!

c) **Read the whole article. Put Zane's day in the correct order:** *1f, 2 ...*

a He does his homework.
b He eats breakfast with his family.
c Zane takes Holly to her school at 8.15.
d He makes a snack.
e Zane goes to bed at 9 o'clock.
f Zane gets up at 7 o'clock, has a shower and gets dressed.
g He meets Holly at her school at 3.20.
h He tidies the kitchen.

5 Looking at language **Simple present**

Erklärfilm

a) Complete the sentences from the article.

1 You ... the winner, readers! (line 4)
2 I ... a wheelchair. (lines 5–6)
3 We all ... breakfast. (line 12)
4 They ... home. (line 17)
5 You ... me a lot. (line 25)
6 He ... long days. (line 7)
7 Zane ... me. (line 8)
8 She ... up at 7.30. (lines 10–11)
9 It ... an hour. (line 19)
10 He ... with his friends. (line 21)

b) Look at the verbs in a). What's different between sentences 1–5 and 6–10? Answer the question in the box below.

Bei regelmäßigen Tätigkeiten und Aktionen verwendest du das *simple present*.
Wann endet das Verb auf *-s*? Bei:
- **I / you / we / they?**
- **he / she / it?**
- **einzelnen Namen, z. B. Zane?**
- **mehreren Namen, z. B. Zane and Holly?**

Be careful with these verbs:
have – has
do – does
go – goes
watch – watches
tidy – tidies

▸ More practice 4, p. 112 ▸ Language file 10, p. 207

6 On Saturdays

Zane's mum tells a friend about the family's weekends. Choose the correct verb.

On Saturdays Zane and Holly (1) get up / gets up late. Eno (2) get up / gets up first and he (3) do / does the shopping. I (4) make / makes breakfast for us and we all (5) eat / eats. In the afternoon Eno (6) work / works in the cafe. The kids and I (7) go / goes to the park or we (8) play / plays a game at home.

▸ More practice 5+6, p. 112 ▸ Challenge 2, p. 113

7 Game **Weekdays**

Talk about your weekdays like this:

Student 1 I get up at six thirty.
Student 2 She gets up at six thirty. I have a shower and get dressed.
Student 3 He has a shower and gets dressed. I eat breakfast.
Student 4 He / She ... I ...

▸ Workbook, pages 43–45

8 SONG Good morning!

a) BEFORE YOU LISTEN **Match the times to the activities.**

1	07.00	a	eat your breakfast
2	07.15	b	go to school
3	07.30	c	have a shower
4	07.45	d	get up
5	08.00	e	brush your teeth

b) **Listen to the song. Compare your answers in a) with the song.**

c) **Listen to verse 6. It's not on this page. Say how the song ends. Then check your answer on p. 110.**

The girl says that it's …

d) ROLE-PLAY **Sing and act out the song.**

▶ Challenge 3, p. 113

The morning song

Get up, it's seven o'clock (It's too early!)
Get up, it's seven o'clock
It's seven already, it's time to get ready
Get up, it's seven o'clock.

Have a shower, it's seven fifteen
(But I'm tired!)
Have a shower, it's seven fifteen
It's seven fifteen, now it's time to get clean
Have a shower, it's seven fifteen.

It's seven thirty, eat your breakfast (I'm not hungry!)
It's seven thirty, eat your breakfast
I say it's the most important meal
of the day
It's seven thirty, eat your breakfast.

It's seven forty-five, brush your teeth
(The bathroom's cold!)
It's seven forty-five, brush your teeth
It's almost eight, you don't want to be late
It's seven forty-five, brush your teeth.

It's eight o'clock, go to school (Wait, Dad …)
It's eight o'clock, go to school (Dad!)
Don't make a fuss, time to catch the bus
It's eight o'clock, go to … (Dad!!!)

My task

9 My school day

WRITING **Read Zane's post. Write a post about your day. You can use the words in the box. Put your post in your** DOSSIER.

in the morning • after school • in the afternoon • in the evening • get up • have a shower • get dressed • walk / go by … • go to school • school starts • have lunch • school ends • go to bed

Hi, Zane
My name is … and I live in … This is my day:
In the morning I get up at …

Hello, everybody
My class has a project about the school day in other countries.
Please tell us about your school day.
Thanks.
Zane

▶ Digital help ▶ More help, p. 113 ▶ Wordbank 10, p. 221

▶ Workbook, p. 45

Digital quiz I can describe my daily routine.

School clubs

1 LISTENING Sports and hobbies

a) BEFORE YOU LISTEN **Look at the sports and hobbies A–M on the list. Which words can you understand?**

A drama
B art
C computer games
D cricket
E cycling
F dancing
G hiking
H music
I running
J singing
K table tennis
L trampolining
M windsurfing

b) **Listen to the Varndean students. Which sports and hobbies from a) can you hear? Write the letters A–M in the correct order. Which letter isn't there?**

c) **Listen again. Write Annie, Brahim, Rin or Liam.**

1 loves drama and singing
2 does competitions
3 is in the school band
4 plays cricket
5 does a sport in the sea

d) **Close your book. Which sports and hobbies can you remember?**

I remember table tennis and … What about you?

e) **Tell your partner about sports and hobbies you like and don't like. You can use the words from 1a).**

Good to know

Most schools in the UK have school clubs. Students can do hobbies and sports there.
– Are there clubs at your school?
– Say which clubs you want at your school.

I like singing because it's fun, but I don't like trampolining because it's hard. What about you?

I like street dance because it's exciting and running because …

► More practice 7, p. 113 ► Challenge 4, p. 114
► Workbook, p. 46

2 How often?

a) **Listen again. Choose the two correct words in each sentence.**

1 Annie A sometimes B often C never plays cricket,
but she A always B sometimes C rarely plays table tennis.

2 Brahim A often B rarely C always does drama,
but he A sometimes B rarely C never goes running.

3 Rin A always B sometimes C often goes hiking
and she A rarely B sometimes C never does dancing.

4 Liam A rarely B always C never does art when he feels stressed,
but he A rarely B sometimes C often plays computer games.

b) **Put the words in the correct place.**

never … … … *always*

3 Looking at language Word order

Erklär-film

a) **Read the sentences.**
Make the rule: Complete the table headings 1–4 with the words on the right: *1 subject, 2 …*

1 …	2 …	3 …	4 …
I	often	play	table tennis.
Brahim	sometimes	plays	music.
She	rarely	does	dancing.
We	always	do	a school show.
My parents	often	watch	cricket matches.

adverb of frequency

subject

object

verb

b) **Write the words in each sentence in the correct order.**

1 *When I feel stressed, … (always / I / swimming / go) because it helps me.*
2 *… (play / I / sometimes / basketball) next to the beach when it's sunny.*
3 *… (football / play / I / rarely), but … (watch / I / often / football matches).*
4 *… (cook / often / I) for my family.*
5 *… (my sister / cook / never) dinner for the family: She's too little.*
6 *… (I / walk / always) to school, but … (goes / Sunita / often) by bus.*

▶ More practice 8, p. 114 ▶ Language file 11, p. 207
▶ Workbook, pages 47–49

4 MEDIATION A very special school club

a) **Read the poster from Varndean school.**
Partner A: You can't understand the poster.
Ask partner B in German. He / She answers in German.

1 Was baut man in dieser AG?
2 Wo findet das jährliche Rennen statt?
3 Arbeiten die Schüler/innen allein oder haben sie Hilfe?
4 Kostet die Teilnahme etwas?

Du brauchst nicht jedes Wort zu übersetzen. Gib nur das Wichtigste wieder.

b) **Swap roles.**
Partner B: You can't understand the poster.
Ask partner A in German. He / She answers in German.

1 Welche Eigenschaften sollte man für die AG haben?
2 Wer darf Mitglied werden?
3 Wer nimmt am Rennen teil?
4 Wann findet die AG statt?

FORMULA 24 CLUB

Are you active and good in a team?
Are you good at sports, maths, art or design and technology?
If you want an interesting hobby, then join Formula 24 club at Varndean!
Students from all years can join.

We plan and make an electric car from old materials. Then we race with 700 other teams from the UK and other countries. The race is in a different city each year, so we always take a cool trip! More than 10,000 students do the race every year!

We meet every Friday afternoon at 3.30 for two hours. Mr Price and Ms Haffar sometimes help us, but we work hard too.
It's always a lot of fun even if we aren't the winner! It's a free club because we make and sell cakes to get money for materials.

▶ Challenge 5, p. 114

5 Speaking Secret sentences

a) Write three sentences for 1 and three sentences for 2. Choose words from the blue boxes for each sentence. Don't show them to your partner.

1 I → often / sometimes / never → play → basketball / table tennis / football → and I → rarely / always / sometimes → go → swimming. / cycling. / running.

2 I like → dancing, / coding, / walking, → but I don't like → singing. / playing music. / trampolining. → My favourite hobby is → cooking. / taking photos. / drawing.

Partner A: Guess your partner's sentences. If you choose the wrong word, start again.
Partner B: Say if your partner is right or wrong.

You never play football and ...

Wrong!

You often play football and ...

Right!

b) Swap roles with your partner.

My task

6 My free time

Read about Annie. Write an online message to her and answer her questions. Write five or more sentences. Use the sentences in 5 to help you.

Hi, I'm Annie from Varndean School. I want a new online friend! Are you in a school club? Tell me what activities you do and how often. What are your other hobbies? I always go to the school computer club on Wednesdays and I often play the guitar in my free time.

Hi, Annie
Nice to meet you! I'm ...

► Digital help ► Wordbank 4, p. 216

Digital quiz I can talk about my free time.

Meeting friends

1 Reading Are you busy?

a) Write the letters to put the messages in the correct order. Check with a partner.

1d, 2 …

b) Choose Lily or Zane for each phrase.

1 wants to meet at the weekend *Lily*
2 is busy all weekend
3 wants to go cycling
4 likes swimming
5 says sorry
6 is sad
7 is always busy

a Oh, OK. Are you free on Sunday? Let's go cycling!

b That's a shame. You're always busy, Zane. I never see you now. ☹

c Sorry, Lily. I'm busy on Saturday.

d Hi, Zane, let's meet on Saturday!

e Sorry, I can't. On Sunday I have a swimming competition.

2 Listening Let's meet

a) Before you listen Copy the table. Write the phrases in the correct place.

Let's … • No, thanks. • I'd love to. • I'm busy • Good idea! • Yes, please! • Are you free on …? • Sorry, I can't. • What about …?

Ask to meet	Say *yes*	Say *no*
…	…	…

b) Now Lily asks to meet Noah. Listen and tick the phrases from your table in 2a) when you hear them. Which phrases are not in the dialogue?

c) Where and when is Lily and Noah's meeting?

Lily and Noah's meeting is at (time) *on* (day) *at* (place).

at 9 o'clock
at the park
on Saturday
on Sunday

3 ROLE-PLAY Can we meet this weekend?

Go to p. 110 and act out Lily and Noah's conversation.
You can use puppets too.

▶ Challenge 6, p. 115

4 Sunday plans

Read the messages from your English friend. Write answers. The sentences on the right can help you.

1 *Are you free on Sunday?*	*Yes, I am.*
2 *Great! Let's go skateboarding.*	*Sorry, I don't like ... Let's ...*
3 *OK! What time?*	*What about ...?*
4 *Sounds good!*	*See you ...!*

5 CHANT Weekend plans

a) BEFORE YOU LISTEN Lily and Sunita want to meet. Match the phrases in blue to the pictures.

1 

2 

3 

4 

Weekend plans

a *Let's go out!*
b *Let's have some fun!*
c *Let's go out to the shops!*
d *Let's see our friends!*
e *Let's go hang out!*
f *Let's go, let's go: Why not?*
g *Let's stay home.*
h *Let's just relax.*
i *Let's watch a film and chill.*
j *Let's eat some snacks.*
k *Let's play a game.*
l *Let's just sit still.*

b) Listen and chant.

▶ Workbook, p. 49

6 Favourite activities with friends

a) Write your top three activities with friends from the box.
I like gaming with friends, hanging out and ...

b) Guess your partner's top three activities. Take turns.
I think your top activities with friends are ...

coding • cooking • cycling • gaming • going to the beach • hanging out • playing football • playing games • playing music • shopping • skateboarding • swimming • watching films

My task

7 Are you free?

a) Copy the calendar.

	Friday	Saturday	Sunday
9.00	*SCHOOL*	*activity:* *with:*	*activity:* *with:*
1.00	*SCHOOL*	*activity:* *with:*	*activity:* *with:*
5.00	*activity:* *with:*	*activity:* *with:*	*activity:* *with:*

b) DOUBLE CIRCLE Choose an activity from the box here or in 6 or your own idea. Talk to a partner.

Let's go to the beach.

Good idea! Are you free on Saturday at 9 o'clock?

Yes, I am. / No, I'm not. Sorry. What about Sunday at 5 o'clock?

Ideas
- *go to the beach*
- *go to the park*
- *go to the skatepark*
- *go skateboarding*
- *go swimming*
- *go cycling*
- *meet at my house / flat*
- *play football*

c) One circle moves to the right. Talk to a new partner. Complete your calendar from a).

d) Tell your partner about your plans.

On Friday at 5 o'clock in the afternoon, I want to go swimming with Lea.

▸ Workbook, p. 50

Digital quiz I can make plans to meet friends.

Background file

1 Cricket and Crackit

a) **Read the text and look at the pictures.**

Cricket is a popular sport in Britain.
There are two teams with eleven players each.
They play on a big field.

b) **Now do the quiz.**

Quiz: Cricket and Crackit

1 Cricket is a sport and the name of an ...
2 A cricket team has 11 ...
3 You play cricket on a big ...
4 Cricket balls are small and ...
5 Students in Varndean's Crackit club design cool ...
6 Students play cricket in the Crackit ...
7 The Crackit club plays in the sports ...

Varndean school has a Crackit club. Students design cool bats and play cricket with them. They play in the sports hall, not on a field.

▸ Workbook, p. 50

The competition

1 Reading About the story

a) Before you read **Look at the title and the pictures. Choose A, B, C or D.**

A Zane wins the competition. But his mum is too ill to go to the prize show.
B Zane is the winner. His family and friends are really happy.
C Zane isn't the winner of the competition. His friends are very sorry.
D Zane wins the competition. His family is happy, but his friends are angry at him.

b) **Read the story and check your answer from 1a). Say which parts (1–6) show the correct answer.**

1
'Hey, Lily! Look at this!' At breakfast Lily's mum shows her the article about Zane in the newspaper.
'What?' Lily is surprised. She reads the article. 'I know Zane's mum is ill. But not that she's in a wheelchair.'
She takes a photo of the article and sends it to Sunita and Noah.

2
The next day Lily, Sunita and Noah talk to Zane after school. 'Hi, Zane,' Sunita says. 'Let's go to the park.'
'Hi, guys.' Zane looks at the ground. 'Erm, sorry. I can't. I ... erm ...'
Noah shows Zane the article on his phone. 'It's OK, Zane, we know about your mum. That's why you're always so busy! But why is it a secret?'

3
'I feel bad for my mum,' says Zane. 'But please don't be sorry for her – she's great. And don't be sorry for me!'
'Zane, you help your mum – that's cool,' says Lily. 'But we're your friends. You can tell us.' 'Don't be angry, Lily,' says Zane. 'People see Mum in her wheelchair and they stare at her. I hate that!'

4

Later at Zane's home ...

'Hello, Louise Adebayo. What? Really? ... That's great! Thank you so much. ... Bye'. 'Zane, come here!' His mum is happy. 'You're the *Best Kids Competition* winner! Well done!'

'Thanks, Mum,' says Zane. 'I love you!'

5

Zane texts his friends with the good news. They are very happy!

Louise gets tickets for the prize show for the family and Zane's friends. She is often tired, but she wants to go to the prize show.

6

At the prize show ...

Zane talks to everybody.

'Hello. Thanks for choosing me as the winner. Mum and Dad and Holly – you're the best! And thanks to my friends Lily, Sunita and Noah! There's some prize money for the winner. I'd like to ...'

2 Headings

Choose headings from a–f for parts 1–6. Or use your own ideas. *1c, 2 ...*

- a Zane says thank you.
- b Zane's friends tell him they know.
- c Zane's friends find out about his mum.
- d Zane tells his friends he's the winner.
- e Zane explains about his mum.
- f Zane's mum is happy.

3 What happens in the story

Read the story again. Complete the sentences.

▶ Parallel exercise, p. 115

1 Lily sends ...
2 Zane says he can't go ...
3 Zane explains about ...
4 Zane's mum tells him that he is ...
5 Zane's mum is tired, but she wants to ...
6 The competition winner gets ...

4 SHOWTIME Freeze!

a) Say how people in the story feel in parts 1–6. The words in the box can help you.

angry • happy • sad • sorry • ~~surprised~~ • tired

In part 1 Lily is surprised. In part 2 Zane is …

b) Choose one of the six parts of the story. Show it as a freeze-frame. Show feelings with your body and face. You can use things (a newspaper, a phone, …) in your freeze-frame too.

c) Show the class. The class says what part it is. Then the class gives feedback.

It's part 5. Zane's friends are happy. His mum is tired.

Your freeze-frame is great!

5 Zane's prize money

a) Zane's prize money is £500. Decide what Zane does with the money. You can use the ideas in the box or your ideas. Agree on two ideas.

Ideas

- *gets a new TV for his family / …*
- *gets a new video console / …*
- *gives some money to his mum and dad*
- *pays for a big party with family and friends*
- *pays for a cleaner*
- *puts it in the bank*

Good to know

The UK's money is the pound (£). In one pound, there are 100 pence (p). How much is £500 in euros?

I think he gets / gives / pays for …

That's a good idea!

I think he …

b) Listen to Zane's ideas in his speech. Are they the same as your group's ideas?

Zane wants to …   Our ideas are the same / different.

6 LIFE SKILLS Be kind

a) THINK Zane is kind because he helps his mum. You can choose one person for a prize. Who is kind in your group of friends, your family or where you live? Think about reasons why: *My basketball trainer is really kind because …*

▶ More help, p. 115

b) PAIR Tell a partner about the person: *My kind person is …*

c) SHARE Tell the class your ideas.

Digital quiz   I can understand feelings in a story.

The Brighton dares: Sports and hobbies

1 About Daisy and Emir

a) BEFORE YOU WATCH **Look at the lists. What are Daisy and Emir's sports and hobbies?**

Daisy plays table tennis and she ...

Emir
do drama
play football

Daisy
play table tennis
go swimming

b) **What other things do you know about the friends? (Pages 35 and 67 can help you.)**

2 VIEWING Time for a new dare

Watch the video. Choose the correct picture (A or B) for each dare.

Daisy's dare for Emir is to ...

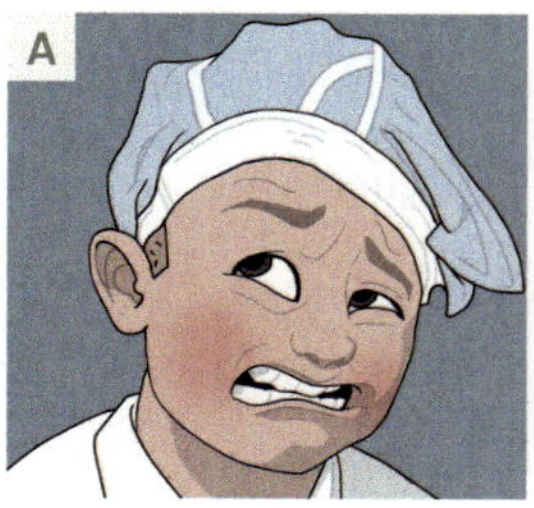

A wear underpants[1] on his head.

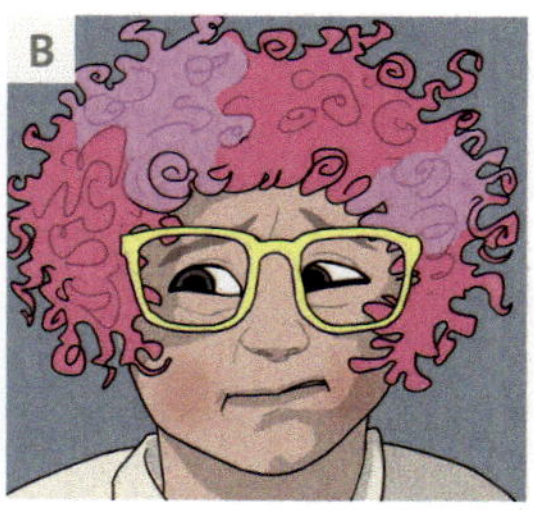

B wear pink hair.

Emir's dare for Daisy is to ...

A make a street drawing.

B play street music.

3 VIEWING Who helps? Who can't help?

a) **Match the people to how they help or can't help. Then watch the video again and check.**

1 Gloria helps Emir.
2 Amal can't help Daisy.
3 Gloria can't help Daisy.
4 Jenny helps Daisy.

a She has a trip to London at the weekend.
b Daisy can play her guitar.
c She can't play the violin for six weeks.
d She gives him a good idea.

b) **Complete how Emir and Daisy do their dares.**

Emir makes a ... from ... *Daisy plays the air[2] ... to her brother's ...*

4 A new sports or hobby dare

Brainstorm new sports or hobbies dares for Daisy and Emir. Then choose the best dare!

What about this? Play table tennis in the canteen.

[1] **underpants** *Unterhose* [2] **air** *Luft*

► Workbook, p. 52

Look up and remember words

1 Look up free-time activities

A new English friend writes to you about free-time activities. You don't know the words in blue.

a) First write the words in a list in alphabetical order.

b) Look up the words in the English-German Dictionary on pages 283–296.

c) Listen and check your answers.

I have a lot of free-time activities! I like crafts, especially jewellery making. I like chess and jigsaw puzzles too. I love collecting things with cats and I love skating.

For words with the same first letter, look at the second letter.

2 Find more free-time activities

Look at Wordbank 4 on free time (p. 216). What are these activities in English?

1 Backen
2 Gitarre spielen
3 Kajakfahren
4 Klettern
5 Nageldesign
6 Reiten

3 Write and remember

Choose five English words from 1 and 2. Write them in your VOCAB FILE.

English	Write a sentence, draw a picture	German & my other languages
collecting	I like collecting rubbers and football cards.	Sammeln, toplamak
jigsaw puzzles		...

4 Odd word out

a) Find the three words in the same word group. Then say the odd word out.

1 running • swimming • cycling • drawing
2 cola • burger • sandwich • fish
3 monkey • parrot • dog • rabbit
4 book • money • words • page
5 kitchen • bathroom • sofa • living room
6 old • big • quiet • house

b) Make an *Odd word out* with four words for the class.

► Skills file 4, p. 197

Digital quiz

I can look up and learn new words.

Share your highlights of the week

Step 1

Think about what you do every week.
Write sentences about the best things.
Choose three to five activities.

On Wednesdays I have a singing lesson at 15.30.
On Saturdays I always get up at 10 o'clock. My dad often takes me to a football match.

Or you can be your favourite singer, a superhero, a TV star, your pet – or me!

► Wordbank 4, p. 216

YOU CHOOSE Step 2

Do task A or B.

Task A	Task B
Draw a comic of your activities from **step 1**. Write your sentences from **step 1** under your comic pictures. You can add speech bubbles too.	Make a video: Record your sentences from **step 1** on your phone. You can show things, for example headphones for music.

Check that the light is good for your video. Speak clearly.

Step 3

Task A	Task B
Show your comic to a partner. Get feedback.	Play your video to a partner. Get feedback.

I like your pictures. Check your spelling.

Your video is really good. Don't speak so fast.

► Let's talk: Feedback, p. 231

Step 4

Look at the comics and watch the videos. Give feedback.

Your comic is great! Your pictures are cool!

► Let's talk: Feedback, p. 231

Digital quiz

I can share the highlights of my week.

1 READING Zara's school journey

I can talk about my school journey.

a) Read the email from Zane's friend Zara.

to Zane
from Zara

Hi, Zane
How are you? My new school in London is great. I have lots of friends now and I like most of the teachers. But I have a problem and that's the journey to school. London is so big and my house isn't near my school. 👎 Sometimes I go to school by car, with my mum, and that's good because it's fast. But most days I go by bus. I don't like the bus because the other people are really loud! 😟 It's slow too: The journey takes 45 minutes. Sometimes I'm late for school and my class teacher isn't happy! What about you? Is your school journey good or bad? Why?

See you later 🤗
Zara

b) Read the sentences. True (T) or false (F)?

1 Zara isn't happy at her school.
2 Her school journey is long.
3 Zara goes to a different school in Brighton.
4 The bus is often quiet.
5 She's sometimes in trouble with her teacher.

c) Answer the questions.

1 Is Zara's car journey good or bad? – *Zara's car journey is ... because it's ...*
2 Is Zara's bus journey good or bad? – *Zara's bus journey is ... because the bus is ... and ...*

d) SPEAKING Talk about your school journey with a partner.

I go to school by 🚗 / 🚲 / 🚆 / 🚌 / ...
I 🚶 to school.
My school journey is 👍 / 👎 because it's long / short / loud / quiet / fast / slow.
That's 👍 / 👎 because ...

Check

2 WORDS Sunita's morning

I can describe my daily routine (simple present).

Sunita talks about her morning routine. Complete her sentences.

1 I ... at six fifteen.

2 At six thirty I ...

3 And I ...

4 After that I ...

5 Then I ...

6 I ... at 8 o'clock.

3 LANGUAGE Sunita's evening

Complete Sunita's sentences. Use the verbs in the box in the correct form.

do (2 x) • eat • go • have (2x) • make • read • take • tidy • watch

I come home from school at 4 p.m. Sometimes Nish (1) ... a snack for us – we're always hungry after school! Then I (2) ... my homework. That (3) ... thirty minutes. We (4) ... dinner at 7 p.m. and then Ben (5) ... the kitchen. After dinner I (6) ... TV and Nish (7) ... his homework on the computer. Nish always (8) ... lots of homework! I'm lucky: I rarely (9) ... much homework. Mum and Ben often (10) ... the newspaper. On weekdays I (11) ... to bed at 9 p.m.

4 SPEAKING A conversation with Ryan

I can talk about my free time.

Ryan asks Lily about her free time. Look at Lily's calendar and say her answers.

Are you in a school club, Lily? Tell me what activities you do and how often.

Phrases

- *(Yes,) I'm in the ... club.*
- *I like/do/play/go to/... too.*
- *I (sometimes/often/always) play/walk/do ...*

Monday	Tuesday	Wednesday	Thursday	Friday	Saturday	Sunday
5.30 p.m.: table tennis		4.30 p.m.: parkour	after school: art club		10 a.m.: parkour	11 a.m.: walk with Dad

Check

5 Words Next weekend

I can make plans to meet friends.

Lily and Alice talk about the weekend. Choose the correct ending for each sentence. There are two extra endings. Copy the sentences into your book.

Lily	Are you free on (1) ...	a shame!
Alice	Sorry Lily, I'm (2) ...	b 11 a.m.
Lily	That's a (3) ...	c have.
Alice	What about Sunday?	d cycling.
	Are you (4) ...	e busy.
Lily	Yes, I (5) ...	f idea!
Alice	Great. Let's go (6) ...	g am.
Lily	Good (7) ...	h 10 p.m.
Alice	Let's meet at the pool at (8) ...	i free?
		j Saturday?

6 Listening Saturday plans

I can understand feelings in a story.

a) Listen to Noah's conversations. What are the students' plans for Saturday? Copy and complete the table. Use the words in the box.

homework • free (3 x) • see grandpa • shopping • swimming • yoga

	Saturday morning	*Saturday afternoon*
1 Zane		
2 Lily		
3 Noah		
4 Sunita		

b) Listen again. Say how they feel. Write the correct ending.

1 Zane is ... 2 Lily is ... 3 Noah is ... 4 Sunita is ...

angry

tired

sad

surprised

happy

sorry

Check

7 STUDY SKILLS The computer club

I can look up and learn new words.

a) Read about the computer club on a British school's website.

b) Look at the text again. Write the blue words in alphabetical order.

c) Look up the words in the Dictionary on pages 283–296.

d) Write the words from b) in the correct group.

Hi, we're the computer club! We swap ideas about technology. We love memes. We help our classmates with computer problems. We give them amazing tips. It's great – we're never stressed. We meet on Wednesdays at 3.30 p.m. in the computer room.

emails	…	*angry*	…	*give*
headphones	*friends*	*sad*	*good*	*tell*
…	*students*	*scared*	*interesting*	*share*
websites	*teachers*	…	*important*	…

8 WRITING Fabian's week

I can share the highlights of my week.

Fabian shares the highlights of his week. Look at the pictures and write his sentences.

On Monday afternoon I go cycling with my friend. …

Monday afternoon – cycling

Tuesday – 16.30 – guitar lesson

Wednesday – grandpa's farm

Thursday – 15.10 – school drama club

Friday evening – computer games

Saturday and Sunday – big breakfast

Check

VARNDEAN Teen Zine

This month's topics: your school journey and free time

Our school magazine: by students for students

School journeys

Hi, I'm **Femi**. I go to school by bike. It only takes ten minutes. I'm lucky! For some kids their school journey takes a long time. There's a great film about four students (11–13) and their school journeys. Read about them here. You can watch the trailer online. Look for the film *On the Way to School.*

Samuel from India uses a wheelchair. Each day his two brothers take him to school. The wheelchair is old and the journey is hard. It takes one hour and fifteen minutes for four kilometres.

Zahira lives in the mountains[1] in Morocco. Every week Zahira and her friends walk 22 km through[2] the mountains to her school. Her journey takes four hours.

Jackson from Kenya walks 15 km to school with his sister every day. It takes two hours. They need to be careful of dangerous[3] elephants!

Carlito lives in Argentina. He rides his horse to school every day and his little sister sits on the horse too. Their journey is 18 km.

[1] **mountain** *Berg* [2] **through** *durch* [3] **dangerous** *gefährlich*

My cool hobby

Two Varndean students tell Teen Zine about their hobbies.

Adam: I have a cool hobby: I collect toothbrushes. I have two hundred and thirty-seven! They're all new. I like the different colours and the different toothbrushes.

Ming: I collect stones and I draw on them. I draw animals and fruit and other things. I find the stones at the beach here in Brighton. It's a fun hobby!

Tell us if you collect something[1]. Or bring some of your things to school and tell your class!

The International Birdman[2] competition

Each year in a small town[3] near Brighton there's a special competition: People jump off[4] the pier and try to[5] fly!

They often wear funny clothes too. They get money for charity[6] and have great fun!

Don't try this at home!
But why not draw your own Birdman costume?
Or think of a cool competition for your school?

[1] **something** *etwas* [2] **birdman** *Vogelmensch* [3] **town** *Stadt* [4] **jump off sth.** *von etwas herunterspringen*
[5] **try to do sth.** *versuchen, etwas zu tun* [6] **charity** *wohltätige Organisation*

Partner page

▸Page 86

3 Speaking The time

Partner A

a) Look at the clocks. Tell your partner the time. Use the 12-hour clock with *a.m.* and *p.m.*

It's ...

1	2	3	4	5
09.10	11.45	15.15	15.35	20.50

b) Ask the time. Listen and write the five times. *What's the time?*

▸Numbers, p. 307

▸Page 89

8 Song Good morning!

c)

What? (Today is Saturday!)
Is it? Well, then
It's eight o'clock, go back to bed
It's eight o'clock, go back to bed
Who gets up at eight when you can
sleep in till late?
It's eight o'clock, go back to bed!

▸Page 95

3 Role-play Can we meet this weekend?

a) Read Lily and Noah's conversation. Then act it out.

Lily Hi, Noah, can we meet this weekend?
Noah I'd love to, Lily.
Lily Great! Let's go to the skatepark.
Noah Sorry, I can't go to the skatepark. It's too loud for me. What about the beach?
Lily Good idea! Are you free on Saturday?
Noah Sorry, I'm busy on Saturday. But I'm free on Sunday.
Lily OK, let's meet at the beach at 10.30 a.m.
Noah Let's ask Sunita too. See you on Sunday!

b) Change the blue words and make a new conversation. Act it out for another pair.

Diff bank

▸ Page 86

More practice 1 Your special numbers

a) Write three special numbers for you. The ideas in the box can help you.

b) Show your partner your numbers. He / She guesses what the number is.

Ideas

- *your birthday*
- *your favourite football shirt number*
- *your favourite number*
- *your house number*
- *your lucky number*
- *how old you are*
- *how old your pet is*

Challenge 1 Let's do some maths

Listen and add the numbers.

▸ Page 86

3 Speaking The time

Partner B

a) Ask the time. Listen and write the five times.

What's the time?

b) Look at the clocks. Tell your partner the time. Use the 12-hour clock with *a. m.* and *p. m.*

It's ...

1	2	3	4	5
06.45	12.05	14.30	18.55	22.40

More practice 2 What's the time?

▸ Numbers, p. 307

a) Listen to five conversations. Write the times in numbers.

b) Then check with a partner.

More practice 3 GAME Match the times

- Each student: Make 3–4 pairs of cards.
- Put all your cards on the table. Mix them up.
- Take turns to turn over two cards.
- Is it a match? Say 'Match!'

▸ Numbers, p. 307

▸ Page 88

More practice 4 Who is it?

Say who it is: Zane, Holly, Louise or Eno. Then listen and check.

1 He watches TV.
2 She uses a wheelchair.
3 He meets his sister at her school.
4 She gets up at 7.30.
5 He does his homework.
6 He makes breakfast.
7 He tidies the kitchen.
8 She goes to school with her brother.

More practice 5 Zane's favourite sport

a) **Find the correct form of the verb.**

Zane (1 go) ... to swimming training every week. He (2 walk) ... to his swimming pool. Zane and the other swimmers (3 have) ... training for an hour. They (4 work) ... really hard. Zane often (5 swim) ... in competitions. All the swimmers (6 want) ... to be the winner! But Zane is really good. He (7 love) ... swimming. His mum often (8 watch) ... the competitions. She (9 take) ... a lot of photos for the swimming club's website.

b) **Tell your partner about a sport you, your family or friends do.**

More practice 6 Funny sentences

Throw the dice and make funny sentences. Make 5–8 different sentences.

he, she it,
das **S** muss mit!

Step 1	Step 2	Step 3
Choose a person.	Choose an action.	Choose a place or time.
1 Zane	1 go / to dancing lessons	1 at 5 a.m.
2 You	2 watch / horror films	2 at school.
3 Mr and Mrs Adebayo	3 cook / spaghetti	3 in the car.
4 Sunita	4 draw / manga pictures	4 at lunchtime.
5 Lily and Noah	5 listen / to loud music	5 at 10 p.m.
6 Our teacher	6 do / yoga	6 on the bus.

Challenge 2 **Scout's routine**

Write about Scout's routine. Use the verbs in the box in the correct form and your own ideas.

eat • ~~get up~~ • go • meet • swim • watch

1 Every day Scout gets up at 7 o'clock. 2 She often ...

▸ Page 89

Challenge 3 **My day**

Write a verse about a time of your day. *It's (time), eat my breakfast / do my homework / ...*

More help **9** MY TASK **My school day**

Write a post about your day. Put your post in your DOSSIER.

Hi, Zane! I'm ... and I live in ... This is my day: In the morning I get up at ... I have breakfast at ... I go to school at ... I walk / I go by ... The journey takes ... minutes. We start school at ... Our first lesson starts at ... We have lunch at ... School ends at ... In the evening I ... I go to bed at ...

▸ Page 90

More practice 7 **My hobbies**

Copy and complete the sentences. Use the words from 1a) on p. 90.

1 I play computer g____.
2 I go h____g.
3 I do t__________g.
4 I play t____t_____.
5 I do d___a.
6 I go r_____g.

Challenge 4 Sports and hobbies

Copy the mind maps.
Add words from 1a) on p. 90, wordbank 4 or your own ideas.

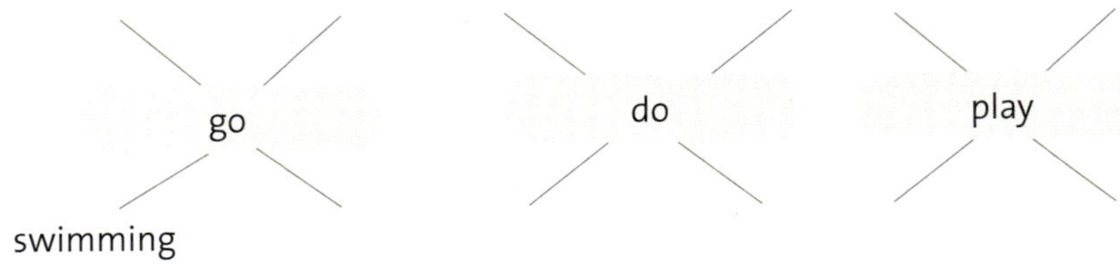

▸ Page 91

More practice 8 Surfing sentences

a) Look at the picture. Make sentences. Your partner checks your verbs.

He sometimes ~~play~~ football. – No, that's wrong. He sometimes plays football.

b) Use the words in the picture and say sentences about you.

▸ Page 92

Challenge 5 A poster

Make a poster in English about a club or sport at your school.
It can be a real club or a dream one. You can get ideas from the posters on p. 90.
Information for the poster:
club name • club description • when the club meets (days and times)

▸ Page 95

Challenge 6 ROLE-PLAY **Let's go to the park**

Act out a new conversation. Use the emojis to help you.

▸ Page 99

Parallel exercise **3 What happens in the story**

Read the story again. Match the sentence parts.

1 Lily sends
2 Zane says he can't go
3 Zane explains about
4 Zane's mum tells him that he is
5 Zane's mum is tired, but she wants to go
6 The competition winner gets

a his mum's illness.
b the winner of the competition.
c some prize money.
d to the park with his friends.
e a newspaper article to Sunita and Noah.
f to the prize show.

▸ Page 100

More help **6** LIFE SKILLS **Be kind**

Zane is kind because he helps his mum. Who is kind at school, in your group of friends, in your family or where you live? Think about reasons why and tell a partner.

My teacher is really kind because ...
My friends are ...

teacher trainer		helps / help	me with my homework / with my computer / at sport / with problems.
brother sister	he she	gives / give	me sweets / books / help.
friends	they	sends / send	me funny messages / pictures / memes.
classmates		shares / share	their lunch / good ideas.

Unit 4
Where I live

1

2

3

1 Viewing This is Brighton

a) Before you watch **Choose a photo. Say what you can see. Your partner guesses the photo.**

I can see	a beach / a building / a cinema / a lot of people / a pier / a skatepark / shops / …
This place is	boring / busy / cool / interesting / modern / nice / old / quiet / …

b) **Watch the video. Match the places (a–g) to the correct photos (1–7).** *1b, 2 …*

a Brighton beach | **b** ~~Brighton Palace Pier~~ | **c** Duke of York's cinema | **d** Hove Skatepark | **e** Brighton Marina | **f** Pavilion Gardens | **g** North Laine

Nach dieser Unit kann ich ...

- ○ Informationen über Brighton verstehen
- ○ meine Nachbarschaft beschreiben
- ○ über meine Stadt oder mein Dorf sprechen
- ○ über Sehenswürdigkeiten und das Wetter reden
- ○ Präsentationen halten

Unit task

- ○ die besten Orte in meiner Umgebung präsentieren

4

5

6

7

c) What are the places in 1–7? Then watch the video again and check.

1 There are a lot of cool shops and cafes here and they're all different.
2 This is a good place for a picnic. You can hear street music here.
3 You can watch old and new films here.
4 People come here to do skateboarding and practise new skills.
5 You can eat fish and chips and play games here.
6 This is a good place for bowling and great food.
7 This place is five miles long.

Good to know

1 mile = 1.6 km

d) Which places in Brighton do you like and why?

I like North Laine because there is / are ... and you can ...

▶ Workbook, p. 59

Digital quiz **I can understand information about Brighton.** ○

My neighbourhood

1 From Lily's window

a) Look at the photo and listen. You're Lily. What can you see, hear and smell?

I can see …	I can hear …	I can smell …
houses	seagulls	the neighbour's cooking
…	…	…

▸ More help, p. 142 ▸ Challenge 1, p. 143

b) Compare your answers. Take turns to say them. Add new ideas to your table.

2 Reading Lily's homework

a) Before you read Make six pairs of opposites to describe a neighbourhood: *big – small, …*

~~big~~ • boring • clean • dirty • friendly • horrible • interesting • loud • nice • quiet • ~~small~~ • unfriendly

b) Read Lily's homework. Say which adjectives from a) Lily uses for:

1 the shop: *small*
2 her neighbours: …
3 activities at the youth centre: …
4 the fields: …
5 some places on the estate: …
6 the cars: …

My neighbourhood

I live in Brighton on Whitehawk Estate. There are a lot of flats and houses and a small shop. We don't have a car – we go into the town centre by bike or bus.
I like our neighbours because they're really friendly. But some people on the estate aren't very nice.
I like the youth centre: It has interesting activities. I sometimes go to the homework club there after school because my parents work long hours. I have a big sister, but she's married and she doesn't live with us.
I like the sports centre. It doesn't have parkour, but I like playing table tennis there. And I like the big fields near the estate too. I walk there with my dad. But we don't go very often because he doesn't have a lot of free days.
Some people don't look after our estate. They don't put rubbish in the bins and some places on the estate are really dirty. I don't like the rubbish – and I don't like all the cars, they're very loud.
My neighbourhood has some problems. But I think it's nice and I like it.

▸ Workbook, p. 60

3 Lily's notes

a) Copy Lily's table with notes for her homework in 2.
Read her homework again and complete her notes.

☺ I like ...	☹ I don't like ...
the neighbours	the rubbish
...	...

b) Say why Lily likes or doesn't like the things in a).

Lily likes ... because ... *She doesn't like ... because ...*

4 Looking at language Simple present: negative sentences

a) Find all the sentences with ***don't*** and ***doesn't*** in Lily's homework in 2.

We don't have a car. *My sister doesn't live with us.*
... ...

b) Complete the rules.

Wenn wir im *simple present* ausdrücken wollen, dass wir etwas nicht machen, verwenden wir:

I
You
We
They
+ ... + have / live / like / go / ...

He
She
It
+ ... + have / live / like / go / ...

Scout **likes** rubbish. Lily **doesn't like** rubbish.

► Language file 12, p. 208

5 Speaking Your neighbourhood

a) Make notes about what you like and don't like about your neighbourhood.

I like ... *I don't like ...*

► More practice 1, p. 143

b) Speed dating Talk to different partners. Make notes.

name	likes	doesn't like
Masoud	his friends	all the dogs
Emma	...	...

Hi, Masoud. I like the sports centre. What about you?

Masoud likes his friends. He doesn't like ...

c) Tell the class about one student.

► Workbook, pages 60–61

6 The youth centre

a) Lily tells her friends about the youth centre. Complete what she says.

1 *It doesn't open at weekends.*

I often go to the youth centre, but not at weekends. It (1 ~~not open~~) … at weekends. There are a lot of activities like cooking, boxing, crafts and football. There's a girls' group on Tuesday, but I (2 not go) … there: I (3 not have) … time then. Sometimes I play pool at the youth centre with my neighbour Niles. He (4 not go) … to Varndean and his school (5 not have) … a lot of clubs. What else? We (6 not pay) … for the activities – they're all free. A lot of people on our estate (7 not have) … a lot of money.

► Parallel exercise, p. 143

b) Talk about the activities in a) with a partner.

I go to / I don't go to	a youth centre.
I like / I don't like	pool / cooking / boxing / football.
I play / I don't play	pool / football.

► More practice 2, p. 143
► Challenge 2, p. 144

7 Words Places (1)

a) Match the places to the explanations. There is one extra explanation.

1 shop	a Kids do interesting activities here.
2 sports centre	b You watch films here.
3 beach	c You eat fish and chips here.
4 cinema	d You do different sports here.
5 field	e You buy things here.
6 youth centre	f You go walking here.
	g You swim in the sea here.

You can explain words in your Vocab file.

b) Start a page in your Vocab file **with a mind map for places. Add the places in a) plus at least four more places from pages 116–120.**

► Skills file 2, p. 194

c) Add explanations for all your words in b).

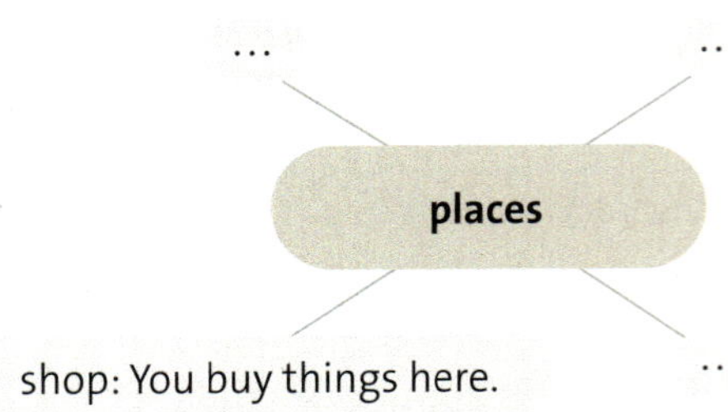

► Workbook, pages 61–62

8 GAME Places

a) Make a table with nine places from your mind map in 7b).

b) When the teacher explains a place:
Put up your hand and say the correct place. Cross it out.
When you have three words →↓↙↘, shout "Here!"

shop	...	...
...	...	...
...	*beach*	...

▸ More practice 3, p. 144

9 READING My neighbourhood

Read the posts. Say what Emma and David think about their neighbourhoods.

Jing likes / doesn't like her neighbourhood because ...
Alexis likes / doesn't like his neighbourhood because ...

www.my-neighbourhood.example.net

Hi, everybody! What's your neighbourhood like?
I live in a big city. It's very loud in my neighbourhood. There are a lot of cars and people. Everybody is very busy and it's also dirty. I don't like my neighbourhood. I'd like to live in a small town.
Jing

I live in a village in the country. Our village doesn't have many interesting places. There's a shop and a lot of fields and animals. It's boring sometimes, but I like living here. Our neighbours are very friendly and there are a lot of other kids.
Alexis

My task

10 A post about my neighbourhood

Write a post like the posts in 9. Write at least six sentences. Put your text in your DOSSIER.

I live in a village / a town / a city / in the country.
My neighbourhood has / doesn't have ...
My neighbourhood is / isn't ...
The neighbours are / aren't ...
☒ *I like / don't like ... because ...*

▸ Digital help ▸ More help, p. 144

Digital quiz I can describe my neighbourhood.

My town or village

1 Words Places (2)

a) Lily's friend Kasia doesn't live in Brighton: She lives in a small town. Lily tells Kasia about Brighton.
Match the places to the pictures.

Lily: Brighton has ...
1 a hospital
2 an ice rink
3 a library
4 a supermarket
5 a museum
6 a shopping centre
7 a stadium
8 a train station

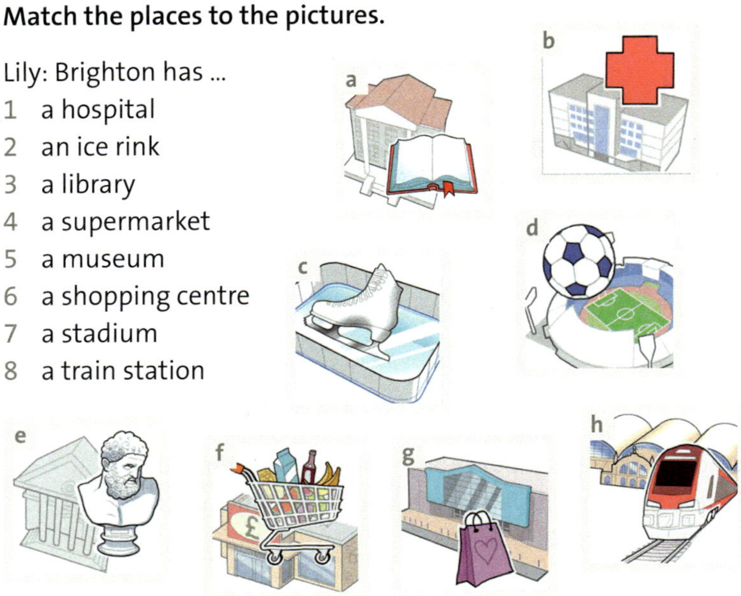

Good to know

Brighton is a city – but it's a small city.
The three biggest UK cities are:
1 London
2 Birmingham
3 Manchester
Find the places on the UK map in your book.

b) Listen and repeat the places in a).

c) Write the places from a) on pieces of paper and put them in a box. Sit in a circle. The first student takes a piece of paper and mimes an activity for the place. A student from the group says the place: *I think it's a hospital*. Then give the box to the next student.

d) Add the places to your mind map from p. 120.

2 Song Kasia's town

a) Close your eyes and listen to Kasia's song. Is Kasia happy with her town or not? Give a 👍 or a 👎.

b) Listen again. What places do you hear? Collect them on the board.

c) Listen again. Complete the song with the places.

d) Say what Kasia likes about her town.

► More practice 4, p. 145

Kasia's town

I think that my town is boring
And I don't like living here.
My town doesn't have a (1) ...
It doesn't have a (2) ... or (3) ...
There isn't anything for me
No (4) ..., no (5) ...
The only thing here that is good
Are my friends in the neighbourhood!

► Workbook, p. 63

3 SPEAKING Different places

a) **Partner B:** Look at p. 142.
Partner A: Look at your picture of a town.
Take turns to ask and answer questions.
Use the places in 1a).

Does your town have a hospital?
– Yes, it does. / No, it doesn't.
– That's the same. / That's different.

b) Now ask and answer questions about your town or village.

► Wordbank 11, p. 222

Do you like your town / village?

Yes, I do. / No, I don't.

Do you have a favourite place? (What is it?)

4 LOOKING AT LANGUAGE Simple present: questions and short answers

Erklärfilm

a) Look at the questions in 3a) and 3b). Complete the rule.

Wenn du eine Entscheidungsfrage stellst, auf die man mit **Ja** oder **Nein** antwortet, verwendest du eine gebeugte Form des Hilfsverbs *do* am Anfang der Frage:

... + I / you / we / they + have / like / ...?
... + he / she / it + have / like / ...?

b) Look at 3a) and 3b) again. Complete these short answers:

Yes, it ... / No, it ...   *Yes, I ... / No, I ...*

► Language file 13+14, pages 208–209

5 Towns and visitors

a) Complete the questions with *do* or *does*.

1 ... visitors sometimes ask you questions in English?
2 ... you have a favourite place in another country?
3 ... your town or village have a lot of visitors?
4 ... you visit other places in Germany?
5 ... your town have a visitor information centre?

b) Listen and check the questions in a).

c) Take turns to ask the questions. Answer with short answers. Give extra information.

► More practice 5, p. 145

► Workbook, p. 63

6 In town with Kasia and Bella

a) **Lily interviews her friend Kasia for some homework. Put the questions in the correct order.**

1 with you / go everywhere / does / Bella / ?
2 you / do / know / the town well / ?
3 have / problems / with Bella / you / in shops / do / ?
4 you and Bella / the bus / use / do / ?

Kasia and her guide dog Bella

b) **Match the questions to Kasia's answers.**

a Yes, I do. I have a map of it in my head.
b Yes, she does. She comes to school too.
c Yes, we do. Everybody on the bus knows Bella!
d No, I don't. Guide dogs can go everywhere.

▸ Challenge 3, p. 146

7 LISTENING Questions from visitors

a) **Listen to six short conversations. Match them to the correct pictures:** *1D, 2 …*

A

B

C
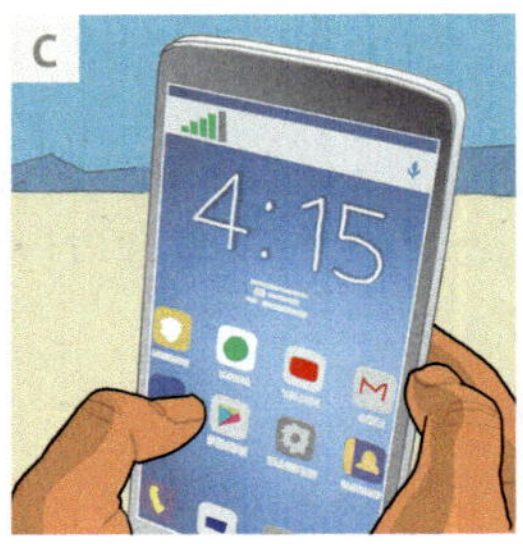

D

b) **Complete the questions in your exercise book.**

1 Does bus 12A go to the …?
2 Do you know a good fish and chip …?
3 Does the Brighton Museum open on …?
4 Do you have the …?
5 Does Brighton have a visitor … centre?
6 Does the … get warm in summer?

E

F

c) **Listen again and check. Does Lily answer *yes* or *no*? Tick (✓) or cross (×).**

d) ROLE-PLAY **Ask the questions in b) and give short answers. Be polite!**

When you ask for information, be polite. Use ***Excuse me*** (before you ask something) and ***Thank you***. When people say ***Thank you***, say ***You're welcome***.

8 SPEAKING Questions about your town

Take turns to ask for tips about your partner's town or village.

Does your town / village have a good …? / Do you know a good …?

▸ Workbook, p. 64

9 MEDIATION Welcome to the pier!

Your family wants to go to Brighton. You find a good website about the pier. Answer your family's questions about it.

1 Wann hat die Seebrücke auf?
2 Muss man dafür Eintritt zahlen?
3 Ich sehe eine Achterbahn und ein Karussell. Was gibt es außerdem?
4 Es gibt Konzerte. Und was noch?
5 Was ist das rosa Zeug auf dem Bild?
6 Was kann man dort essen? Gibt es auch etwas Gesundes?

www.brightonpier.example.com

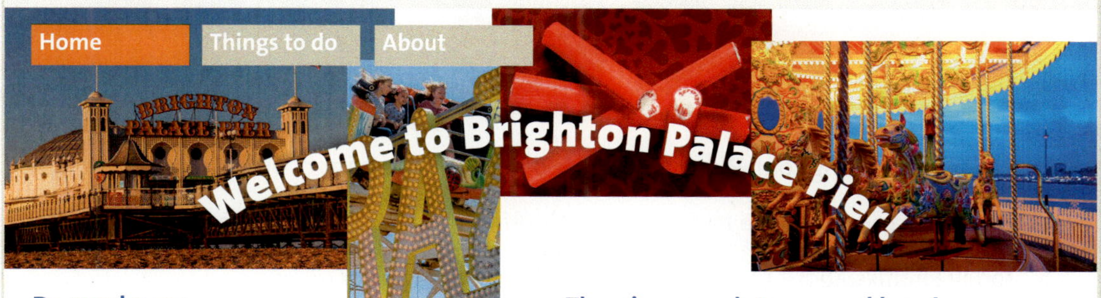

Do you know ...

... Brighton Pier is over 120 years old?
... it's open from 10 a.m. to 6 p.m. every day?
... it's free to visit the pier? (But you must pay for rides.)

There's so much to do!

There are great rides for all the family.
Try the trampolines.
Play games and win prizes.

There's so much to see and hear!

We have concerts, firework shows and special Halloween and Christmas activities.

There's so much to eat!

Are you hungry? You can choose from fish and chips, hot dogs, pizza, crepes, salads and ice cream. Don't miss Brighton Rock! It's pink, it's sweet, it's bad for your teeth – but it's part of Brighton!

My task

10 Five questions about places

a) Work in pairs. Agree on a place from your mind maps on p. 120.

b) Work with another pair. Pair 1 asks five *yes/no*-questions to guess the place.
Pair 2 gives short answers.
Pair 1 gets one point for the correct place.

c) The pairs swap roles.

Remember: You can also ask questions with forms of ***be***:
Is it free? – No, it ***isn't***.
Are there shops? – Yes, there ***are***.

▸ Digital help ▸ More help, p. 146

Digital quiz I can talk about my town or village.

Brighton in all weathers

1 LISTENING A walking tour

a) BEFORE YOU LISTEN **Find the correct picture.**

1 It's rainy.
2 It's sunny.
3 It's snowy.
4 It's cloudy.
5 It's windy.

Hi, Sunita! My uncle Aleksander and my aunt Svetlana from Russia are here in Brighton on holiday. We're on a walking tour now!

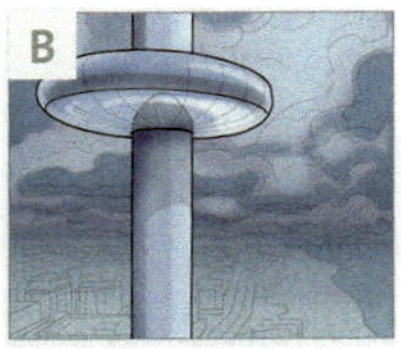

b) **Listen to the walking tour. Put the weather pictures in the correct order.**

c) **Listen to Eli's tour from the next day. What's different? Choose the correct words.**

1 Today Eli talks about the Pavilion when it's snowy / sunny / rainy.
2 He says you can have a party / barbecue / picnic outside the Pavilion.
3 Today on the beach it isn't windy / cold / warm.
4 On the pier it's very sunny / rainy / windy.
5 Today the wind takes a woman's hat / sandwich / phone.
6 At the end the tourists can visit the i360 because it isn't cloudy / cold / snowy.

▶ More practice 6, p. 146

2 LOOKING AT LANGUAGE Simple present: *wh*-questions (and how)

Erklär-film

a) **Read the questions about the i360 tower from people on the tour. Match them to the correct answers (a–d).**

1 When does the i360 open today?
2 How often does it go up and down?
3 How fast does it travel?
4 What do you see from the top?
5 Why do you think it's interesting?
6 Where do you buy tickets?

a You buy tickets online or at the ticket office.
b It goes up and down every 30 minutes.
c It opens at 10 o'clock.
d You see amazing views of Brighton from the top.
e Because you can take great photos from the top.
f It travels 16 metres per second.

b) **Look at these *yes/no* questions and the questions in a). What's different? Complete the sentences in the box.**

Does the i360 open today?
Do you think it's interesting?

Ja/Nein-Fragen fangen mit ... an.
Wh-Fragen fangen mit ... an.

▶ Language file 15, p. 209 ▶ Workbook, p. 65

3 More questions on the tour

Put the words in each question about Brighton in the correct order.

1 the shops / when / open / do / ?
2 buy train tickets / do / I / how / ?
3 you / do / why / love Brighton / ?
4 where / stop / the bus / does / ?
5 does / how much / cost / a bus ticket / ?
6 like / do / food / what / you / ?

4 The Upside Down House

Lily's aunt and uncle want to visit the Upside Down House.
Partner B: Look at p. 142.

a) **Partner A: Look at the review. Answer partner B's questions.**

www.upsidedown.example.com

We love this place! We come here to take really cool photos inside the house. It closes at 9 p.m., so we can also visit in the evening. And it isn't too expensive – tickets cost £5.

b) **Partner A: Ask partner B these questions. Use the correct question word and add *do* or *does*.**

1 Who / What / When ... the Upside Down House open?
2 Where / What / Why ... I buy tickets?
3 What / How / Who ... we take funny photos?

► Challenge 4, p. 147

5 Plans for the week

Lily's aunt and uncle want to make plans for the week. Look at the weather and answer their questions in complete sentences.

Good to know

Brighton isn't very warm in the summer or very cold in the winter. There are a lot of rainy and cloudy days, but not a lot of snowy days.

Monday	Tuesday	Wednesday	Thursday	Friday	Saturday	Sunday
16°	17°	18°	21°	23°	19°	22°

1 How many days are rainy this week?
2 We want to go to the beach on a warm, sunny day. What's the best day?
3 Why isn't Tuesday good for the beach?
4 Is Wednesday good for the i360? Why or why not?
5 What's good for Sunday: swimming or the museum? Why?
6 What's a good day for a walk in the park? Why?

► Workbook, pages 65–67

6 What can we do today?

a) **Partner A:** Ask your partner about the weather today.
What's the weather like today?

Partner B: Choose two or more words from the box.
Tell your partner the weather for today in Brighton.
It's rainy and windy today.

cloudy • cold • hot • rainy • snowy • sunny • warm • windy

Partner A: Your partner tells you the weather in Brighton.
Choose a place or an activity in Brighton for that weather.
Tell your partner why it's a good idea for the weather.
Let's go to the ... *It's inside / outside. / We can ... there.*

beach • cinema • i360 • marina • North Laine • park • pier • Upside Down House

Partner B: Give an answer: *Great idea! / No, let's ... / ...*
Find a new partner.

b) What's the weather like in your town today?
What's a good activity or place for the weather?

I think ... is a good ... because ...

My task

7 Quiz-quiz-swap

a) Write one question about your town or village and the weather on a card.
Use the notes in the table to help you.

What do you do when it's snowy?

What ... do Where ... go How ... travel	when it's	cloudy / cold / hot / rainy / snowy / sunny / warm / windy?

b) WALK AROUND
Find a partner and ask your question.
Answer your partner's question.

When it's hot, I go swimming.

► Digital help ► More help, p. 147

c) Swap cards and walk around again. Find a new partner and ask your new question.

Digital quiz **I can talk about sights and the weather.**

Background file

1 Talking about the weather

What you can say:

Looks like rain / snow / ...!

What a beautiful / horrible / ... day!

Terrible / Great / ... weather, isn't it?

Good to know

In Britain you can always talk about the weather when you meet people. It's a way to be friendly and make small talk. Because Britain is an island, there's a lot of rain and the weather changes often. Be careful: Bring an umbrella!

Look at the pictures. What's the weather like? Use phrases from the top of the page.

A

B

C

2 Weather phrases

Match the weather phrases (1–4) to the meanings (a–d).

1 (to) have a moment in the sun
2 (to) have your head in the clouds
3 (to) rain cats and dogs
4 come rain or shine

a gedankenverloren sein
b stark regnen
c kurz im Mittelpunkt stehen
d bei jedem Wetter; was auch immer geschieht

What goes up when the rain comes down?

▶ Workbook, p. 67

Lily's idea

1 Before you read Where Lily lives

a) **What can you remember about Lily's neighbourhood? Collect information with the class.**

She lives on an ... The neighbours are ...
The neighbourhood is ... There's a lot of ...

b) You choose **What rubbish or things can you find on the streets near your school? Do 1 or 2.**

1 **Make a list and share with your class.**

2 **Take photos and describe them to your class.**

2 Reading Clean-up day

a) **Lily makes a poster for a clean-up day on her estate. Read the first page of the story and complete the poster.**

HELLO, NEIGHBOURS!

Come to our ... day

When? ..., 2 April at ... Where? At the ...
Do you get angry about ... everywhere?
Do you want to live on a clean ...?

Then help us to clean up!

b) **Now read the whole story. Say what Buddy finds in the ground.**

It's 9 o'clock on a Sunday morning and there's a big group in front of the youth centre. 'It's a great idea to have a clean-up day, Lily!' says her sister Chloe. 'Look at all these people!'

'I guess a lot of people want a clean place to live!' says Lily.

Mr Davies is there too. He lives next to the Hall family. He sees Lily and Chloe's mum, Olga, and speaks to her.

'Mrs Hall, who are these people?' asks Mr Davies. 'I don't know them! And they're too loud. It's Sunday! Today is a quiet day.'

'Hello, Mr Davies. Today is the clean-up day. A lot of people are angry about rubbish everywhere,' says Olga. 'They want to live on a clean estate.'

'Well, I don't like this noise! I want to live on a quiet estate,' says Mr Davies. He walks away.

Olga looks at Chloe and Lily. 'It's OK, Mum. We can be quiet!' says Lily.

'Yeah! No problem,' says Zane.

'OK. Well, let's start! Hello everybody. Welcome to clean-up day!' says Olga. 'We have lots of big rubbish bags.'

'What about things for the Swap Place?' asks Lily's neighbour Dosia. 'So other people can use them.'

'Ah, yes,' Olga answers. 'Let's put good things over there. And let's meet here at 12 o'clock for lunch. Also, please don't forget: Some neighbours want to have a quiet day today.'

Lily, Chloe and Noah work together. Buddy wants to help too. First he finds a dead mouse. 'Yuck,' says Noah. Next Buddy brings an old shoe to Lily. 'Thanks, Buddy,' says Lily. Then Buddy digs in the ground for a long time. He barks. 'What do you have now?' asks Noah. 'Wow! Good dog! Hey, Lily, look at this.'

It's a gold ring. 'It has "Jack and Maria" in it,' Lily finds out.

'It's a wedding ring,' says Chloe. 'It looks old. But how do we find Jack and Maria?'

The neighbours meet at the youth centre at 12 o'clock. They have over fifty bags of rubbish! They also have some old furniture, a bike, shoes and a lot of other things for the Swap Place. They take them to the Swap Place garage. They eat lunch and Lily tells the others about the ring.

'Why don't we put up notices?' asks Zane. 'Maybe somebody knows Jack and Maria.'

'Good idea, Zane,' Lily answers.

c) Now listen to the end of the story.

3 Characters in the story

Who are they? Complete the sentences.

1 Chloe is ...
2 Olga is ...
3 Dosia is ...
4 J ... and M ... are the names in ...

4 Why, what and how?

Answer the questions.

1 Why is Mr Davies angry?
2 What two things does Buddy find before the ring?
3 How many bags of rubbish does the group collect?
4 When does Lily tell everyone about the ring?
5 How do the kids find Jack and Maria?
6 How does Mr Davies want to say thank you?

▸ More help, p. 147

5 Words in the text

Find words in the story with these meanings.

1 to find something in the ground you … (line 37)
2 when a dog 'speaks' (line 38)
3 things like tables and chairs (line 47)
4 where people put their car (line 50)
5 a paper with information (line 52)

6 The Whitehawk Swap Place

a) **True (T) or false (F)?**

1 *(To) swap* means to give something to somebody and take another thing.
2 Olga asks about the Swap Place.
3 Things for the Swap Place are things that other people can use.
4 The neighbours don't find many things for the Swap Place.
5 The Swap Place is in the youth centre.

b) **Correct the false sentences.**

7 SHOWTIME Missing scenes

Act out a scene that's not in the story for another group. You can use the ideas in the box or your own ideas.

- Dosia's group cleans up rubbish.
- The kids make notices about the ring.
- People take things from the Swap Place.
- Mr Davies helps at the next clean-up.

8 LIFE SKILLS Go green!

a) **You can organize a Swap Place in your class or at your school. Think of things at home and make an A–Z of things for a Swap Place:** *A – animals (toys), B – books, …*
Then compare your ideas with the class.

b) **Make a poster for your Swap Place with information about it.**

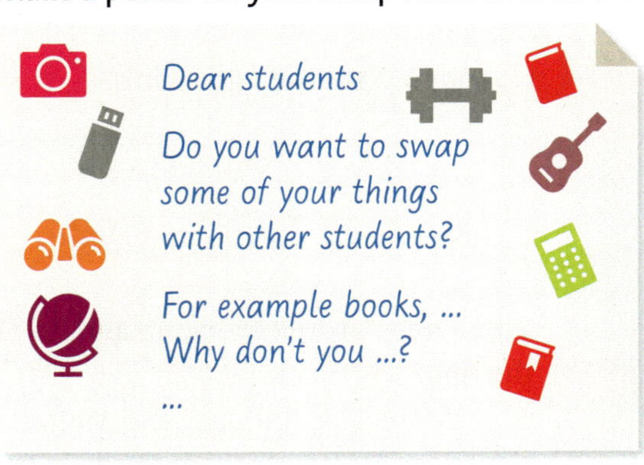

c) **Choose the best poster and start to swap!**

▸ Workbook, p. 68

I can understand a story about green activities.

The Brighton dares: In town

1 In Brighton

BEFORE YOU WATCH **Look at the dares. Answer the questions.**

1 Do you think this dare is hard or easy for Emir? Why?
2 What sights[1] can Daisy show people on her tour of Brighton?

1

Daisy's dare for Emir:
Change the time on the Queen's Park Clock Tower.

2

Emir's dare for Daisy:
Give a free tour of Brighton to a tourist (in a swimming cap).

I think the dare is hard/ easy for Emir because ...

Daisy can show people ...

2 VIEWING How they do the dares

a) **Team A:** **Read the notes about Daisy.** **Team B:** **Read the notes about Emir. Watch the video and complete the notes about Daisy or Emir.**

Daisy ...
1 asks people on the ...
2 goes to Volk's ... Railway.
3 meets Mara, a tourist from the ...
4 takes the number ... bus.

Emir ...
1 takes a mirror from ... to the clock.
2 takes a photo of the time on the clock: It's ...
3 takes a photo in the mirror. The time is ...
4 Emir shows Daisy and Mara the ...

b) **Team A:** **Find another A student and compare notes.**
Team B: **Find another B student and compare notes.**

c) **Two A students make a group with two B students. Present your notes. Listen and complete the notes in a) about the other person. Then watch the video again and check.**

3 Try Emir's trick

a) **Write the name of a Brighton sight. Look in a mirror and copy it. Or use these mirror letters.**

b) **Read your partner's sight! Use a mirror or these letters.**

[1] **sight** *Sehenswürdigkeit*

Give a presentation

1 Plan the presentation

Put topics A-F in the correct order for Scout's presentation about her favourite place in Brighton.

A Explain what the presentation is about.
B Explain why it's my favourite place.
C Greet my audience.
D Ask for questions.
E Say thank you and end the presentation.
F Say what my favourite place is.

2 Make a slide show

Scout's notes are too long on this slide.
Help her choose five keywords or phrases for her notes: *– My favourite place – ...*

My favourite place
My favourite place in Brighton is the beach because a lot of people come here and they often eat fish and chips or sandwiches. And I love fish and chips too!

Make the title big.
Use short notes.
Use some colour.
Choose big pictures.

3 Find useful phrases

Copy the table. Put the phrases in the correct place. Add other phrases you know.

In this photo you can see • ~~I'd like to talk about~~ • Finally • Next • Do you have any questions? • Let's look at this picture of • My presentation is about • Thank you for listening.

Start the presentation	Continue the presentation	Talk about pictures	End the presentation
I'd like to talk about	...	...	...

4 Practise the presentation

a) **Give your presentation on Scout's favourite place to a partner or film yourself.**

b) **Give your partner or yourself feedback. Draw one, two or three ☺ or ☹.**

Speak loudly: ... *Speak clearly: ...* *Look at your partner/group: ...*

▸ Skills file 5, p. 199

Digital quiz — I can plan and practise a presentation.

Present your top three places for kids

Step 1

Use a placemat in a group. First write ideas about your top places for kids. Then compare your ideas. Write the best ideas in the middle of your placemat.

What about the park?

That's a good idea! You can play football and ride bikes.

I like the zoo.

Sorry, I don't like the zoo. It isn't nice for animals.

The science museum is interesting. It's fun and it's free.

The cinema is good on rainy days. The popcorn is great.

So our top three are ...

When you work in a group you can also collect ideas in an online group file.

► Digital help ► Wordbank 11, p. 222

Step 2

Find your top three places on an online map. Make a slide: Show where your places are.

Step 3

Make a slide for each place. Add a photo or picture.
Write short notes for each place:

park: play football, ride bikes
science museum: fun, free
cinema: good on rainy days, great popcorn

Use Creative Commons photos. Find them in your browser. Then write the place or topic.

Step 4

Practise your group presentation. Then give feedback.

Please speak loudly.
Don't speak so fast, please.
Please look at me.

► Let's talk: Feedback, p. 231

Step 5

Give your presentation to another group or the class.
Ask another group 2–3 questions. Give feedback.

Do kids pay to go there?

Does the museum have a cafe?

► Study skills, p. 134

Digital quiz — I can give a presentation to a group.

1 Mediation Jack's favourite place

I can understand information about Brighton.

a) Read the message from your British friend Jack and tell your family about it. Choose the best description A, B or C.

A Jack will, dass wir ihn und seine Familie in Brighton besuchen.
B Jacks Familie ist oft im *Hove Skatepark*.
C Jack meint, dass wir den *Hove Skatepark* in Brighton besuchen sollten.

Hi
Your family wants to visit Brighton? Cool! You must visit Hove Skatepark. It's my favourite place. I often go skateboarding there. It's not in the town centre, but Portslade train station and Wish Road South bus stop are near the park. And what's best: The park is next to the beach. It's free to get in and it's always open! Have fun!
Jack

b) Answer your family's questions in German.

1 Ist der Skatepark im Zentrum?
2 Wie kommt man dorthin?
3 Muss man Eintritt zahlen?
4 Bis wann ist der Skatepark offen?

2 Language We live in Hove

I can describe my neighbourhood (simple present: negative sentences).

Read about Sunita's neighbourhood. Complete the sentences. Use *don't* or *doesn't*.

I live with my family in Hove.
Our neighbourhood has nice shops and parks, but it (1) ... have a cinema.
There's a great beach in Hove. Nish and I often go there after school, but we (2) ... go there at the weekend because it's really busy.
There's a museum too, but I (3) ... go there very often. I (4) ... like museums!
I like my neighbourhood, but Nish (5) ... like it. He wants to live in London, but my mum and Ben say no: They (6) ... want to live there!

3 Writing Lea's neighbourhood

Read Lea's notes about her neighbourhood. Then write Lea's message to Sunita.

Hi, Sunita! I don't live in a ...

- ~~city~~: small village
- clean
- fields, 3 shops, nice cinema ☺
- no youth centre ☹
- ~~lots of activities~~: boring

Check

4 A tour of Chester

I can talk about my town or village (simple present: questions and short answers).

a) LANGUAGE **Zane visits his cousin Sophie and asks questions about her town. Complete the sentences.**

Zane (1) ... like your town?
Sophie Yes, (2) ... It's a nice place.
Zane (3) ... have a good park?
Sophie Yes, (4) ... I often go cycling there.
Zane (5) ... have a beach?
Sophie No, (6) ... It's a shame!

b) WORDS **Write the names of the places a–f.**

a 
b 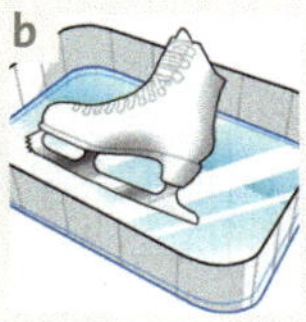
c 
d 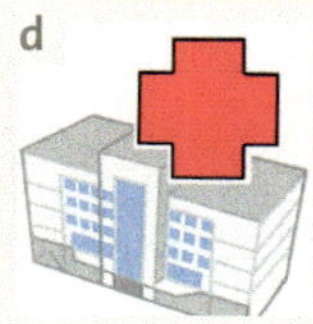
e 
f 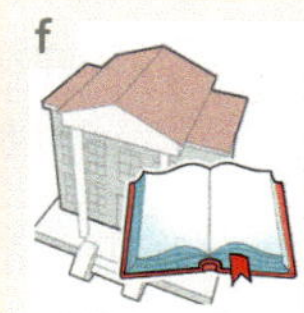

c) LISTENING **Listen to the tour. Where do Zane and Sophie go? Write the letters a–f from b) in the correct order:** *1c, 2 ...*

5 Photos of Brighton

I can talk about sights and the weather (simple present: *wh*-questions).

a) LANGUAGE **Write the questions in the correct order.**

1 see / in the picture / what / you / do / ?
2 like / the weather / what's / ?
3 do / like / why / you / the picture / ?

b) SPEAKING **Choose your favourite photo (A or B). Your partner asks you the questions from a). Answer the questions. Then swap roles.**

A

B

Phrases

- *I can see ...*
- *There's / There are ...*
- *The weather is ...*
- *I like picture A/B because ...*

6 READING At the Swap Place

I can understand a story about green activities.

a) BEFORE YOU READ **Look at the title and the pictures. Choose the correct answer.**

The story is about A Zane's family B Zane's day at school C Zane's things.

At the Swap Place

It's Saturday morning and Zane wants to meet his friends at the park. 'Dad, where's my scooter?' asks Zane. 'I can't find it. It isn't in the flat and it isn't outside.'

'It's at the Swap Place, Zane,' says Eno. 'We have too many things. And you don't need those old toys.'

'But Dad! It's my scooter and I still use it sometimes!' says Zane.

'Ah, I'm really sorry, Zane. Go to the Swap Place now. Maybe it's still there.'

'Excuse me,' says Zane when he gets there. 'I think my dad ...'

The woman in the Swap Place doesn't say hello. She looks sad.

'Are you OK? What's wrong?' asks Zane.

'Oh yes, I'm OK,' says the woman. 'But we have so many things here. The place is really messy. I want to tidy it, but I don't know where to start.'

'I can help you with that!'

Two hours later, Zane goes home. 'Hi, Dad. Sorry I'm late. I don't have my scooter, but I have some other things! Two footballs, a console, a book and a jigsaw puzzle. The Swap Place is great.'

'Hi, Zane. More things! That's ... erm ... great.'

b) **Read the story: true (T) or false (F)? Correct the false sentences.**

1 Zane's scooter isn't in the flat.
2 Eno doesn't know where the scooter is.
3 The Swap Place is very tidy.
4 Zane helps the woman in the Swap Place.
5 Zane brings his scooter home.

c) **Find words in the story with these meanings.**

1 the day after Friday (line 1)
2 kids play with them (line 6)
3 not tidy (line 17)
4 where someone lives (line 20)
5 a game with a lot of parts (lines 22–23)

Check

7 STUDY SKILLS Buddy's favourite places

I can plan and practise a presentation.

a) Look at Noah's slides. Which slide is the best? Why? Talk to your partner.

1 The first place is the Pavilion Gardens.

2 **The beach**

– we walk
– the sea

3 Buddy loves our garden too because all his toys are there.

I think slide number 1/2/3 is the best because it has a big title/short notes/a big picture.

I think you're right.

I think you're wrong and slide number 1/2/3 is the best because ...

b) Copy and complete Noah's sentences with words from the box. There is one extra word.

end • listening • look • next • photo • presentation • questions

1 My ... is about Buddy's favourite places.
2 In this ... you can see the Pavilion Gardens.
3 In the ... photo we have the beach.
4 Let's ... at these pictures of Buddy's toys in the garden.
5 Thank you for ...
6 Do you have any ... ?

8 SPEAKING Ideas for a rainy day

I can give a presentation to a group.

Tim wants to talk about places to go on a rainy day. Look at his slides and give his presentation.

Ideas for a rainy day
– hello
– my presentation

the sports centre
– a lot of activities
– not expensive

the ice rink
– costs 10 euros
– fun

the cinema
– interesting films
– nice cafe

Questions?
– thank you
– any questions

Check

VARNDEAN Teen Zine

This month's topic: Brighton

Our school magazine: by students for students

Questions and answers: The Real Junk Food Project

What is it?
It's a cafe in Brighton.

Why is it different?
The cafe uses waste[1] food and there are no prices[2].

Where does the food come from?
When shops in Brighton don't sell[3] all their food, they don't put the rest in the bin – they give it to the cafe!

How much do meals cost?
People pay what they can. People with more money pay more and homeless[4] people eat for free. And everybody sits together!

Who are the cooks?
They're volunteers – people who help for no money –, but they're still very good at cooking!

Puzzle time

Where in Brighton am I?

1 I'm not land and I'm not sea
But to walk on water, you can walk on me!

2 I'm high in the sky
With a big round[5] eye
But I'm not a bird and I can't fly!

Joke[6] time
What do you call it when it's rainy for two days in Brighton?
The weekend!

---

[1] **waste** *überschüssig; hier: Lebensmittel, die weggeworfen werden sollten* [2] **price** *Preis* [3] **sell** *verkaufen*
[4] **homeless** *obdachlos* [5] **round** *rund* [6] **joke** *Witz*

A postcard from Brighton

Dear Annie

Brighton is great! My favourite place here is Snooper's Paradise. It's a really cool shop and it sells ... everything[1]! Hats, skateboards, photos, guitars, clocks, toys, books, posters ...

It's very big. Even[2] the people who work in the shop don't know everything they sell! But you can always find something different. Wish you were here![3]

Leena xx

TO

What's your favourite shop?

Fergal's reading tip:

My favourite book is 'A Brighton birthday'. It's a cool story with lots of places in Brighton and great puzzles. What happens? It's Saturday morning and Alice wakes up - it's her birthday! But there are no birthday messages, no presents and everyone is busy. Then she gets a mysterious message with a puzzle ...

[1] **everything** *alles* [2] **even** *sogar* [3] **Wish you were here!** *Ich wünschte, du wärst hier!*

Partner page

▸ Page 123

3 SPEAKING Different places

a) **Partner B:** Look at your picture. Take turns to ask and answer questions. Use the places in the box.

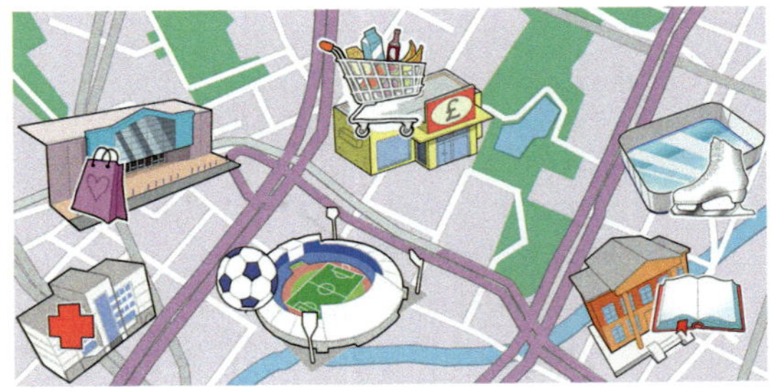

Partner A: *Does your town have a supermarket?*
Partner B: *Yes, it does. / No, it doesn't.*
Partner A: *That's the same. / That's different.*
Partner B: *Does your town have ...*

a hospital • an ice rink • a library • a museum • a shopping centre • a stadium • a supermarket • a train station

▸ Page 127

4 The Upside Down House

a) **Partner B: Ask partner A these questions. Use the correct question word and add *do* or *does*.**

1. Who / What / Why ... people do inside the house?
2. Where / Who / When ... the Upside Down House close?
3. How much / How fast / How often ... tickets cost?

b) **Look at the online review. Answer partner A's questions.**

www.upsidedown.example.com

The Upside Down house is great! It's good to be there at 10 a. m. when it opens, so there aren't too many people. You don't need to buy tickets online – you buy tickets at the kiosk. My tip: Take funny photos – put your hands up, then turn the photo upside down!

Diff bank

▸ Page 118

More help 1 From Lily's window

a) **Look at the photo and listen. You're Lily. What can you see, hear and smell?**

I can see ...
I can hear ...
I can smell ...

babies • buses • cars • dogs • doors • flats • grass • houses • kids • loud / nice music • my neighbour's TV • a police car • rubbish • streets

Challenge 1 **From my window**

What can you see, hear and smell from your window at home? Write five or more sentences.
I can see / hear / smell ...

▸ Page 119

More practice 1 **We don't like ...**

the colour green • dancing • dogs • drawing • football • homework • loud people • maths • messy rooms • rubbish • snakes • sport • swimming in the sea

a) **Draw something that you don't like. You can use an idea from the box or your own idea. You have two minutes.**

b) **Take turns to show your pictures. One student says what the picture shows:** *You don't like fish.*

c) **Tell the class about your group:** *Otto doesn't like pizza, Mariam doesn't like cats, ...*

▸ Page 120

Parallel exercise **6 The youth centre**

a) **Lily tells her friends about the youth centre. Choose *don't* or *doesn't*:** *1 It doesn't open ...*

I often go to the youth centre, but not at weekends. It (1) don't / doesn't open at weekends. There are a lot of activities like cooking, boxing, crafts and football. There's a girls' group on Tuesday, but I (2) don't / doesn't go there: I (3) don't / doesn't have time then. Sometimes I play pool at the youth centre with my neighbour Niles. He (4) don't / doesn't go to Varndean and his school (5) don't / doesn't have a lot of clubs. What else? We (6) don't / doesn't pay for the activities – they're all free. A lot of people on our estate (7) don't / doesn't have a lot of money.

More practice 2 **New activities**

a) **The youth centre wants to plan new activities. Lily asks her friends what they do at the youth centre. Use the table to complete Lily's sentences with *don't* or *doesn't*.**

	Lily	Bob	Ayse	Joshua
act in plays	x	✓	✓	✓
make jewellery	x	x	✓	✓
do sports	✓	x	✓	x
play chess	✓	✓	x	x
watch films	✓	✓	✓	x
do homework	✓	x	✓	✓

1 *I don't act in plays.*
2 *Bob ... homework.*
3 *Joshua and Bob ... sports.*
4 *Joshua ... films.*
5 *Bob and I ... jewellery.*
6 *Ayse and Joshua ... chess.*

▸Page 120

Challenge 2 My family and friends

Write five sentences about you, your family and friends.

I My family My best friend My friends	(don't / doesn't)	have / has like / likes play / plays go to / goes to	…

▸Page 121

More practice 3 On Lily's estate

WORDS **Lily tells a new boy at the youth centre about her neighbourhood and Brighton. Complete what she says with the correct places from the box. There are two extra places.**

beach • cafe • cinema • fields • hospital • ice rink • pier • shop • sports centre

You can buy everything at the (1) … on the estate. There's a small (2) … next to it. They have great hot chocolate! There's a (3) … here too – you can do a lot of different sports there.
You can see the sea from our estate and the (4) … isn't far. We go there to swim in the summer. You can walk with your dog in the (5) … near the estate.
The (6) … is near the beach. It looks great at night when there are lots of lights. I meet my friends there to eat fish and chips and play games.
What else? Oh, yes. I often watch films at home, but there's a great (7) … in Brighton.

More help 10 MY TASK A post about my neighbourhood

Write a post like in 9. Write at least six sentences.

I live in	a village / a town / a city / the country / …
My neighbourhood is / isn't	boring / clean / dirty / horrible / interesting / loud / nice / quiet / ….
My neighbourhood has / doesn't have	a cinema / a park / a swimming pool / a youth centre / shops / …
The neighbours are / aren't	friendly / loud / nice / quiet / unfriendly / …
I like / don't like	my neighbourhood.

▸Page 122

More practice 4 A puzzle: Places in town

Read the descriptions and look at the map. Write the missing places for 1–8.

There's a tree in front of the market.
The library is between the train station and the market.
The museum is behind the library.
The stadium isn't in town. It's three miles away.
The ice rink is in front of the market and next to the shopping centre.
The shopping centre is between the ice rink and the hospital.

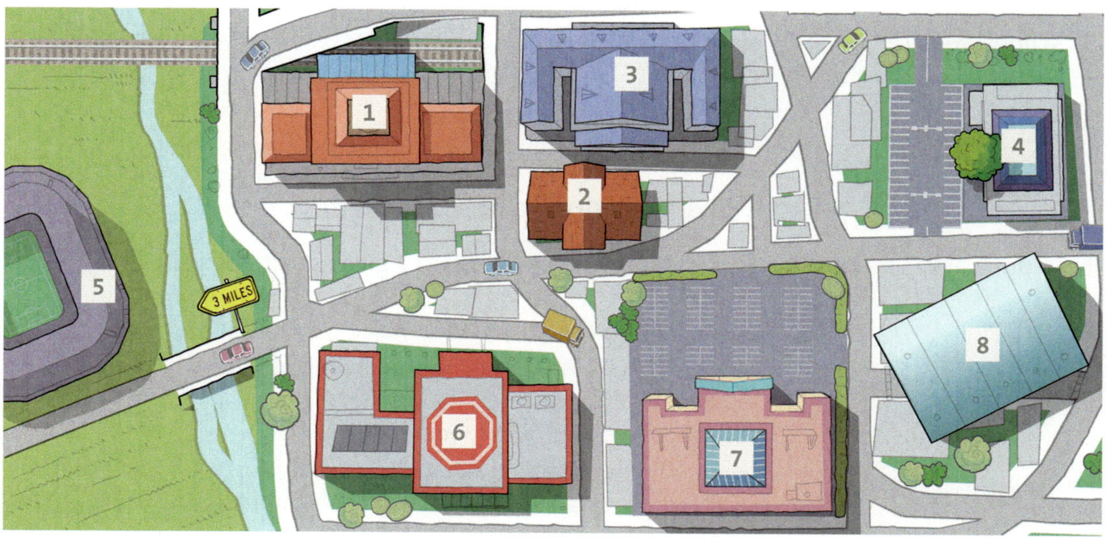

▸Page 123

More practice 5 I'm lost!

A visitor asks Lily for help. Complete the questions in the conversation with *do* or *does*.

Visitor	Excuse me, (1) ... you live here?
Lily	Yes, I do. (2) ... you need help?
Visitor	Yes, I do. I'm lost. I want to go to the visitor information centre. Is it in this street?
Lily	Yes, it is. (3) ... your phone have a map?
Visitor	Yes, it does, but my phone is dead.
Lily	OK, let's look on my phone. (4) ... you see this place? We're here. And here's the visitor information centre in this building.
Visitor	(5) ... the building have a name?
Lily	Yes, it does. It's the Brighton Centre. It isn't far down there, on the right. (6) ... that help?
Visitor	Yes, it does. Thank you very much.
Lily	You're welcome.

▸ Page 124

Challenge 3 Do you like your neighbourhood?

a) Write five interview questions for students in your class. You can use the sentence starters in the box or your own ideas.

b) Find a partner and ask your questions. Answer your partner's questions. Use short answers and add more information.

c) Write a short article about your partner for your school website.

> Do you go ...? • Do you play ...? • Do you like ...?• Do you have ...? • Does your brother / sister ...? • Does your mum / dad ...?

▸ Page 125

More help 10 My task Five questions about places

b) Team 1 asks *yes/no*-questions to guess the place. Team 2 gives short answers.

Does this place	sell	clothes / drinks / food / something / ...?
	have	books / films / football matches / games / grass / old things / table tennis / trains / trees / water / ...? a lot of people with books / young people / ...?
Is it the		beach / cinema / hospital / library / museum / park / shopping centre / sports centre / stadium / swimming pool / train station / youth centre / ...?

▸ Page 126

More practice 6 The weather for next week

Lily looks at the weather for next week. Complete the sentences with the words from the box.

1 On M..., it's ... and ...
2 On Tu..., it's ... and ...
3 On W..., it's ...
4 On Th..., it's ... and ...

> cloudy • cold • rainy • snowy • sunny • warm • windy

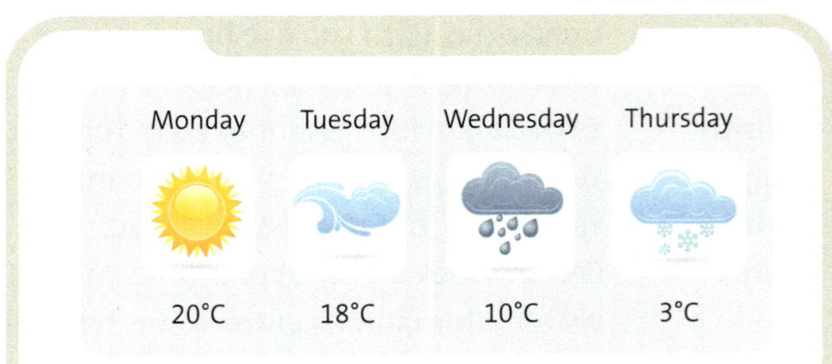

▸ Page 127

Challenge 4 **Questions for Scout**

Look at Scout's answers. What are the questions? Use the words in the boxes.

how • what • when • where • who • why	eat • get up • like • live • love • travel

1 I live in Brighton.

2 I get up at 5 a.m.

3 I eat sandwiches and chips and fish.

4 I fly everywhere.

5 I like Noah, Sunita, Zane and Lily.

6 Because I love the sea and the food on the beach.

▸ Page 128

More help **7** My task **Quiz-quiz-swap**

b) Walk around

Find a partner and ask your question. Answer your partner's question about your town.

When it's	sunny / rainy / snowy / cloudy / windy / hot / cold / warm,	I	have a picnic / stay at home / visit my friends / go to the cinema / go swimming / ...
		I go to	the beach / the park / the shops / ...
		I travel by ... (I walk.)	bus / bike / car / train / ...

▸ Page 131

More help **4 Why, what and how?**

Match the answers to the questions on p. 131.

a They put up notices.
b He wants to give the youth centre some money.
c Because it's loud.
d Over fifty.
e A dead mouse and an old shoe.
f At lunch.

Unit 5
Enjoy!

My favourite dessert is trifle. Dad always makes it for my birthday and at Christmas. In trifle there is fruit and red jelly, then custard and then cream and then more fruit. A lot of people put strawberries on trifle, but I'm allergic to strawberries.

Noah's birthday dessert

1 Words **Food**

a) Look at Noah and Sunita's pages in 7C's class recipe book. Which words in blue do you understand? Use the photos or words from German and other languages.

I think 'fruit' is 'Obst'. It's like 'Frucht' in German and 'frukty' (фрукты) *in Russian.*

b) Listen, find and repeat the correct blue food word.

c) Start a page in your Vocab file. Make lists or a mind map for other food words. You can draw pictures and add words in other languages. Add more new words later.

▸ More practice 1, p. 177

Nach dieser Unit kann ich ...

- ○ über Essen sprechen
- ○ über Geburtstage und Feste sprechen
- ○ mein Lieblingsgericht beschreiben
- ○ über Unterschiede sprechen
- ○ unbekannte Wörter erklären

Unit task

- ○ ein Rezeptbuch erstellen

A lot of people in the UK go to Indian restaurants. We eat a lot of Indian food at home. There are a lot of Indian dishes with meat, but we eat vegetarian food. This is my favourite dish – mattar paneer. It's Indian cheese and peas in a tomato sauce with a lot of spices. We usually eat it with bread or rice and some vegetables.

Sunita's favourite dish

2 Speaking Our food

a) Read Noah and Sunita's pages again. Complete the sentences.

1 You make trifle with ...
2 Noah is allergic to ...
3 Sunita doesn't eat ... She's a ...
4 You make mattar paneer with ...

Good to know

A lot of people in the UK eat vegetarian or vegan food. Some people are vegetarians or vegans for health reasons, others for religious reasons or because they love animals.

b) What about you? Talk about the food on these pages.

I love ... *I don't like ...* *I often/never eat ... (because ...)* *I'm allergic to ...*

▶ Workbook, p. 74

Digital quiz I can talk about food.

Time for a party

1 Reading Noah's invitation

a) Before you read **What do you usually do on your birthday? Tell a partner.**

I always / never / ... have a birthday party.
We usually eat sausages and birthday cake.
We often go bowling. – What about you?

b) **Read Noah's invitation. Answer the questions.**

1. How old is Noah on his birthday?
2. What day of the week is his birthday party?
3. What time does the party start?
4. Where's the party?
5. What activities are there?
6. What food is there?
7. How can Noah's friends answer the invitation?

► More practice 2, p. 177 ► Challenge 1, p. 177

2 Words Months and seasons

a) Song **Listen and sing. Then listen again and stand up for your birthday month.**

b) Walk around **Find out from different partners what their birthday month is.**

A When's your birthday?
B It's in spring.
A Is it in March?
B No, it isn't.
A Is it in ...?
B Yes, it is. When's your birthday?

winter	spring	summer	autumn

December January February	March April May	June July August	September October November

► More practice 3, p. 178

3 Birthday dates

a) Look at the list of numbers on p. 307.
Listen and repeat the numbers from 1st to 31st.

b) Look how Scout says and writes her birthday.
Then listen to eight students.
Write their birthdays.

1 Noah: 30th May
2 Lily: ... April
3 Zane: ... August
4 Sunita: ... March
5 Theo: ... February
6 Ivy: ... January
7 Tareq: ... July
8 Marta: ... October

c) Check your answers with a partner.

Lily's birthday is on the ... of ... – That's right. / That's wrong. I think it's on ...

► Numbers, p. 307 ► More practice 4 + 5, p. 178

4 Speaking My birthday

a) Make two groups.
Make a line in your group in order of your birthdays.
Which group is quicker?

b) Check: Are you in the right place in the line?
Take turns: Say your birthday.

5 Writing My birthday invitation

a) Look at Noah's invitation in 1 again. Change the parts in blue and write an invitation to your birthday party. Make it look good!

b) Gallery walk Look at all the invitations. What do you think? Make notes.

Which invitation ...
1 looks the best (colours, photos, ...)?
2 has the best place?
3 has the best activity?
4 has the best food?

► Workbook, p. 75

6 Zane calls Noah

**Look at the picture and read the phone conversation.
What's different? What are Noah and Buddy really doing?**

1 Noah is resting / playing with Buddy / juggling.
2 Buddy is playing ball / sleeping / watching Noah.

Zane Hi, Noah! What are you doing?
Noah Hi, Zane. Erm, I'm not telling you. It's a secret. ... Erm, I'm playing with Buddy. Yes ... he's playing ball now.
Zane Oh, I'm calling to ask: Do you need help with your party?
Noah Erm, thanks a lot, but no. What are you doing?
Zane I'm not busy. I'm listening to music at the moment.
Noah OK. Sorry, I must go, Zane! My dad is calling me. See you!

7 Looking at language Present progressive

Erklär-film

a) Complete the examples from 6.

What **are** you	...	?
I'm	...	with Buddy.
He's	...	ball now.
I'm not	...	you.

Mit dem *present progressive* sprechen wir darüber, was in diesem Moment *(now, at the moment)* geschieht. Wir beschreiben mit dem *present progressive* auch, was auf Bildern passiert.

► Language file 16, p. 210

b) Look at the examples in a). Complete the rule.

Wir bilden das *present progressive* mit ...

I	am / 'm / 'm not	
he / she	is / isn't	*verb* (sleep / ...) + ...
you / we / they	are / aren't	

8 Double circle What are you doing?

Have a phone call with different partners. Use the ideas in the box or your ideas.

A Hi [name]. What are you doing? Are you free?
B Hi [name]. Sorry, no, I'm busy. **I'm** ...
A That sounds fun / interesting / great / ...
B What are you doing?
A **I'm** ... OK – see you!

cleaning my room • coding • eating a kebab • playing cards • playing with my pet snake • standing on my head • teaching my parrot to sing • watching a film • writing a post • ...

► Workbook, p. 76

9 A birthday photo

Zane is showing his mum a photo of his friend's birthday party. Complete his sentences with *'m, is, 's, are, 're* and the *-ing* form of the words in the box.

draw • eat • lie • ~~listen~~ • play • sit • take • wear

1 Sunita and Ruby *are listening* to music.
2 I ... birthday cake.
3 Ju ... a gold hat.
4 Noah ... on a chair with a cat.
5 He ... photos with his phone.
6 Max and Albie have balloons. They ... with them.
7 Lily is at the table. She ... a picture.
8 Amina and Vicky ... on the floor.

The spelling of some verbs with *-ing* is different:
sit – sitting
take – taking
lie – lying

▶ Parallel exercise, p. 178 ▶ More practice 6 + 7, p. 179

10 Speaking Find the differences

Partner B: Look at p. 176.
Partner A: Look at this picture.
Take turns and find six differences.

In my picture a boy and a girl in blue T-shirts are singing karaoke.

In my picture they are / aren't ...
In my picture a dog is ...

▶ Challenge 2, p. 179

My task

11 My party photos

You choose **Do task A or B.**

Task A: Bring photos of family parties to class or show them on your phone to your partner. Describe them.

This is my birthday party. It's the 26th of February.
Look, I'm wearing ... We're eating / playing / ...

Task B: Describe the photos on p. 176.

▶ Digital help

▶ Workbook, pages 76–77

Digital quiz **I can talk about birthdays and parties.**

Party shopping

1 LISTENING A present for Noah

a) BEFORE YOU LISTEN **Say what things in the box Noah likes or doesn't like.**

animals • circus tricks • cycling • strawberries • walking

He likes … He doesn't like …

b) **Sunita and Lily are looking online for a birthday present for Noah. Look at the website. Then listen. What ideas do they have?**

c) **Say what they choose and why.**

d) **Listen again. Complete the phrases.**

What about a …?
Why don't we buy …?
Let's get some / a / the …

☹ *I'm n… sure.*
It's too …
Noah already has …

☺ *It's a great …!*
That's a … idea.
That's p…!

2 SPEAKING Find a present

a) **Brainstorm a list of cool birthday presents on the board.**

b) **Find a birthday present for each student in your group. Use the presents from 1b) and 2a) and phrases from 1d). The 'birthday boy / girl' listens.**

First let's find a present for Samir.
OK. Why don't we buy …?
That's a great idea, but Samir already has / doesn't like / can't …

c) **The 'birthday boy / girl' says thank you and comments on the present:** *Thanks, guys! A … is a great present. …*

▸ Workbook, p. 78

3 Listening Party food and drinks

a) Before you listen **Can you remember ...**

- What kind of party is Noah's birthday party?
- Where's the party?
- What's his birthday dessert?

b) **Look at the party menu. Listen to Noah and his parents. What two things are wrong?**

Noah's party menu

Food
ham sandwiches, cheese sandwiches, sausages, pasta salad, carrots, trifle, melon

Drinks
cola, lemonade

4 Words The shopping list

a) **Read the conversation. Write Noah's shopping list for the party.**

Noah I'm writing the shopping list. How much bread do we need?
Dad For the sandwiches? We need a lot of bread! Two packets. And three packets of cheese and two packets of ham.
Noah OK. And how many tomatoes? Ten?
Dad Hmm, let's get six.
Noah How much pasta?
Dad A big bag of pasta.
Noah And how many carrots do we need? One bag?
Dad Yes, we don't need many. And one big melon.
Noah OK. How many lemons do we need for the lemonade? And how much sugar?
Dad Let's get twelve lemons. We already have sugar.

sandwich bread: 2 packets
...

b) **Compare your list with your partner. Then listen and check.**

5 Looking at language *much, many, a lot of*

Erklär-film

a) **Complete the table with food and drinks from 4a).**

b) **Complete the box with *much* and *many*.**

How much ...?	How many ...?
bread	tomatoes
...	...

- Zählbare Wörter haben eine Pluralform (Mehrzahl): *six tomatoes, twelve lemons.*
- Nicht zählbare Wörter verwendet man nicht im Plural: *bread, lemonade, meat, sugar, water.*
- Wir verwenden ■ mit zählbaren Wörtern und ■ mit nicht zählbaren Wörtern.
- *A lot of* kann man in Aussagesätzen mit zählbaren und mit nicht zählbaren Wörtern benutzen.

► Language file 17, p. 211 ► More practice 8, p. 180

6 GAME *How much ...? – How many ...? – A lot of ...!*

Look in the fridge and write five questions. Then close your books. In turns, ask your questions and write your partner's answers:

How many strawberries are there? – Not many. There are five strawberries.
How much pasta is there? – There's a lot of pasta – four packets.
How much cheese is there? – Not much. One small piece.

Open your books again and check. The partner with more correct answers wins.

► Challenge 3, p. 180

7 SONG The shopping song

a) BEFORE YOU LISTEN **Ask and answer the questions about food shopping.**

1 How often do you go food shopping?
I never / sometimes / often go ...
2 Do you usually go with your parents or do you sometimes go alone?
I usually / sometimes / ... go ...
3 Where do you usually go shopping?
In the supermarket. / In small shops. / At the market.

b) **Listen to the song. Write the letters of the foods (A–N) in the order of the song. Check on p. 181.**

c) **Listen again and say which food words in the song rhyme. Then sing!**

► Workbook, p. 79

8 MEDIATION A party game

It's your friend's birthday soon. He sends you a message with a link to a party game description.
Write back and answer his questions.

www.birthdaygames.example.com

Guck mal, Schokolade mit Messer und Gabel essen – das Spiel gibt's auch in England! Wie ging das nochmal? Ist hier etwas anders, als wir es kennen? Wenn ja, was?

www.birthdaygames.example.com

The chocolate game
Here's a great party game for your birthday!
It's really easy to play and it's a lot of fun!

You need:
- some chocolate on a plate
- a knife and a fork
- sunglasses
- gloves
- a dice

To play:
- Take turns to throw the dice. When you get a six, say 'Six'! Now you can eat some chocolate! But you must wear the sunglasses and gloves and use a knife and fork.
- While you're eating, another person rolls the dice. The next person with a six takes the sunglasses, the gloves, a clean knife and fork, and eats some chocolate.
- The game ends when there isn't any more chocolate!

My task

9 Our party

a) **Plan a party for your class. Work in groups. In your group decide on a kind of party (a dance / film / garden / magic / ... party).**

What about ...?

b) **In your group make notes / posters about these things:**
- your party food
- your party music / playlist
- games and activities

▸ Digital help ▸ Wordbank 12, p. 223

c) **Tell the class about your party. The class chooses the best party plan.**

This is our party menu: ...

This is our music playlist. First ... by ...

We want to watch a film / ...

Digital quiz **I can talk about party food and activities.**

Let's cook!

1 Before you watch What are you cooking?

Read Zane's notes.
What kind of cake is he making?

I think it's a ... cake.

Hey, Zane! What are you doing?

Hi, Lily. I'm watching a cooking video. I want to make this for Noah's birthday party.

For the cake:
250 g flour
60 ml oil
120 g sugar
50 g cocoa
30 ml milk
2 eggs
salt
½ teaspoon vanilla
2 teaspoons baking powder

For the icing:
200 g butter
100 g chocolate
400 g icing sugar

2 Viewing A cooking video

a) Watch the first part of the video until 0:40. Which things in the list in 1 does Maiku forget to say?

b) Watch the whole video. Put the photos in the correct order.

A He is ... the mixture in the oven (180° C for 50 minutes).

B He's ... the eggs.

C Now Maiku is ... the cake.

D Maiku is ... the flour, cocoa and baking powder.

E He is ... the eggs, vanilla, oil, sugar and salt.

F He's ... the icing with chocolate, butter and sugar.

c) Complete the sentences in b) with words from the box. There are two extra words. Then watch again and check.

adding • breaking • decorating • drawing • making • mixing • putting • sending

► Workbook, p. 80

3 Britain's favourite dishes

a) At the bottom of the page are three of Britain's favourite dishes. Which is best for you? Answer the questions and find out! You can find a recipe for scones on p. 161.

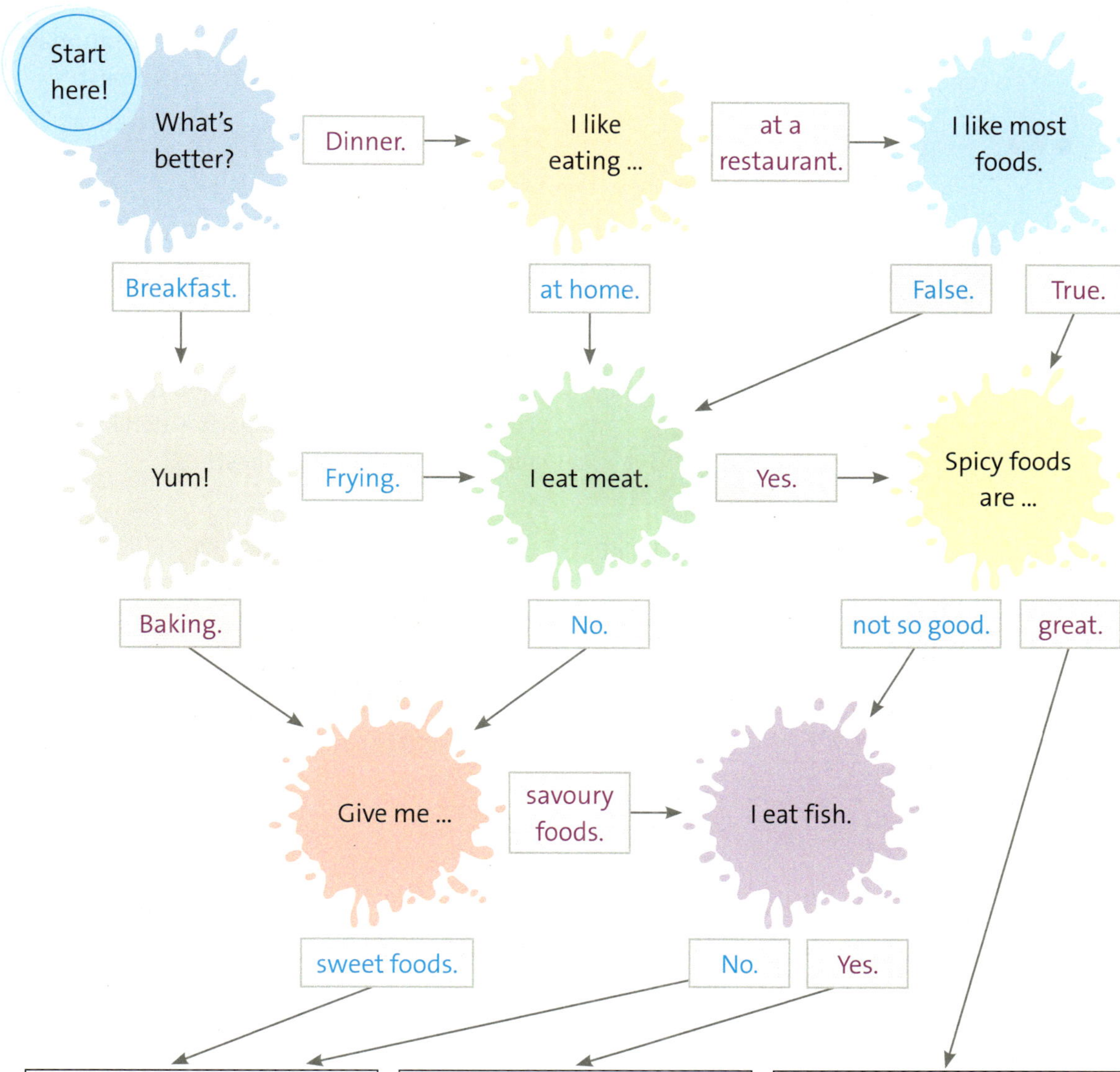

Scones!
Small, round cakes. You eat them with cream or butter and jam.

Fish and chips!
You usually buy these in a shop. The shop puts them in paper.

Chicken tikka masala!
People love this spicy dish! It sounds and tastes Indian, but it comes from England.

4 READING Zane's favourite dish

Read Zane's blog post. Write if these sentences are true (T), false (F), or not in the text (NT). Correct the false sentences.

1 Zane's favourite dish is from India.
2 Jollof rice is a main course.
3 It's a vegetarian dish.
4 Zane likes plantain.
5 Zane's dad cooks jollof rice every Saturday.
6 Zane thinks that his dad cooks it best.

www.cooking-with-zane.example.net

This is my favourite dish. It's called jollof rice and it's from Nigeria.
It's a spicy dish and a main course. You make it with rice, tomatoes, onions, peppers, chicken – and a lot of spices!
It's delicious and I love it!

We eat it with plantain – it's a kind of banana. It isn't sweet, so we fry it with honey. Yum!
This is an important dish for my family and my dad cooks it every week. And sometimes I cook it when we have a party – don't tell him, but I think I cook it best! 😉

My task

5 My favourite dish

Use Zane's blog post in 4 and these questions to write about your favourite dish. Put your text in your DOSSIER.

- What kind of dish is it? A main course? A dessert?
- Is it sweet?
- What culture or country does it come from?
- What's in the dish?
- When do you eat it? Who cooks it?
- Do you eat it with your family?
- What do you drink with it?

▶ Digital help ▶ More help, p. 181 ▶ Wordbank 12, p. 223

Good to know

Food and drinks in the UK
- Modern food has a lot of traditions. We eat food from everywhere.
- Chinese stir-fry with vegetables and noodles is the favourite dish in the UK.
- A lot of people drink tea (often with milk and sugar), but a lot of people drink coffee too.

▶ Workbook, p. 81

Digital quiz I can **describe my favourite dish.**

Background file

1 Britain's favourite dishes: Scones

a) **Find out more about one of the dishes from p. 159. How and when do you eat scones?**

Many people in Britain eat their scones with clotted cream, but you usually can't buy it in Germany. Clotted cream looks like whipped cream, but it tastes like butter. It's not sweet. You can make clotted cream at home, but it takes two or three days. Butter or whipped cream are also good with scones!
Scones are popular for afternoon tea. Afternoon tea is a small meal between lunch and dinner. People usually drink tea (of course!) and eat small sandwiches, scones or cake.

b) **Read this quick and easy recipe for scones. Try it out!**

50 g butter · 225 g flour · 50 g sugar · 3 teaspoons baking powder · ½ teaspoon salt · 75 ml milk · 1 egg

1 Preheat oven to 230°C.
2 Mix butter, flour, sugar, baking powder and salt.
3 Mix the butter and the flour with your fingers. Add milk and egg and mix it all together.
4 Roll out dough.
5 Use a glass to cut out scones.
6 Put the scones in the oven for 8–10 minutes.
7 Cut a scone and eat it with butter or cream and jam.

2 More favourite dishes

a) **What's in the three dishes on this page? Read and find out. The main ingredients are in blue.**

fish · potatoes · egg · milk · flour · cornflake crumbs

chicken · rice · onion · garlic · spices · tomato sauce · tomato paste · chicken stock · cream

b) **Is your dish from p. 159 really a good match for you? Why or why not? Discuss.**

Fish and chips are / aren't good for me because I like / don't like ...

▸ Workbook, p. 82

A different kind of party

1 Reading What's happening in the story?

a) Before you read **Look at the first picture and choose the correct word:** ***are • aren't • is • isn't***

1 Lily, Zane and Sunita ... meeting Noah.
2 Zane ... bringing a drink.
3 Noah and his family ... sitting in the park.
4 Buddy ... running in the park.
5 It ... raining.
6 The kids ... wearing school uniforms.

b) **Read the story and answer the questions.**

1 Why is it a different kind of party?
2 What three things are problems for Lily and Zane?
3 Does Noah think these are problems too?

1

Lily This is Hove Park and it's two o'clock. But where are Noah and his family?
Zane Look, there they are! Noah's waving. Oh, and here's Sunita!
Sunita Hi! What are you bringing to the party, Zane?
Zane It's my special chocolate cake.
Lily It looks delicious! You're so good at baking, Zane.

2

Zane Happy birthday, Noah! Here's a dessert for you.
Noah Thanks! Mum and Dad, my friends are here.
Mum Hello! Nice to meet you.
Lily I have some strawberries for the party!
Dad Thanks, Lily ... that's very kind of you. Noah is allergic to strawberries, but I love them!

3

Sunita Zane, are you OK? You're very quiet.
Zane Erm, this is a very different kind of party. I mean, we're just sitting and talking. There's no music, people aren't dancing ... It isn't the kind of party that I like!
Sunita Well, it is a little different. But Noah doesn't like loud music or dancing. So I think this is the kind of party that he likes.

4

Dad Do you want to open your presents now, Noah?
Noah No, let's eat my birthday trifle first!
Dad OK, it's in my bag over there ... Oh no! Stop, Buddy!
Noah Is Buddy OK?
Mum Yes, he's fine. There's no chocolate in the trifle, so it's OK. But we can't eat it now! I'm sorry, Noah.

5

Lily Hey, Noah! Are you enjoying the party?
Noah Yeah, it's great!
Lily Oh, I'm happy to hear that. You can't eat my strawberries and now there's no trifle! I want your party to be fun for you!

6

Noah This is the best birthday party ever! I'm having a picnic with my family and my best friends and my dog. It isn't too loud, so I'm feeling good. It's sunny, I have presents and we can eat Zane's chocolate cake. It's the perfect party for me!
Lily That's true ...
Noah So don't worry. You know ... I think it's really funny! The look on Mum's face about Buddy and the trifle!
Lily You're right! Hahaha!
Noah Now you're smiling!

7

Noah And now – my secret: Watch this!
Sunita Wow! Noah, that's amazing!
Zane You're really good at juggling!
Dad Yes, when Noah wants to learn something, he works really hard.
Noah Ta-dah! Well, this is a circus birthday party, right? Now it's your turn – I can show you how to juggle too! And then ... my magic show!
Zane Wow, this is a great party! It's a new kind of party for me, but it's great fun. Thanks, Noah!

2 Who is it?

Complete the sentences with a name or names.

1 ... makes some food for the party.
2 ... can't eat strawberries.
3 ... loves eating strawberries.
4 ... and ... think the party is too quiet at first.
5 ... eats the trifle.
6 ... is worrying about the party.
7 ... thinks the party is perfect.
8 ... thinks something different about the party at the end.

▶ More practice 9, p. 181

3 SHOWTIME Miming scenes

a) **Choose a scene from the story and mime it.**

b) **One student says a sentence and the group mimes the new scene.**

Noah Lily Sunita Zane Noah's mum / dad Buddy	is / are	dancing. eating the cake. juggling. opening a present. smiling. waving.

4 LIFE SKILLS People are different

a) **Read the sentences about Noah and his friends. Write how you are the same or different.**

1 Noah likes quiet parties. *I like quiet parties too. / I don't like quiet parties.*
2 Zane likes loud music.
3 Noah's dad loves strawberries.
4 Sunita doesn't eat meat.
5 Lily likes parkour.

b) **Talk to your partner. What's the same and what's different?**

c) **Tell the class one thing that is the same for you and your partner and one that's different.**

Digital quiz **I can understand and talk about differences.**

The Brighton dares: A birthday

1 Birthday words

a) Before you watch **Make a mind map for the word *birthday*. Add as many words as you can.**

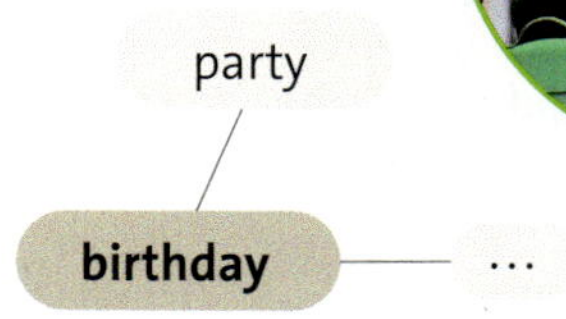

b) **Compare with a partner and add his / her ideas.**

2 Viewing The party

a) **Watch the video from 00:00 to 04:17. Complete the invitation and the information about Daisy's friend.**

Daisy's imaginary[1] friend

Dare: *Take an imaginary friend to Gloria's party*
Name of friend: *Sota*
From: *Japan*
Hobby: (4) ...
Likes England? (5) ...
Likes best? (6) ...

b) **Now watch the video from 04:18 to 06:27. Choose the correct answers about Emir's dare.**

1 Emir does his dare ... A at his home. B at the party. C in the supermarket.
2 Emir feels ... A brave. B nervous. C angry.
3 Daisy makes a video of Emir: He's ... A dancing. B singing. C singing and dancing.
4 Other people look ... A surprised but happy. B angry. C embarrassed[2].
5 The video is ... A for dancing at the party. B a present for Gloria. C for a video channel[3].
6 Emir buys a toy dog as a birthday present from ... A himself. B Daisy. C Sota.

c) **Watch the video from 06:28 to 09:17 and answer the questions.**

1 Which birthday things from your mind map in 1 can you see and hear? Make notes.
2 What is everybody doing when the video ends?

3 All the dares

Think about all the dares in this book (pages 35, 67, 101, 133 and 165). Which is the best dare and why? Discuss in your group and then tell the class.

[1] **imaginary** *Fantasie- (vorgestellt)* [2] **embarrassed** *verlegen, peinlich berührt* [3] **video channel** *Video-Kanal*

► Workbook, p. 83

Explaining words

1 Use umbrella words

a) Match the food and drinks to the correct umbrella words.

1e, 2 …

~~1 watermelon~~	a It's a kind of pasta.
2 chicken	b It's a kind of Chinese food.
3 pepper	c It's a kind of meat.
4 stir-fry	d It's a kind of drink.
5 spaghetti	~~e It's a kind of fruit.~~
6 milk	f It's a kind of vegetable.

b) Now describe these food and drinks with umbrella words.

1 ham 2 trifle 3 onion 4 water 5 lemon 6 noodles

2 Describe it

Describe the food and drinks. Think of colours and use words from the box.

watermelon: *It's green outside and red inside. It's a big, round and sweet fruit.*

1 cola 2 carrot 3 curry 4 sugar 5 tea 6 pea

big • cold • dish • drink • food • hot • long • round • small • spicy • sweet • vegetable

3 Add more information

Complete the descriptions in 1–3.

1 **watermelon:** You eat it in summer.
strawberries: You eat them in …
2 **spaghetti:** You make it with tomato sauce.
curry: You make it with …
3 **stir-fry:** You eat it as a main dish.
trifle: You eat it for …

4 GAME Explain it!

Start in groups of three. Each student writes two words (food, drinks, dishes) on pieces of paper. Swap words with another group, but don't show them. In each group, a student takes a piece of paper and explains the word. The group has one minute to guess it.

▶ Skills file 6, p. 201

Digital quiz I can explain words.

Make a class recipe book

Step 1: Research and plan your recipe

Research your dish. You can use your favourite dish from p. 160.
Make a mind map with food, cooking things and useful verbs.

Pad Thai
- food: noodles, tamarind, …
- cooking things: wok, cooking spoon, …
- useful verbs: cook, fry, boil, mix, add, stir, …

▶ Wordbank 12, p. 223 ▶ Wordbank 13, p. 224

Step 2: Write the introduction

You can use your description from p. 160.
Add a list of food and cooking words. Explain food words.

A tamarind is a kind of fruit. It's brown and sweet.
You make a sauce from it.

> Not sure how to cook it?
> Ask your family or look online.
> Use " " to look for a phrase.

▶ Study skills, p. 166 ▶ Wordbank 12, p. 223 ▶ Wordbank 13, p. 224

Step 3: Write the instructions

Write how to cook the dish.

▶ Wordbank 13, p. 224

Step 4: Decorate your page

Add pictures of the dish and of you cooking or eating it.
Use photos or draw pictures.
Write what's happening in them.

1 *I'm boiling the water and adding the noodles.*
2 *I'm mixing the tamarind sauce and …*
3 *…*

Step 5: Give feedback

Put all the recipes on tables or the walls. Look at the recipes and write notes with your feedback. Put each note on the correct recipe page.

Your recipe looks delicious!

The instructions are very clear.

I'd like to see more pictures.

I want to cook this!

▶ Let's talk: Feedback, p. 231

Digital quiz I can research and write a recipe.

1 A film night

I can talk about food.

a) WORDS Look at the food and drinks. What things can you see? Write the correct word.

1

2

3

4

5

6

7

8

b) SPEAKING You and your partner are having a film night. You talk about what you want to buy for food and drinks. Choose three things from a).

Let's buy some ... / I want to buy ...
I love ... / I often eat / drink ...
Do you like ...?

Yes, that's a good idea. /
No, I don't want to buy ..., but let's buy ...
I don't like ... / I never eat / drink ... / I'm allergic to ...

c) Now tell your partner about another favourite snack. Why do you like it?

2 LANGUAGE A very bad picnic

I can talk about birthdays and parties (present progressive).

Sunita shows her friends a photo of a bad family party. Complete her sentences with the *-ing* form of the words in the box.

bark • decorate • eat • listen • play • sit • text • wear

1 Willow's birthday is in August, so we're ... T-shirts, but it's cold and rainy.
2 Mum is ... a tree, but it's very windy.
3 We're ... on the grass because there are no chairs.
4 A dog is ... because it wants our food.
5 Nish is on his phone. He's ... his friends.
6 A seagull is ... my sandwich.
7 Ben is ... the guitar.
8 But just one person is ... to Ben's music!

Check

3 Language After the party

I can talk about party food and activities *(much, many, a lot of)*.

a) Complete the questions with *much* or *many*.

1 How ... lemonade is there?
2 How ... sandwiches are there?
3 How ... salad is there?
4 How ... sausages are there?
5 How ... carrots are there?

b) Look at the picture. Answer the questions from a). Use *much*, *many* or *a lot of*.

1 There isn't ... lemonade.
2 There aren't ...
3 There's a ...
4 There are ...
5 There aren't ...

4 Reading Zane's dream party

a) Look at the title of the website and the pictures. Where's Zane's dream party?

www.stadium-birthday-party.example.net

The stadium: The perfect place for your birthday party

Why?
- The stadium is a special and interesting place.

Party activities:
- A tour of the stadium.
- A football skills lesson with our trainers.
- You and your friends play a football match.

When?
- Sunday mornings: 10 a.m. – 12 p.m.

What about food?
- Enjoy a delicious lunch of sandwiches, fruit and birthday cake.

b) Read the website. Answer the questions. Write in sentences.

1 Why is the stadium a good place for a party?
2 What activities are there?
3 What day of the week are the parties?
4 How long are the parties?
5 What food is there?

c) Where's your dream party? Why? You can use the ideas in the box.

home • ice rink • museum • park • skatepark • stadium • zoo

Check

5 MEDIATION My favourite evening meal

I can describe my favourite dish.

You want to tell your mum about your new favourite dish. You find the recipe on the internet and show it to her. Answer your mum's questions:

1 Isst man das zum Frühstück oder zu Abend?
2 Welche Zutaten braucht man dafür?
3 Was macht man mit den Würstchen?
4 Wie lange wird es im Ofen gebacken?

www.delicious-dinners.example.net

Toad in the hole

Today I want to tell you about my favourite evening meal: toad in the hole. I often eat it in winter. The name sounds weird, but the ingredients aren't weird!

You need:
- 3 eggs
- 300 ml milk
- 8 sausages
- 175 g flour
- oil

How to make it:
1 Mix the eggs, milk and flour.
2 Cook the sausages in oil until they are brown.
3 Add the mixture to the sausages.
4 Cook in the oven for 30 minutes.

6 LISTENING Dinner at Sunita's house

I can understand and talk about differences.

a) **Zane is at Sunita's house. Listen. Which picture is Sunita's dining room?**

A

B

b) **Listen again. Write 'Zane's family' or 'Sunita's family'.**

1 ... eats dinner in a big dining room.
2 ... has a small dining room.
3 ... eats dinner in the living room.
4 ... doesn't eat meat.
5 ... has no animals.

Check

7 STUDY SKILLS Explaining new words

I can explain words.

a) **Daniel is explaining some new words, but there are some mistakes. Find the mistake in each sentence.**

1 carrot: It's a kind of fruit.
2 chicken: It's a kind of cake.
3 dessert: It's the meal before dinner.
4 milk: It's a kind of food.
5 cornflakes: You eat them with a knife.
6 tea: It's a cold drink.
7 shopping list: You need it at school.
8 vegetables: They are bad for you.

b) **Write the correct sentences (1–8).**

1 carrot: It's a kind of …

8 WRITING A banana and chocolate crepe

I can research and write a recipe.

Luisa wants to write a blog post about her favourite dessert recipe: a banana and chocolate crepe. Look at the pictures and read her notes. Then write her post. Use the sentence starters to help you.

I want to tell you about … • You make it with … • You also need … • First … • Then … • After two minutes … • Finally …

1

125 g flour, 2 eggs, 360 ml milk, 1 tablespoon sugar, chocolate sauce, a banana

2

need • cooking spoon, frying pan

3

mix • flour, eggs, milk and sugar

4

fry • for two minutes

5

turn over • fry other side

6

put on • plate • add • chocolate and banana

Check

VARNDEAN Teen Zine

This month's topics: food and parties

Our school magazine: by students for students

Varndean food by Otis

I eat breakfast at school and get a hot lunch every day in the canteen. I'm a vegan so it's great that there is always a vegan menu. In the breaks I get snacks like fruit.

Monday	Tuesday	Wednesday	Thursday	Friday
Sausages / Vegan sausages with potatoes and green vegetables	Beef[1] and vegetable lasagne / Vegan lasagne and garlic bread	Burgers / Vegan burgers with salad	Chicken and pepper burritos / Bean[2] and pepper burritos with brown rice	Fish / Vegan nuggets with chips, baked beans and ketchup

What do you think of our school food? If you're at a different school: Tell us about about your school food. What's on your menu this week? What can you buy in breaks? What would you like to change?

Kian's tongue twisters

Listen to my tongue twisters[3]. How fast can you say them? You can have a class competition!

I scream, you scream, we all scream for ice cream!

How many cookies could[4] a good cook cook if a good cook could cook cookies?

Fresh fried fish, fish fresh fried, fried fish fresh, fish fried fresh.

[1] **beef** *Rindfleisch* [2] **bean** *Bohne* [3] **tongue twister** *Zungenbrecher* [4] **he / she could** *er / sie könnte*

Baking with Betty

Hi, guys! Today we're making blueberry[1] muffins. Perfect for parties!

You need:
260 g flour
2 teaspoons baking powder
2 teaspoons vanilla sugar
1 egg
150 g sugar
100 ml sunflower[2] oil
300 ml buttermilk
250 g blueberries

1

I'm mixing the flour, the baking powder and the vanilla sugar in a bowl[3].

2

In another bowl, I'm mixing the buttermilk, the oil, the egg and the sugar.

3

I'm adding the buttermilk mixture to the flour mixture and mixing everything[4].

4

Now I'm washing the blueberries and I'm adding them to the bowl.

5

I'm making twelve muffins and I'm putting the muffins in the oven.

6

Bake at 180 °C for 20–25 minutes. Well done! Twelve blueberry muffins.

[1] **blueberry** *Blaubeere* [2] **sunflower** *Sonnenblume* [3] **bowl** *Schüssel* [4] **everything** *alles*

Assistance dogs

Working animals

Most people have jobs. But some animals also have jobs! We call them working animals. They do things like work on farms or with the police. Assistance animals help people – for example **deaf** or blind people. Most assistance animals are dogs, but other animals can also help people. Small horses can help people walk. Monkeys can get things for their **owners** and do helpful little jobs with their hands.

Guide dogs

Guide dogs help blind people. They show their owners where to walk and when to stop, for example at a street. The owner holds the dog with a special **harness**. Some guide dogs can also get things for their owners. Golden retrievers, Labradors and **German shepherds** are good **breeds** for guide dogs.

Hearing dogs

Deaf people can use **hearing dogs**. They give their owners a signal when there's a sound like the phone, an alarm or a doorbell ringing, a person saying the owner's name, or a car in the street. **Poodles** and cocker spaniels can be good hearing dogs.

Good to know

If you see an assistance animal, leave it alone. It's working!

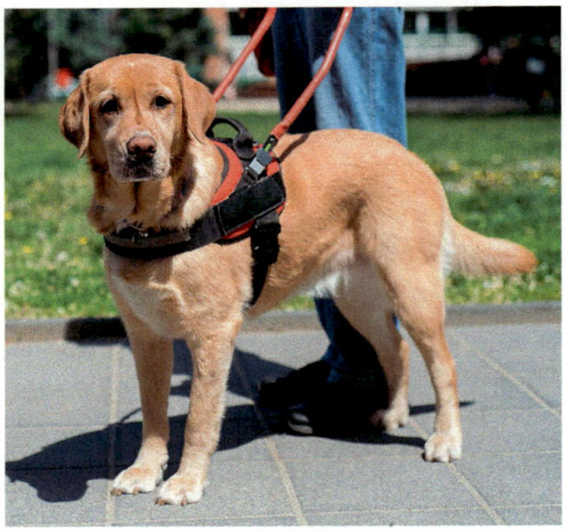

A guide dog. Its owner is holding it with a special harness.

Key terms

Assistance dogs
- autism *der Autismus*
- breed *die Rasse, die Züchtung*
- deaf *taub*
- German shepherd *der Deutsche Schäferhund*
- guide dog *der Blinden(führ)hund*
- hearing dog *der Signalhund (für Hörbehinderte)*
- harness *das (Hunde-)Geschirr, das Führgeschirr*
- hearing *das Gehör*
- owner *der Besitzer, die Besitzerin*
- physical disability *die körperliche Behinderung*
- poodle *der Pudel*
- sensory overload *die Reizüberflutung*
- therapy dog *der Therapiehund*
- warn sb. *jn. warnen*

Why are poodles good assistance dogs?

- Most poodles aren't very big.
- They're very smart.
- Most people aren't allergic to poodles.

[1] **doorbell** *Türklingel*

Therapy dogs
Assistance dogs don't just do physical jobs. Some dogs help their owners when they're sad or scared. Some **therapy dogs** help kids with **autism**. It's sometimes hard to talk to people, but easy to talk to a dog. When people with autism experience **sensory overload**, they sometimes stop listening. A therapy dog gives them a signal for important information.

Assistance dogs for other physical disabilities
Dogs can also help with other **physical disabilities**. They can open and close doors, **turn lights on and off**, or get help if there's a problem. Some assistance dogs smell things their owners are allergic to and **warn** them. Other assistance dogs can even smell when their owner is ill.

Training an assistance dog
Guide dogs and hearing dogs begin training when they're one year old. It takes almost two years to train them. The owners also go to training for about five weeks. They learn how to work with the dog.

A therapy dog in a hospital.

Good to know

You can use *he* or *she* for animals, but you can also use *it*.

1 Good assistance dogs

Describe a good assistance dog.
You can use the words and phrases in the green box.

2 Dog breeds

With a partner, choose a dog breed from p. 174 and explain why it makes a good assistance dog. Make a poster. Use the poster on p. 174 as an example and the words and phrases in the green box.

Use your words and phrases

Describing working animals
A good assistance dog is smart / ...
It can learn to help / guide people ...
It likes people / helping / learning ...
Assistance dogs open ...
... are good assistance / working animals. They ...

3 Other working animals

Research another working animal (for example dolphins, rats, ...).
Why is it a good working animal? You can use the words and phrases in the green box.
Write a text and put it in your DOSSIER.

[1] **physical** *körperlich* [2] **turn a light on / off** *ein Licht ein-/ausschalten*

Partner page

▸ Page 153

10 SPEAKING Find the differences

Partner B: Look at this picture.
Take turns and find six differences:

In my picture the boy and girl in blue T-shirts are singing karaoke.

In my picture they are / aren't ...
In my picture a dog is ...

▸ Page 153

11 My party photos

Diff bank

▸ Page 148

More practice 1 Food words

a) **What am I? Choose four of the food words from the box.**

bread • cheese • cream • meat • pea • rice • strawberry • tomato • spice

1 I'm a very small, green vegetable.
2 I come from animals. Vegetarians don't eat me.
3 I'm a sweet red fruit.
4 People eat me with cake or fruit or in a dessert.

☒ b) **Write sentences for the other food words in the box. The sentences in a) can help you.**

▸ Page 150

More practice 2 Thanks for the invitation!

Sunita and Ryan write messages to Noah. Put their messages in the correct order.

a Bye – see you in the park on Saturday!
b I'd love to come to your party – thanks!
c Love Sunita xox
d I love picnics!
e Hello, Noah
f A circus theme is a great idea.

a I have an important basketball game.
b Bye and happy birthday from Ryan
c I'm sorry, but I can't come.
d Hi, Noah
e Have a great party!
f Thanks for the invitation.

Challenge 1 Ella's party

You get this invitation. Write a message to Ella. Say *yes* (like Sunita) or *no* (like Ryan).

When? On Sunday 2nd June
What time? From 1 p.m. to 4 p.m.
Where? At Ella's house, 135 Preston Road, Brighton
What? It's a cupcake party! We can make a lot of different cupcakes. (But there's other food too!)

RSVP to Ella by text or phone.

More practice 3 A poem about the months of the year

a) Listen to and read the poem. Then say it.

b) Answer the questions.

1 Which months have 30 days?
2 Which months have 31 days?
3 Which month has 28 or 29 days?

Thirty days have September,
April, June and November.
All the rest have 31.
February's great with 28
And a leap year's fine with 29!

▸ Page 151

More practice 4 The calendar for July

Look at the calendar for July. Take turns to ask and answer the questions.

1 What day of the week is 3rd July? – *It's ...*
2 What date is the second Thursday in July?
3 What date is the last day in July?
4 Today is 13th July. What date is the next Saturday?
5 What day and date is Ezra's birthday? (Look at the red circle.) – *It's on ...*

JULY

Mon	Tue	Wed	Thur	Fri	Sat	Sun
	1	2	3	4	5	6
7	8	9	10	11	12	13
14	15	16	17	18	19	20
21	22	23	24	25	26	27
28	29	30	31			

More practice 5 My important dates

a) What dates are important to you? Write five dates: *13th December: my dog's birthday*

b) Tell your partner about your dates.

My dog's birthday is on the 13th of December.

▸ Page 153

Parallel exercise 9 A birthday photo

Zane is showing a photo of his friend's birthday party to his mum. Complete his sentences with the *-ing* form.

1 Sunita and Ruby are (listen) *listening* to music.
2 I'm (eat) ... birthday cake.
3 Ju is (wear) ... a gold hat.
4 Noah is (sit) ... on a chair with a cat.
5 He's (take) ... photos with his phone.
6 Max and Albie have balloons. They're (play) ... with them.
7 Lily is at the table. She's (draw) ... a picture.
8 Amina and Vicky are (lie) ... on the floor.

The spelling of some verbs with *-ing* is different:
sit – sitting
take – taking
lie – lying

More practice 6 What are they doing?

a) **Look at the pictures. What are people doing in different places? Write sentences.**

A girl / boy / family is ... *A girl and her dad are ...*

1

Mexico City, 6 a.m.

2

New York, 7 a.m.

3

London, 12 o'clock

4

Berlin, 1 p.m.

5

Tokyo, 8 p.m.

6

Sydney, 9 p.m.

☒ b) **Write what you're doing now. Write what people in your family are doing now.**

I'm sitting in the classroom. I'm ... *My little brother is playing at home. ...*

More practice 7 What's happening?

a) **Listen to the sounds. What's happening? Write a sentence. Choose words from the box.**

box • cook • dance • drink • eat • close • play • send • skateboard • swim

Somebody is ... / Two people are ...

Challenge 2 A hot day in Brighton

Write the conversation.

Scout Hi, George. (1) What / you / do?
George (2) I / rest. (3) I / not / feel / well. The sun is too hot and (4) my head / burn.
Scout Yes, it's hot. But we're lucky – (5) it / rain / not / now!
George Yes, you're right. (6) You / wear / a nice hat, Scout.
Scout Thanks. (7) It / keep / me cool. (8) You / not / wear a hat. You need a hat, George!

▸ Page 155

More practice 8 In the kitchen

**Complete the conversation with *much, many* or *a lot of*.
What dish are Zane and his dad making?**

Dad Have we got everything?
Zane How (1) ... tomatoes do we need?
Dad Five or six.
Zane And how (2) ... meat?
Dad You can use the whole packet. There isn't (3) ... meat in there.
Zane And how (4) ... carrots?
Dad Just two, that's fine. They're big carrots, so you don't need (5) ... .
Zane How (6) ... water do I need for the pasta?
Dad You need to cook it in (7) ... water.
Zane And how (8) ... pasta do we need?
Dad A lot – we're all hungry!

(Spaghetti bolognese)

▸ Page 156

Challenge 3 At the supermarket

Noah and his dad are at the supermarket. Complete each sentence with the correct simple present form of the verb and *much, many* or *a lot of*.

1 We *don't have* (not have) *much* bread at home; let's buy more.
2 Look, I ... (have) ... sausages here already.
3 Lily ... (not eat) ... meat, but she's not a vegetarian.
4 How ... carrots ... (be) in the bag?
5 I'm happy there ... (not be) ... people in the supermarket today!
6 I can't remember: How ... pasta ... we ... (need)?
7 The lemons ... (not cost) ... money.
8 But the supermarket ... (not have) ... lemons today.
9 ... (be) there still ... things on our shopping list?
10 ... your friends ... (eat) ... fruit?

▸ Page 156

7 SONG The shopping song

I'm going to the supermarket today
Where's my shopping list? I'm on my way.
I have my bags and my money 'cause I
Have a lot of food I need to buy:

Cheese and peas and aubergines,
Avocados and tomatoes and baked beans,
Meat and sweets and nectarines,
Lemons, melons, ham and jam and lamb.
And ...

I'm going to the supermarket today ...

▸ Page 160

More help 5 My favourite dish

My favourite dish is It's	a dessert / a main course / a cake / a drink / ... cold / delicious / hot / spicy / sweet / ...
It comes from	my dad's / mum's / family's culture / ... China / Germany / India / Poland / Turkey / South Africa / ...
You make it with	cheese / chocolate / meat / onions / pasta / rice / sugar / tomatoes / ...
I eat / cook it My family eats it My dad / mum cooks it	at a restaurant / with my friends / ... every day / every week / every Friday / at parties / ...
I drink it with	water / tea / cola / ...

▸ Page 164

More practice 9 Words in the story

Find the words in the story for the descriptions.

1 moving your hand to say hello (part 1)
2 when food is really good (part 1)
3 eating in the park with friends (part 6)
4 when your face shows that you are happy (part 6)
5 when something is really great (part 7)

The lost dog

1 READING Activities at the beach

a) BEFORE YOU READ **Look at the picture below. Zane and Holly are collecting sea glass at the beach. Talk to a partner about activities at the beach. Make a top three list together.**

b) **Read the story. Then talk to a partner about your version of the story.**

In my version Zane and Holly ...
In my version they don't ...

!

The lost dog is a different kind of story: **You decide** what happens next several times!

Good to know

Sea glass is old pieces of glass: People throw glass, for example glass bottles, into the sea. The water and the sand make the glass smooth and cloudy. You find sea glass on the beach. Because Brighton Beach has rocks, not sand, it's a great place to collect sea glass.

Part 1

It's a sunny day in the summer holidays. Zane and his sister Holly are at the beach. "Let's collect sea glass," Zane says. "Oh yes, let's," Holly shouts. An hour later they have lots of smooth, colourful glass. "OK," says Zane. "Let's go home now. We can get some chips on the way."

The kids get their chips and sit down outside Harry's fish and chip shop. They start to count their pieces of sea glass. "So many pieces!" Holly says. "We're a good team, Zane." "That's right, Holly!" Zane answers.

"Hey, let's eat our chips. They're getting cold!" Zane says. At that moment a dog comes to the kids. He looks at Holly with his big brown eyes. "You're hungry, right?" asks Holly. "You can have this chip." She gives the dog a chip. "Holly!" Zane says. "Dogs can't eat chips! They're not healthy for dogs." "But he's hungry!" Holly cries. "Poor dog." "I'm sure his owners are here," Zane says. "Come on – let's go home now."

The kids walk home. Holly looks behind her. "Look, Zane!" she shouts. "He's following us." "Who is following us?" Zane asks. "The hungry dog!" Holly laughs. "Erm ... Zane, can we take him home with us?" "But he isn't our dog," Zane answers. The dog comes to Zane and looks at him. Then he licks Zane's hand. Zane looks up and down the street. But he and Holly are alone with the dog. "Maybe you're right, Holly," Zane says. "We can't just leave him here. Come on, boy, you can come with us."

Part 2

At home the kids play with the dog in the living room. Mrs Adebayo comes into the room. "Hi," she smiles. "I'm glad you're back from ..." Then her smile goes away. "Where is that dog from?" she asks. "Harry's fish and chip shop," Zane says. "Chip is hungry! And alone." "Chip?" asks his mother. "Yes, Chip," Zane answers. "Isn't it a great name? It's Holly's idea." "Zane, Holly, that dog can't stay here." "But why not?" Holly asks. "Because he isn't our dog," Mrs Adebayo answers and takes her phone.

"Hello. My name is Louise Adebayo. I'm calling about a dog. He's at our house, but he's not our dog. ... Yes, that's right. ... He's brown and white. He's a spaniel, I think. ... You can't collect him? Why not? ... Yes, I think that he's happy here. He's playing with my children. ... Yes, maybe. OK, we can do that. But I hope that you find the owner soon! OK. Goodbye. Thank you." "The animal shelter has no information about a lost spaniel," Mrs Adebayo explains. "So can we keep Chip?" Holly asks. "Just for a few days," Mrs Adebayo answers. "Hey, Zane," Holly whispers. "Let's hope they don't find the owner. Then Chip can live here with us."

Part 3

Two days later Chip is still with the Adebayo family. Before Zane goes to bed, he writes in his diary.

21st JULY
Today was Chip's 3rd day with us. He's already part of the family. Mum was not happy at first, but she really likes him now. Noah and Buddy came to see him yesterday. We all played together in the garden. We had a lot of fun! Lily wants to meet him too: maybe tomorrow.

Lily kicks the ball to the end of the garden. "Run for it, Chip," she shouts. A moment later Chip comes back with the ball in his mouth. "He's fun," Lily laughs. "He really likes it here," Zane answers. "Yes," Lily says. "But maybe he misses his family." "Lily!" Holly cries. "We're his family now." "Oh, right," Lily says. "Hey guys, I must go now. It's my big sister's birthday today and there's a party this evening."

After dinner that evening the Adebayo family goes into the living room. Zane is looking at his phone.

"Let's watch a film," Mrs. Adebayo says. "Come here, Chip, you can sit with me."

"Hey, Zane," Mr Adebayo says. "Please put your phone away. We want to watch a film together." "I don't want to watch a film," he says. He goes into his room.

Mrs and Mr Adebayo look at each other. They're worried. What's wrong with Zane? In his room Zane looks at the text from Lily again.

You decide!

Does Zane tell his parents about Lily's message?
Yes. → Go to part 4.
No. → Go to part 5.

► Workbook, pages 91–93

Part 4

Mrs Adebayo comes into Zane's room. "What's wrong, love?" she asks. Zane looks at his mother. There are tears in his eyes. "Look," he says. "It's from Lily." "Oh no," Mrs Adebayo says and kisses Zane's head. "I'm so sorry."

An hour later the doorbell rings. "Come in, please," says Mrs Adebayo and opens the door. An old woman comes in. "I'm Elsa Brown. Thank you so much, Mrs Adebayo," she says. A moment later Chip runs in. He wags his tail and barks. "He's happy to see you," Mrs Adebayo says. "And I'm so happy to see Bonzo," Mrs Brown smiles. "He's my best friend."

"It's time to say goodbye to Chip," Mrs Adebayo calls. Zane and Holly come into the hall. "Don't cry, Holly," Zane whispers. "Chip must go home."

"I'm sorry," says Mrs Brown. "I can see that you really like Bonzo." "We love him a lot," Holly says. "But he's your dog," Zane adds. "It's good that you're together again. Goodbye, Chip. You're a great dog!" "I have an idea," says Mrs Brown. "Maybe you can help me with Bonzo! Usually my granddaughter helps me. She's about your age. She takes Bonzo for walks and helps me take him to the vet. Those jobs are really hard for me. Bonzo is a very strong dog!" "Why can't she help you now?" asks Holly. "She's on holiday in the US with her parents," says Mrs Brown. "You know Bonzo now. He likes you. Can you help me?"

You decide!

Do Zane and Holly help Mrs Brown?

Yes. → Go to part 6.
No. → Go to part 7.

Part 5

Zane closes the message and goes back into the living room. He watches the film and doesn't tell his family about the message. He wants to keep Chip!

On Saturday morning Zane and Holly are walking with Chip in the park. Chip stops and looks at an old woman on the other side of the park. He starts to run. "Stop, Chip," shouts Holly. But Chip doesn't stop. Chip runs to the woman. "Bonzo!" the woman shouts. "There you are!" She hugs the dog. Then she looks at Zane and Holly. She looks angry. "Why do you have my dog?" she asks. "Erm ...," says Zane.

The woman takes Bonzo. "Come Bonzo," she says. "Let's go home!" Zane looks at Holly. She's crying. "I'm so sorry, Holly," says Zane.

The next day Zane has an idea. He goes back to the park in the morning. Zane wants to find the old woman again. It works! He sees her with Bonzo. Zane goes to the woman. He explains about Bonzo at the fish and chip shop, about the animal shelter and about Lily's message.

"I'm really, really sorry," he says. "We love Bonzo. But he's your dog." "He's my best friend," says the old woman. "But maybe you can help me with Bonzo. Usually my granddaughter helps me. She's about your age. She takes Bonzo for walks and helps me take him to the vet. Those jobs are really hard for me. Bonzo is a very strong dog!" "Why can't she help you now?" asks Zane. "She's on holiday with her parents in the US," says Mrs Brown. "You know Bonzo now. He likes you. Can you help me?"

You decide!

Zane doesn't have time. → Go to part 7.
Zane wants to help Mrs Brown. → Go to part 8.

Part 6

"I want to help!" cries Holly. "Me too," says Zane. "I miss Bonzo already!"
Mrs Adebayo thinks. "The kids are usually very busy. But in the summer holidays they have time." "Wonderful!" says Mrs Brown. "I live in the next street. How often can you come?" "Our family holiday is already over. We can come every morning and evening this week and next week. Is that enough?" "That's a big help," says Mrs Brown. "I can put Bonzo in the garden in the afternoon. But he likes two nice long walks every day. And I can pay you each ten pounds per week." "Oh, we don't want money," says Holly. "We just want to see Bonzo!" "And we want to help you, of course," Zane adds.

"Thank you very much," says Mrs Brown. "But I also pay my granddaughter to walk Bonzo. It's a very important job. See you tomorrow!"

Mrs Adebayo looks at the children. "Great! You can see the dog every day, get some money AND help someone." "You're right," says Zane. "I'm happy that Bonzo is with Mrs Brown now." He sends Lily a text:

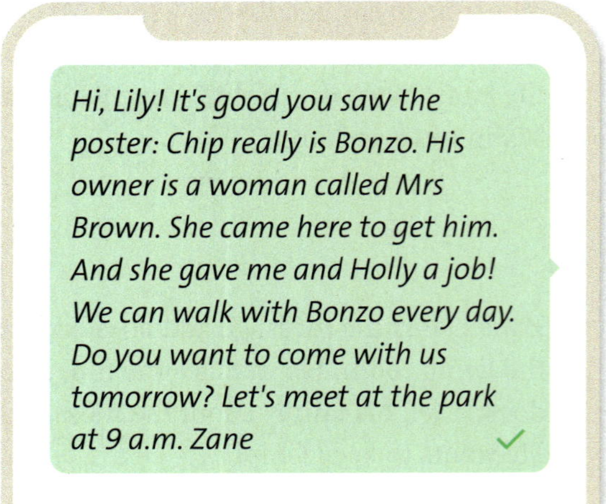

!

→ Now go to part 9.

Part 7

"I don't know," says Zane. "I really like Bonzo, but I'm very busy. I want to hang out with my friends every day. And I go swimming at the beach a lot. And play rugby. Sorry!"
"Oh dear," says Mrs Brown. "I don't want Bonzo to get lost again!"

"I have an idea," says Zane. "I can ask my friend Lily. She loves Bonzo. She really wants a pet, but her flat is too small. Maybe she can help. I'll send her a message."
Seconds later there's an answer from Lily.

YES YES YES!!!

That night Zane gets another text from Lily.

Thanks again, Zane. I talked to Mrs Brown. I got the job! Can you and Holly come to the park tomorrow and help me with Bonzo?

!

→ Now go to part 9.

Part 8

"Oh, thanks!" says Zane. "That's great! How often do you need help?"
"I can put Bonzo in the garden in the afternoon," says Mrs Brown, "but he likes a nice long walk in the morning and in the evening."
"My sister Holly and I have time then," answers Zane. "But I must ask my mum."
"Of course," says Mrs Brown. "I can pay you each ten pounds per week. Please call me in the evening. I hope your mum says yes!"
She gives Zane her phone number and they say goodbye.

At home Zane asks his mum and she says yes. Holly says yes too! She misses Bonzo. Zane sends Lily a text:

Hi, Lily! Chip really is Bonzo. His owner is a woman named Mrs Brown. She gave me and Holly a job! We can walk with Bonzo every day. Do you want to come with us tomorrow? Let's meet at the park at 9 a.m. Zane

Part 9

The next day Zane and Holly meet Lily at the park. The three kids walk and play with Bonzo. He's a very friendly dog. He likes to meet new people. But when a tall man with red hair says hi to the dog, Bonzo isn't friendly! He barks at the man. Zane and Holly are surprised. "I'm sorry," says Zane. "I don't understand. Bonzo is always very friendly!" The man doesn't answer. He walks away. "Zane," whispers Holly. "I also don't like that man!" Holly, Zane and Lily walk through the park. Holly watches the man. She says to Zane, "Look! That man's hand is in that woman's bag! The woman with the blue blazer and the green bag! He's taking her mobile!" Zane and Lily look, but the man is walking away.

You decide!

What do the kids do?

Follow the man. → Go to part 10.
Call the police. → Go to part 11.

Part 10

"Are you sure?" Lily asks Holly. "Yes!" says Holly. "OK," Lily says. "Let's see where he goes." The kids follow the man. The man sits down next to a bag. The owner of the bag is a father, but he's playing with his baby. He's not watching his bag. The tall man puts his hand in the bag and takes the father's mobile. He puts it in his pocket and walks away.

!

Lily shouts to the father. "Hey! That man with the red hair has your mobile!" Bonzo barks. He's really loud! Lily shouts more. The father looks at the man. He looks very angry. The woman with the blue blazer cries, "My mobile isn't in my bag! I think that man has it!"

More people look. Some football players run to the man with the red hair. The man starts to run, but he falls down. Two policewomen run over. They listen to the people. Then they look in the man's pockets. He has six mobile phones! More police officers come. They all call Bonzo a good dog. The woman with the blue blazer and the father say thank you to the kids. "You're very brave," the father tells the kids. "With Bonzo we're not scared!" says Holly. "He IS a good dog! And very loud!"

The end → Now go to p. 189 and do exercises 2–3.

Part 11

"Are you sure?" Lily asks Holly.
"Yes!" she says. "OK," Lily says. "Let's see where he goes." Lily starts to follow the man, but Zane stops her. "We can call the police and tell them about the man." Lily calls 999 for the police. "Hello, my name is Lily Hall," she says. She tells the police about the man and where they are. "The man is going out of the park," she tells the police. "I think that he's going to West Drive. He's very tall and has red hair. He's wearing a grey blazer, blue jeans and black shoes."

The kids look back at the woman with the blue blazer. She's looking in her bag and in her pocket. "Are you looking for your phone?" asks Zane. "Yes, I am!" says the woman. "I think a man has it," says Holly. "But the police are looking for him now!"

The next morning Zane calls Lily. "We're in the newspaper!" he says. "Again?" Lily asks. "You're always in the newspaper, Zane!" "Right," says Zane. "But this time, you're in the newspaper too. Look!"

The end

2 Looking at language **Writing about the past**

a) **Find the past form of each word below in Zane's diary on p. 184 and in the newspaper article on this page.**

1 call 2 come 3 describe 4 have 5 is 6 look 7 play 8 see

b) **Write about your places for yesterday.**

At seven o'clock I was in bed / in the kitchen / at the bus stop / ….

3 Showtime **The lost dog**

Make groups of four: Zane, Holly, Lily and the tall man with the red hair.
Act out what happens after part 9. You choose A or B:

A Your show can be like part 10 or 11.

B You can find a new end for the story.

▸ Workbook, pages 91–93

Digital quiz — I can understand a story.

Skills file – Übersicht

Auf den ***Skills file***-Seiten findest du Methoden und Tipps, die dir helfen, z. B. Wortschatz zu lernen, Informationen zu sammeln, Wörter zu umschreiben oder kleine Vorträge zu halten.

Inhalt

Die mit diesem Symbol gekennzeichneten Abschnitte enthalten Hinweise und Tipps, die dir dabei helfen, elektronische Medien beim Englischlernen einzusetzen.

Erklärfilm: Dieses Symbol zeigt dir, dass du einen Erklärfilm zu diesem Thema in der App findest.

Lösungen der Merkaufgaben:

SF 2, Merkaufgabe:
a) *Thema: animals • Oberbegriffe: farm animals, wild animals, pets • Unterbegriffe: chicken, snake, dog*

SF 3, Merkaufgabe:
- *Sea:* [es] – [iː] – [eɪ]
- *Lanes:* [el] – [eɪ] – [en] – [iː] – [es]
- *BN2 1PS:* [biː] – [en] – two – one – [piː] – [es]
- *Brighton:* [biː] – [ɑː] – [aɪ] – [dʒiː] – [eɪtʃ] – [tiː] – [əʊ] – [en]

SF 4, Merkaufgabe 1:
beach, because, bed

SF 4, Merkaufgabe 2:
a) *Haupteintrag: opinion*
b) *Haupteintrag: colour*
c) *Haupteintrag: shopping*

SF 4, Merkaufgabe 3:
a) *question: questions* **b)** *mouse: mice*
c) *potato: potatoes*

SF 4, Merkaufgabe 4:
a) *drink: 1. das Getränk;*
2. trinken
b) *love: 1. die Liebe;*
2. der Liebling;
3. lieben, sehr mögen
c) *mean: 1. gemein, fies;*
2. bedeuten;
3. meinen (sagen wollen)

SF 5, Merkaufgabe 1:
a) *Karte für den Abschluss* **b)** *That's the end of my presentation. Thank you for listening. Do you have any questions?*

SF 5, Merkaufgabe 2:
b) *I like your presentation. Your pictures are very nice. Please don't speak so fast.*

SF 6, Merkaufgabe 1:
a) *room* **b)** *fruit*

SF 6, Merkaufgabe 2:
It's a place at school. You do sports there.

SF 1

Erklär-
film

Wörter lernen leichtgemacht

▸ Unit 1 | p. 36

Alle neuen Wörter und Wendungen des Buches findest du im *Vocabulary*, S. 233–281.
Alle fett gedruckten Wörter aus der linken und der rechten Spalte musst du lernen.

Wie kann ich Wörter lernen?

Lerne immer nur fünf bis zehn Wörter auf einmal.

Es gibt viele Möglichkeiten, wie du Wörter lernen kannst.

Hier stellen wir dir einige vor. Probiere sie aus und finde heraus, welche Methoden am besten zu dir passen.

1 Wörter lernen mit dem *Vocabulary*

Auf S. 233 kannst du sehen, wie das *Vocabulary* aufgebaut ist und welche Symbole und Abkürzungen dort verwendet werden. Hier ist ein Beispiel von S. 238:

hat	der Hut, die Mütze	 **hats**
(to) **sing**	singen	**singing** = das Singen **singer** = der Sänger, die Sängerin
Sorry. / I'm sorry.	Tut mir leid. / Entschuldigung.	Don't eat my sandwich! – Oh, **I'm sorry.**

- Lies dir zunächst das englische Wort laut vor.
- Lies dann die deutsche Übersetzung und die Beispiele und Hinweise in der rechten Spalte.
- Schreibe das englische Wort auf und präge dir so die Schreibweise ein.
- Wiederhole diese Schritte mehrfach hintereinander, um dir die Wörter gut zu merken. Wechsle dabei auch die Leserichtung: Beginne mit der deutschen Übersetzung, sage dann das englische Wort.
- Teste dich nun selbst: Decke die deutsche Übersetzung ab, lies das englische Wort. Weißt du noch, was es auf Deutsch bedeutet? Kannst du auch die englischen Beispiele nennen?
- Du kannst auch jemanden bitten dich abzufragen.

Merkaufgabe 1

Probiere das gleich einmal aus: Wähle fünf bis zehn Wörter aus deinem *Vocabulary* und lerne sie wie oben beschrieben. Lasse dich von deinem Partner oder deiner Partnerin abfragen.

2 Wörter lernen mit digitalen Medien

Vokabeln kannst du auch digital auf deinem Smartphone, Tablet oder PC üben.

Am Ende kannst du dich oft mit einem Quiz testen und bekommst ein Feedback zu deinem Lernergebnis.

Oft kannst du die Wörter auch anhören. So lernst du die richtige Aussprache gleich mit!

Denke daran, dass du mit deinen Eltern sprichst, bevor du eine kostenpflichtige App herunterlädst.

Wie kann ich mir Wörter besser merken?

Manche Wörter wollen einfach nicht im Gedächtnis bleiben! Dann können dir Merktechniken helfen:

- Schreibe das Wort auf einen Klebezettel und bringe ihn an einer Stelle an, wo du oft hinschaust.
- Male ein **Bild** zum Wort.
- Verbinde das Wort mit einer passenden **Geste** oder **Bewegung**.
- Suche passende **Reimwörter**: *house – mouse*
- Finde Wörter aus der gleichen **Wortfamilie**:
  dance → dancing
  swim → swimmer
- Erfinde **Bildwörter**.
- Verwende das Wort in einem Satz oder einer typischen **Redewendung**:
  how → How are you?
  ride → ride a bike
- Finde **Gegensatzpaare**:
  big – small
  sunny – rainy
- Finde **Oberbegriffe** *(umbrella words)*:
  football → sport
  monkey → animal

Das *Vocabulary* (S. 233–281) enthält in der dritten Spalte viele Merkhilfen, die du beim Lernen nutzen kannst.

ein Bild zum Wort

ein Bildwort

ein Gegensatzpaar

Merkaufgabe 2

Wähle aus deinem *Vocabulary* drei Wörter, die du dir bisher noch nicht merken konntest. Wende drei verschiedene Merktechniken an.

Wörter sammeln und ordnen in einem *Vocab file*

In einem Vokabelordner *(Vocab file)* kannst du Wörter sammeln und in Listen, Mindmaps und Tabellen ordnen.

Dadurch kannst du sie nicht nur besser lernen und behalten, sondern auch noch später nutzen, z. B. wenn du über ein Thema sprechen oder schreiben möchtest.

Zudem kannst du neue Wörter und Seiten an jeder Stelle beliebig ergänzen.

So gestaltest du die Seiten deines *Vocab files*:

- Lege Mindmaps zu bestimmten Themen an, wie z. B. zu *food*. Schreibe das Thema in die Mitte.
- Ergänze Oberbegriffe *(umbrella words)* und suche passende Wörter oder auch Unterbegriffe dazu (z. B. *lunch: fish and chips, sandwich, salad, ...*).
- Erstelle nach und nach weitere Listen, Mindmaps und Tabellen und hefte sie in deinen Ordner. Ergänze deine Listen, wenn du neue Wörter lernst.

Wenn deine Sammlung umfangreicher wird, kannst du ein farbiges Register einfügen, um den Überblick zu behalten.

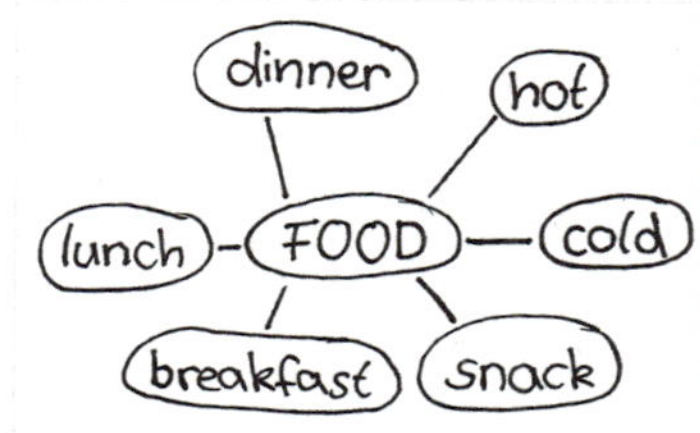

English	write a sentence	German
collecting	I like collecting books.	sammeln
dancing	I like dancing to music.	tanzen

Merkaufgabe 3

Besorge dir einen Schnellhefter oder Ordner. Lege deine erste Wortliste an und suche im *Vocabulary* passende Wörter dazu, z. B.:

- Reimwörter *(rhyme words)*
- Gegensatzpaare *(opposites)*
- schwierige Wörter *(difficult words)*
- Lieblingswörter *(my favourite words)*

In den *Wordbanks* auf S. 214–224 findest du viele nützliche Wörter, Sätze und Ausdrücke zu bestimmten Themen wie z.B. Schule, Tiere oder Freizeitaktivitäten.

SF 2

Sammeln und ordnen – Mindmaps

▸ Unit 1 | p. 36

Wobei kann mir eine Mindmap helfen?

Eine Mindmap (englisch *mind map*) hilft dir beim Sammeln und Ordnen von Ideen. Du kannst sie bei der Planung von Projekten oder Präsentationen, beim Wörterlernen, bei der Strukturierung von eigenen Texten oder auch bei der Erarbeitung von Lesetexten verwenden.

Wie erstelle ich eine Mindmap?

1 Das Thema

Nimm dir ein leeres Blatt und schreibe das Thema in Großbuchstaben in die Mitte. Umrahme das Thema mit einem Kreis oder einer Wolke.

2 Oberbegriffe

Finde Oberbegriffe zu deinem Thema.
Verwende für jeden Oberbegriff eine neue Farbe.
Jetzt hat deine Mindmap Hauptäste.

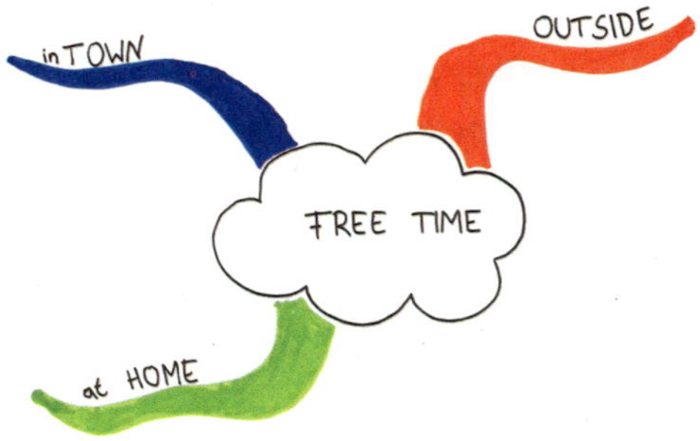

3 Unterbegriffe

Ergänze nun weitere Ideen zu den Oberbegriffen als Unterbegriffe. Verwende dieselbe Farbe wie für den Oberbegriff.

Deine Hauptäste haben nun Nebenäste. An diese kannst du noch weitere Ideen als Unteräste anhängen.

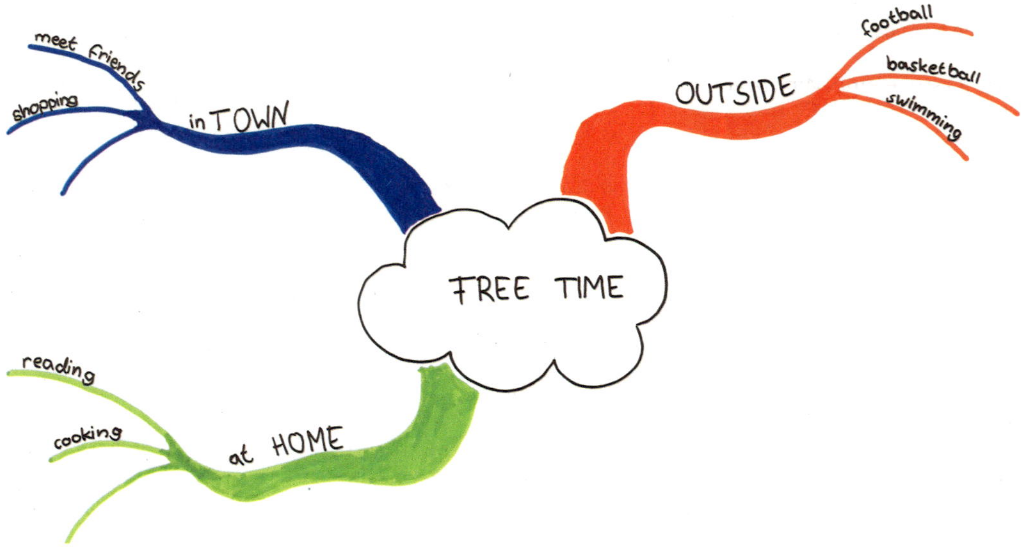

4 Überarbeiten

Gehe alles noch einmal durch und mache deine Mindmap noch anschaulicher: Lassen sich vielleicht Verbindungen zwischen den einzelnen Hauptästen oder den Nebenästen herstellen? Mit Zeichnungen und Symbolen kannst du die Ideen deiner Mindmap weiter verdeutlichen.

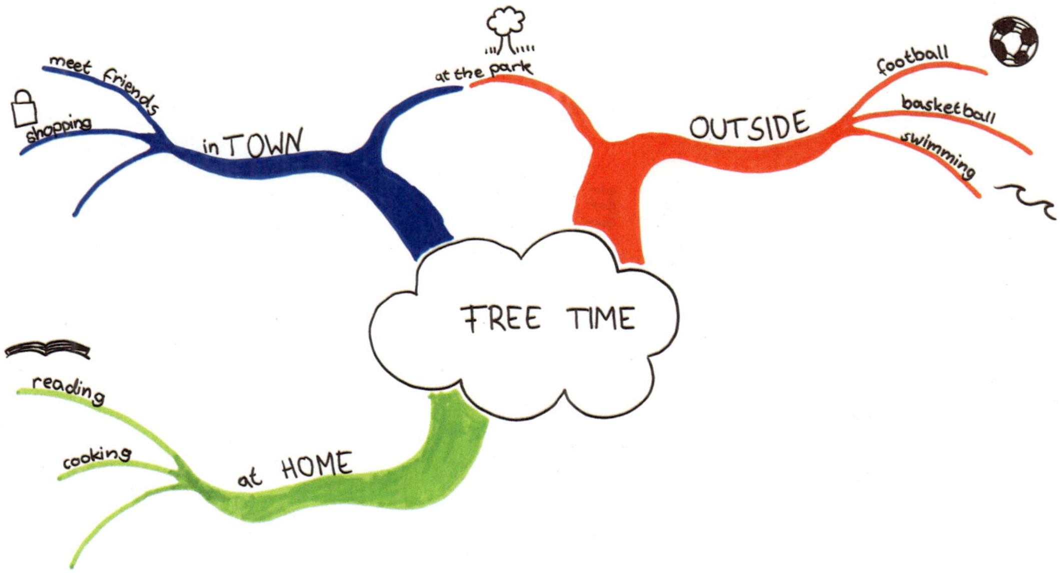

Merkaufgabe

a) Sortiere die folgenden Begriffe:

dog • farm animals • pets • wild animals • snake • animals • chicken

- Was ist das Thema?
- Was sind die Oberbegriffe?
- Welches sind mögliche Unterbegriffe?

(Die Lösung findest du auf S. 190.)

b) Erstelle eine Mindmap zu diesem Thema. Gehe wie oben beschrieben (1–4) vor.

SF 3

Buchstabieren

▶ Unit 2 | p. 68

Oft spricht man Wörter oder auch Namen auf Englisch ganz anders aus, als man sie schreibt. Um sie nicht falsch zu schreiben, bittet man darum, sie zu buchstabieren.

Dazu brauchst du das englische Alphabet:

A [eɪ]	B [bi:]	C [si:]	D [di:]	E [i:]
F [ef]	G [dʒi:]	H [eɪtʃ]	I [aɪ]	J [dʒeɪ]
K [keɪ]	L [el]	M [em]	N [en]	O [əʊ]
P [pi:]	Q [kju:]	R [ɑ:]	S [es]	T [ti:]
U [ju:]	V [vi:]	W ['dʌbəlju:]		
X [eks]	Y [waɪ]	Z [zed]		

Einige Laute haben in der Lautschrift besondere Zeichen, z. B.

- [ʃ] sprichst du wie „sch".
- [ʤ] sprichst du wie „dsch" (z. B. in „Dschungel").
- [:] Dieses Zeichen sieht wie ein Doppelpunkt aus. Es soll dir sagen, dass der Laut davor lang gesprochen wird.

▶ English sounds, p. 212

Wie übe ich buchstabieren auf Englisch?

- Höre dir das Alphabet in der App an und lies jeden Buchstaben laut mit, z. B. oben oder auf S. 212.
- Versuche danach, das Alphabet alleine zu sprechen. Die Lautschrift in eckigen Klammern kann dir helfen, dich an die Aussprache zu erinnern.

Merkaufgabe

Buchstabiere Scouts Adresse: *Sea Lanes, BN2 1PS, Brighton*

(Die Lösung findest du auf S. 190.)

Wenn dir jemand etwas buchstabiert, schreibe zuerst die einzelnen Buchstaben auf. Danach lies das ganze Wort oder den ganzen Namen.

Arbeit mit dem Wörterbuch

▶ Unit 3 | p. 102

Wenn du die Bedeutung eines englischen Wortes nicht weißt, kannst du das *English-German Dictionary* deines Englischbuchs (S. 283–296) oder ein Online-Wörterbuch zu Hilfe nehmen.

Wie finde ich Wörter und Ausdrücke im *Dictionary*?

1 In deinem *English-German Dictionary* (und in anderen Wörterbüchern) sind die Wörter alphabetisch geordnet:

g kommt vor h
ga kommt vor ge
gal kommt vor gam

Merkaufgabe 1

Schreibe die folgenden Wörter in der richtigen alphabetischen Reihenfolge untereinander auf:

1 *because* **2** *beach* **3** *bed*

Suche die Wörter anschließend in deinem *English-German Dictionary* (S. 283–296). Überprüfe, ob sie in der gleichen Reihenfolge erscheinen wie deine Wörter.

(Die Lösung findest du auch auf S. 190.)

°**furthest** [ˈfɜːðəst] am weitesten (entfernt)
°**fuss** [fʌs]: **make a fuss (of/over)** Theater/Wirbel machen (wegen)

G

°**gallery** [ˈɡæləri] die Galerie
game [ɡeɪm] das Spiel 2 (61)
°**gap** [ɡæp] die Lücke
garage [ˈɡærɑːʒ] die Garage 2 (54)
garden [ˈɡɑːdn] der Garten 2 (54)
geography [dʒiˈɒɡrəfi] die Geografie, die Erdkunde 1 (26)
German [ˈdʒɜːmən] deutsch; Deutsch; der/die Deutsche 1 (27)
Germany [ˈdʒɜːməni] Deutschland 4 (118)
get [ɡet]:
1. bekommen 3 (93)
get sth. *(sich etwas)* holen/besorgen 3 (93)
2. werden 4 (118)
get dressed sich anziehen 3 (83)
get warm warm werden 4 (118)
°**get ready (for)** sich fertig machen

2 Zusammengesetzte Wörter und längere Ausdrücke findest du bei einem Haupteintrag. Der Haupteintrag steht farbig oder **fett** am Anfang, Untereinträge kommen nach dem Haupteintrag. Schaue dir rechts den Eintrag für *name* an.

name [neɪm] der Name (10/11) **family name** der Familienname, der Nachname 2 (64) **first name** der Vorname 2 (64) **What's your name?** Wie heißt du? (10/11)

Merkaufgabe 2

Finde den Haupteintrag zu folgenden Redewendungen:

a) *in my opinion* **b)** *What colour is ...?* **c)** *go shopping*

(Die Lösung findest du auf S. 190.)

Was erfahre ich alles aus dem *Dictionary?*

- Im *English-German Dictionary* findest du die deutsche Übersetzung zu den englischen Wörtern aus deinem Buch.
- Außerdem kannst du die richtige Schreibweise eines Wortes überprüfen.
- Du erfährst auch, wie das Wort ausgesprochen wird. Schaue dir dafür die Lautschrift hinter dem Wort an.
- Und du kannst herausfinden, ob ein Wort einen unregelmäßigen Plural hat. Ist die Pluralform regelmäßig, findest du keinen Zusatz.

Kingdom [ˈkɪŋdəm]: **the United Kingdom (the UK)** das Vereinigte Königreich 3 (82)
kiosk [ˈkiːɒsk] der Kiosk, die Verkaufsbude, der Verkaufsstand 4 (121)
kitchen [ˈkɪtʃɪn] die Küche 2 (55)
knife [naɪf], *pl* **knives** das Messer 5 (150)
knives [naɪvz] *Plural von* **knife**
know [nəʊ] wissen; kennen 1 (20)

Merkaufgabe 3

Finde den Plural von **a)** *question* **b)** *mouse* **c)** *potato*

(Die Lösung findest du auf S. 190.)

- An den Ziffern 1., 2., ... kannst du sehen, dass ein Wort mehrere Bedeutungen hat. Lies daher immer den ganzen Eintrag und entscheide dann, welche Bedeutung in deinem Fall die richtige ist.

text [tekst]:
1. der Text 4 (124)
2. die SMS 5 (142)
3. **text sb.** jm. eine SMS schicken 5 (142)

Merkaufgabe 4

Diese Wörter können unterschiedliche Bedeutungen haben:

a) *drink* **b)** *love* **c)** *mean*

Schlage im *English-German Dictionary* nach, was sie bedeuten.

(Die Lösung findest du auf S. 190.)

Wie finde ich Wörter in einem Online-Wörterbuch?

Es gibt sehr viele Online-Wörterbücher im Internet oder als App. Frage deine Lehrkraft, welches Online-Wörterbuch sie dir empfehlen kann. Mit einem Online-Wörterbuch kannst du Wörter sehr schnell finden. So gehst du vor:

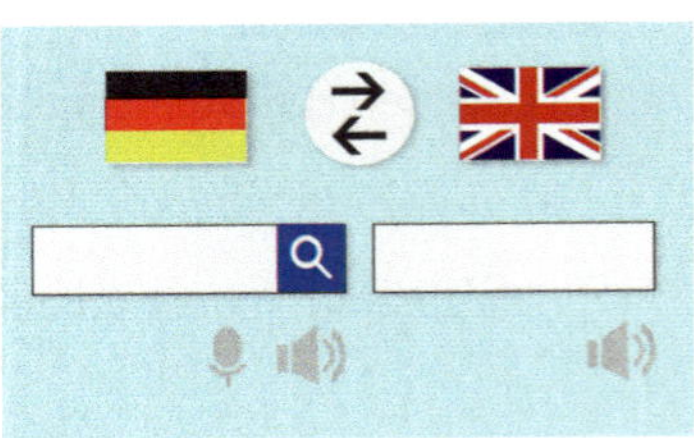

Zunächst musst du die Sprachen und die Suchrichtung eingeben (Englisch – Deutsch oder Deutsch – Englisch) und dann das Wort in das Suchfeld tippen. Gibt es ein Lautsprechersymbol, kannst du dir das gesuchte Wort auch anhören.

Manchmal kannst du das Wort direkt per Spracheingabe suchen. Vielleicht findest du dazu ein Mikrofonsymbol?

SF 5

Einen Kurzvortrag halten

▶ Unit 4 | p. 134

Ab und zu sollst du vor deiner Klasse etwas vortragen oder präsentieren. Hier erfährst du, wie du dich darauf gut vorbereiten kannst.

Wie bereite ich einen Kurzvortrag vor?

1 Sammeln und aufschreiben

Sammle Ideen und Informationen zu deinem Thema als Stichpunkte und ordne sie, z. B. mithilfe einer Mindmap (SF 2, S. 194) oder in einer Tabelle.

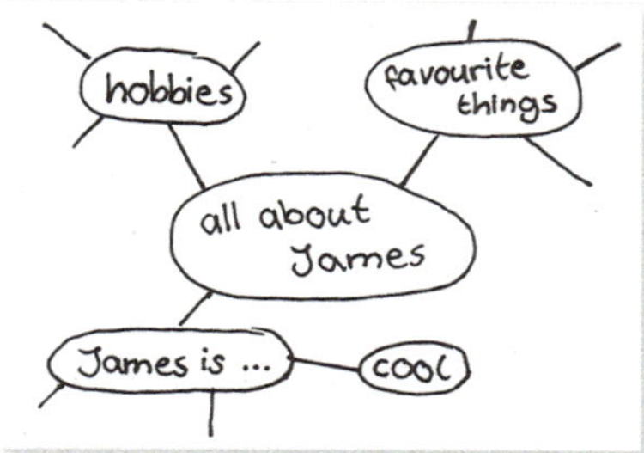

2 Veranschaulichen

Überlege, welche Bilder du zeigen kannst und wie du sie präsentieren möchtest, z. B. als Poster oder am Computer.

Bei einer Präsentation am Computer:

- Wähle ein einfaches Layout.
- Wähle eine gut lesbare Schrift und verwende eine Schriftgröße von mindestens 16 Punkt.
- Schreibe nur wenig Text.
- Wähle nur ein Bild pro Folie. Schreibe dazu, woher du dein Bild hast, z. B. den Namen der Internetseite.

3 Ordnen

Ein Kurzvortrag sollte folgendermaßen aufgebaut sein:

- **Einleitung:** Nenne das Thema.
- **Hauptteil:** Nenne deine Hauptpunkte. Erzähle dann mehr zu jedem Punkt.
- **Abschluss:** Bedanke dich fürs Zuhören. Erkundige dich, ob jemand eine Frage hat.

I'd like to talk about ...

First I'd like to talk about ...
Then I'd like to tell you about ...
I'd also like to talk about ...
This picture shows ...

That's the end of my presentation.
Thank you for listening.
Do you have any questions?

4 Notizen auf Karteikarten

Mache dir kurze Notizen auf Karteikarten. Du kannst dabei auch Symbole benutzen (z. B. „?" bedeutet: *Do you have any questions?*).

Nummeriere die Karteikarten, damit du beim Vortragen den Überblick behältst.

Merkaufgabe 1

Lies den Text auf der Karte.

a) Ist es die Karte für die Einleitung, den Hauptteil oder den Abschluss?

b) Formuliere aus den Notizen vollständige Sätze.

(Die Lösungen findest du auf S. 190.)

5 Üben

Übe deinen Vortrag mithilfe deiner Notizen vor dem Spiegel oder mit einem Partner oder einer Partnerin. Du kannst dich auch selbst mit einem Smartphone aufnehmen. Achte auf die Zeit.

Worauf muss ich beim Vortragen achten?

Überprüfe zu Beginn, ob alles vorbereitet ist: Ist das Poster aufgehängt? Ist der Computer bereit? Liegen die Vortragskarten richtig sortiert? Dann beginne deinen Vortrag:

- Schaue dein Publikum an und warte, bis es ruhig ist.
- Sprich langsam, laut und deutlich.
- Zeige während deines Vortrags auf Bilder oder dein Poster.

Feedback

Hole dir eine Rückmeldung darüber, wie deine Präsentation bei anderen ankommt. Vielleicht ist ein guter Tipp dabei, wie du dich verbessern kannst.

Can you give me some feedback, please?

Bitten dich andere um ein Feedback, sei respektvoll:

- Nenne zuerst Gelungenes, denn Lob tut gut und spornt an! Sage, was dir besonders gefallen hat.
- Dann mache Verbesserungsvorschläge.

Merkaufgabe 2

Die Präsentation eines Mitschülers hat dir gut gefallen. Seine Zeichnungen sind besonders schön, aber er hat etwas zu schnell gesprochen. Welches Feedback ist besser?

a) *Please don't speak so fast. Your pictures are very nice.*

b) *I like your presentation. Your pictures are very nice. Please don't speak so fast.*

Wörter umschreiben

▶ Unit 5 | p. 166

Gerade beim Sprechen kommt es häufig vor, dass dir ein englisches Wort fehlt oder nicht einfällt. Dann kannst du versuchen, es zu umschreiben.

It's an umbrella, Scout!

Wie umschreibe ich etwas?

1 Erkläre das Wort, indem du zunächst einen passenden Oberbegriff *(umbrella word)* auswählst. In dieser Tabelle findest du besonders häufige Oberbegriffe:

	umbrella words
Personen	boy • child • girl • man • person • woman • ...
Orte	building • country • place • room • ...
Dinge	drink • food • fruit • game • musical instrument • sport • thing • vegetable • ...

Hier ein Beispiel:
- gesuchtes Wort: *waitress*
- passende Oberbegriffe: *person, woman*

Merkaufgabe 1

Finde unter den vier Wörtern den Oberbegriff *(umbrella word)*:

a) *kitchen • hall • room • bedroom*

b) *apple • orange • fruit • banana*

(Die Lösungen findest du auf S. 190.)

2 Nenne dann nähere Details, z. B. wo die Person arbeitet:

It's a woman. She works in a restaurant.

	umbrella word	**Umschreibung**
waitress	It's a woman.	She works in a restaurant.
kitchen	It's a room in the house.	You make food there.
banana	It's a kind of fruit.	It's long and yellow.

Merkaufgabe 2

Finde eine passende Umschreibung für *sports hall.*

(Die Lösung findest du auf S. 190.)

Das sind Redewendungen, die du zum Umschreiben nutzen kannst:

It's a kind of ...
It's a person ...
It's a place ...
It's a thing ...

Inhalt

Erklär-film: Dieses Symbol zeigt dir, dass du einen Erklärfilm zu diesem Thema in der App findest.

LF 1

Der *s*-Genitiv und die *of*-Fügung
(The possessive form and the of-phrase)

▶ Hello! + Unit 1

Der s-Genitiv *(The possessive form)*

Noah's phone
Noahs Handy

Scout's hat
Scouts Hut

the dog's colour
die Farbe des Hundes

the girls' bikes
die Fahrräder der Mädchen

Mit dem *s*-Genitiv drückst du aus, dass etwas jemandem oder zu jemandem gehört.

Anders als im Deutschen wird im Englischen **bei Personen und Tieren** im Singular das s mit einem Apostroph (') angehängt.

Im Plural enden viele Hauptwörter bereits auf s, dann hängst du kein zweites s, sondern nur einen Apostroph (') an.

Die *of*-Fügung *(The of-phrase)*

the end of the game
das Ende des Spiels

a kilo of apples
ein Kilo Äpfel

Wenn zwei **Sachen** zusammengehören, verwendest du die ***of***-Fügung.
Man gebraucht sie auch bei Mengenbezeichnungen.

LF 2

Der Artikel *(The article)*

▸ Unit 1 | p. 21

Der unbestimmte Artikel *(The indefinite article)*

a bag
a girl

an apple
an elephant

an hour [ən ˈaʊə]
a uniform [eɪ ˈjuːnɪfɔːm]

Der unbestimmte Artikel (ein, eine) heißt im Englischen *a* oder *an*.
Du verwendest,
- *a*, wenn das folgende Wort mit einem Konsonanten (b, c, d, ..., z) beginnt,
- *an*, wenn das folgende Wort mit einem Vokal (a, e, i, o, u) beginnt.

! Entscheidend ist die Aussprache des Wortes, nicht die Schreibung.

Der bestimmte Artikel *(The definite article)*

the [ðə] ruler
the [ðə] classroom

the [ði] elephant
the [ði] English book

Der bestimmte Artikel (der, die, das) heißt im Englischen immer nur *the*.
Du sprichst
- [ðə], wenn das folgende Wort mit einem Konsonanten beginnt,
- [ði], wenn das folgende Wort mit einem Vokal beginnt.

LF 3

Der Plural der Nomen *(The plural of nouns)*

▸ Unit 1 | p. 22

a book	two books
a table	two tables
a bus	two buses
a beach	two beaches
a story	two stories
a pony	three ponies
man	men
woman	women
child	children
jeans	Jeans
trousers	Hose
clothes	Kleidung

Bei den meisten Nomen wird im Plural die Endung *-s* angehängt.

Nach *-s, -x, -ch* oder *-sh* wird *-es* angehängt.

Bei Nomen, die auf Konsonant + *y* enden, wird *y* zu *-ies*.

Einige Pluralformen sind unregelmäßig. Diese musst du lernen.

Einige Nomen haben keine Singularform und werden nur im Plural gebraucht:
The trousers are new. – Die Hose ist neu.

LF 4

Die Personalpronomen *(The personal pronouns)*

▸ Unit 1 | p. 24

I *(ich)*

you *(du)*

he *(er)*

she *(sie)*

it *(er, sie, es)*

we *(wir)*

you *(ihr)*

they *(sie)*

Personalpronomen ersetzen Nomen *(table ⇨ it)* oder Eigennamen *(Ben ⇨ he)*.

Das Pronomen *I* (ich) wird im Englischen immer großgeschrieben.

Das Pronomen *it* steht für Dinge und Tiere und entspricht „er", „sie" oder „es":

It's short. Er ist kurz.

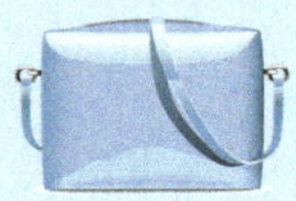

It's blue. Sie ist blau.

It's new. Es ist neu.

Bei Tieren, die du nicht kennst, verwendest du *it*: *It's a dog.*
Über Haustiere, deren Namen du kennst, sprichst du mit *he* oder *she*: *She's my dog.*

LF 5

Die Possessivbegleiter *(The possessive determiners)*

▸ Units 1–2

Is this your book?
Ist das dein Buch?

I	my room	*mein Zimmer*
you	your bike	*dein Fahrrad*
he	his drink	*sein Getränk*
she	her ball	*ihr Ball*
it	its name	*sein/ihr Name*
we	our dog	*unser Hund*
you	your teacher	*euer Lehrer*
they	their class	*ihre Klasse*

Possessivbegleiter zeigen an, wem etwas gehört.

This is my favourite hat.

! Nicht verwechseln:
their = ihr/e
they're = sie sind

LF 6

Das Verb *be* *(The verb be)*

Erklärfilm

a) Bejahte Aussagesätze *(Positive statements)*

▶ Unit 1 | p. 24

Kurzform	Langform
I'm eleven.	I am eleven.
You're ten.	You are ten.
He's nice.	He is nice.
She's in my class.	She is in my class.
It's a dog.	It is a dog.
We're here.	We are here.
You're from London.	You are from London.
They're from Hove.	They are from Hove.

Kurzform	
I'm	
You're	
He's / She's / It's	from Brighton.
We're	
You're	
They're	

Langform	
Zane is	from Brighton.
Sunita and Noah are	

Es gibt Kurz- und Langformen. Bei den Kurzformen ist ein Buchstabe weggefallen. Dafür steht ein Apostroph (').

Kurzformen werden eher beim Sprechen und in persönlichen E-Mails oder Chats verwendet.
Sie stehen meist nach Pronomen *(I, you, he, she, it, we, you, they)*.

Langformen benutzt du meist nach Eigennamen *(Zane, Sunita)* oder Nomen *(bike, teachers)*. Man verwendet sie außerdem bei offiziellen Schreiben.

LF 7

b) Verneinte Aussagesätze *(Negative statements)*

▶ Unit 1 | p. 29

Kurzform	Langform
I'm not old.	I am not old.
You aren't old.	You are not old.
He isn't old.	He is not old.
She isn't old.	She is not old.
It isn't old.	It is not old.
We aren't old.	We are not old.
You aren't old.	You are not old.
They aren't old.	They are not old.

Bei der Verneinung benutzt du fast immer die Kurzformen.

LF 8

Erklär-film

Das Verb *be* (*The verb be*)

c) Fragen und Kurzantworten *(Questions and short answers)*

▸ Unit 2 | p. 53

Are you eleven? Yes, I am. / No, I'm not.
Bist du elf? Ja. / Nein.

Is your room OK? Yes, it is. / No, it isn't.
Ist dein Zimmer OK? Ja. / Nein.

Fragen	Kurzantworten
Are you here, Ali?	Yes, I am. No, I'm not.
Are you all OK?	Yes, we are. No, we aren't.
Is Timo at home?	Yes, he is. No, he isn't.
Is Mum tired?	Yes, she is. No, she isn't.
Is your room nice?	Yes, it is. No, it isn't.
Are the cats here?	Yes, they are. No, they aren't.

Antworte auf eine Frage im Englischen nicht einfach mit *yes* oder *no*. Das klingt meist unhöflich. Verwende Kurzantworten.

LF 9

There is … / There are …

▸ Unit 2 | p. 56

There's a beach in Brighton.
Es gibt einen Strand in Brighton.

There are two girls in the pool.
Da sind zwei Mädchen im Pool.

There's	a man. a bike.
There are	two boys. three dogs.

Mit *there is* (= *there's*) oder *there are* sagst du, dass etwas vorhanden ist.

Im Deutschen heißt es meist:
Es gibt …
Da sind …
Es stehen …
Da liegen …

LF 10

Die einfache Form der Gegenwart *(The simple present)*

Erklär-film

a) Bejahte Aussagesätze *(Positive statements)*

▶ Unit 3 | p. 88

I often get up at 7 o'clock.
Ich stehe oft um 7 Uhr auf.

Dad always makes breakfast.
Papa macht immer das Frühstück.

I You We They	start.

He She It	starts.

do [duː] – *does* [dʌz]
go – *goes*
watch [wɒtʃ] – *watches* [wɒtʃɪz]
wash – *washes*
tidy – *tidies*
have – *has*

Mit dem *simple present* sagst du, was oft oder jeden Tag passiert oder auch selten oder nie geschieht.

Diese Signalwörter findest du oft in Sätzen im *simple present:*
always, often, sometimes, rarely, never.

Mit *he, she* und *it* musst du immer ein *-s* ans Verb anhängen.

He, she, it – ein ***-s*** muss mit!

! Wenn ein Verb auf ***-ss***, ***-x***, ***-sh***, ***-ch*** oder ***-o*** endet, fügst du bei *he/she/it* ***-es*** hinzu. Endet ein Verb auf ***-y***, fügst du bei *he/she/it* ***-ies*** hinzu.

Für das Verb *have* benutzt du bei *he/she/it* die Form ***has***.

LF 11

b) Die Wortstellung *(Word order)*

Erklär-film

▶ Unit 3 | p. 91

s	v	o
Deniz	loves	old cars.

s	a	v	o
Mia	*always*	walks	to school.
Yusuf	*sometimes*	goes	by bike.

In Aussagesätzen ist die Wortstellung wie im Deutschen: *subject* – *verb* – *object*.

Mit Häufigkeitsadverbien *(always, often, sometimes, rarely, never)* kannst du sagen, wie oft etwas geschieht.

Anders als im Deutschen stehen sie im Englischen meist direkt vor dem Hauptverb.

Dad always *makes* breakfast.

Papa *macht* immer das Frühstück.

LF 12

Die einfache Form der Gegenwart *(The simple present)*

Erklär-film

c) Verneinte Aussagesätze *(Negative statements)*

▶ Unit 4 | p. 119

We don't live in town.
Wir wohnen nicht in der Stadt.

My dad doesn't like snakes.
Mein Papa mag keine Schlangen.

I You We They	don't start.
He She It	doesn't start.

Aussagen im *simple present* kannst du mit ***don't*** oder ***doesn't*** verneinen.

Bei *I, you, we, they* verwendest du ***don't***.

Bei *he, she, it* verwendest du ***doesn't***.

LF 13

d) Fragen mit *do / does (Do / Does-questions)*

▶ Unit 4 | p. 123

Do you like this game?
Magst du dieses Spiel?

Does your sister play football?
Spielt deine Schwester Fußball?

Fragen		
Do	I you we they / your parents	like music?
Does	he / your dad she / Lily it	like music?

Fragen, auf die man mit „ja" oder „nein" antworten kann, heißen Entscheidungsfragen. Sie beginnen mit *Do* oder *Does*.

Mit *I, you, we, they* verwendest du *Do*.

Mit *he, she, it* verwendest du *Does*.

LF 14

Erklär-
film

Die einfache Form der Gegenwart *(The simple present)*

e) Kurzantworten *(Short answers)*

▶ Unit 4 | p. 123

Kurzantworten	
Yes, I do.	No, I don't.
Yes, he does.	No, he doesn't.
Yes, she does.	No, she doesn't.
Yes, it does.	No, it doesn't.
Yes, you do.	No, you don't.
Yes, we do.	No, we don't.
Yes, they do.	No, they don't.

Es ist unhöflich, auf Entscheidungsfragen nur mit *yes* oder *no* zu antworten. Besser ist eine Kurzantwort.

LF 15

f) Fragen mit Fragewörtern *(Questions with question words)*

▶ Unit 4 | p. 126

Where does your pet sleep?
Wo schläft dein Haustier?

What do snakes eat?
Was fressen Schlangen?

Auch Fragen mit Fragewörtern stellst du mit *do* oder *does*. Das Fragewort steht wie im Deutschen am Anfang.

How?	Wie?
What?	Was?
When?	Wann?
Why?	Warum?

Who cooks lunch?
Wer kocht das Mittagessen?

What makes you sad?
Was macht dich traurig?

Wenn mit *Who* oder *What* nach dem Subjekt des Satzes gefragt wird, bildest du die Frage ohne *do* oder *does*.

LF 16

Die Verlaufsform der Gegenwart *(The present progressive)*

Erklär-
film

▸ Unit 5 | p. 152

I'm reading a comic.
Ich lese gerade einen Comic.

Dad is cooking dinner.
Papa macht gerade das Abendessen.

What are you doing at the moment?
Was machst du jetzt gerade?

Aussagesätze (Yes)	
I'm You're He's She's It's We're They're	working.

Verneinte Sätze (No)	
I'm not You aren't He isn't She isn't It isn't We aren't They aren't	working.

Fragen (?)	
Am I Are you Is he Is she Is it Are we Are they	working?

Mit dem *present progressive* sagst du, was jemand jetzt gerade tut. Damit beschreibst du auch, was auf Bildern passiert.

Diese Zeitangaben findest du oft in Sätzen im *present progressive*:
now, at the moment, today.

Das *present progressive* besteht aus zwei Teilen:

'm oder 're oder 's	+	Verb + *-ing*

Bei Verben, die auf *-e* enden, fällt das *-e* bei der *ing*-Form weg:

have – having
make – making
ride – riding

Bei einigen Verben wird der letzte Buchstabe verdoppelt:

plan – planning
stop – stopping
sit – sitting

Erklärfilm

Much – many – a lot of

▶ Unit 5 | p. 155

zählbar

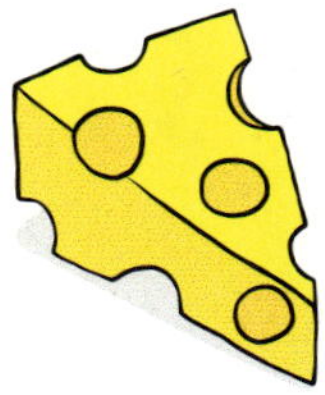

nicht zählbar

Bejahte Aussagesätze

We've got a lot of apples.
I eat a lot of fruit.

Verneinte Aussagesätze

My dad doesn't watch many films.
I don't like much sugar in my tea.

Fragen

How many apples do we need?
How much money do you have?

Mit *much, many* oder *a lot of* kannst du über unbestimmte, größere Mengen sprechen. Dabei ist es wichtig, ob es sich um zählbare oder nicht zählbare Nomen handelt.

Zählbare Nomen haben eine Pluralform: *one apple – two apples.*
Nicht zählbare Nomen kannst du nicht in die Mehrzahl setzen: *cheese, fruit, music, love.*

In bejahten Sätzen verwende *a lot of* – bei zählbaren und nicht zählbaren Nomen.

In verneinten Sätzen und Fragen verwendest du
- *many* bei zählbaren Nomen (viele),
- *much* bei nicht zählbaren Nomen (viel).

Lassen sich die Nomen zählen,
musst du immer *many* wählen.

Grammatical terms *(Grammatische Fachbegriffe in diesem Buch)*

adjective	das Adjektiv: *good, old, nice, ...*
adverb (of frequency)	das (Häufigkeits-)Adverb: *always, often, sometimes, rarely, never*
article	der Artikel: ***a / the** book* ***an / the** apple*
conjuction	die Konjunktion: ***before** you read*
form	die Form
long form	die Langform: *I **am**, do **not**, you **are***
negative	die negative Form: ***don't** go, **can't** make, **aren't** going, **doesn't** want, ...*
noun	das Nomen / Substantiv: *friend, car*
object	das Objekt: *I like **cats**.*
personal pronoun	Personalpronomen: *I, you, he, she, it, we, they*
plural	Plural, Mehrzahlform: *books, children, potatoes, stories, ...*
positive	die positive Form: *do, can, ...*
possessive determiner	Possessivbegleiter: *my, your, his, her, its, our, their*
preposition	die Präposition: ***before** school*
present progressive	die Verlaufsform der Gegenwart: ***I'm** speak**ing***
short answer	die Kurzantwort: *Yes, I do. / No, I'm not. / Yes, she does. / ...*
short form	die Kurzform: ***I'm**, **don't***
simple present	die einfache Gegenwart: *I **speak** English, he **likes** it*
statement	Aussage(satz)
subject	das Subjekt: ***They** eat dinner.*
verb	das Verb: *(to) go, (to) do, (to) have, (to) love, (to) think, ...*
wh-question	die Frage mit Fragewort: *What's this? Who are you?*

The English alphabet

a	[eɪ]	h	[dʒiː]	o	[əʊ]	v	[viː]
b	[biː]	i	[ɑɪ]	p	[piː]	w	['dʌbljuː]
c	[siː]	j	[dʒeɪ]	q	[kjuː]	x	[eks]
d	[diː]	k	[keɪ]	r	[ɑː]	y	[waɪ]
e	[iː]	l	[el]	s	[es]	z	[zed]
f	[ef]	m	[em]	t	[tiː]		
g	[dʒiː]	n	[en]	u	[juː]		

English sounds

Die Lautschrift zeigt dir die Aussprache von Wörtern und Lauten *(sounds)*.

Einige dieser Laute kommen im Deutschen nicht vor oder werden anders geschrieben. Sie sind hier mit einem Ausrufezeichen gekennzeichnet: **!**. Übe sie mit Hilfe der App.

	[iː]	green, he, sea
	[ɑː]	ask, class, car, park
!	[ɔː]	or, ball, door, four, morning
	[uː]	ruler, blue, too, two, you
	[ɜː]	early, her, girl, work, T-shirt
	[ɪ]	in, big, expensive
	[e]	yes, bed, again, breakfast
	[æ]	animal, apple, black, cat
	[ʌ]	mum, bus, colour
	[ɒ]	song, on, dog, what
	[ʊ]	book, good, put, bully
	[ə]	again, today, a sister
	[i]	happy, monkey
	[eɪ]	name, eight, play, great
	[aɪ]	I, time, right, my
	[ɔɪ]	boy, toilet, noise
	[əʊ]	old, no, road, yellow
	[aʊ]	now, house
	[ɪə]	where, pair, share, their
	[eə]	here, material, really, year
	[ʊə]	tour
	[b]	bike, table, verb
	[p]	pen, paper, shop
	[d]	day, window, good
	[t]	ten, letter, at
	[g]	go, again, bag
	[k]	kitchen, car, back
	[m]	man, remember, mum
	[n]	no, one, ten
!	[ŋ]	wrong, young, uncle, thanks
	[l]	like, old, small
	[r]	ruler, friend, sorry
!	[w]	we, where, one
	[j]	yes, you, uniform
	[f]	family, after, laugh
!	[v]	very, seven, have
	[s]	six, poster, yes
!	[z]	zoo, quiz, his, music, please
	[ʃ]	she, station, English
!	[ʒ]	ususally, revision, garage
	[tʃ]	chain, teacher, watch
!	[dʒ]	job, German, project, orange
!	[θ]	thing, three, bathroom, north
!	[ð]	the, weather, with
	[h]	house, who, behind

Words with silent letters

Manche Wörter enthalten Buchstaben, die du schreibst, aber die entsprechenden Laute sprichst du **nicht**. Deshalb heißen sie auch „stille Buchstaben" *(silent letters)*. Höre dir diese Wörter in der App an und sprich sie nach. So merkst du sie dir leicht.

b lam**b**

c s**c**ience

d san**d**wich, gran**d**ma/gran**d**pa/gran**d**parents/gran**d**son/gran**d**daughter, We**d**nesday

g desi**g**n

h tec**h**nology, C**h**ristmas, **h**our

i fru**i**t

k (to) **k**now, **k**nife

l (to) wa**l**k, (to) ta**l**k

u g**u**itar, b**u**ilding, g**u**ide dog

t (to) lis**t**en

w (to) ans**w**er, t**w**o, **w**rong, (to) **w**rite

Wordbank 1: Numbers

▸ Hello! | p. 10

one two three four five

six seven eight nine ten

eleven twelve thirteen fourteen fifteen

Wordbank 2: Colours

▸ Hello! | p. 12

Wordbank 3: Animals

► Hello! | p. 14

cat, dog, elephant, fish, horse, lion, monkey, parrot, seagull, snake, ...

a bear

a butterfly

a crocodile

a dolphin

a duck

a llama

a meerkat[1]

My favourite animal is ...

an owl

a panda

a penguin

a rhinoceros / rhino

a spider

a tiger

a whale

[1] **meerkat** *Erdmännchen*

Wordbank 4: Free time

▶ Hello! | p. 15

dancing, drawing, football, listening to music, taking photos, swimming, ...

baking

climbing

coding

cycling

doing nail art

gaming

gymnastics

My favourite hobby is ...
My favourite sport is ...
I like ...
I love ...
I don't like ...

hanging out with friends

horse riding

judo

kayaking

playing (the) guitar

reading

singing

Wordbank 5: School subjects

▶ Unit 1 | p. 27

art, computing, design and technology, English, French, maths, music, PE, ...

 German *(Deutsch)*	 media studies *(Medienkompetenz)*	 school club *(AG)*
 business and employment studies: technology, economics, home economics *(Arbeitslehre: Technik, Wirtschaft, Hauswirtschaft)*	 science: biology, chemistry, physics *(Naturwissenschaften: Biologie, Chemie, Physik)*	 social studies: history, geography, politics *(Gesellschaftswissenschaften: Geschichte, Geografie, Politik)*
 ethics *(Ethik)*	 RE: religious education *(Religion)*	 philosophy *(Philosophie)*
 special needs support *(Förderunterricht)*	 study time *(Arbeitsstunde, Eigenarbeit, Hausaufgabenbetreuung)*	 tutor time *(Klassenlehrkraftstunde / Verfügungsstunde)*

Wordbank 6: Places in school

► Unit 1 | p. 30

art room, canteen, classroom, computer room, corridor, sports hall, theatre, ...

assembly hall / auditorium

cinema

dance studio

drama room

games room

library

music room

office

playground

(running) track

school garden

science lab

sports field

staff room

swimming pool

Wordbank 7: Family

▸ Unit 2 | p. 51

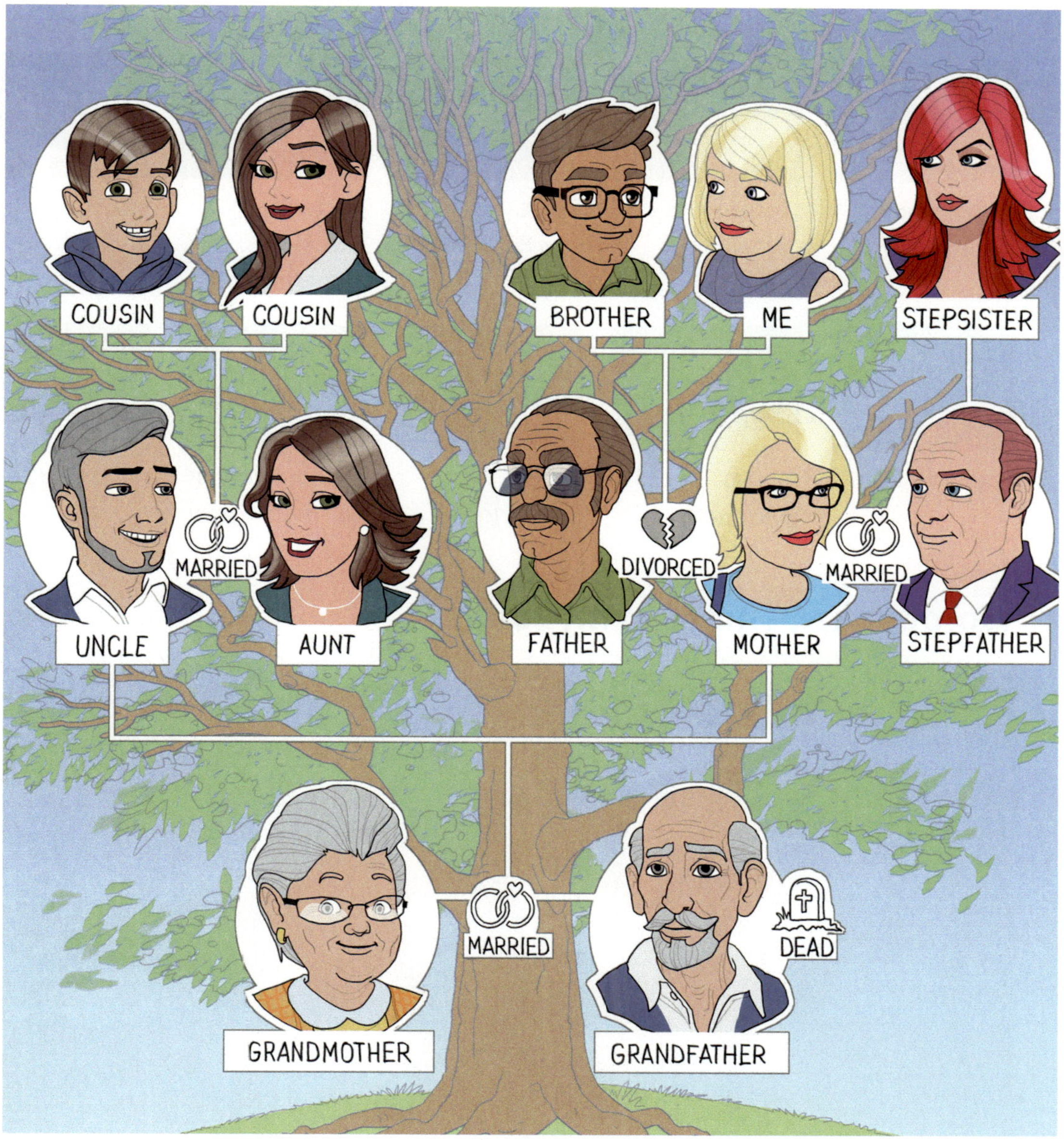

parents / grandparents	die Eltern / die Großeltern
child / children	das Kind / die Kinder
son / daughter	der Sohn / die Tochter
grandson / granddaughter	der Enkel / die Enkelin
blended family	die Patchworkfamilie
separated	getrennt
husband / wife	der Ehemann / die Ehefrau
single	alleinstehend
niece / nephew	Nichte / Neffe

Wordbank 8: Pets

▶ Unit 2 | p. 55

cat, dog, fish, hamster, horse, parrot, rabbit, snake, ...

budgie *(der Wellensittich)*

chicken *(das Huhn)*

ferret *(das Frettchen)*

guinea pig *(das Meerschweinchen)*

kitten *(das Kätzchen)*

lizard *(die Echse)*

mouse *(die Maus)*

puppy *(der Welpe)*

bearded dragon *(die Bartagame)*

rat *(die Ratte)*

Wordbank 9: Things in my room

▶ Unit 2 | p. 63

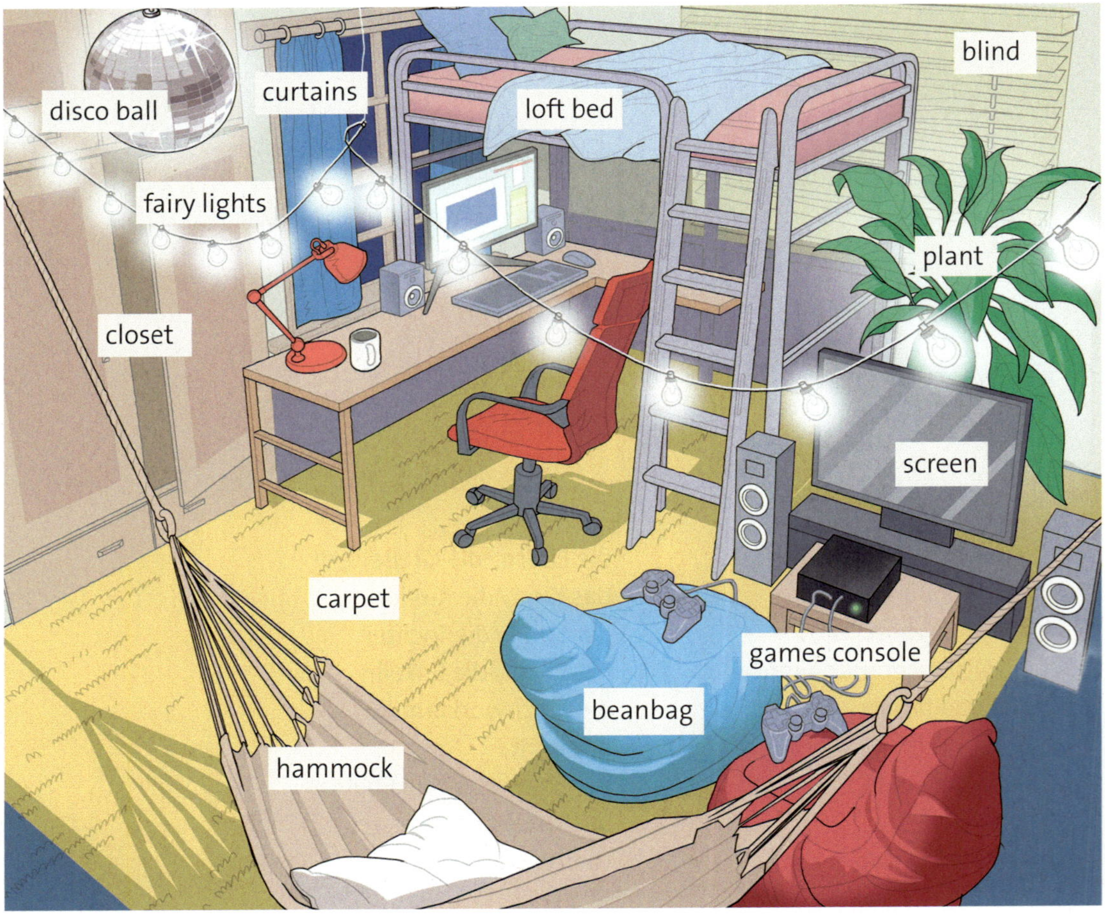

Wordbank 10: The times of the day

▸ Unit 3 | p. 86

Wordbank 11: Places

▸ Unit 4 | p. 123

bakery

supermarket

ice rink

places

- *shopping*
  - bakery
  - supermarket
  - shopping centre
  - market
- *sports*
  - ice rink
  - sports centre
  - stadium
  - skate park
- *learning*
  - museum
  - library
  - school
- *fun*
  - cinema
  - youth centre
  - theme park
- *other*
  - mosque
  - synagogue
  - church
  - temple
  - town hall
  - park
  - hospital
- *transport*
  - bus stop
  - train station
  - bike rack
  - car park

theme park

mosque

synagogue

church

bus stop

temple

bike rack

car park

town hall

▶ Unit 5 | p. 160

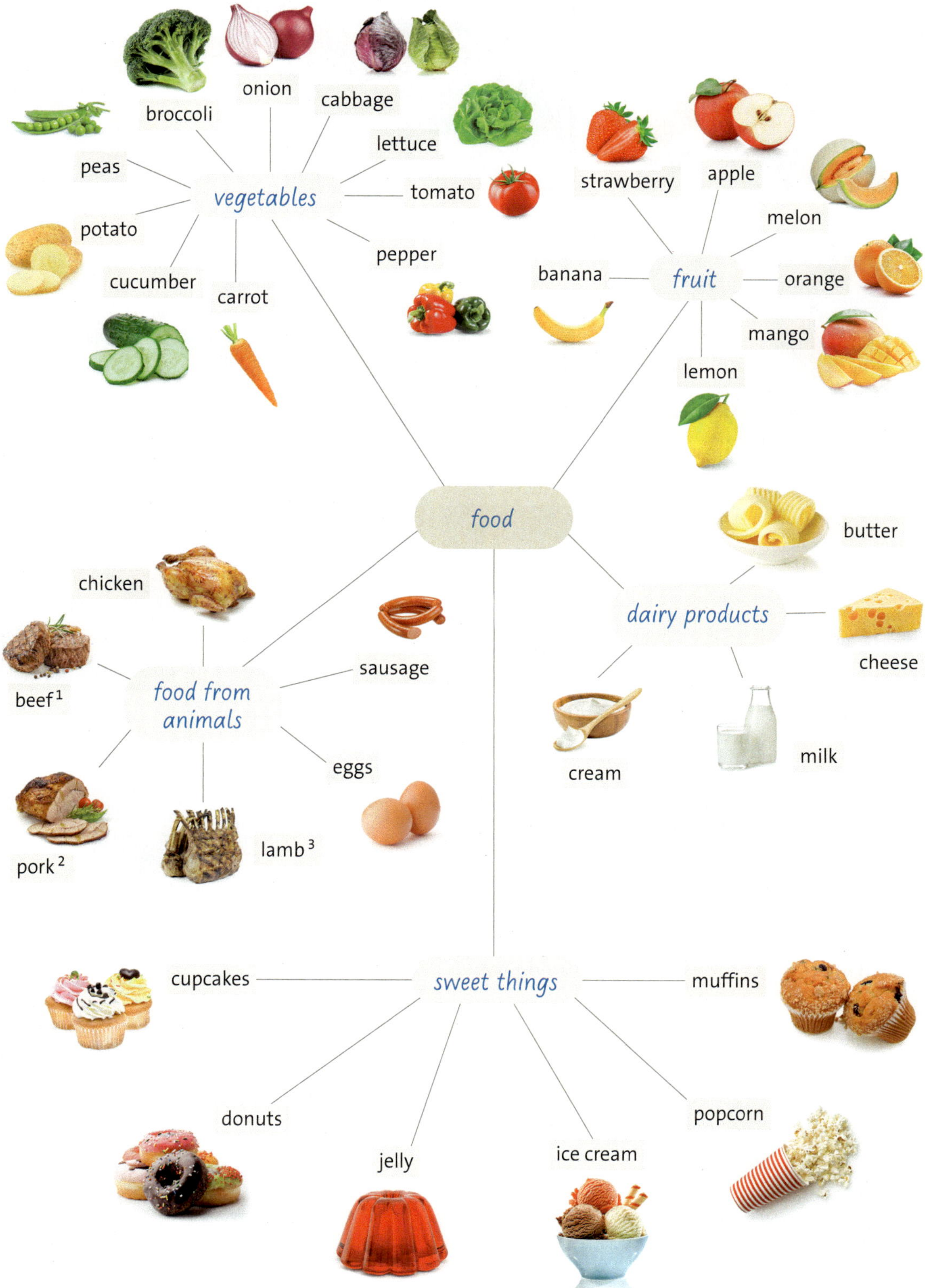

[1] **beef** *Rindfleisch* [2] **pork** *Schweinefleisch* [2] **lamb** *Lamm; Lammfleisch*

Wordbank 13: Cooking

▶ Unit 5 | p. 167

(to) add

(to) bake

(to) boil

(to) cut

(to) fry

(to) mix

(to) pour

(to) roll out

(to) stir

baking tray

frying pan

oven

pot

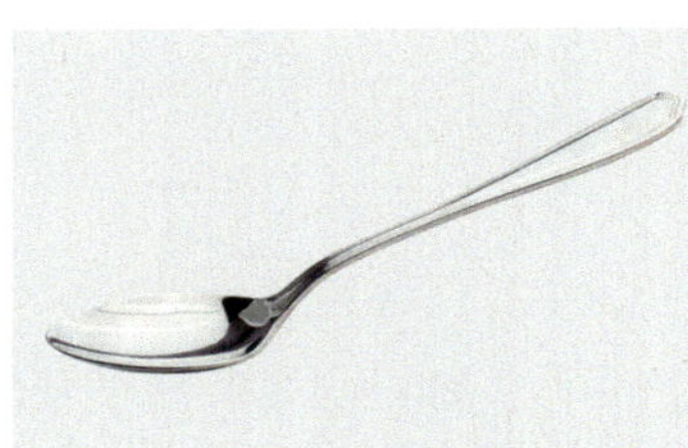
spoon

whisk

Hier findest du englische Sätze mit ihrer deutschen Übersetzung. Höre sie dir in der App an. Da jede Sprache anders funktioniert, ist eine wortwörtliche Übersetzung oft nicht möglich: Achte daher auf die kleinen Unterschiede.

1 Sich und andere vorstellen

Über den Namen und das Alter sprechen

Hello!	Hello, I'm ... / Hi! I'm ...	Hallo, ich bin ...
	What's your name?	Wie heißt du?
	How old are you?	Wie alt bist du?
	I'm ... (years old). What about you?	Ich bin ... (Jahre alt). Und du?
Unit 1	(Sunita) is 12 years old.	(Sunita) ist 12 Jahre alt.
	I'm 12 too.	Ich bin auch 12.
Unit 5	When's your birthday?	Wann hast du Geburtstag?
	My birthday is on the first of May.	Mein Geburtstag ist am ersten Mai.

Sich begrüßen und verabschieden

Hello!	Hi! / Hello!	Hi! / Hallo!
	Bye!	Tschüs!
	Goodbye.	Auf Wiedersehen.
	Nice to meet you.	Freut mich, dich / euch / Sie kennenzulernen.
	Nice to meet you too.	(Freut) Mich auch.
Unit 1	See you soon.	Bis bald.
	See you.	Bis dann. / Tschüs.
Unit 2	Speak later.	Tschüs. / Bis später.
Unit 3	Hello everybody!	Hallo allerseits!
	I'd love / like to meet you.	Ich würde mich (liebend) gerne mit dir / euch treffen.
	See you later / tomorrow.	Bis später.
Unit 4	Welcome to (our house).	Willkommen in (unserem Haus).

Über die Familie und Freunde sprechen ► Wordbank 7, p. 219

Unit 1	This is my best friend (Noah).	Das ist meine beste Freundin / mein bester Freund (Noah).
	We are / aren't friends.	Wir sind / sind keine Freunde.
	These are my new friends (Lily and Harry).	Das sind meine neuen Freunde (Lily und Harry).
	Good friends are always helpful.	Gute Freunde sind immer hilfsbereit.
Unit 2	That's me. / This is me.	Das bin ich.
	That's my family.	Das ist meine Familie.
	This is me and my big sister Rahel.	Das bin ich und meine große Schwester Rahel.
	Next to me is my little brother Nick.	Neben mir ist mein kleiner Bruder Nick.

	These are my parents.	Das sind meine Eltern.
	Grandma and Grandpa live in the neighborhood.	Oma und Opa leben in der Nachbarschaft.
	My uncle and my aunt are from Russia.	Mein Onkel und meine Tante sind aus Russland.
	They have a daughter and two sons.	Sie haben eine Tochter und zwei Söhne.
	So, I have three cousins.	Also habe ich drei Cousinen und Cousins.
Unit 4	My parents often work late.	Meine Eltern arbeiten oft lange.
	I have a lot of friends at school.	Ich habe viele Freunde in der Schule.
	Do you have brothers and sisters?	Hast du Geschwister?
	No, I don't have brothers and sisters.	Nein, ich habe keine Geschwister.
	But I have three cousins.	Aber ich habe drei Cousinen und Cousins.

Über Hobbys, Vorlieben und Abneigungen sprechen ► Wordbank 4, p. 216

Hello!	I like / love sandwiches.	Ich mag / liebe Sandwiches.
	My favourite animal is a fish.	Meine Lieblingstiere sind Fische.
	What's your favourite ...?	Was ist dein Lieblings...?
	My favourite sport / hobby is (tennis). What about you?	Mein Lieblingssport / Lieblingshobby ist (Tennis). Und deins?
	I like / love dancing.	Ich mag / liebe Tanzen.
	I don't like football.	Ich mag Fußball nicht. / Ich mag keinen Fußball.
Unit 1	Let's go to the beach!	Lass uns / Lasst uns an den Strand gehen!
	Let's play football!	Lass uns / Lasst uns Fußball spielen!
Unit 2	My dream pet is a cute little dog.	Mein Traum-Haustier ist ein süßer kleiner Hund.
Unit 3	Let's go cycling!	Lass uns / Lasst uns Fahrrad fahren!
	I hate that.	Ich hasse das.
Unit 4	Which places / things do you like?	Welche Orte / Dinge magst du?
	I like my neighbourhood / friends.	Ich mag meine Nachbarschaft / Freunde.
	I don't like rubbish.	Ich mag Müll nicht.
	Why do you love (Brighton)?	Warum liebst du (Brighton)?
	I love (Brighton) because ...	Ich liebe (Brighton), weil ...
	I like living here because ...	Ich lebe gern hier, weil ...

Das eigene Zuhause / Zimmer beschreiben ► Wordbank 9, p. 220

Unit 2	This is my home.	Das ist mein Zuhause.
	I live in a flat / house.	Ich wohne in einer Wohnung / in einem Haus.
	Our house has a garden / balcony.	Unser Haus hat einen Garten / Balkon.
	Where is your room?	Wo ist dein Zimmer?
	It's on the ground / first / top floor.	Es ist im Erdgeschoss / ersten Stock / Obergeschoss.
	What's in your room?	Was ist / gibt es in deinem Zimmer?

	There's / There are (a bed / two chairs).	Da ist / Da sind / Es gibt (ein Bett / zwei Stühle).
	There are a lot of books on the shelves.	Es gibt / Es stehen viele Bücher in den Regalen.
	I have my own room.	Ich habe ein eigenes Zimmer.
	Is your room messy or tidy?	Ist dein Zimmer unordentlich oder aufgeräumt?
	Is it loud or quiet in your room?	Ist es laut oder leise in deinem Zimmer?
	Are you at home?	Bist du zu Hause?
	I'm home.	Ich bin zu Hause.
	My room is small, but it's perfect for me.	Mein Zimmer ist klein, aber es ist perfekt für mich.
	I live with my parents and my brother.	Ich lebe zusammen mit meinen Eltern und meinem Bruder.
	We live in a small house near (Bremen).	Wir leben in einem kleinen Haus bei (Bremen).
	There's a kitchen, a living room, two bedrooms and a bathroom.	Es gibt eine Küche, ein Wohnzimmer, zwei Schlafzimmer und ein Bad.
Unit 5	Do you often clean your room?	Machst du dein Zimmer oft sauber?
	Yes, I do. But it's always messy.	Ja, manchmal. Aber es ist immer unordentlich.

Über den Wohnort und die Nachbarschaft sprechen

Hello!	Where are you from?	Wo kommst du her? / Wo wohnst du?
	I'm from ...	Ich bin / komme aus ...
Unit 2	I live in ...	Ich wohne in ...
	I live with my mum and dad.	Ich wohne zusammen mit meiner Mutter und meinem Vater.
	We live in a flat / a house in ...	Wir wohnen in einer Wohnung / einem Haus in ...
	Tell me about your home.	Erzähl mir was über dein Zuhause.
	Where's your home?	Wo bist du zu Hause?
	Who are your neighbours?	Wer sind eure Nachbarn?
Unit 3	Where's your house?	Wo ist dein / euer Haus?
	Our house isn't near my school.	Unser Haus ist nicht in der Nähe meiner Schule.
Unit 4	Where do you live?	Wo wohnst du?
	I live in a village / town / city / in the country.	Ich wohne in einem Dorf / einer (Klein-)Stadt / einer (Groß-)Stadt / auf dem Land.
	What's your neighbourhood like?	Wie sieht deine Nachbarschaft aus?
	It's busy, but nice.	Es ist ziemlich viel los, aber es ist nett.
	I like our neighbours, they're really friendly.	Ich mag unsere Nachbarn. Sie sind wirklich freundlich.
	My neighbourhood has some problems	Es gibt einige Probleme in der Nachbarschaft.
	A lot of people on our estate don't have a lot of money.	Viele Leute in unserer Wohngegend haben nicht viel Geld.

2 Über Gefühle, Wünsche und Empfindungen sprechen

Hello!	How are you?	Wie geht es dir?
	I'm fine / I'm OK, thanks.	Danke, mir geht es gut.
Unit 1	I'm not scared of school / snakes.	Ich habe keine Angst vor der Schule / vor Schlangen.
	Why are you angry / happy / sad / tired?	Warum bist du wütend / glücklich / traurig / müde?
	I'm happy because I have good friends.	Ich bin glücklich, weil ich gute Freunde habe.
	I'm not alone.	Ich bin nicht alleine.
	Go away!	Hau ab! / Haut ab!
	You're in trouble now!	Jetzt bekommst du Ärger!
	If I'm in trouble, my friends help me.	Wenn ich Ärger habe, helfen mir meine Freunde.
	Who's scared?	Wer hat Angst?
	We aren't scared of (them / the bullies)!	Wir haben keine Angst vor (denen / den Mobbern)!
	Sometimes people are mean to me.	Manchmal sind Leute echt fies zu mir.
	They think I'm different or difficult.	Sie glauben, ich bin anders oder schwierig.
	But I'm just quiet / clever.	Dabei bin ich nur ruhig / schlau.
Unit 2	I'd like to go away.	Ich würde am liebsten weggehen.
	I'd like to be back at home.	Ich wäre am liebsten wieder zurück zu Hause.
	Don't be so rude!	Sei nicht so unhöflich / frech!
	How do you feel?	Wie fühlst du dich?
Unit 3	Sometimes people think I'm stupid.	Manchmal denken Leute, ich bin blöd.
	Well, I'm not!	Bin ich aber nicht!
	I'm really surprised.	Ich bin echt überrascht.
	Sometimes I'm in trouble with my parents.	Ich habe manchmal Ärger mit meinen Eltern.
	Don't be sorry for me.	Sei nicht traurig wegen mir.
Unit 4	Why are you angry?	Warum bist du wütend?
	I'm angry because my neigbourhood is really dirty.	Ich bin wütend, weil es in der Nachbarschaft so dreckig ist.
	Sometimes school is boring.	Manchmal ist es langweilig in der Schule.
Unit 5	I feel sad / great.	Ich bin traurig / Ich fühle mich toll.

3 Über den Schulalltag sprechen

▸ Wordbank 5, 6, pages 217–218

Unit 1	We're in the same class.	Wir sind in der gleichen Klasse.
	Mr Lee is my class teacher and English teacher.	Herr Lee ist mein Klassenlehrer und Englischlehrer.
	I'm at a new school.	Ich bin an einer neuen Schule.
	What about your new school?	(Sag mal) Wie ist es an der neuen Schule?
	I'm lucky. The students in my class are really nice.	Ich habe Glück. Meine Mitschülerinnen / Mitschüler in meiner Klasse sind echt nett.

	Where are your English lessons?	Wo finden deine / eure Englischstunden statt?
	They're in room 2.	Die sind in Raum 2.
	On Monday morning I have (maths).	Montagmorgen habe ich (Mathematik).
	The next lesson is ...	Die nächste Stunde ist ...
	I'm in class 7B.	Ich bin in Klasse 7b.
	Where's the canteen?	Wo ist die Kantine?
	The name of my school is ...	Meine Schule heißt ...
	I'm at ... school.	Ich bin auf der ... Schule.
	My timetable is great.	Mein Stundenplan ist super.
	The classrooms aren't near the canteen.	Die Klassenräume sind nicht in der Nähe der Kantine.
Unit 2	Is it hard to do your homework?	Fällt es dir schwer deine Hausaufgaben zu machen?
	The (English) homework is hard.	Die (Englisch-)Hausaufgaben sind schwer.
Unit 3	Our first lesson starts at ...	Unsere erste Stunde fängt um ... an.
	Lunchtime at school is at twelve thirty.	Mittagessen in der Schule ist um halb eins.
	After school I do my homework.	Nach der Schule mache ich meine Hausaufgaben.
	I have a lot of homework.	Ich habe viele Hausaufgaben auf.
	Me too.	Ich auch.
	My school journey is short.	Mein Schulweg ist kurz.
	I go to school (by bus).	Ich fahre (mit dem Bus) zur Schule.
	The start of school is at 9 a.m. / School starts at 9 a.m.	Die Schule fängt um 9 Uhr an.
	I come home from school at 4 p.m.	Ich komme um 16 Uhr aus der Schule nach Hause.
	My homework takes 30 minutes.	Ich brauche 30 Minuten für die Hausaufgaben.
Unit 5	Are you good at (sports / maths)?	Bist du gut in (Sport / Mathematik)?

4 Über den Tagesablauf sprechen, über Verabredungen sprechen

Unit 3	My parents work long days.	Meine Eltern arbeiten sehr lang.
	In the morning I get up at (7 o'clock), have a shower and get dressed.	Morgens stehe ich um (7 Uhr) auf, dusche und ziehe mich an.
	Sometimes I meet my friends in the afternoon.	Manchmal treffe ich mich nachmittags mit meinen Freunden.
	We meet every Friday afternoon at 3.30.	Wir treffen uns jeden Freitagnachmittag um halb vier.
	In the evening I often play computer games.	Abends spiele ich oft Computerspiele.
	On weekdays I always go to bed at (9 o'clock).	An Wochentagen gehe ich immer um (9 Uhr) ins Bett.
	How often do you play (tennis)?	Wie oft spielst du (Tennis).
	I never / rarely play (tennis).	Ich spiele nie / selten (Tennis).

	Let's meet in the afternoon.	Lass uns nachmittags / am Nachmittag treffen.
	Let's meet on Saturday!	Lass uns am Samstag treffen!
	Sorry, I'm busy on Saturday.	Tut mir leid, ich bin beschäftigt am Samstag.
	Are you free on Sunday?	Hast du Sonntag Zeit?
	I'd love to, but I can't.	Ich würde gerne, aber ich kann nicht.
	What do you do in your free time?	Was machst du in deiner Freizeit?
Unit 4	I practise the guitar every day.	Ich übe jeden Tag auf der Gitarre.
	On Saturday mornings I always look after my little sister.	Samstagvormittags passe ich immer auf meine kleine Schwester auf.
Unit 5	What are you doing?	Was machst du gerade?
	What do you usually do at the weekend?	Was machst du / macht ihr normalerweise am Wochenende?
	We usually stay at home.	Normalerweise bleiben wir zu Hause.
	Where's the party?	Wo findet die Party statt?
	Thanks for the invitation.	Danke für die Einladung.
	Send me a message if you can come or not.	Sende mir eine Nachricht, ob du kommen kannst oder nicht.

5 Seine Meinung äußern und diskutieren

Unit 1	Sorry, can you say that again?	Entschuldigung. kannst du das noch einmal sagen?
	Listen, (Tony)!	Hör zu, (Tony)!
	Listen to (Gina).	Hör / Hört (Gina) zu.
	You're welcome.	Bitte, gern geschehen. / Nichts zu danken.
	I think ...	Ich denke / glaube ...
	Let me think.	Lass mich nachdenken.
	I don't know.	Das weiß ich nicht.
Unit 2	Good / Great / Clever idea!	Gute / Tolle / Schlaue Idee!
	We can talk about problems.	Wir können über Probleme reden.
	Please be polite.	Sei bitte höflich.
Unit 3	Yes, that's right.	Ja, das stimmt.
	No, that's wrong.	Nein, das ist falsch.
	I think you're right / wrong.	Ich glaube, da hast du recht / unrecht.
	I think that's false.	Ich glaube, das ist falsch.
Unit 4	Do you think it's interesting?	Denkst du, es ist interessant?
	Why do you think it's interesting?	Warum denkst du, es ist interessant?
	Do you have any questions?	Hast du / Habt ihr Fragen?
Unit 5	What do you think?	Was denkst du?
	What do you mean?	Was meinst du?

6 Über Essen und Lebensmittel sprechen

► Wordbank 12, 13, pages 223–224

Unit 1	I'm really hungry.	Ich habe echt Hunger. / Ich bin echt hungrig.
	We're always hungry.	Wir haben immer Hunger.
Unit 4	Are you hungry?	Hast du Hunger?
	Try the pizza.	Probier mal die Pizza.
	No, I'm not hungry.	Nein, ich habe keinen Hunger.
	Where do you buy your food?	Wo kaufst du / kauft ihr Essen / Lebensmittel ein?
	We buy our food in the supermarket / at the market.	Wir kaufen unser Essen im Supermarkt / auf dem Markt.
Unit 5	What food do you eat?	Was isst du so?
	We at a lot of fruit and vegetables.	Wir essen viel Obst und Gemüse.
	I'm not vegan, but I eat vegan food sometimes.	Ich bin kein/e Veganer/in, aber ich esse manchmal vegan.
	I like vegetarian food because it's healthy.	Ich mag vegetarisches Essen, weil es gesund ist.
	Eating too much meat is not healthy.	Zu viel Fleisch ist ungesund.
	My favourite dish is (pizza).	Mein Lieblingsgericht ist (Pizza).
	I'm allergic to ...	Ich bin allergisch gegen ...
	Enjoy your food.	Guten Appetit. / Genieß dein Essen. / Lass es dir schmecken.

7 Feedback geben

Unit 1	I like the photos in your poster.	Ich mag die Fotos auf deinem Poster.
	Your poster is really good / great.	Dein Poster ist wirklich gut / toll.
	You can use more words or pictures.	Du kannst mehr Wörter oder Bilder verwenden.
Unit 2	Your presentation about (your dream room) is cool / very nice.	Deine Präsentation zu (deinem Traumzimmer) ist cool / sehr schön.
	Your presentation was too long.	Deine Präsentation war zu lang.
Unit 3	Please speak more loudly.	Sprich bitte ein bisschen lauter.
	Don't speak so fast.	Sprich nicht so schnell.
	Speak clearly, please.	Sprich bitte deutlich.
	Well done!	Gut gemacht!
	Great job!	Tolle Arbeit!
Unit 4	That was useful information.	Das waren nützliche Informationen.
	Please check that again.	Überprüfe das bitte noch einmal.
	Remember to make notes.	Denk daran, Notizen zu machen.
	Your notes are helpful.	Deine Notizen sind nützlich.
Unit 5	I'd like to see more pictures.	Ich würde gerne mehr Bilder sehen.
	The instructions are very clear.	Die Anweisungen sind sehr klar.

Classroom English

You and your teacher	Du und deine Lehrerin / dein Lehrer
Good morning, Mr / Mrs / Ms ... (bis 12 Uhr)	Guten Morgen, Herr / Frau ...
Good afternoon, Mr / Mrs / Ms ... (ab 12 Uhr)	Guten Tag, Herr / Frau ...
Sorry, I'm late.	Entschuldigung, dass ich zu spät komme.
Can I open / close the window, please?	Kann ich bitte das Fenster öffnen / zumachen?
Can I go to the toilet, please?	Kann ich bitte zur Toilette gehen?
Goodbye. / See you tomorrow.	Auf Wiedersehen! / Bis morgen.

Homework and exercises	Hausaufgaben und Übungen
Sorry, I have no exercise book.	Es tut mir leid, ich habe mein Schulheft nicht dabei.
I don't understand this exercise.	Ich verstehe die Übung nicht.
I can't do number 3.	Ich kann Nummer 3 nicht lösen.
Sorry, I haven't finished.	Entschuldigung, ich bin noch nicht fertig.
I have ... Is that right?	Ich habe ... Ist das auch richtig?
Sorry, I don't know.	Es tut mir leid, das weiß ich nicht.
What's for homework?	Was haben wir (als Hausaufgabe) auf?

You need help	Du brauchst Hilfe
Can you help me, please?	Können Sie / Kannst du mir bitte helfen?
What page is it, please?	Auf welcher Seite sind wir / steht das?
What's ... in English / German?	Was heißt ... auf Englisch / Deutsch?
Can you write it on the board, please?	Können Sie das bitte an die Tafel schreiben?
Can I say it in German?	Kann ich das auf Deutsch sagen?
Can you speak louder, please?	Können Sie / Kannst du bitte lauter sprechen?
Can you say / play that again, please?	Können Sie das bitte noch einmal sagen / abspielen?

Work with a partner	Partnerarbeit
Can I work with Julian?	Kann ich mit Julian arbeiten?
Can I use your (pen), please?	Kann ich deinen (Stift) benutzen?
Yes, here you are.	Hier, bitte.
It's my / your turn.	Ich bin / Du bist dran.
Let's make / draw a ...	Lass uns ein ... machen / zeichnen.
Let's act out the story / dialogue.	Lass uns die Geschichte / den Dialog spielen.

What your teacher says	Was deine Lehrerin / dein Lehrer sagt
Let's go.	Lasst uns anfangen. / Los geht's.
Listen, please. / Quiet, please.	Hört bitte zu. / Ruhe bitte.
Open your books at page 24, please.	Schlagt bitte Seite 24 auf.
Do exercise 5 for homework, please.	Macht bitte Übung 5 als Hausaufgabe.
Write the correct words.	Schreibt die richtigen Wörter (hin).
Correct the false sentences.	Korrigiert die falschen Sätze.
Where's your book, David?	Wo ist dein Buch, David?
Try again!	Versuche es noch einmal.
That's all for today. You can go.	Das ist alles für heute. Ihr könnt gehen.

Im ***Vocabulary*** findest du alle neuen Wörter und Wendungen, die du lernen musst. Sie stehen in der Reihenfolge, in der sie im Buch zum ersten Mal vorkommen. Höre dir in der App jedes Wort beim Lernen genau an und sprich es nach.

Inhalt

Symbole und Abkürzungen

► p. 12 ► pp. 18/19	Die Seitenzahl in der linken Spalte zeigt dir, wo das Wort zum ersten Mal in diesem Buch vorkommt (*p. = page*, Seite; *pp. = pages*, Seiten).
►► Hello	Die doppelten Pfeile weisen auf ein Wort mit gleicher Bedeutung hin, das du gelernt hast. Blaue Wörter kennst du aus der Grundschule.
(to) **close** ◄► (to) **open**	Das „Gegenteil“-Zeichen bedeutet: *(to) close* ist das Gegenteil von *(to) open*.
! *English:* I'm **at** school. *German:* Ich bin **in** der Schule.	Das ! zeigt: Vorsicht, hier keinen Fehler machen!
a – an **a d**og **an e**lephant **a n**ice picture **an o**ld picture	In den Merkboxen findest du wichtige Hinweise zu den neuen Wörtern und Wendungen.
sb. / sth.	*somebody* (jemand) / *something* (etwas)
infml.	*informal* (informell, umgangssprachlich)
pl.	*plural* (Plural, Mehrzahlform)

Hinweise

Tipps zum Vokabellernen findest du im **Skills file** auf S. 191–193. Die **Wordbanks** (S. 214–224) bieten dir nach Themen sortierten Wortschatz. **Let's talk** (S. 225–232) enthält Wendungen für wichtige Situationen, z.B.: seine Meinung äußern und diskutieren.
Englische Wörter, die Wörtern im Deutschen ähnlich sind, findest du auf S. 282.
Im **Dictionary** (S. 283–306) kannst du englische und deutsche Wörter nachschlagen.

Hello! Nice to meet you

▸ pp. 10/11 **Hello.**	Hallo.	
Nice to meet you.	Freut mich, dich/euch/Sie kennenzulernen.	
nice	nett, schön	
(to) **meet**	kennenlernen; (sich) treffen	
you	du; dich; dir; ihr; euch; Sie; Ihnen	
I'm (= I am)	ich bin	**I** = ich ! "I" wird immer großgeschrieben – auch wenn es nicht am Satzanfang steht.
hungry	hungrig	**I'm hungry.** = Ich habe Hunger.
careful	vorsichtig	**Careful,** Leo! = Vorsicht, Leo! (*wörtlich*: (Sei) vorsichtig!)
a seagull	eine Möwe	**a seagull – seagulls** **a** = ein, eine 
it's (= it is)	es ist *(bei Sachen und Tieren auch:* er ist; sie ist)	**it** = es *(bei Sachen und Tieren auch: er; sie)* **is** = ist
the	der, die, das	**the** computer – **der** Computer **the** show – **die** Show **the** baby – **das** Baby
What's your name?	Wie heißt du? (*wörtlich:* Was ist dein Name?)	**What ...?** = Was ...? **name** = der Name

you	du, dir *(Dativ)*, dich *(Akkusativ)*	ihr, euch *(Dativ)*, euch *(Akkusativ)*
your	dein, deine	euer, eure

Hi.	Hallo.	►► Hello.
number	die Zahl, die Ziffer, die Nummer	

1 one	**2** two	**3** three	**4** four	**5** five	**6** six	**7** seven
8 eight	**9** nine	**10** ten	**11** eleven	**12** twelve	**13** thirteen	**14** fourteen

► Numbers, p. 307

year	das Jahr; der Jahrgang	Scout the seagull is six **years old**.
old	alt	
How old are you?	Wie alt bist du?	**How ...?** = Wie ...? **you are** = du bist / ihr seid
Where are you from?	Wo kommst du her?	**Where ...?** = Wo ...? **from** Hove = aus Hove
(to) **like**	mögen	
What about you?	Und du? / Was ist mit dir?	
football	der Fußball	
thank you, thanks	danke (schön)	
colour	die Farbe	! *English:* What colour **is** ...? – It's white. *German:* Welche Farbe **hat** ...?

colours

black schwarz **blue** blau **brown** braun **green** grün **grey** grau **pink** pink, rosa
purple violett, lila **orange** orange; die Orange **red** rot **yellow** gelb **white** weiß

and	und	
right	richtig	
wrong	falsch	**right** ◄ ► **wrong**
class	die Klasse; der Unterricht; der Kurs	! one **class** – two **classes** **in class** = im Unterricht
too	auch	! *English:* I'm hungry **too**. *German:* Ich habe **auch** Hunger.
Bye. **Goodbye.**	Tschüs. Auf Wiedersehen.	**Hello.** ◄ ► **Bye. / Goodbye.**

Goodbye, holidays!

► p. 12	**holiday(s)**	der Urlaub; die Ferien; Urlaubs-	! **on holiday** = **im / in den** Urlaub
	in the picture	auf dem Bild	**picture** = Bild **in** = in; auf
	mum	die Mama, die Mutti	
	dad	der Papa, der Vati	
	Leo's mum	Leos Mama / Leos Mutti	
	animal	das Tier	
	drink	das Getränk	noun: **drink** – verb: (to) **drink** (trinken)
	thing	das Ding, die Sache	
	(to) **eat**	essen; fressen	
	things **to** eat	Dinge zum Essen	**to** = (um) zu Nice **to** meet you! = Schön, dich/euch/Sie kennen**zu**lernen!
	other	andere(r, s)	the **others** = die anderen
	here	hier; hierher	**Here's** (= **Here is**) Scout.
	I can see ... **I can't (= cannot) see ...**	ich kann ... sehen ich kann ... nicht sehen	(to) **see** = sehen **can** = können **can't** (= **cannot**) = nicht können

	dog	der Hund	
	(to) **remember**	daran denken, nicht vergessen; sich erinnern an	Can you **remember** my name? (dich erinnern an) **Remember,** seagulls like sandwiches too! (Denk dran!)
▸ p. 13	**How are you?**	Wie geht's? / Wie geht es dir/euch/ Ihnen?	
	I'm fine. / Leo is fine.	Mir/Leo geht es gut.	I'm **fine**. = I'm **OK**.
	I'm not ...	ich bin nicht ...; ich bin kein/e ...	I'm **not** ten. And I'm **not** a seagull. Ich bin **nicht** zehn. Und ich bin **keine** Möwe.
	so **good**	so gut	Are you OK? – I'm not **so good**. I'm hungry! = Mir geht's nicht so gut.

About me

▸ p. 14	**about me/you/...**	über mich/dich/...	**!** **me** = **1.** mir; **2.** mich; **3.** ich *(in bestimmten Wendungen)* 
	my	mein/e	**my** name (**mein** Name) **my** class (**meine** Klasse)
	favourite animal	das Lieblingstier	adjective: **favourite** – noun: **favourite** (der Liebling, der Favorit, die Favoritin)
	there's (= there is) **there are**	es ist ... / es gibt ... es sind ... / es gibt ...	**there** = da, dort; dahin, dorthin
	cat	die Katze	
	an elephant	ein Elefant	**a – an** **a d**og — **an e**lephant **a n**ice picture — **an o**ld picture 
	horse	das Pferd	
	lion	der Löwe	
	monkey	der Affe	
	parrot	der Papagei	
	snake	die Schlange	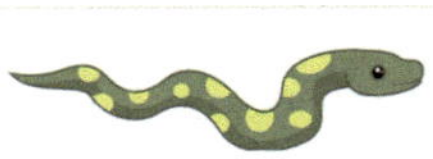
	fish, *pl* **fish**	der Fisch, die Fische	**!**  one **fish**  two **fish**
▸ p. 15	**hobby**	das Hobby	**!** *English:* one **hobby** – two,three **hobbies** *German:* ein **Hobby** – zwei,drei **Hobbys**

sport	der Sport; die Sportart	
(to) **listen (to)**	(sich etwas) anhören; zuhören	**Listen,** Scout! – Hör zu, Scout! **Listen to** Leo. – Hör(t) Leo zu. **Listen to** the song. – Hört euch das Lied an.
music	die Musik	! Betonung auf der 1. Silbe: <u>mu</u>sic
(to) **draw**	zeichnen	verb: (to) **draw** (zeichnen) – noun: **drawing** (die Zeichnung; das Zeichnen)
(to) **dance**	tanzen	nouns: **dance** (der Tanz); *(hobby:)* **dancing** (das Tanzen); *(person):* **dancer** (der Tänzer, die Tänzerin)
(to) **swim**	schwimmen	nouns: *(hobby:)* **swimming** (das Schwimmen); *(person):* **swimmer** (der/die Schwimmer/in)
photo	das Foto	! **in the photo** = **auf** dem Foto
(to) **take photos**	Fotos machen	! *English:* Can you **take** a **photo** of us? *German:* ... ein **Foto** von uns **machen**?
(to) **love**	lieben, sehr mögen	verb: (to) **love** – noun: **love** (die Liebe)
I don't like football.	Ich mag Fußball nicht. / Ich mag keinen Fußball.	
guitar	die Gitarre	(to) **play** = spielen (to) **play the guitar** = Gitarre spielen **player** = der Spieler, die Spielerin

bike	das Fahrrad	

cap	die (Schirm-)Mütze, die Kappe	
chain	die Kette	

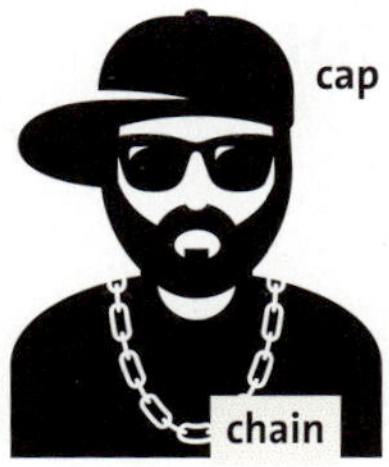

book	das Buch	
phone	das Handy, das Telefon	noun: **phone** – verb: (to) **phone** (anrufen; telefonieren) **phone number** = die Telefonnummer ! "Handy" klingt zwar englisch, aber das (Mobil-)Telefon heißt auf Englisch **phone**, manchmal auch **mobile phone**.
scooter	der (Tret-)Roller	
small	klein	

	new	neu	**new** ◀ ▶ **old**
	big	groß	**big** ◀ ▶ **small**
	this	dies; diese(r, s)	**This** is Scout. – Hello, Scout! Nice to meet you.
	gold	das Gold; goldfarben	 **gold**
	silver	das Silber; silberfarben	 **silver**
	with	mit; bei	! **1.** Is Max the kid **with** the red bike? (mit) **2.** Where's Scout? – Scout is **with** Leo. (bei)
	(to) **read**	lesen	**reader** = der Leser, die Leserin
	(to) **put**	*(etwas wohin)* tun, legen, stellen, stecken	**Put** your books and your sandwich in your rucksack.
▶ p. 16	**but**	aber	I like reading, **but** I like sport too.
	of	von	• the colour **of** my bike (... meines Rades) • the names **of** the animals (... der Tiere)
	all	alle(s)	Are **all** your school things in your rucksack?
	(to) **do**	machen, tun	my favourite thing to **do** = das, was ich am liebsten tue
	hat	der Hut, die Mütze	 **hats**
	(to) **sing**	singen	**singing** = das Singen **singer** = der Sänger, die Sängerin
	Sorry. / I'm sorry.	Tut mir leid. / Entschuldigung.	Don't eat my sandwich! – Oh, **I'm sorry.**
	that	das (dort)	**that's** (= **that is**) = das (da) ist **Is that** a seagull? – Yes, **that's** Scout.

Ready for school

▶ p. 17	**ready**	fertig, bereit	Are you **ready**? Where's your rucksack?
	for	für	Is that drink **for** me? – No, it's my drink!
	school	die Schule	This is my new **school** and I'm in class 5C.
	please	bitte	Sing that song for me, **please**.
	quiet	ruhig, still, leise	It's **quiet** and I can read my book. Super!
	(to) **stand up**	aufstehen	
	(to) **sit down**	sich hinsetzen	(to) **sit down** ◀ ▶ (to) **stand up**
	(to) **look at** sth.	sich etwas anschauen	(to) **look** = sehen, schauen
	board	die Tafel	Please look at the **board**.
	(to) **open**	öffnen; aufschlagen *(Buch)*	verb: (to) **open** – adjective: **open** (offen, geöffnet)

(to) **put your hand(s) up**	sich melden, aufzeigen	**hand** = die Hand  (to) **put your hand up** = (to) **put up your hand**
(to) **close**	schließen, zumachen	(to) **close** ◄► (to) **open**

Unit 1: My new school

► pp. 18/19	(to) **code**	programmieren *(Computer)*; kodieren	**coding** = das Programmieren verb: (to) **code** – noun: **code** (der Code; die Vorwahl(nummer))
	(to) **walk**	(zu Fuß) gehen, wandern	**walking** = das Wandern verb: (to) **walk** – noun: **walk** (der Spaziergang)
	(to) **cook**	kochen	**cooking** = das Kochen verb: (to) **cook** – noun: **cook** (der Koch, die Köchin)
	student	der Schüler, die Schülerin; der Student, die Studentin	! Betonung auf der 1. Silbe: <u>**stu**</u>dent
	at	an; in; bei; auf	! **at school** = **in** der Schule **at this school** = **auf/an** dieser Schule

Topic 1

► p. 20	**time**	die Zeit; die Uhrzeit	I'm hungry! Is it **time** to eat?
	girl	das Mädchen	
	boy	der Junge	
	friend	der Freund, die Freundin	Scout the seagull is Leo's **friend**.
	... **are** friends.	... sind Freunde/Freundinnen.	Scout and Leo **are** friends.
	(to) **be busy**	(viel) beschäftigt sein, (viel) zu tun haben	Sorry, Scout, I can't play with you. I'm **busy**. **busy** = (viel)beschäftigt (to) **be** = sein
	tired	müde	Are you two **tired**? 
	tie	die Krawatte	
	(to) **be scared (of)**	Angst haben (vor)	Scout, be quiet! I'm not **scared of** you.

	(school) uniform	die (Schul-)Uniform	**school uniforms** 
	the same	gleich; derselbe/dieselbe/dasselbe; dieselben	Sunita and Noah are in **the same** class.
	(to) **know**	wissen; kennen	I'm from Hove, not from Brighton. – I **know**!
	British	britisch	adjective: **British** – noun: **(Great) Britain** (Großbritannien)
	(to) **have**	haben	Are you hungry? You can **have** my sandwich!
	often	oft	I love cooking. I **often** cook nice things to eat.
	great	großartig, toll	I like my new school. It's **great**!
	horrible	schrecklich	**horrible** ◄ ► **great**
► p. 21	**desk**	der Schreibtisch	
	art	die Kunst	I like drawing pictures. I love **art**!
	folder	die Mappe, der Ordner	All my drawings are in my art **folder**.
	exercise book	das Schulheft, das Übungsheft	**exercise** = die Übung, die Aufgabe
	English	das Englisch; englisch	**!** Ländernamen, -adjektive und Sprachen werden im Englischen immer groß-geschrieben: **England, English** **!** in **English** = **auf** Englisch
	pencil case	das Federmäppchen	**pencil** = der Bleistift **case** = das Etui, der Behälter, der Kasten
	pen	der Kugelschreiber, der Stift; der Füller	
	glue stick	der Klebestift	**glue** = der Kleber, der Klebstoff 
	apple	der Apfel	
	rubber	das Radiergummi	
	pencil sharpener	der Bleistift(an)spitzer	
	ruler	das Lineal	
► p. 22	**different (to)**	verschieden; anders (als)	six **different** colours 

Mr Lee	Herr Lee	**Mr** Lee **Ms** Lee / **Mrs** Lee  ! **Ms** = allgemeine Anrede für Frauen **Mrs** = Anrede für verheiratete Frauen
teacher	der Lehrer, die Lehrerin	**class teacher** = der/die Klassenlehrer/in
I'm late.	Ich habe mich verspätet.	**late** = (zu) spät
Don't be late.	Verspäte dich nicht.	Scout! **Don't** eat my sandwiches!
again	wieder, noch einmal	Stand up. – Thanks, you can sit down **again**.
window	das Fenster	
yes	ja	**yes** ◄► **no** (nein)
(to) **go**	gehen; fahren	Can I **go** to the toilet, please? (gehen) I often **go** to Plymouth. (fahren)
to	zu, nach	! **to** = **1.** (um) zu: things **to** eat; **2.** zu, nach: I go **to** school.
toilet	die Toilette	
now	nun, jetzt	Ah, great! I love sport. But **now** I'm hungry.
(to) **take**	(mit)nehmen; bringen	Please **take** your book and read exercise 10. (nehmen) Remember: **Take** your sandwiches with you! (mitnehmen) Can you **take** the new kids to the toilet? (bringen)
(to) **say**	sagen	Be quiet! – Listen, it's nice to **say** "please".
(to) **talk (to)**	sprechen, reden (mit)	**Talk to** your friends **about** your hobbies. verb: (to) **talk** – noun: **talk** (das Gespräch; die Rede, der Vortrag)
Let's ..., Let us ...	Lass uns ... / Lasst uns ...	**Let us** go now.
us	uns	Do you want to go with **us**?
(to) **start**	beginnen, anfangen (mit)	verb: (to) **start** – noun: **start** (Anfang, Start)
secondary school	die weiterführende Schule	I'm 11. I go to **secondary school** now.
► p. 23 **What page ...?**	Welche Seite ...?	! **what?** = **1.** welche(r, s)?; **2.** was?
page (= p.)	die (Buch-/Heft-)Seite	**on page 15 / on p. 15** = auf Seite 15 / auf S. 15 **Open** your books **at page 10**. (**auf** Seite 10)
(to) **understand**	verstehen	In English, please. I don't **understand** German.
(to) **help**	helfen	verb: (to) **help** – noun: **help** (die Hilfe)

question	die Frage	"What's this?" is a **question**.
answer	die Antwort	**question ◄ ► answer** noun: **answer** – verb: (to) **answer** (antworten (auf), beantworten)
the answer **to the question**	die Antwort auf die Frage	**!** **to** = **1.** auf: the answer **to** the question; **2.** (um) zu: things **to** eat; **3.** zu, nach: I go **to** school.
(to) **use**	benutzen, verwenden	**user** = der (Be-)Nutzer, die (Be-)Nutzerin
Here you are.	Bitte schön. / Hier, bitte.	

You're welcome.	Bitte, gern geschehen. / Nichts zu danken.	

"bitte"

• in Aufforderungen und Bitten:	**please**	Close the window, **please.** / Where's the toilet, **please**? (Schließ das Fenster, bitte. / Wo ist die Toilette, bitte?)
• wenn du jemandem etwas gibst:	**Here you are.**	Can I use your pen, please? – Yes, **here you are.** (Kann ich deinen Stift benutzen? – Hier, bitte.)
• wenn sich jemand bedankt hat:	**You're welcome.**	I can help you. – Thanks. – **You're welcome.** (Ich kann dir helfen. – Danke. – Bitte, gern geschehen.)

(to) **ask**	fragen	What page is it? – Don't **ask** me. I don't know. **!** *English:* Can I **ask** you a **question**? *German:* Kann ich dir eine **Frage** **stellen**?
classroom	das Klassenzimmer	

Topic 2

► p. 24	**timetable**	der Stundenplan	Look at your **timetable**, please.
	lesson	die (Unterrichts-)Stunde	Can you see your English **lessons**? **lessons** *(pl)* = Unterricht(sstunden)
	they're (= they are) **they aren't**	sie sind sie sind nicht	**they** = sie *(Plural)*
	room	der Raum, das Zimmer	The English lessons are in **room** number 201.
	he's (= he is) **he isn't (= he is not)**	er ist er ist nicht	**he** = er
	(to) **be asleep**	schlafen	My cat is **asleep**.

(to) **think**	denken, meinen, glauben	**I think ...** = Ich denke/meine/glaube/finde, ...
(to) **be right**	Recht haben	**You're right.** = Du hast Recht. (to) **be right** ◄ ► (to) **be wrong** (Unrecht haben)
she's (= she is)	sie ist	**she** = sie (*weibliche Person*)
's (is) (= ist) he**'s** (he is) she**'s** (she is)	He**'s** my dad. She**'s** my mum.	it**'s** (it is) / that**'s** (that is) what**'s** (what is) It**'s**/That**'s** nice. What**'s** your name?
we're (= we are)	wir sind	you**'re** (you are) – du **bist**; ihr **seid** we**'re** (we are) – wir **sind** they**'re** (they are) – sie **sind**
break	die Pause	My favourite time at school is the **break**! ! at **break** = in der Pause
soon	bald	Don't eat in class. It's time for break **soon**!
minute	die Minute	! Betonung auf der 1. Silbe: **min**ute
people *(pl)*	die Leute, die Menschen	four **people** 
▶ p. 25 **message**	die Nachricht, die Mitteilung	noun: **message** – verb: (to) **message** (sb.) ((jm.) Nachrichten schicken, Nachrichten austauschen (mit jm.)) ! **message** *(noun)* = **1**. die Nachricht, die Mitteilung; **2**. die Botschaft, die Aussage
(to) **be lucky**	Glück haben	**You're lucky.** = Du hast Glück. **lucky** (number) = Glücks-(zahl) my **lucky** colour = meine Glücksfarbe ! Sie **hat Glück.** = She's **lucky**. Sie **ist glücklich**. = She's **happy**.
See you.	Bis dann. / Tschüs.	**See you soon.** = Bis bald!
Dear ...	Liebe/r ...	
(to) **be fun**	Spaß machen; lustig sein	**fun** = der Spaß (to) **have fun** = Spaß haben
yours	deine, deiner, deins; eurer, eure, eures; Ihrer, Ihre, Ihres	! Am Briefschluss: **Yours** Jill (Deine/Ihre/Eure Jill)
day	der Tag	
week	die Woche	Oh no! School starts this **week**. (diese Woche)

	on Monday	am Montag	**on Sundays** = an jedem Sonntag, sonntags ! **on** = **1.** an/am: School starts late on Monday.; **2.** auf: My books are **on** my desk.
	Monday (der) Montag **Thursday** (der) Donnerstag **Sunday** (der) Sonntag	**Tuesday** (der) Dienstag **Friday** (der) Freitag	**Wednesday** (der) Mittwoch **Saturday** (der) Samstag
		! Die Wochentage werden immer großgeschrieben.	
▸ p. 26	**subject**	das (Schul-)Fach	What's your favourite **subject** at school?
	registration	*die Anwesenheitskontrolle und Ankündigung aktueller Ereignisse vor dem Unterricht*	
	(to) **check**	(über)prüfen, kontrollieren	verb: (to) **check** – noun: **check** (die (Über-)Prüfung, die Kontrolle)
	assembly	die Schulversammlung	All my days at school start with **assembly**.
	history	die Geschichte *(vergangene Zeiten)*	
	geography	die Geografie, die Erdkunde	! Betonung auf der 2. Silbe: geography
	lunch	das Mittagessen	! What's for **lunch**? = Was gibt es **zum** Mittagessen? at **lunch** = **beim** Mittagessen
	maths	die Mathe(matik)	a **maths** exercise 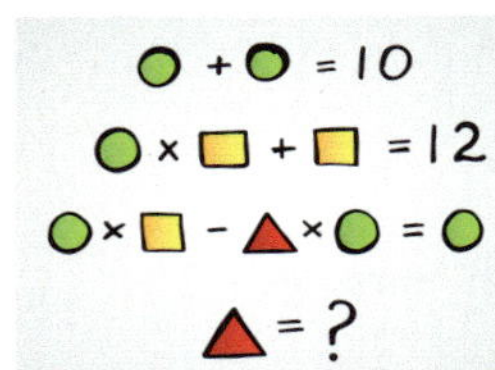
	science	die Naturwissenschaft	a **science** lesson 
	French	das Französisch; französisch	
	design and technology	das Werken, der Werkunterricht	**design** = Gestaltung, Design **technology** = Technik(unterricht); Technologie
	computing	die Informatik	
	PE (physical education)	der (Schul-)Sport	
▸ p. 27	**biology**	die Biologie	! Betonung auf der 2. Silbe: biology
	because	weil	I'm happy **because** now we have PE.
	hard	schwer, schwierig; hart	This exercise is so **hard**. Help me, please!
	German	deutsch; das Deutsch; Deutsche/r	adjective/language: **German** – noun/country: **Germany** (Deutschland)
	laboratory, *infml auch* **lab**	das Labor	

Topic 3

► p. 28	**place**	der Ort, der Platz	Put it there. That's the right **place**. ! in **this place** = **an** diesem Ort
	alone	allein	I often walk **alone** and think.
	our	unser/e	**our** poster (**unser** Poster) **our** class (**unsere** Klasse)
	bag	die Tasche	**bags** 
	canteen	die Kantine, die (Schul-)Mensa	Time for lunch! Let's go to the **canteen**.
	maybe	vielleicht	Let me think – **maybe** this is the answer: ...
	corridor	der Korridor	
	map	die Landkarte, der Stadtplan	
	building	das Gebäude	What's that **building**, Mum? – My old school!
	hall	die Halle, der Saal	**sports hall** = die Sporthalle ! **hall** = **1.** die Halle, der Saal; **2.** der Flur, die Diele
	near	nahe (bei), in der Nähe von	Hove is **near** Brighton.
	really	wirklich	Our teachers are **really** nice.
	always	immer	You're a great friend. You're **always** so nice!
► p. 29	**food**	das Essen, das Lebensmittel; das Futter	►► things to eat
	bad	schlecht; schlimm	**bad** ◄► **good**
	today	heute	What's our first lesson **today**? – French.
	activity	die Aktivität, die Tätigkeit	! Betonung auf der 2. Silbe: ac<u>tiv</u>ity
	(to) **get**	*(sich etwas)* holen/besorgen; bekommen	Where can I **get** help? (bekommen) Let's **get** sandwiches. (holen/besorgen)
► p. 30	**after** lesson 1 / **after** school	nach der ersten Unterrichtsstunde / nach der Schule	I don't have time for all my hobbies **after** school. preposition *(plus noun)*: **after** school (**nach** der Schule) – conjunction *(plus sentence)*: **after** you read the text (**nachdem** du ... liest)
	library	die Bücherei, die Bibliothek	I often get books from the **library**. at **the library** = in der Bücherei / Bibliothek
	playground	der Schulhof; der Spielplatz	At break we go to the school **playground**.
	theatre	das Theater	Let's go and see the new show at the **theatre**.

very big	sehr groß	London is **very** big. You can't see all nice places there in one day.
grandma	die Oma	

Background file

▸ p. 31 (the) **most** schools/time/...	die meisten Schulen / am meisten Zeit / ...	**Most** students in my class go to school clubs.
(to) **wear**	tragen, anhaben *(Kleidung)*	At English schools students **wear** uniforms.
or	oder; sonst	Do you like cats **or** dogs? – I love cats!
trousers *(pl)*	die Hose	! Das Wort **trousers** steht immer im Plural! **Are** your **trousers** new? **They're** cool! (**Ist** deine Hose neu? Sie **ist** cool!)
sock	die Socke	
skirt	der Rock	
shoe	der Schuh	
he / she / it **has**	er/sie/es hat	I **have** you **have** we **have** they **have** he **has** she **has** it **has**
goat	die Ziege	
(school) club	die Arbeitsgemeinschaft (AG) *(in der Schule)*	**club** = **1.** der Klub, der Verein; **2. school club** = die AG
gate	das Tor, das Gatter	Oh no, the **gate** is open! Where's our dog?
away	weg, fort	(to) **walk/go away** = weggehen
(to) **give**	geben	Can you **give** me that book, please? 
friendly	freundlich, nett	Don't be scared. They're **friendly** dogs. 
kind	freundlich, nett	►► friendly

Story

► p. 32

brave	mutig	! **brave** = mutig – Sunita is **brave**. **good** = brav – **Good** dog!
helpful	hilfsbereit; hilfreich, nützlich	You often help other people. You're very **helpful**. (hilfsbereit) This exercise is hard, but there are **helpful** tips on page 85. (hilfreiche/nützliche Tipps)
mean	gemein, fies	**mean ◄ ► kind, friendly** They're horrible people. They're really **mean**.
character	der Charakter; die Figur *(aus einer Geschichte)*	I love Brighton. It has **character**! (Charakter) This **character** in the story is so cool. (Figur) ! Betonung auf der 1. Silbe: **char**acter
who	wer	**how?** wie? **where?** wo? **what?** was? **who?** wer?
sad	traurig	**sad ◄ ► happy**
then	dann, danach	Now it's assembly time, **then** we have maths.
free	frei; kostenlos	**free time** = Freizeit, freie Zeit **Are you free** after school? = Hast du nach der Schule Zeit?
beach	der Strand	Let's go **to the beach**. (= zum Strand, an den Strand) ! **on the beach** = **am** Strand
(to) **move**	(sich) bewegen	Please don't **move** now ... 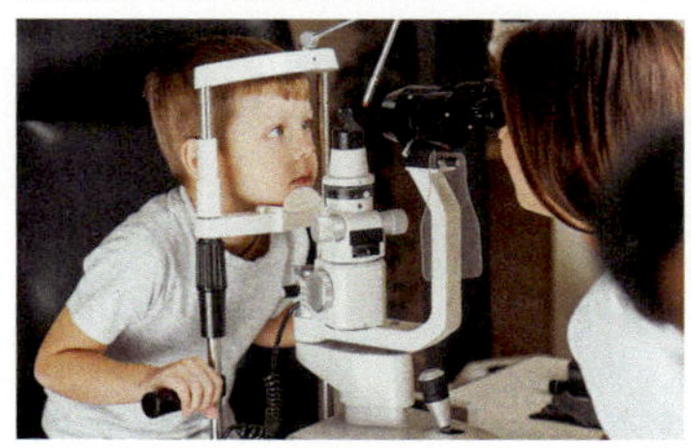
slow	langsam	This animal is very **slow**. 
too slow	zu langsam	Let's go to the beach. – Sorry, I'm **too** busy.
weird	seltsam, komisch	That's **weird**. My sandwich isn't in my bag, but Scout is very happy ...
bully	der Mobber, die Mobberin; der Tyrann, die Tyrannin	noun: **bully** – verb: (to) **bully** (tyrannisieren, mobben)
trouble	der Ärger, die Schwierigkeiten	He is **in trouble**. = Er hat Ärger. / Er ist in Schwierigkeiten.
those	die dort, jene (dort)	! **Those** kann mit Nomen stehen: I don't like **those** people. They're mean. Oder es kann alleine stehen: Hey! **Those** are my things!

	them	sie, ihnen	**I – me** **he – him** **we – us** **they – them**
	some	einige, ein paar; etwas, ein wenig	There are **some** books in my bag. (einige) I understand **some** French. (etwas, ein wenig)
▶ p. 33	**him**	ihm, ihn	There's Tom. Can you see **him**? (ihn) Let's talk to **him**. (mit ihm)
	still	(immer) noch; trotzdem	It's 4.30 and Joe **still** isn't here. (noch) I know you're tired! **Still** – please listen. (trotzdem)
	her friends	ihre Freunde/Freundinnen	**I – my** **we – our** **she – her** **you – your** **he – his**
	his friends	seine Freunde/Freundinnen	
	These are my friends.	Das hier sind meine Freunde/ Freundinnen.	

this, that – these, those

- Wenn etwas näher beim Sprecher / bei der Sprecherin ist, verwendet man eher **this** und **these.** — **This** dog is so nice and I love **these** cats.
- Wenn etwas weiter entfernt ist, verwendet man eher **that** und **those.** — **That** snake and **those** seagulls ... no, I'm scared.

	I'm happy that ...	Ich bin froh, dass ...	I'm happy **that** I still have my sandwich. I know **that** Scout is always hungry! ! Kein Komma im Englischen: *English*: she **says that** ... *German*: sie **sagt, dass** ... ! **that** = **1.** dass *(Konjunktion)*; **2.** das (dort) *(Pronomen)*
	first	erste(r, s)	**at first** = zuerst, am Anfang ! **first** = **1.** erste/r/s; **2.** zuerst, als Erstes
▶ p. 34	(to) **act**	aufführen, spielen	**acting** = die Schauspielerei (to) **act** sth. **out** = etwas vorspielen, aufführen
	loud	laut	Quiet, please. You're too **loud**. **louder** = lauter
	opinion (of)	die Meinung (zu/bezüglich)	! in **my opinion** = meiner Meinung **nach**
	next	nächste(r, s)	**the next day** = am nächsten Tag

Study skills

▶ p. 36	(to) **learn**	lernen	It's hard to **learn** all these new words. Can I **learn** to play the guitar, Mum?
	vocabulary, *infml auch* **vocab**	der Wortschatz, das Vokabular; das Vokabelverzeichnis	Reading English books is good for your **vocabulary**. (Wortschatz) Learn the new words on these **vocabulary** pages. (Vokabeln, Vokabelverzeichnis)
	mind map	die Gedankenkarte, das Wörter-netz, die Mindmap	

way	der Weg; die Art und Weise	You're in the **way**. (im Weg) Do it **(in) this way**! (auf diese Art/Weise) ! You can do it **in different ways**. (**auf** unterschiedliche Art/Weise)
file	die Datei; der Ordner, die Liste	I have a **file** on my computer with all the new words from my French lessons.
word	das Wort	What's the English **word** for "Handy"? – The correct **word** is "phone".
(from) A **to** Z	(von) A bis Z	We go to school **from** Monday **to** Friday. ! **to** = **1.** bis: from Monday **to** Friday; **2.** (um) zu: things **to** eat; **3.** zu, nach: I go **to** school.; **4.** auf: the answer **to** your question

Unit task

► p. 37 (to) **make**	machen, herstellen	Let's **make** music! I play the guitar and you can sing.
step	die Stufe; der Schritt	Let's sit down on the **steps** and look at the map. 
useful	nützlich, hilfreich	These exercises are too hard? Here are some **useful** tips. (= these tips can help you)
before you take a photo	bevor du ein Foto machst	

	before		◄►	**after**	
preposition *(plus noun)*	**before** school	(vor der Schule)	◄►	**after** school	(nach der Schule)
conjunction *(plus sentence)*	**before** you read	(bevor du liest)	◄►	**after** you read	(nachdem du liest)

difficult	schwierig, schwer	This exercise is really **difficult**. (= really hard)

Unit 2: My family and home

► pp. 50/51 **family**	die Familie	! Betonung auf der 1. Silbe: family
home	das Heim, das Zuhause	(to) go **home** = nach Hause gehen ! at **home** = **zu** Hause
aunt	die Tante	**aunt** ◄► **uncle**
uncle	der Onkel	
brother	der Bruder	**brother** ◄► **sister**
sister	die Schwester	
cousin	der Cousin, die Cousine	! Betonung auf der 1. Silbe: cousin

daughter	die Tochter	Do they have kids? – Yes, they have one **daughter,** Jane, and one **son,** Jack.
son	der Sohn	
circle	der Kreis	drawing a **circle** 
neighbour	der Nachbar, die Nachbarin	**neighbourhood** = die Nachbarschaft, die Gegend, das Viertel There's a bike shop in my **neighbourhood.**
stepmum	die Stiefmutter	**step-** ("Stief-") **stepmother** **stepsister** **stepfather** **stepbrother** **stepmum** **stepdaughter** **stepdad** **stepson**

(to) marry (heiraten)

Alex loves Dave. They can **marry**.	Alex liebt Dave. Sie können heiraten.
Alex can **marry** Dave.	Alex kann Dave heiraten.
Then Alex is **married to** Dave.	Dann ist Alex mit Dave verheiratet.
They are **married.**	Sie sind verheiratet.

Topic 1

▸ p.52 **pet**	das (Haus-)Tier	Are seagulls good **pets**? – No, they aren't!
a lot (of) **lots (of)**	viel/e; sehr viel/e	I have **a lot of** books in my room. (viele) I like the breaks at school **a lot.** (sehr)
rabbit	das Kaninchen	
hamster	der Hamster	
(to) **be lost**	sich verlaufen/verirrt haben	**Are you lost?** = Hast du dich verlaufen/verirrt? – Yes, **I'm lost.** Can you help me, please?
angry	wütend	Scout has my sandwich. I'm so **angry**!
vet	der Tierarzt, die Tierärztin	a **vet** with a dog 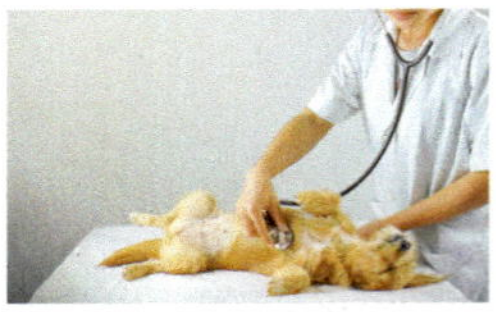
weekend	das Wochenende	**!** at **the weekend** = **am** Wochenende at **weekends** = **an** den Wochenenden (= an vielen/allen Wochenenden)
so	also, daher	It's Sunday, **so** we don't go to school. **!** **so** = **1. so** big/cold/... = so groß/kalt/... **2.** also, daher

	work	die Arbeit	**!** at **work** = **bei** der Arbeit, **am** Arbeitsplatz noun: **work** – verb: (to) **work** = **1.** arbeiten: **Work** with a partner. **2.** funktionieren: It's not a great computer, but it **works**.
	house	das Haus	
	messy	unordentlich	adjective: **messy** – noun: **mess** (das Chaos, die Unordnung)
► p.53	**polite**	höflich	
	only	nur, bloß; erst	I **only** have one pet. (nur) My sister is **only** two. (erst)
► p.54	**homework**	die Hausaufgabe(n)	What's for **homework?** = Was haben wir als Hausaufgabe(n) auf? **!** *English:* (to) do **your homework** *German:* **(deine) Hausaufgaben** machen **homework hat** keinen Plural: **Homework** is horrible. **Hausaufgaben sind** schrecklich.
	missing	vermisst	We can help you to find your **missing** pet.
	(to) **fly**	fliegen	Seagulls and parrots can **fly.**
	when	wenn (*zeitlich*)	**!** **when** = **1.** wann: **When**'s lunch? **2.** wenn: I eat a sandwich **when** I'm hungry.
	(to) **call**	nennen; rufen; anrufen	• This is Fiona, but we **call** her Fi. (nennen) • It's time for a snack – **call** the kids! (rufen) • **Call** me on this phone number: ... (anrufen) verb: (to) **call** – noun: **(phone) call** (der Ruf; der (Telefon-)Anruf)
	if	wenn, falls	What **if** ...? =Was wäre, wenn ...? **!** **if** = **1.** falls: **If** you see our missing cat, please phone us. **2.** ob: I don't know **if** this is the right answer.
	(to) **find**	finden	I can't **find** my bag. Where is it?
► p.55	(to) **want**	wollen	**!** • **want sth.** = etwas (haben) wollen I **want** a new computer. • **want to do sth.** = etwas tun wollen I **want to have** it now.
	active	aktiv	**active** ◄► **passive** (passiv)
	cute	niedlich, süß	Our rabbit is still very small and he's so **cute**!

	fast	schnell	I like my bike, but it isn't very **fast**.
	interesting	interessant	Books about animals are very **interesting**.
	special	besondere(r, s)	... **is special** = ... ist etwas Besonderes ! What's **special** about this place? = Was ist das Besondere **an** diesem Ort?
	lizard	die Eidechse	
	quite	ziemlich, ganz	My homework is **quite** hard. (ziemlich schwer) My maths teacher is **quite** nice. (ganz nett)
	dream	der Traum	I'm a vet. It's my **dream** job. I love it. noun: **dream** – verb: (to) **dream (of/about sth.)** (träumen (von etwas))

Topic 2

► p.56	**tree**	der Baum	
	garden	der Garten	
	ground floor	das Erdgeschoss	**ground** = der (Erd-)Boden ! **floor** = **1.** die Etage, das Stock(werk); **2.** der Fußboden
	top	die Spitze, das obere Ende	**at the top (of** sth.) = oben; am oberen Ende (von etwas); an der Spitze (von etwas) **top floor** = das Dach-/Obergeschoss, das oberste Stockwerk, die oberste Etage
	flat	die Wohnung	some **flats** with **balconies** 
	balcony	der Balkon	
	garage	die Garage	! Betonung auf der 1. Silbe: **ga**rage
	each	jede(r, s) (einzelne), jeweils	**Each** student can ask one question. = You can ask one question **each.** (jeweils eine Frage)
	lamp	die Lampe	
	no	kein, keine; verboten	I have **no** brothers or sisters. Sorry, **no** dogs! (Hunde verboten!) ! **no** = **1.** kein/e; verboten; **2.** nein
► p.57	**tour (of)**	die Tour, die Reise, der Rundgang / die Rundfahrt (durch)	! a **tour** of Brighton = ein Rundgang / eine Rundfahrt / eine Reise **durch** Brighton
	bedroom	das Schlafzimmer	
	bathroom	das Bad(ezimmer)	
	dining room	das Esszimmer	

	kitchen	die Küche	
	living room	das Wohnzimmer	
	office	das Büro	
► p.58	**sunny**	sonnig	 **It's sunny.** = Die Sonne scheint. adjective: **sunny** – noun: **sun** (die Sonne)
	modern	modern	! Betonung auf der 1. Silbe: <u>**mo**</u>dern
	street	die Straße (*in Ortschaften*)	**street music** = die Straßenmusik **street dance** = der Streetdance (*Tanzstil*) ! in **the street** = **auf** der Straße
	(to) **live**	leben, wohnen	Leo **lives** in Hove.
	(to) **tell**	erzählen, sagen	**Tell** the class about your hobbies. Please **tell** me how I can help you.

Background file

► p.59	**block**	der (Wohn-)Block	**block of flats** = das Mehrfamilienhaus
	terraced home/house	das Reihenhaus	
	detached home/house	das frei stehende Haus	
	semi-detached home/ house	die Doppelhaushälfte	
	their	ihr/e (*Plural*)	the students (**they**) and **their** teacher
	(to) **describe**	beschreiben	verb: (to) **describe** – noun: **description** (die Beschreibung) ! *English:* **Describe** the picture to <u>**him / her**</u>. *German:* **Beschreibe** <u>**ihm / ihr**</u> das Bild.
	cottage	das Häuschen, das Cottage (*kleines Haus, meist auf dem Land*)	 a nice old **cottage**
	little	klein	►► small We have a cute **little** rabbit.

Topic 3

► p.60	**bed**	das Bett	(to) **go to bed** = ins Bett gehen
	cushion	das Kissen	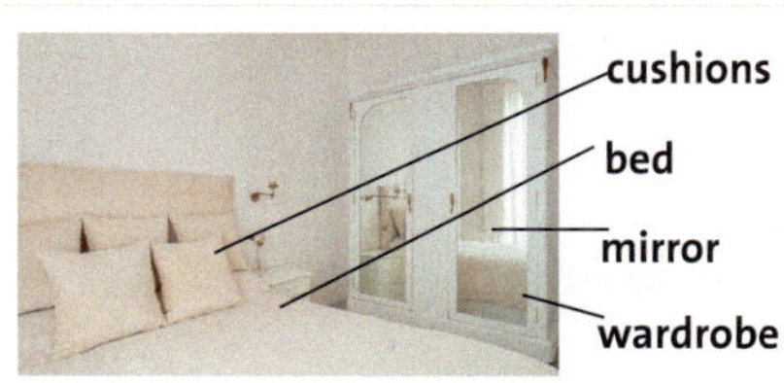
	wardrobe	der Kleiderschrank	
	mirror	der Spiegel	

	clothes *(pl)*	die Kleidung, die Kleidungsstücke	! *English:* **All** her **clothes are** black. *German:* Ihre gesamte **Kleidung ist** schwarz.
	shelf, *pl* **shelves**	das Regal	! one **shelf** – two **shelves**
	robot	der Roboter	Hello, **robot!** 
	chocolate	die Schokolade	! Betonung auf der 1. Silbe: <u>choc</u>olate
	chair	der Stuhl	
	under	unter	**on ◀ ▶ under**
	in front of	vor	
	behind	hinter	
	next to	neben	
	over	über; mehr als	
	between	zwischen	
	table	der Tisch	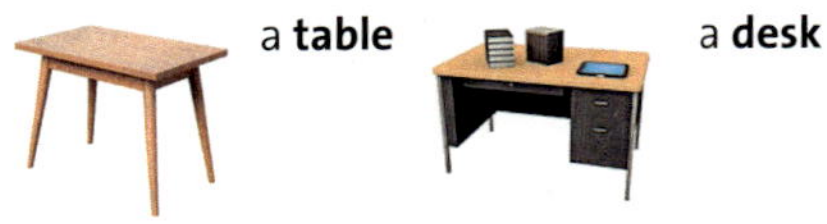
▶ p.61	**door**	die Tür	
	tidy	ordentlich	• adjective: **tidy** My room is always very **tidy**. – • verb: (to) **tidy** (aufräumen) I often **tidy** my room. **tidy ◀ ▶ messy**
▶ p.62	**person**	die Person	! Nur selten wird der Plural **persons** benutzt. Normalerweise: one **person** – five **people**
▶ p.63	**sweets** *(pl)*	die Bonbons, die Süßigkeiten	noun: **sweets** – adjective: **sweet** (süß)
	its terrarium	sein Terrarium / ihr Terrarium	! I have a pet. It's (= **It is**) a cute hamster. Its name is Joe. (= the hamster's name) **I – my name** / **we – our names** **you – your name** / **you – your names** **he – his name** / **it – its name** **she – her name**
	your **own** room	dein/ein eigenes Zimmer	! *English:* Do you have **your own** room? *German:* Hast du **ein eigenes** Zimmer?
	wall	die Wand, die Mauer	! **on the wall** = **an** der Wand; **an** die Wand

Story

► p.64	**expensive**	teuer	£6 for a sandwich? That's very **expensive**!
	perfect	perfekt	! Betonung auf der 1. Silbe: **per**fect
	enough	genug	Is one sandwich **enough**? Or are you still hungry?
	problem	das Problem	! Betonung auf der 1. Silbe: **prob**lem
	parents *(pl)*	die Eltern	►► your mum and dad
	of course	natürlich, selbstverständlich	Where's my phone? Oh, in my bag, **of course**!
	funny	witzig, lustig; seltsam	• All those animals in the house – it's not **funny!** (witzig, lustig) • What's so **funny** about a horse in the living room? (Was ist so lustig **an** ...?) • That's **funny** ... my phone isn't in my bag ... where is it? (seltsam) ! Hamsters are funny. = ... **sind witzig.** Swimming is fun. = ... **macht Spaß.**
	(to) **speak (to)**	sprechen (mit)	Can I **speak to** you after the lesson, Mr Lee? **speaking** = das Sprechen (to) **speak loudly** = laut sprechen
	later	später	**Speak later.** = Tschüs. / Bis später.
► p.65	**dinner**	das Abendessen	I'm hungry! **What's for** dinner, dad? = Was gibt es zum Abendessen? ! for **lunch** / for **dinner** = **zum** Mittagessen / **zum** Abendessen
	love	der Liebling	! **love** = **1.** der Liebling; **2.** die Liebe; **3.** lieben
	rude	unhöflich, frech	**polite** ◄► **rude**
	part (of)	der Teil (von)	What **part of** England are you from? = Aus welchem Teil Englands kommst du? A pet is always **part of** the family.
	electric	elektrisch, Elektro-	I play the **electric** guitar in our band.
	headphones *(pl)*	der Kopfhörer	! *English:* These are my new **headphones.** *German:* Dies ist mein neuer **Kopfhörer.** 
	game	das Spiel	Let's meet at Jo's and play some nice **games.**
	back	zurück	Mum is **back** at home. (wieder zu Hause)
► p.66	**on the phone**	am Telefon	! **on** = **1.** auf: **on** the desk **2.** an/am: **on** Monday, **on** the phone
	idea	die Idee	Can't we do it this way? – Of course! Good **idea.**
	noise	das Geräusch; der Lärm	Listen! What's that **noise?** (Geräusch) All that **noise!** I can't do my homework. (Lärm)
	long	lang	**(for) a long time** = lange, (für) eine lange Zeit Sorry, I can't talk to you **for a long time.** Twelve pages? That's a **long** story!

	solution (to a problem)	die Lösung (eines Problems)	! *English:* the **solution** to this problem. *German:* die **Lösung** für dieses Problem / die **Lösung** dieses Problems

Study skills

▸ p.68	(to) **spell**	buchstabieren	verb: (to) **spell** – noun: **spelling** (die Schreibweise, die Rechtschreibung)
	alphabet	das Alphabet	! Betonung auf der 1. Silbe: alphabet
	address	die Adresse	Where do you live? What's your **address?** ! Beachte die Schreibweise: a**dd**re**ss**
	like this	so, auf diese Art	►► (in) this way Look, it's not hard if you do it **like this.** ! **1.** it's always **like this** (so) **2.** a story **like this** (so/solch eine Geschichte)
	oh (= zero)	Null (*im gesprochenen Englisch*)	

15 fifteen	**21 twenty-one**	**40 forty**	**100 a/one hundred**
16 sixteen	**22 twenty-two**	**50 fifty**	**101 a/one hundred and one**
17 seventeen	**(...)**	**60 sixty**	**102 a/one hundred and two**
18 eighteen	**30 thirty**	**70 seventy**	**103 a/one hundred and three**
19 nineteen	**31 thirty-one**	**80 eighty**	**(...)**
20 twenty	**(...)**	**90 ninety**	

▶ Numbers, p. 307

	(to) **write**	schreiben	First **write** your text, then check the spelling!

Unit task

▸ p.69	(to) **present** sth. **(to** sb.)	(jm.) etwas präsentieren, vorstellen	verb: (to) **present** sth. **to** sb. – noun: **presentation** (das Referat, die Präsentation) (to) **give a presentation** = ein Referat halten ! *English:* **Present** your idea **to** your friends. *German:* Stelle deinen Freunden deine Idee vor. (*nicht:* ~~Present them your idea~~.)
	photographer	der Fotograf, die Fotografin	! Betonung auf der 2. Silbe: pho**to**grapher

Unit 3: My day

▸ pp. 84/85	**journey**	die Reise, die Fahrt; der Weg	It's not a long **journey** from here to Hove. You can walk or take the bus.
	(to) **come**	(mit)kommen	**Come** to our disco on Saturday! (kommen) Your friends can **come** too! (mitkommen)
	bus	der Bus	! on **the bus** = **im** Bus
	by bike/bus/...	mit dem Fahrrad/Bus/...	Let's not walk there, let's go **by** bus.
	car	das Auto	

	train	der Zug, die Eisenbahn	! on **the train** = **im** Zug
	short	kurz; klein *(Person; Körpergröße)*	**short ◄► long** It's a **short** walk. (= not a long walk) My little brother is still **short.** (klein *(Körpergröße)*)

Topic 1

► p. 86	**weekday**	der Werktag, der Wochentag	Monday to Friday are **weekdays.** **weekdays ◄► weekend**
	at 8 o'clock	um 8 Uhr	It's **1 o'clock** now. 
	4 p.m.	4 Uhr nachmittags, 16 Uhr	**9 p.m.** = 9 Uhr abends, 21 Uhr
	4 a.m.	4 Uhr (früh)morgens	**9 a.m.** = 9 Uhr vormittags
	the United Kingdom (= the UK)	das Vereinigte Königreich	►► England, Scotland, Wales and Northern Ireland
	hour	die Stunde	! Das "h" wird nicht gesprochen. Das Wort klingt genau wie "our".
	clock	die (Wand-, Stand-, Turm-)Uhr	
	morning	der Morgen	
	evening	der Abend	

• **in** the morning	morgens, am Morgen	• **on** Monday	am Montag
in the afternoon	nachmittags, am Nachmittag	**on** Tuesdays	dienstags, an Dienstagen
in the evening	abends, am Abend	**on** Friday morning	freitagmorgens, am Freitagmorgen

	lunchtime	die Mittagszeit	! at **lunchtime** = **zur** Mittagszeit
	end	das Ende, der Schluss	noun: **end** – verb: (to) **end** (enden; beenden)

in **the end**	schließlich; zum Schluss	Walk or take the bus? **In the end** I often go by bus.
at **the end (of)**	am Ende (von)	**At the end of** a long school day I'm always tired.

	What's the time?	Wie spät ist es?	**What's the time? ►► What time is it?** Let's meet on Saturday. – Good idea! **What time?** (Um wie viel Uhr?)
► p. 87	**why**	warum	**what?** was? **when** wann? **where?** wo(hin)? **why?** warum? **who?** wer? **how?** wie?
	newspaper (*kurz auch:* **paper)**	die (Tages-)Zeitung	! **paper** = **1.** die (Tages-)Zeitung I read the **paper** / **newspaper** in the morning. **2.** das Papier I can draw an elephant. Do you have a pen and some **paper?**

letter	der Brief	I often write **letters** to my grandma. ! letter = **1.** der Brief; **2.** der Buchstabe
competition	der Wettbewerb	One of my photos is in an art **competition.**
best	beste(r, s); am besten	You're my **best** friend!
(to) **choose**	(aus)wählen	Walk or go by bike? You can **choose.**
(to) **win**	gewinnen	I feel good when my football team **wins**. verb: (to) **win** – noun: **winner** (der Gewinner, die Gewinnerin / der Sieger, die Siegerin)
illness	die Krankheit	noun: **illness** – adjective: **ill** (krank)
wheelchair	der Rollstuhl	a **wheelchair** 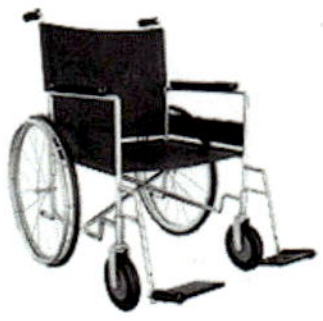
husband	der Ehemann	Zoe and Carl are married. Carl is Zoe's **husband**. Zoe is Carl's **wife**. **wife**, *pl* **wives** = die (Ehe-)Frau
cafe	das Café	! Betonung auf der 1. Silbe: <u>ca</u>fe
(to) **get up**	aufstehen	On weekdays I **get up** at 7 a.m.
shower	die Dusche	(to) **have a shower** = (sich) duschen 
(to) **get dressed**	sich anziehen	You're late! **Get dressed!** Where are your clothes?
breakfast	das Frühstück	
(to) **take**	dauern, *(Zeit)* brauchen, in Anspruch nehmen	The journey from London to Brighton **takes** an hour by train. ! (to) **take** = **1.** dauern, *(Zeit)* brauchen, in Anspruch nehmen; **2.** (mit)nehmen; bringen; **3.** (to) **take photos** = Fotos machen
(to) **watch** (sth.)	(sich etwas) anschauen; (etwas) beobachten	(to) **look** • (to) **see** • (to) **watch** • **Look** at the picture. ((an)schauen) • Can you **see** me? (sehen) • Can I **watch** the football game? (anschauen) Let's **watch** the dogs. (beobachten)
► p. 88 **line**	die Zeile; die Reihe	a **line** of houses 

	shopping	das Einkaufen; die Einkäufe	(to) **do the shopping** = die Einkäufe erledigen, einkaufen gehen (to) **go shopping** = einkaufen gehen
▶ p. 89	(to) **brush**	bürsten	verb: (to) **brush** – noun: **brush** (die Bürste)
	tooth, *pl* **teeth**	der Zahn	(to) **brush your teeth** = (sich) die Zähne putzen
	everybody	jeder; alle	**Hello everybody!** = Hallo allerseits! Mr Lee is really nice. **Everybody** likes him.
	project	das Projekt	! Betonung auf der 1. Silbe: **pro**ject
	country	das Land, *(auch:)* die ländliche Gegend	! *English:* **in the country** *German:* **auf** dem Land

Topic 2

▶ p. 90	**drama**	das Schauspiel, die darstellende Kunst	
	(to) **cycle**	Rad fahren	**cycling** = das Radfahren 
	(to) **hike**	wandern	**hiking** = das Wandern We often go **hiking** at the weekend.
	(to) **run**	rennen, laufen	**running** = das Laufen *(Sport)*
	trampolining	das Trampolinspringen/-turnen	**trampoline** = das Trampolin
	Which clubs ...?	Welche AGs ...?	**Which** school club do you like?
	(to) **join** a club	bei einer AG mitmachen, in einen Klub eintreten	• (to) **join** sb./sth. = sich jm. anschließen; bei etwas mitmachen • I love drawing. I want to **join** the art club. (bei einer AG mitmachen) • Are you free this afternoon? We're going to the beach. **Join** us! (sich anschließen, mitkommen (mit))
	how to do sth.	wie man etwas tut / tun kann / tun soll	I don't know ... **... what to do / what to say.** **... how to answer.** **... where to go.**
	every	jede(r, s)	I go to the drama club **every** Tuesday. **every 30 minutes** = alle 30 Minuten
	month	der Monat	August is a **month** with 31 days.
	sea	das Meer, die See	! **by the sea** = **am** Meer, **an** der See
	exciting	aufregend	Parkour? Wow, that's an **exciting** hobby, Lily!
▶ p. 91	**sometimes**	manchmal	**always** **often** **sometimes** **rarely** **never**
	never	nie, niemals	

	rarely	selten *(Adv.)*	adverb: **rarely** (I **rarely** read old books.) adjective: **rare** (a **rare** old book)
	(to) **feel**	sich fühlen; fühlen	I **feel** great when I make music.
	stressed	gestresst	Homework for six subjects! I feel so **stressed**.
	match	das Spiel, der Wettkampf	a football **match** ►► a football game
► p. 93	**secret**	geheim; das Geheimnis	This is a **secret** message. (geheim) It's our **secret.** (Geheimnis)
	sentence	der Satz	"I like you." is a short English **sentence.**

Topic 3

► p. 94	**all weekend**	das ganze Wochenende	**all the time** = die ganze Zeit, ständig
	a shame	schade; eine Schande	You're not free this afternoon? **That's a shame!** (Das ist schade!) **What a shame!** (Wie schade!)
	I'd love to. **(= I would love to.)**	Sehr gerne. / Das würde ich sehr gerne.	**Would you like** a drink? – Oh yes, please, **I'd love** a cola! • **I'd like/love ...** (= **I would like/love ...**) = Ich hätte (liebend) gern ... / Ich möchte (liebend gern) ... • **I'd love/like to meet** Zane. = Ich würde mich (liebend) gern mit Zane treffen.
	(to) **ask** sb. **to do** sth.	jn. bitten, etwas zu tun	Can I **ask** you **to help** me? = Can I **ask** you **for** some help? **!** (to) **ask** = **1.** fragen; **2.** (to) **ask** sb. **for** sth. = jn. um etwas bitten
► p. 95	**plan**	der Plan	noun: **plan** – verb: (to) **plan** (planen) I'm **planning** dinner with my friends. – Oh, nice! What do you **plan to cook?** (... planst du / plant ihr zu kochen?)
	(to) **sound**	klingen *(sich ... anhören)*	Going to the beach? **Sounds** great! (Klingt toll!) verb: (to) **sound** – noun: **sound** (das Geräusch; der Klang, der Laut)
► p. 96	(to) **hang out**	rumhängen, abhängen	My friends and I often **hang out** in the park.

Background file

► p. 97	(to) **crack**	lösen *(z.B. Problem)*, knacken *(z.B. Code)*	How can we **crack** this problem? (= find a solution)
	popular	beliebt, populär	Football is very **popular**. Lots of kids love it. **!** The word **pop music** (or: **pop**) is short for **popular music**.
	field	das Spielfeld, der Platz	Look! There are only 10 players on the **field**!
	cricket	die Grille *(Insekt)*	**!** **cricket** = **1.** die Grille *(Insekt)*; **2.** das Kricket *(Mannschaftssportart)*

	bat	der Schläger *(Sport)*	
	ball	der Ball	Our dog likes to play with **balls**.
	(to) **design**	entwerfen, gestalten	verb: (to) **design** – noun: **design** (die Gestaltung, das Design)

Story

▶ p. 98	**prize**	der Preis, der Gewinn	The **prize** for the winner of this competition is a weekend in Paris.
	(to) **show**	zeigen	**Show** your teacher your story. = **Show** your story **to** your teacher. (Zeige deinem Lehrer / deiner Lehrerin deinen Text.) verb: (to) **show** – noun: **show** (die Show, die Aufführung; die Ausstellung)
	her	sie; ihr	! **her** = **1.** sie; ihr: I can see **her**. (sie) / I can help **her**. (ihr) **2.** ihr/e (wessen?): **her** dog, **her** room
	article	der Artikel	! Betonung auf der 1. Silbe: <u>ar</u>ticle
	surprised	überrascht	This bike for only £150? I'm really **surprised.**
	(to) **send**	senden, schicken	I'd like to **send** my sister a message. = I'd like to **send** a message **to** my sister. (Ich würde meiner Schwester gern eine Nachricht schicken.)
	guys *(pl)*	Leute *(als Anrede verwendet)*	Hey, **guys,** great to see you!
	(to) **be/feel sorry for** sb.	Mitleid haben mit jm.	I**'m** / I **feel sorry for** him. = Ich habe Mitleid mit ihm. / Er tut mir leid.
	(to) **stare (at)**	(an)starren	It's rude to **stare** at people. verb: (to) **stare (at)** – noun: **stare** (das Starren, der starre Blick)
	(to) **hate**	hassen	verbs: (to) **love** ◀ ▶ (to) **hate** nouns: **love** ◀ ▶ **hate** (der Hass)
▶ p. 99	**much**	viel; sehr	**How much** time do we have? (viel) I like Zane **so much.** (so sehr) **Thank you very much.** = Vielen Dank. / Danke vielmals.
	Well done.	Gut gemacht!	**well** = gut *(Adv.)* • adjective: **good** Your English is very **good.** – • adverb: **well** You speak English very **well.**
	(to) **text** sb.	jm. eine SMS schicken	**Text** me when you're back from London, OK? ! **text** = **1.** der Text; **2.** die SMS; **3.** (to) **text** sb. = jm. eine SMS schicken
	news	die Nachrichten	**news** hat <u>keinen Plural</u>: **That is** good news. **Das <u>sind</u>** gute Nachrichten.

	as the winner	als Gewinner/in	! *English:* **as** the winner / **as** a teacher *German:* **als** Gewinner/in / **als** Lehrer/in
	money	das Geld	Nice bike ... how much **money** do I have?
	heading	Überschrift	The **heading** is at the top of a page or where a new part or unit of a book starts.
	(to) **find out (about)**	herausfinden; sich informieren (über)	• Let's **find out** when the show starts. (herausfinden) • **Find out about** the cricket club at our school and tell your friends. (sich informieren über)
	(to) **explain** sth. **to** sb.	jm. etwas erklären	! *English:* Please **explain** it to me. *German:* **Erkläre** es mir bitte.
	(to) **happen** (**to** sb.)	(jm.) geschehen, passieren	Tell us what **happen**s in the story.
► p. 100	(to) **freeze**	(ge)frieren; erstarren	**freeze-frame** = das Standbild *(Film)*
	(to) **pay (for** sth.**)**	zahlen; (etwas) bezahlen	! *English:* Let me **pay** for the pizzas. *German:* Lass mich die Pizzas **bezahlen.**
	cleaner	die Reinigungskraft	
	bank	die Bank *(Geldinstitut)*	(to) put money in **a bank** = Geld **zur Bank** / **auf die Bank** bringen
	pound (£)	das Pfund *(britische Währung)*	! you write: **£ 5** – you say: five **pounds**
	penny (= p), *pl* **pence**	der Penny, Pence *(Plural)*	

Pounds and euros

In **England** you have **pounds** and **pence.**		In **Germany** you have **euros** and **cents.**	
You say:	*You write:*	*You say:*	*You write:*
fifty p / fifty pence	**50 p**	**fifty cents**	**€ 0.50**
one pound / a pound	**£ 1**	**one euro / a euro**	**€ 1**
two pounds fifty	**£ 2.50**	**two euros fifty**	**€ 2.50**

Study skills

► p. 102	(to) **look** sth. **up**	etwas nachschlagen, nachschauen	What's "Möwe" in English? – Sorry, I don't know. Let's **look** it **up.**
	jigsaw (puzzle)	das Puzzle	**puzzle** = das Rätsel
	(to) **collect**	(ein)sammeln	My friend Jamie **collects** old clocks.
	second (2nd)	zweite(r, s)	First we have maths and our **second** lesson today is music.
	card	die Karte	**playing cards** = die Spielkarten 
	language	die Sprache	She speaks three **languages:** English, German and French.
	group	die Gruppe	Please work in **groups** of 3 or 4 students. noun: **group** – verb: (to) **group** (gruppieren)

Unit task

► p. 103	(to) **share**	teilen	I **share** a room **with** my brother. = We **share** a room. = Wir teilen uns ein Zimmer. verb: (to) **share** – noun: **share** (der (An-)Teil)
	(to) **think about**	nachdenken über	Work in groups and **think about** this problem. Can you crack it?
	superhero, *pl* **superheroes**	der Superheld, die Superheldin	This character helps everybody. She's my **superhero**!
	task	die Aufgabe	(to) **do a task** = eine Aufgabe machen/erledigen
	(to) **add**	hinzufügen, addieren	When you **add** blue **to/and** yellow, you get green.
	speech bubble	Sprechblase	What do the characters say? Write some funny text for **speech bubbles**.
	(to) **record**	aufnehmen, aufzeichnen	Our school band wants to **record** a CD.
	example	das Beispiel	**for example** = zum Beispiel
	light	das Licht; die Lampe	I have good **lights** on my bike. **car light** = der Autoscheinwerfer
	clear	klar, deutlich	adjective: **clear** Is the task **clear**? – adverb: **clearly** Please speak **clearly**. (deutlich sprechen)

Unit 4: Where I live

p. 116/117	**cinema**	das Kino	! at **the cinema** = **im** Kino
	pier	der Pier, die Seebrücke	
	boring	langweilig	Maths isn't **boring!** It's very interesting. **boring** ◄► **exciting/interesting**
	busy	hektisch, belebt	It's too **busy** in the shops. Let's go home. ! **busy** = **1.** hektisch, belebt; **2.** (viel) beschäftigt
	palace	der Palast, das Schloss	! Betonung auf der 1. Silbe: <u>pal</u>ace
	duke	der Herzog	
	marina	der Jachthafen	
	north	der Norden; nördlich; Nord-	York is in the **north** of England.
	picnic	das Picknick	(to) **have a picnic** = ein Picknick machen
	(to) **hear**	hören	! (to) **hear** = hören (können) (to) **listen** (to) = zuhören, horchen **Listen!** Can you **hear** that noise?

	(to) **practise**	üben	I **practise** the guitar every day. verb: (to) **practise** – noun: **practice** (die Übung(en))
	skill	die Fähigkeit, die Fertigkeit	
	chips *(pl)*	die Pommes frites	**fish and chips** = Fisch mit Pommes frites
	mile	die Meile ***(ca. 1,6 km)***	**per** = pro ! **at 30 miles per hour** = **mit** 30 Meilen pro Stunde
	kilometre (km)	der Kilometer	**1,000 metres** = **1 kilometre** **1 mile** = **1.6 km**
	1.6 (one point six)	1,6 (eins Komma sechs)	! **point** = **1.** der Punkt You get one **point** for each correct answer. **2.** das Komma *(Dezimalzeichen)* One mile is **one point six** / **1.6** kilometres.

Im Englischen steht ein **Punkt,** im Deutschen ein **Komma.**

English: 1.6 = one **point** six   *German:* 1,6 = eins **Komma** sechs

Topic 1

► p. 118	(to) **smell**	riechen; schlecht riechen	verb: (to) **smell** – noun: **smell** (der Geruch; der Gestank)
	cooking	das Kochen, das *(gekochte)* Essen	my **cooking** = mein (gekochtes) Essen verb: (to) **cook** – nouns: *(person)* **cook**; *(what you cook/eat; a hobby)* **cooking**
	clean	sauber	adjective: **clean** – verb: (to) **clean** (sauber machen, putzen)
	dirty	schmutzig	**dirty** ◄ ► **clean**
	youth centre	das Jugendzentrum	**youth** = die Jugend; der Jugendliche **centre** = das Zentrum; die Mitte
	field	das Feld; die Weide; die Wiese	! in the field **auf** der Weide **field** = **1.** das Feld; die Weide; die Wiese **2.** das Spielfeld
	estate	die Wohnsiedlung; das Gewerbegebiet	! **on our estate** = **in** unserer Wohnsiedlung
	town	die Stadt	**in town** = in der Stadt **town centre** = das Stadtzentrum
	into the town centre	ins Stadtzentrum (hinein)	
	(to) **look after**	sich kümmern um; aufpassen auf	I sometimes **look after** my baby sister. People don't **look after** our town well: there's a lot of rubbish in the streets.
	rubbish	der (Haus-)Müll, der Abfall	Please put your **rubbish** in the **bin.** 
	bin	der (Müll-)Eimer	
► p. 119	**note**	die Notiz; der kurze Brief	(to) **make notes** = (sich) Notizen machen *(zur Vorbereitung)*

► p. 120	**like**	wie; wie zum Beispiel	• My bike is **like** your bike. (wie) • I like team sports **like** cricket, basketball or football. (wie zum Beispiel) • What's your new school **like**? (Wie ist ...?)
	(to) **box**	boxen	**boxing** = das Boxen
	crafts *(pl)*	das Kunsthandwerk, das Basteln	I'm in the **crafts** club at school because I like making things.
	a girls' class	ein Mädchenkurs, ein Kurs für Mädchen	

Apostroph + s: Etwas gehört (zu) jemandem. Aber beachte die **Stellung des** Apostrophs!

Singular + Apostroph + s: **eine** Person

the **girl's** dog
der Hund **des Mädchens**

Plural-s + Apostroph: **mehrere** Personen

the **girls'** dogs
die Hunde **der Mädchen**

	What else?	Was sonst noch?	Coding, dancing – **what else** do you do in your free time?
	(to) **buy**	kaufen	►► (to) get sth. I'm hungry. Let's **buy** some sandwiches.
► p. 121	**also**	auch	I like music and I **also** like dancing. = I like music and I like dancing too.
	village	das Dorf	a very small town in the country
	many	viele	You have **many** fish in your aquarium! **How many** are there?

much („viel") – **many** („viele")

How much time do we have?
Wie viel Zeit ...?

We do**n't** have **much** time, but we have **a lot of** / **lots of** work.
nicht viel Zeit — **viel** Arbeit

How many shops are in your village?
Wie viele Geschäfte ...?

There are**n't many** shops, but there are **a lot of** / **lots of** fields.
nicht viele Geschäfte — **viele** Felder

Topic 2

► p. 122	**hospital**	das Krankenhaus	When you're very ill, you go **to hospital.** (ins Krankenhaus) Is he very ill? Is he **in hospital?** (im Krankenhaus)
	ice rink	die Schlittschuhbahn	
	library	die Bücherei, die Bibliothek	I don't always buy books, I often get them from the **library**. ! **at the library** = **in** der Bücherei/Bibliothek
	supermarket	der Supermarkt	I buy my food **at the supermarket (im** Supermarkt) or **at the market** (**auf** dem Markt).
	museum	das Museum	! **at the museum** = **im** Museum
	stadium	das Stadion	! **at the stadium** = **im** Stadium
	(train) station	der Bahnhof	! Betonung auf der 1. Silbe: station

	biggest	der/die/das größte; am größten	• What's the **biggest** building in this town? (das größte Gebäude) • Which city is **biggest:** London, Berlin, Madrid? (am größten)
	things **that** are good	Dinge, die gut sind	! Kein Komma im Englischen: *English:* **sports that** I don't like *German:* **Sportarten, die** ich nicht mag
► p. 124	**everywhere**	überall	There's rubbish **everywhere** in the park. It's horrible!
	head	der Kopf	a snake with three **heads** 
	guide dog	der Blindenhund	I have a **guide dog** because I can't see very well, and my dog helps me. noun: **(tour) guide** (der Reiseleiter, die Reiseleiterin / der Fremdenführer, die Fremdenführerin) – verb: (to) **guide** (führen, leiten)
	fish and chip shop	*die Imbissstube, die Fisch mit Pommes frites verkauft*	
	warm	warm	
	(to) **get** warm	warm werden	In the north of Canada it never **gets** very warm.
	summer	der Sommer	summer ◄► winter
	Excuse me, ...	Entschuldigung, ... / Entschuldigen Sie, ...	**Excuse me,** please. Where's the train station?
	something	etwas	Can I ask you **something**? I'm hungry! Can I have **something** to eat?
► p. 125	**Welcome to ...**	Willkommen in/an ...	**Welcome to** our house! Let me show you my room.
	ice cream	das (Speise-)Eis	

Topic 3

► p. 126	**weather**	das Wetter, die Witterung	What's the **weather** like? Can we go to the beach?
	rainy	regnerisch	It's a **rainy** day. = It's **raining.** adjective: **rainy** – noun: **rain** (der Regen) – verb: (to) **rain** (regnen) 
	snowy	schneebedeckt; verschneit	adjective: **snowy** – noun: **snow** (der Schnee) – verb: (to) **snow** (schneien)

Verben und Nomen, die dieselbe Form haben

answer	**1.** (be)antworten	**2.** die Antwort	**phone**	**1.** anrufen	**2.** das Telefon
cook	**1.** kochen	**2.** der Koch, die Köchin	**plan**	**1.** planen	**2.** der Plan
dance	**1.** tanzen	**2.** der Tanz	**rain**	**1.** regnen	**2.** der Regen
drink	**1.** trinken	**2.** das Getränk	**snow**	**1.** schneien	**2.** der Schnee
help	**1.** helfen	**2.** die Hilfe	**walk**	**1.** (zu Fuß) gehen	**2.** der Spaziergang
love	**1.** lieben	**2.** die Liebe	**work**	**1.** arbeiten	**2.** die Arbeit

cloudy	wolkig, bewölkt	adjective: **cloudy** – noun: **cloud** (die Wolke)
windy	windig	It's **windy.** adjective: **windy** – noun: **wind** (der Wind) 
Russia	Russland	• nouns: *(country)* **Russia** – Sergej is from **Russia**. *(person)* **a Russian** (ein Russe, eine Russin) He's **Russian**. (... ist Russe.) – • adjective: **Russian** (russisch, Russisch) – This is a **Russian** dessert. Yum! (russisch) I speak English, French and **Russian**. (Russisch)
outside the Pavilion	außerhalb des Pavilion	**outside** ◄ ► **inside**

	preposition (+ noun)	**adverb** (Where?)
inside	Do your rabbits live **inside your house**? (innerhalb (von))	They're never **inside**. (= in the house) ((nach) (dr)innen)
outside	No, they live **outside the house**. (außerhalb (von))	They're always **outside**. (= in the garden) ((nach) draußen)

cold	kalt	adjective: **cold** – noun: **cold** (die Kälte; die Erkältung) (to) **be cold** = frieren (to) **have a cold** = erkältet sein
woman, *pl* **women**	die Frau	! one **woman** – two **women** one **man** – two **men** (ein Mann / zwei Männer) *German* **Frau**: • She's a nice **woman**. (eine nette Frau) • **That's Mrs/Ms** Smith. (Frau Smith) • **This is** Anne, my **wife**. (meine Frau)
up	hinauf, hoch	**up** ◄ ► **down** (hinunter, herunter)
(to) **travel**	reisen, fahren	verb: (to) **travel** – noun: **travel** (das Reisen)
amazing	erstaunlich; großartig	24,000,000 people live in Shanghai? **Amazing!** (erstaunlich) This museum is so great – really **amazing.** (großartig)
view	der (An-)Blick, die (Aus-)Sicht	noun: **view** – verb: (to) **view** (anschauen)

	second	die Sekunde	**for 30 seconds** = für 30 Sekunden, 30 Sekunden lang
▶ p. 127	**more**	mehr, weitere	I only go to the cycling club. I don't have time for **more** clubs. Please write **three more** words into the mind map. (noch drei Wörter, drei weitere Wörter)
	(to) **stop**	(an)halten; stoppen; aufhören (mit)	(to) **start** ◀ ▶ (to) **stop** The bus **stops** here. (anhalten) Please **stop** talking and listen. (aufhören mit) verb: (to) **stop** – noun: **stop** (der Halt, der Haltepunkt; die Unterbrechung) **bus stop** = die Bushaltestelle
	(to) **cost**	kosten	How much does this phone **cost?** verb: (to) **cost** – noun: **cost** (die Kosten; der Preis)
	upside down	verkehrt herum, auf dem Kopf	the **upside down house** = das Haus, das auf dem Kopf steht
	degree (°)	das/der Grad	It's very cold today, only 5 **degrees**! (= 5°)
	(to) **need** sth. (to) **need to do** sth.	etwas brauchen etwas tun müssen	I **need** money. I **need to buy** a new bike.
	tip	der Tipp	Thanks for those **tips!** They're very helpful.
	(to) **turn** sth. **(over)**	etwas umdrehen	**Turn** it upside down. = Dreh/Stell es auf den Kopf. (to) **turn** = (sich) umdrehen
▶ p. 128	**hot**	heiß, warm	**cold – warm – hot** **hot chocolate** = der Kakao, die heiße (Trink-)Schokolade
	swap	der Tausch	• noun: **swap** My friends and I like to have **clothes swaps**. (der Kleidertausch, die Kleidertauschparty) • verb: (to) **swap** (tauschen) I **swap** clothes with my friends.

Background file

▶ p. 129	(to) **look**	aussehen	It **looks** like rain. (Es sieht nach Regen aus.) What does it **look** like? (Wie sieht es aus?)
	beautiful	wunderschön	Horses are **beautiful** animals. It's a **beautiful** day! Let's go outside.
	terrible	schrecklich, fürchterlich	▶▶ horrible
	It's great, **isn't it?**	Es ist großartig/toll, nicht wahr?	Parkour is very exciting, **isn't it?**
	island	die Insel	

(to) **change (into)**	(sich) (ver)ändern (zu/in); wechseln; (sich) verwandeln (in), werden (zu)	verb: (to) **change** – noun: **change** (die Veränderung, der Wechsel, die Verwandlung)
(to) **bring**	bringen, mitbringen	Daisy, **bring** me the shoe! 
umbrella	der Regenschirm	An **umbrella** is useful for rainy weather – but not when it's too windy!
moment	der Moment	! Betonung auf der 1. Silbe: <u>mo</u>ment **at the moment** = **im** Moment, zurzeit
shine	der (Sonnen-)Schein; der Glanz	noun: **shine** – verb: (to) **shine** (scheinen *(Sonne)*; strahlen, glänzen)

Weather phrases

(to) **have a moment in the sun**	kurz im Mittelpunkt stehen
(to) **have your head in the clouds**	in Gedanken verloren sein; unrealistisch sein
(to) **rain cats and dogs**	stark regnen
..., **come rain or shine**	... bei jedem Wetter; ... was auch (immer) geschieht

(to) **go up**	aufgehen *(z. B. Sonne)*; (an)steigen	Every morning the sun **goes up**. (aufgehen) When it starts to rain, the umbrellas **go up**. (aufgehen) Costs for food and other things are **going up** all the time. ((an)steigen)

Story

▶ p. 130	(to) **clean** sth. **up**	etwas aufräumen, sauber machen	verb: (to) **clean up** – noun: **clean-up** (die Säuberung) **clean-up day** = der Dreck-weg-Tag *(Aktionstag zum Müllsammeln)*
	(to) **guess**	(er)raten	

(to) guess / guess

verb: (to) **guess**
Guess what my favourite animal is! (Rate mal, was ...)
I **guess** Jo is late again. (Ich nehme an, ... / Ich glaube, ...)
Guess what! (Stell dir / Stellt euch (mal) vor!)

noun: **guess** (Vermutung)
Make / Have / Take a **guess**! (Rate mal!)
My **guess** is that Jo is late again.

	Well, ...	Nun, .../ Also, .../ Na ja, ...	! **well** = **1.** Nun, .../ Also, .../ Na ja, ... Cycle to school in the rain? **Well,** I'm not sure ... **2.** gut *(Adv.)* You speak English really **well.**
▶ p. 131	**so (that)**	sodass	! **so** = **1.** also, daher **2.** (*auch* **so that**) sodass **3. so** big/cold/... (so groß/kalt/...)
	over there	da drüben, dort drüben	**over here** ◀ ▶ **over there**

(to) **forget**	vergessen	**forget ◄ ► remember** There's a maths test on Monday. Don't **forget** it! Don't **forget**. = Vergiss (es) nicht. / Denk dran!
together	zusammen	Work in groups and find answers to these questions **together.**
dead	tot	Fish and chips? No, I don't eat **dead** animals.
mouse, *pl* **mice**	die Maus	two **mice** 
Next ...	Als Nächstes ...	**Next** I'd like to look at some photos with you. **!** **next** = **1.** der/die/das nächste; **2.** als Nächstes
(to) **dig**	graben	My dog likes **digging** in the sand.
(to) **bark (at** sb.**)**	(jn. an)bellen	My dog never **barks at** you: he knows you!
wedding	die Hochzeit	Jack marries Jo next week. I need to buy them a **wedding present**. (das Hochzeitsge-schenk) **wedding ring** = der Ehering
bags **of** rubbish	Tüten/Säcke (mit/voller) Müll	**!** **of** = **1.** von – the last day **of** the holidays **2.** mit, voller *(oft auch unübersetzt)* – a bag **of** rubbish
furniture *(no pl)*	die Möbel(stücke), das Mobiliar	**!** **furniture** hat keinen Plural: The **furniture is** new. Die **Möbel sind** neu.
(to) **put** sth. **up**	etwas aufhängen *(an der Wand)*	Design your own posters and **put** them **up** on the classroom wall.
notice	der Anschlag, die Bekanntmachung *(an einem Schwarzen Brett)*	• noun: **notice** Look, there's a **notice** over there: "Missing parrot!" – • verb: (to) **notice** ((be)merken) „If you **notice** a parrot in your garden, phone this number."
somebody **someone**	jemand	**!** **somebody** *or* **someone** = jemand **everybody** *or* **everyone** = jeder; alle There's **someone/somebody** at the door.
► p. 132 (to) **mean**	bedeuten; meinen *(sagen wollen)*	What does this word **mean?** (bedeuten) What do you **mean?** (meinen) verb: (to) **mean** – noun: **meaning** (die Bedeutung)
scene	die Szene	
(to) **go green**	grün/umweltfreundlich werden	(to) **go red** = erröten, rot werden
toy	das Spielzeug	Little Emma likes to play with **toy** cars.

Study skills

► p. 134	(to) **greet**	begrüßen	verb: (to) **greet** – noun: **greeting** (die Begrüßung; der Gruß) "**Greetings** from York! I'm having a great time."
	audience	das Publikum; die Zuschauer/innen, die Zuhörer/innen	Look at your **audience** when you talk to them.
	title	der Titel, die Überschrift	I like the band and their music, but some of their song **titles** are really weird.
	phrase	der Ausdruck, die (Rede-)Wendung	A **phrase** is a group of words with a special meaning, for example "for seven seconds".
	Do you have any questions?	Habt ihr / Hast du (irgendwelche) Fragen?	**Are there any** cats in your photo? – No, **there aren't any** cats in my photo. **Are there any …?** = Gibt es (irgendwelche) …? **There aren't any …** = Es gibt/sind kein/e … **I don't have any …** = Ich habe kein/e …
	(to) **continue**	fortfahren, weitermachen; (sich) fortsetzen, weitergehen	Let's stop now and **continue** later. / … and **continue to write** our presentation later. (to) **continue to do** sth. = etwas weiterhin tun, (mit) etwas weitermachen, fortfahren

Unit task

► p. 135	**zoo**	der Zoo	Do you like going to the **zoo** and looking at all the animals?
	(to) **ride (a bike)**	(mit dem Fahrrad) fahren	►► (to) cycle
	topic	das Thema	The **topic** of my presentation is "animals in zoos".

Unit 5: Enjoy

p. 148/149	(to) **enjoy**	genießen	**enjoy doing sth.** = genießen, etwas zu tun **Enjoy!** = Viel Vergnügen!
	dessert	die Nachspeise, das Dessert	! Weiches **-ss-** in der Wortmitte: **dessert** for **dessert** = **zum/als** Nachtisch
	birthday	der Geburtstag	! on **my birthday** = **an** meinem Geburtstag

Happy **birthday!** Herzlichen Glückwunsch zum Geburtstag!	When's your **birthday?** Wann hast du Geburtstag?	My **birthday** is in April. Ich habe im April Geburtstag.

Christmas	(das) Weihnachten	**Christmas Day** = der 1. Weihnachtstag (25. 12.)
fruit	das Obst	
jelly	das Gelee; der Wackelpudding	
cream	die Sahne	**clotted cream** = die besonders dicke Sahne, der Streichrahm **whipped cream** = die Schlagsahne, die geschlagene Sahne
strawberry	die Erdbeere	**strawberries** and **cream**

allergic (to)	allergisch (gegen)	It's sad, but I can't eat strawberries. I'm **allergic to** them.
Indian	indisch; der Inder, die Inderin	adjective/person: **Indian** – noun: **India** (Indien)
restaurant	das Restaurant	Let's eat **at a restaurant** this evening. (= **in** einem Restaurant)
dish	das Gericht *(die Mahlzeit)*	This is my favourite Indian **dish.** ►► meal ! **dish** = **1.** das Gericht *(die Mahlzeit);* **2.** die Schüssel, die Schale
meat	das Fleisch	I don't eat **meat.**
vegetarian, *infml auch:* **veggie**	vegetarisch; der/die Vegetarier/in	... I'm a **vegetarian.** **vegan** = vegan; der Veganer, die Veganerin ! Betonung auf der 1. Silbe: **ve**gan No meat for me, please, and no cheese or butter: I'm a **vegan.**
cheese	der Käse	
pea	die Erbse	**peas** 
tomato, *pl* **tomatoes**	die Tomate	**tomato sauce** (die Tomatensoße)  **tomato**
spice	das Gewürz	noun: **spice** – adjective: **spicy** (würzig) **noun + -y → adjective** cloud → cloudy, rain → rainy mess → messy, snow → snowy ***but:*** fun → fu**nn**y, sun → su**nn**y spic**e** → spicy
usually	normalerweise, meistens	
bread	das Brot	**white bread**  **black bread** 
rice	der Reis	**rice** with **vegetables** 
vegetables *(pl)*	das Gemüse	
recipe	das (Koch-)Rezept	**recipe book** = das Kochbuch
health	die Gesundheit	Do sport and eat **healthy** food – it's good for your **health!** noun: **health** – adjective: **healthy** (gesund)

reason	der Grund, die Begründung	! for **this reason** = **aus** diesem Grund
religious	religiös	adjective: **religious** – noun: **religion** (die Religion) ! Betonung auf der 2. Silbe: religious / religion

Topic 1

► p. 150	**invitation (to)**	die Einladung (zu, nach)	I have an **invitation to** Jill's party. noun: **invitation** – verb: (to) **invite** (einladen)
	sausage	das (Brat-, Bock-)Würstchen, die Wurst	
	cake	der Kuchen, die Torte	
	twelfth (12th) birthday	der zwölfte Geburtstag	

1st	2nd	3rd	4th	5th	8th	9th	12th
first	**second**	**third**	**fourth**	**fifth**	**eighth**	**ninth**	**twelfth**
erste(r, s)	zweite(r, s)	dritte(r, s)	vierte(r, s)	fünfte(r, s)	achte(r, s)	neunte(r, s)	zwölfte(r, s)

► Numbers, p. 307

The months (die Monate)

1 January der Januar	**4 April** der April	**7 July** der Juli	**10 October** der Oktober
2 February der Februar	**5 May** der Mai	**8 August** der August	**11 November** der November
3 March der März	**6 June** der Juni	**9 September** der September	**12 December** der Dezember

	circus	der Zirkus	
	by phone	per Telefon / telefonisch	Please phone me and let me know. = Please let me know **by phone.**
	season	die Jahreszeit; die Saison	There are four seasons: **spring** (der Frühling), **summer, autumn** (der Herbst), **winter.**
► p. 151	**date**	das Datum	**date of birth** = das Geburtsdatum
	the first of April (1st April)	der erste April	
► p. 152	(to) **rest**	ruhen; sich ausruhen	verb: (to) **rest** – noun: **rest** (Ruhe, Pause, Erholung) (to) **take** a **rest** = eine Pause machen
	(to) **juggle**	jonglieren	He's **juggling** with balls. 
	(to) **sleep**	schlafen	verb: (to) **sleep** – noun: **sleep** (der Schlaf)
	must	müssen	**I must go.** = Ich muss Schluss machen. *(am Telefon/Briefschluss)* ! Kein **-s** bei *he / she / it:* Noah **must** go.
	(to) **teach**	lehren, unterrichten	Mr Schwarz is a teacher. He **teaches** English. My sister is **teaching** me to play the guitar. (... bringt mir das Gitarrespielen bei.)
► p. 153	(to) **lie**	liegen	! *-ing*-Form: **lying** – I'm **lying** on the sofa.
	balloon	der Ballon	

Topic 2

▶ p. 154	**present**	das Geschenk	a **present** 
	magic set	der Zauberkasten	**magic** = magisch, Zauber-; die Zauberei Let me show you a **magic trick**. (der Zaubertrick) Can you **do magic?** (Kannst du zaubern?)
	What about a … ?	Wie wäre es mit einer/einem … ?	! **What about …?** = **1. What about another sandwich?** Wie wär's mit noch einem Sandwich? **2. What about you?** Und du? / Was ist mit dir?
	sure	sicher	The next lesson is art. – Are you **sure?** Can you help me? – **Sure.** (Sicher! / Na klar!)
	already	schon	Get up! It's 7 o'clock **already!** – Go away! It's Sunday! ! Wortstellung: Noah **already** has bike lights. Noah hat **schon** Fahrradleuchten.
▶ p. 155	**kind (of)**	die Art (von), die Sorte (von)	• **What kind of** shoes do you usually wear? • all **kinds of** things (lauter Dinge, alles mögliche)
	menu	die Speisekarte	What can we eat at this restaurant? Let's look at the **menu.**
	ham	der Schinken	**salad** with **ham** 
	salad	der Salat *(als Gericht oder Beilage)*	
	carrot	die Möhre, die Karotte	
	melon	die Melone	! Betonung auf der 1. Silbe: **me**lon **watermelon** = die Wassermelone **water** = das Wasser
	lemonade	die Limonade	**Lemonade** is a sweet cold drink.
	shopping list	die Einkaufsliste	What do we need to buy at the supermarket? Let's make a **shopping list.** noun: **list** (die Liste) – verb: (to) **list** ((auf)listen)
	packet	die Packung, das Päckchen	a **packet** of **bread** (eine Packung Brot) 
	lemon	die Zitrone	**lemons** 
	sugar	der Zucker	There's a lot of **sugar** in these sweets.

▶ p. 156	**piece**	das Stück, der/das Teil	Your cake is great! Can I have another **piece,** please? **piece of paper** = das Stück Papier, der Zettel

Topic 3

▶ p. 158	**gram (g)**	das Gramm	100 **grams** of rice (100 Gramm Reis) 
	flour	das Mehl	You need **flour,** sugar and lemons to make these muffins.
	millilitre (ml)	der Milliliter	You need 200 **millilitres** of milk. (200 ml Milch)
	oil	das Öl	Oh no, look, now there's **oil** everywhere! 
	cocoa	der Kakao	! Beachte Aussprache und Schreibung! • Betonung auf der 1. Silbe: cocoa • *English:* **cocoa** – *German:* Kakao
	milk	die Milch	Cheese? **Milk** chocolate? No thanks, not for me. I'm vegan.
	egg	das Ei	**eggs, milk, flour, sugar** 
	salt	das Salz	I always put **salt** on my chips, but too much.
	teaspoon	der Teelöffel	**spoon** = der Löffel  **knife,** *pl* **knives** = das Messer **fork** = die Gabel **tablespoon** = der Esslöffel **teaspoon** = der Teelöffel
	vanilla	die Vanille	I like this dessert with custard or **vanilla** sauce.
	baking powder	das Backpulver	(to) **bake** = backen **powder** = das Pulver
	icing	die Glasur, der Zuckerguss	**icing sugar** = der Puderzucker
	butter	die Butter	You need milk to make **butter** or cream.
	mixture	die Mischung	noun: **mixture** – verb: (to) **mix** = mischen

	oven	der Backofen	Put the cake in the **oven** and bake it for 45 minutes.
	(to) **break** sth.	etwas zerbrechen	Let's **break** the chocolate **up,** then each of us can have some pieces.
	(to) **decorate**	dekorieren, schmücken	verb: (to) **decorate** – noun: **decoration** (die Dekoration, der Schmuck, die Verzierung) ! Achte auf die Betonung: (to) decorate / decoration
► p. 159	**better**	besser	**good – better – best** (to) **like sth. better** = etwas lieber mögen
	false	falsch, unrichtig	
	true	wahr, richtig	Is it **true** that you're the winner of the competition? Wow! Well done! **true ◄► false**
	(to) **fry**	braten; frittieren	I often **fry** vegetables in some oil and eat them with tomato sauce.
	savoury	herzhaft, salzig	**sweet** food **◄► savoury** food
	scone	*das kleine runde Milchbrötchen, leicht süß, oft mit Rosinen*	
	round	rund	! **round** = **1.** *(adjective)* A ball is **round.** (rund) **2.** *(noun)* Let's play a **round** of golf. (die Runde) **3.** *(preposition)* Let's walk **round** the park. (um (herum), in ... umher)
	jam	die Marmelade	**scones** with **cream** and **jam** 
	chicken	das Huhn; das (Brat-)Hähnchen	I'm a vegetarian, so I don't eat **chicken.**
	(to) **taste**	schmecken; kosten, probieren	• **Taste** these home-made burgers! (kosten, probieren) • They **taste** wonderful. (schmecken) verb: (to) **taste** – noun: **taste** (der Geschmack) – adjective: **tasty** (schmackhaft, lecker)
► p. 160	**main course**	das Hauptgericht	**►► main dish** **main** = Haupt-, wichtigste(r, s)
	(to) **be called**	heißen	• Our dog **is called** Fido. = Our dog's name is Fido. • We have a dog **called** Fido. (einen Hund, der Fido heißt / einen Hund mit Namen Fido)
	Nigeria	Nigeria	noun/country: **Nigeria** – adjective/person: **Nigerian** (nigerianisch; der Nigerianer, die Nigerianerin)

onion	die Zwiebel	an **onion** 
pepper	die Paprika, die Peperoni; der Pfeffer	
delicious	köstlich, lecker	This dessert with strawberries and cream is **delicious!** Can I have some more, please?
banana	die Banane	I love fruit like **bananas,** strawberries or melons.
honey	der Honig	**Honey** is sweet. Most vegan people don't eat it because it comes from animals.
important	wichtig	Listen, please. This is very **important.**
culture	die Kultur	! Betonung auf der 1. Silbe: **cul**ture
tradition	die Tradition	noun: **tradition** – adjective: **traditional** (traditionell) ! Betonung auf der 2. Silbe: tra**di**tion / tra**di**tional
Chinese	chinesisch; Chinesisch	adjective / language: **Chinese** – nouns: *(people)* **the Chinese** (die Chinesen, die Chinesinnen); *(country)* **China**
stir-fry	*das Gericht aus kurz angebratenen Zutaten, z.B. kleinen Stücken Fleisch, Fisch und/oder Gemüse*	noun: **stir-fry** verb: (to) **stir-fry sth.** (etwas unter Rühren scharf anbraten) I often **stir-fry** vegetables and eat the **stir-fry** with rice. (to) **stir** = (um)rühren
noodles *(pl)*	die Nudeln	! In China people have **noodles** in their meals. In Italy people eat **pasta.**
tea	der Tee	
coffee	der Kaffee	

Background file

▶ p. 161 **afternoon tea**	der Nachmittagstee, der Fünfuhrtee	
meal	die Mahlzeit, das Essen	Do you eat a hot **meal** at lunchtime? (warme Mahlzeit)
(to) **preheat (the oven to …)**	(den Backofen) vorheizen (auf)	verb: (to) **heat** (erwärmen, erhitzen) – noun: **heat** (die Hitze, die Wärme) – adjective: **hot**
(to) **roll (out)**	rollen; ausrollen *(Teig)*	**rolling out dough** 
dough	der Teig	

„Stumme" Buchstaben (Silent letters)
Manche Buchstaben, die in Wörtern geschrieben werden, sind „stumm" – du sprichst sie nicht aus:

Stummes d	Stummes gh	Stummes h	Stummes k	Stummes u	Stummes w
sandwich	**dough**	**hour**	**knife, knives**	**guess**	**answer**
Wednesday	**eight**	**what**	**know**	**guide**	**write**
	neighbour	**when**		**guitar**	**wrong**
	right				

▶ Words with silent letters, p. 213

glass	das Glas	! **a glass** of milk = ein Glas Milch
(to) **cut**	schneiden	(to) **cut sth. out** = etwas ausschneiden verb: (to) **cut** – noun: **cut** (der Schnitt)
potato, *pl* **potatoes**	die Kartoffel	
crumb	die Flocke, der Krümel	**cornflake crumbs** *(pl)* = die zerbröselten Cornflakes
garlic	der Knoblauch	**garlic** 

Story

▶ p. 162	(to) **wave (to** sb.**)**	(jm. zu)winken	Oh, there they are, but they don't see us! **Wave to** them! / Give them a **wave!** verb: (to) **wave** – noun: **wave** (das Winken) (to) **give sb. a wave** = jm. zuwinken
	(to) **be good at** sth. **/ at doing** sth.	etwas gut können; gut in etwas sein	You speak French, English and Russian? You're **good at** learning languages!
	just	nur, bloß; einfach	**Just** listen to me for five minutes, please. Don't **just** sit there! Get up and help me.
	a little	ein wenig, ein bisschen	Would you like sugar in your tea? – Yes, please, but only **a little.** (= not much) ! **little** = klein **a little** = ein wenig, ein bisschen
▶ p. 163	(to) **worry (about)**	sich Sorgen machen (wegen, um)	verb: (to) **worry (about)** – I **worry about** Dave. Why is he so sad? **Don't worry.** (Mach dir keine Sorgen.) adjective: **worried (about)** – I'**m worried about** Dave. (Ich bin beunruhigt/besorgt wegen ...)
	face	das Gesicht	
	(to) **smile**	lächeln	(to) **smile at sb.** = jn. anlächeln verb: (to) **smile** – noun: **smile** (das Lächeln)
	it is sb.'s **turn (to do** sth.**)**	jm. ist dran / an der Reihe (etwas zu tun	

When is (it) my turn (to play)?	Wann bin ich dran / an der Reihe (zu spielen)?
We're **taking turns** to play. = We're **taking it in turns** to play.	Wir wechseln uns (beim Spielen) ab. / Wir wechseln uns dabei ab, zu spielen.
Now **it's your turn** (to play).	Jetzt bist du dran / an der Reihe (zu spielen). / Jetzt bist du (beim Spielen) dran / an der Reihe.

Unit task

► p. 167	(to) **research**	erforschen, untersuchen, recherchieren	verb: (to) **research** – I'd like to **research** this topic. noun: **research** (die Forschung(en), die Recherche(n)) – I'd like to **do** some **research.** (recherchieren)
	(to) **boil**	kochen (in Wasser); sieden	! *German* **„kochen":** Let's **cook** a curry. (Mahlzeit zubereiten) Let's **boil** some eggs. ((in Wasser) kochen) The water is **boiling**. (sieden)
	introduction	die Einführung, die Einleitung	the first part of a presentation, a text, a book etc. where you tell people what you want to talk/write about
	instruction	die Anweisung	Do you always read the **instructions** when you get a new phone?

°Unit 6: The lost dog

Die Unit 6 ist keine Pflicht-Unit, deshalb sind die neuen Wörter alle mit einem Kringel (°) markiert.
Wenn du die Story liest, kannst du die neuen Wörter lernen, aber sie werden nicht in Band 2 vorausgesetzt.

► p. 182	°**bottle**	die Flasche	
	°**smooth**	gleichmäßig, glatt	
	°**cloudy**	trüb, milchig	
	°**rock**	der Fels(en)	! **rock** = der Fels(en) – **skirt** = der Rock
	°**several**	mehrere, einige	We have **several** bikes for under £400 in our shop.
	°**colourful**	farbig, bunt	a **colourful** toy train 
	°(to) **cry**	rufen, schreien; weinen	Babies **cry** when they're hungry.
	°**poor**	arm	**Poor dog!** = Der arme Hund!
	°**owner**	der Besitzer, die Besitzerin	Is this your dog? Are you its **owner?**
► p. 183	°**I'm glad**	ich bin froh	! Don't use **glad** in front of nouns: • **I'm glad / She's glad / We're glad that ...** • but: **a happy smile/day/child/family/...**
	°**(to) collect**	(ab)holen	! (to) **collect** = **1.** (ab)holen; **2.** (ein)sammeln
	°**child,** *pl* **children**	das Kind, die Kinder	►► kid(s) ! **one child – two children**
	°(to) **hope**	hoffen	Are there problems? I **hope** you're OK!

	°**animal shelter**	das Tierheim	Our dog is missing! Let's phone the **animal shelter.** Maybe they have him there.
	°(to) **keep**	behalten; halten	Can I use your pen? – Of course. You can **keep** it! I have lots of pens.
	°**a few**	ein paar, einige	You're hungry? There are still **a few** sandwiches in the kitchen. **a few ◄ ► a lot of / lots of / many**
	°(to) **whisper**	flüstern	Why are you **whispering?** – I think there's someone at the door.
	°(to) **follow**	(ver)folgen	Is someone **following** us? (= Is someone walking behind us?)
	°(to) **laugh (at)**	lachen (über)	Dad, that's not really funny. – So why are you **laughing**?
	°(to) **lick**	(ab)lecken	
	°(to) **leave**	lassen; zurücklassen	You can **leave** your bags in the classroom.
► p. 184	°**diary**	das Tagebuch; der Kalender	Sunday? Let me look in my **diary** ... 
	°(to) **be: it was**	sein: es war; es ist gewesen	The maths test **was** really hard.
	°(to) **come: they came**	kommen: sie kamen (mit); sie sind (mit)gekommen	They **came** to see him. = Sie kamen ihn besuchen.
	°**yesterday**	gestern	**Yesterday** was Monday, so today is Tuesday.
	°(to) **play: we played**	spielen: wir spielten; wir haben gespielt	I always **played** this game with my friends when I was a kid.
	°(to) **have: we had**	haben: wir hatten; wir haben gehabt	I **had** some problems with this exercise at first. It was really hard.
	°**tomorrow**	morgen	Yesterday was Friday, today is Saturday, **tomorrow** is Sunday.
	°(to) **kick**	treten; *(Sport)* schießen	Lily **kicks** the ball ...
	°(to) **run for** sth.	hinter etwas herlaufen	... and her dog **runs for** it.
	°**What's wrong?**	Was ist los? / Was/Wo ist das Problem?	**What's wrong with Zane?** = Was ist mit Zane los?
	°(to) **see: they saw**	sehen: sie sahen; sie haben gesehen	I was at the beach and **saw** lots of seagulls!
	°(to) **look for**	suchen; Ausschau halten nach	I'm **looking for** my red T-shirt. Do you know where it is?
► p. 185	°**tear**	die Träne	When you cry, there are **tears** in your eyes.
	°(to) **kiss**	(sich) küssen	
	°**doorbell**	die (Tür-)Klingel	
	°**in**	herein; hinein	**Come in!** = Komm/Kommt/Kommen Sie herein!

	°(to) **wag**	wedeln (mit)	The dog's **tail** is **wagging.** (wedeln) The dog is **wagging its tail.** (wedeln mit)
	°**tail**	der Schwanz	
	°**granddaughter**	die Enkelin	►► your child's daughter
	°**age**	das Alter	**She's your age.** = Sie ist in deinem/eurem Alter
	°**about**	ungefähr	We get up at **about** 8.30 on Sundays. **!** **about** = **1.** ungefähr; **2.** von, über (Präposition)
	°**strong**	stark	**strong** 
	°(to) **hug** (sb.)	(jn.) umarmen; einander umarmen	I'm so happy to see you! Let me **hug** you.
► p. 186	°**wonderful**	wunderbar	►► very good, great
	°(to) **give: she gave**	geben: sie gab; sie hat gegeben	We all **gave** some money for Zoe's birthday present.
► p. 187	°**tonight**	heute Abend, heute Nacht	I'm going to the cinema **tonight**. Are you free?
► p. 188	°**tall**	groß *(Person);* hoch *(Gebäude)*	Only a **tall** person can put something on the top of that shelf.
	°**hair**	das Haar, die Haare	*English:* Your **hair is** black. *German:* Deine **Haare sind** schwarz.
	°**through**	durch	Let's walk **through** the park, not down the street.
	°**police** *(pl)*	die Polizei	**!** Das Wort **police** steht immer im Plural! Where **are** the **police**? Call **them**! (Wo ist die Polizei? Ruf sie!)
	°**pocket**	die Tasche *(an Kleidungsstücken)*	This anorak has a special **pocket** for a phone.
	°(to) **fall down**	hinfallen	
	°**policewoman,** *pl* **policewomen**	die Polizistin	Jane works for the police: she's a **policewoman**.
	°(to) **run over**	hinüber-/herüberrennen	
	°**police officer**	der Polizeibeamte, die Polizeibeamtin	That **police officer** is waving at us. Stop the car!
► p. 189	°**out of ...**	aus ... (heraus/hinaus)	Take the cake **out of** the oven after 45 minutes. **out of ...** ◄► **into ...**
	°(to) **find: they found**	finden: sie fanden; sie haben gefunden	When we had our clean-up day, we **found** interesting things.
	°**past**	die Vergangenheit	"Yesterday was Sunday." is a sentence about the **past.**

Ähnliche Wörter im Englischen und Deutschen

Viele englische Wörter ähneln deutschen Wörtern: *a cowboy* = ein Cowboy.
Beachte aber die Unterschiede 1–3!
(1) Nomen werden im Deutschen großgeschrieben, aber im Englischen klein.
(2) Verben haben im Deutschen andere Endungen, aber einen ähnlichen Stamm, z.B. planen – *(to) plan.*
(3) Oft unterscheidet sich die Aussprache. Höre dir die blau markierten Wörter in der App an und sprich sie nach.

active / activity
address
allergic (to)
alphabet
app
April
article
August
badminton
balcony
ball
banana
band
barbecue
basketball
biology
blazer
bowling
box
(to) bring
British
browser
burger
bus
butter
cafe
card
check
chocolate
circus
city
class
classroom
clever
club
coffee
cola
comic
computer
console
cool
corridor
cost / (to) cost
cousin
culture
curry

dance / (to) dance
December
drama
drink / (to) drink
electric
elephant
end / (to) end
England / English
family
fan
February
feedback
film
(to) find
fish
football
Friday
friend / friendly
garage
garden
gold
group
hamster
happy
Hello
highlight
hockey
hot dog
house
hungry
idea
information
internet
January
July
June
karaoke
kebab
kid
kilometre (km)
kiosk
lamp
market
maths
melon
milk

millilitre
mini
minute
modern
moment
Monday
museum
music
name
November
number
October
online
park
parkour
partner
party
pasta
perfect
person
photo
picnic
plan / (to) plan
playlist
pool
popcorn
post
poster
problem
project
restaurant
ring
robot
room
rucksack
salad
sandwich
sauce
school
(to) send
September
shopping centre
silver
skateboard
skatepark
smart

snack
sofa
software
song
sport
star
stop
story
street dance
student
summer
Sunday
supermarket
surfing
sweatshirt
(to) swim
swimmer
test / (to) test
text / (to) text
ticket
tip
title
toilet
tomato
top
tourist
tradition
trainer / training
trick
T-shirt
uniform
vanilla
vegan
vegetarian / veggie
video
warm
website
wind
winner
winter
word
yoga
zoo

Im *Dictionary* kannst du nachschlagen, was ein Wort bedeutet oder wie es ausgesprochen wird.

Im *Dictionary* werden folgende **Abkürzungen und Symbole** verwendet:

Infml = informal (umgangssprachlich)
sb. = somebody (jemand)
jd. = jemand
jm. = jemandem
pl = plural (Mehrzahl)
sth. = something (etwas)
jn. = jemanden

° Mit diesem Kringel sind Wörter markiert, die nicht zum Lernwortschatz gehören.

Die **Fundstellenangaben** zeigen, wo ein Wort zum ersten Mal vorkommt. Die Ziffern in Klammern bezeichnen Seitenzahlen.

1 (26) = Unit 1, Seite 26

A

a [ə] ein, eine (10/11) **a seagull** eine Möwe (10/11)
about [əˈbaʊt]:
1. **about me/you/...** über mich/dich/... (14)
What about a ... ? Wie wäre es mit einer/einem ... ? 5 (154)
What about you? Und du? / Was ist mit dir? (10/11)
°2. ungefähr
act [ækt] aufführen, spielen 1 (34)
act sth. out etwas vorspielen, aufführen 1 (34)
acting [ˈæktɪŋ] die Schauspielerei 1 (34)
°action [ˈækʃn] die Aktion, die Handlung
active [ˈæktɪv] aktiv 2 (55)
activity [ækˈtɪvəti] die Aktivität, die Tätigkeit 1 (29)
add [æd] hinzufügen, addieren 3 (103)
address [əˈdres] die Adresse 2 (68)
after [ˈɑːftə]:
1. **after (school)** nach (der Schule) 1 (30)
°Repeat after me: .... Sprich mir nach: .... / Wiederhole: ....
2. **after (you read)** nachdem (du liest) 1 (30)
afternoon [ɑːftəˈnuːn] der Nachmittag 3 (86) **in the afternoon** nachmittags, am Nachmittag 3 (86)
afternoon tea [ɑːftənuːn ˈtiː] der Nachmittagstee, der Fünfuhrtee 5 (161)
again [əˈgen] wieder, noch einmal 1 (22)
°age [eɪdʒ] das Alter **She's your age.** Sie ist in deinem/eurem Alter.
°agree on [əˈgriː ɒn] sich einigen auf
all [ɔːl] alle(s) (16) **all the time** die ganze Zeit, ständig 3 (94) **all weekend** das ganze Wochenende 3 (94) **°all the family** die ganze Familie
allergic (to) [əˈlɜːdʒɪk] allergisch (gegen) 5 (148/149)
°almost [ˈɔːlməʊst] fast, nahezu, beinahe
alone [əˈləʊn] allein 1 (28)
alphabet [ˈælfəbet] das Alphabet 2 (68)
°alphabetical [ælfəˈbetɪkl] alphabetisch
already [ɔːlˈredi] schon 5 (154)
also [ˈɔːlsəʊ] auch 4 (121)
always [ˈɔːlweɪz] immer 1 (28)
am [æm]: **I'm (= I am)** ich bin (10/11)
a.m. [eɪˈem]: **4 a.m.** 4 Uhr (früh) morgens 3 (86) **9 a.m.** 9 Uhr vormittags 3 (86)
amazing [əˈmeɪzɪŋ] erstaunlich; großartig 4 (126)
an [ən] ein/e *(vor Vokalen)* (14)
and [ænd], [ənd] und (10/11)
angry [ˈæŋgri] wütend 2 (52)
animal [ˈænɪml] das Tier (12)
°animal shelter [ˈænɪml ʃeltə] das Tierheim
another [əˈnʌðə] ein/e andere/r/s; noch ein/e 4 (123)
answer [ˈɑːnsə]:
1. die Antwort 1 (23)
2. (be)antworten 1 (23)
any [ˈeni]: **Do you have any questions?** Habt ihr / Hast du (irgendwelche) Fragen? 4 (134)
there aren't any ... es gibt keine ... 4 (134)
°anything [ˈeniθɪŋ]: **not (...) anything** nichts
app [æp] die App 1 (36)
apple [ˈæpl] der Apfel 1 (21)
April [ˈeɪprəl] der April 4 (130)
are [ɑː]: **we/they are** wir/sie sind 1 (24) **we/they aren't** wir/sie sind nicht 1 (24) **you are** du bist / ihr seid (10/11)
art [ɑːt] die Kunst 1 (21)
article [ˈɑːtɪkl] der Artikel 3 (98)
as [æz], [əz]: **as the winner** als Gewinner/in 3 (99) **°as many as you can** so viele (wie) du kannst
ask [ɑːsk]:
1. fragen 1 (23)
ask a question eine Frage stellen 1 (23)
2. **ask sb. for sth.** jn. um etwas bitten 3 (94)
ask sb. to do sth. jn. bitten, etwas zu tun 3 (94)
asleep [əˈsliːp]: **be asleep** schlafen 1 (24)
assembly [əˈsembli] die Schulversammlung 1 (26)
at [æt], [ət] an; in; bei; auf 1 (18/19)
at 8 o'clock um 8 Uhr 3 (86)
at night nachts, in der Nacht 1 (25)
at the cinema im Kino 4 (116/117)
at work bei der Arbeit, am Arbeitsplatz 2 (52) **be good at sth. / at doing sth.** etwas gut können; gut in etwas sein 5 (162) **Open your books at page 10.** Schlagt eure Bücher auf Seite 10 auf. (17)
°at least wenigstens, **°at three** um drei (Uhr)
°aubergine [ˈəʊbəʒiːn] die Aubergine
audience [ˈɔːdiəns] das Publikum; die Zuschauer/innen, die Zuhörer/innen 4 (134)
August [ˈɔːgəst] der August 5 (150)
aunt [ɑːnt] die Tante 2 (50/51)
autumn [ˈɔːtəm] der Herbst 5 (150)
°avocado [ævəˈkɑːdəʊ] die Avocado
away [əˈweɪ] weg, fort 1 (31)

B

back [bæk]:
1. zurück 2 (65)
back at home wieder zu Hause 2 (65)
°2. der Rücken; die Rückseite, der hintere Teil
°at the back hinten **°at the back of your book** hinten in deinem Buch **°on the back of the card** auf der Rückseite der Karte
°background [ˈbækgraʊnd] der Hintergrund
°background file [ˈbækgraʊnd faɪl] die Hintergrundinformation(en)
bad [bæd] schlecht; schlimm 1 (29)
badminton [ˈbædmɪntən] das Badminton, der Federball *(Spiel)* 1 (18/19)
bag [bæg] die Tasche 1 (28)
bake [beɪk] backen 5 (158)
°baked beans *(pl)* [beɪkt ˈbiːnz] die weißen Bohnen in Tomatensauce
baking powder [ˈbeɪkɪŋ paʊdə] das Backpulver 5 (158)
balcony [ˈbælkəni] der Balkon 2 (56)

ball [bɔːl] der Ball 3 (97)
balloon [bəˈluːn] der Ballon 5 (153)
banana [bəˈnɑːnə] die Banane 5 (160)
band [bænd] die Band, die Musikgruppe 1 (30)
bank [bæŋk] die Bank *(Geldinstitut)* 3 (100)
barbecue [ˈbɑːbɪkjuː] das Grillfest, das Grillen 4 (126)
bark [bɑːk]:
1. das Bellen 4 (131)
2. **bark (at sb.)** (jn. an)bellen 4 (131)
basketball [ˈbɑːskɪtbɔːl] der Basketball 1 (18/19)
bat [bæt] der Schläger *(Sport)* 3 (97)
bathroom [ˈbɑːθruːm] das Bad(ezimmer) 2 (57)
be [biː] sein 1 (20)
beach [biːtʃ] der Strand 1 (32) **on the beach** am Strand 1 (32) **to the beach** zum Strand, an den Strand 1 (32)
beautiful [ˈbjuːtɪfl] wunderschön 4 (129)
because [bɪˈkɒz] weil 1 (27)
bed [bed] das Bett 2 (60) **go to bed** ins Bett gehen 2 (60)
bedroom [ˈbedruːm] das Schlafzimmer 2 (57)
before [bɪˈfɔː]:
1. **before (the lesson)** vor (der Unterrichtsstunde) 1 (37)
2. **before (you take a photo)** bevor (du ein Foto machst) 1 (37)
behind [bɪˈhaɪnd] hinter 2 (60)
°**below** [bɪˈləʊ] unten; unter(halb von)
best [best] beste(r, s); am besten 3 (87)
better [ˈbetə] besser 5 (159) **like sth. better** etwas lieber mögen 5 (159)
between [bɪˈtwiːn] zwischen 2 (60)
big [bɪg] groß (15)
biggest [ˈbɪgɪst] der/die/das größte; am größten 4 (122)
bike [baɪk] das Fahrrad (15)
bin [bɪn] der (Müll-)Eimer 4 (118)
biology [baɪˈɒlədʒi] die Biologie 1 (27)
°**bird** [bɜːd] der Vogel
birthday [ˈbɜːθdeɪ] der Geburtstag 5 (148/149) **Happy birthday!** Herzlichen Glückwunsch zum Geburtstag! 5 (148/149) **My birthday is in April.** Ich habe im April Geburtstag. 5 (148/149) **on my birthday** an meinem Geburtstag 5 (148/149) **When's your birthday?** Wann hast du Geburtstag? 5 (148/149)
black [blæk] schwarz (10/11)
blazer [ˈbleɪzə] der Blazer *(Jackett)* 1 (20)
block [blɒk] der (Wohn-)Block 2 (59)
block of flats [blɒk əv ˈflæts] das Mehrfamilienhaus 2 (59)
blue [bluː] blau (10/11)
board [bɔːd]:
1. die Tafel (17)
°2. das Spielbrett
°**board game** [ˈbɔːd geɪm] das Brettspiel
°**body** [ˈbɒdi] der Körper
boil [bɔɪl] kochen *(in Wasser)*; sieden 5 (167)
book [bʊk] das Buch (15)
boring [ˈbɔːrɪŋ] langweilig 4 (116/117)
°**bottle** [ˈbɒtl] die Flasche
°**bottom** [ˈbɒtəm] **at the bottom of the page** unten auf der Seite
bowling [ˈbəʊlɪŋ] das Bowling, das Kegeln 4 (116/117)
°**box** [bɒks] die Box, der Kasten
box [bɒks] boxen 4 (120)
boxing [ˈbɒksɪŋ] das Boxen 4 (120)
boy [bɔɪ] der Junge 1 (20)
°**brainstorm** [ˈbreɪnstɔːm] Ideen (ungeordnet) sammeln
brave [breɪv] mutig 1 (32)
bread [bred] das Brot 5 (148/149)
break [breɪk] die Pause 1 (24) **at break** in der Pause 1 (24)
break sth. [breɪk] etwas zerbrechen 5 (158)
breakfast [ˈbrekfəst] das Frühstück 3 (87)
bring [brɪŋ] bringen, mitbringen 4 (129)
Britain [ˈbrɪtn] Großbritannien 1 (20)
British [ˈbrɪtɪʃ] britisch 1 (20)
°**bro** [brəʊ] *(infml für* **brother***)* der Bruder, der Kumpel
brother [ˈbrʌðə] der Bruder 2 (50/51)
brown [braʊn] braun (10/11)
browser [ˈbraʊzə] der Browser *(Computerprogramm zum Finden und Lesen von Websites)* 4 (135)
brush [brʌʃ]:
1. die Bürste 3 (89)
2. bürsten 3 (89)
brush your teeth (sich) die Zähne putzen 3 (89)
building [ˈbɪldɪŋ] das Gebäude 1 (28)
bully [ˈbʊli]:
1. der Mobber, die Mobberin / der Tyrann, die Tyrannin 1 (32)
2. tyrannisieren, mobben 1 (32)
burger [ˈbɜːgə] der Hamburger *(Frikadelle)* 3 (102)
°**burn** [bɜːn] brennen
bus [bʌs] der Bus 3 (84/85) **by bus** mit dem Bus 3 (84/85) **on the bus** im Bus 3 (84/85) °**catch the bus** den Bus nehmen, erwischen
bus stop [ˈbʌs stɒp] die Bushaltestelle 4 (127)
busy [ˈbɪzi]:
1. hektisch, belebt 4 (116/117)
2. (viel)beschäftigt 1 (20)
be busy (viel) beschäftigt sein, (viel) zu tun haben 1 (20)
but [bʌt], [bət] aber (16)
butter [ˈbʌtə] die Butter 5 (158)
buy [baɪ] kaufen 4 (120)
by [baɪ]: **by bus** mit dem Bus 3 (84/85) **by phone** per Telefon / telefonisch 5 (150) **by the sea** am Meer, an der See 3 (90)
Bye. [baɪ] Tschüs. / Auf Wiedersehen. (10/11)

C

cafe [ˈkæfeɪ] das Café 3 (87)
cake [keɪk] der Kuchen, die Torte 5 (150)
°**calendar** [ˈkælɪndə] der Kalender
call [kɔːl]:
1. nennen; rufen; anrufen 2 (54)
be called heißen 5 (160)
2. der Ruf 2 (54)
3. *(kurz für:* **phone call***)* der (Telefon-)Anruf 2 (54)
called ... [kɔːld] mit Namen ..., der/die ... heißt 5 (160)
°**came** [keɪm]: **they came** sie kamen (mit); sie sind (mit)gekommen **They came to see him.** Sie kamen ihn besuchen.
can [kæn], [kən] können (12) **I can't (= cannot) see ....** Ich kann ... nicht sehen. (12)
canteen [kænˈtiːn] die Kantine, die (Schul-)Mensa 1 (28)
cap [kæp] die (Schirm-)Mütze, die Kappe (15)
car [kɑː] das Auto 3 (84/85)
car light [ˈkɑː laɪt] der Autoscheinwerfer 3 (103)
card [kɑːd] die Karte 3 (102) **playing card** die Spielkarte 3 (102)
careful [ˈkeəfl] vorsichtig (10/11)
carrot [ˈkærət] die Möhre, die Karotte 5 (155)
case [keɪs] das Etui, der Behälter, der Kasten 1 (21)
cat [kæt] die Katze (14) **rain cats and dogs** stark regnen 4 (129)
°**catch** [kætʃ] **catch the bus** den Bus nehmen, erwischen
°**'cause** [kɔːz] *(infml)* weil (= because)
°**Celsius** [ˈselsiəs]: **degree Celsius (°C)** das/der Grad Celsius
cent [sent] der Cent 3 (100)
centre [ˈsentə] das Zentrum; die Mitte 4 (118)
chain [tʃeɪn] die Kette (15)
chair [tʃeə] der Stuhl 2 (60)
°**challenge** [ˈtʃælɪndʒ] die Herausforderung
change [tʃeɪndʒ]:
1. **change (into)** (sich) (ver)ändern (zu/in); wechseln; (sich) verwandeln (in), werden (zu) 4 (129)
2. die Veränderung, der Wechsel, die Verwandlung 4 (129)
°**chant** [tʃɑːnt]:
1. der Sprechchor, der (Sprech-)Gesang
2. singen *(Sprechgesänge)*
character [ˈkærəktə] der Charakter; die Figur *(aus einer Geschichte)* 1 (32)
check [tʃek]:
1. (über)prüfen, kontrollieren 1 (26)
2. die (Über-)Prüfung, die Kontrolle 1 (26)
°**checkpoint** [ˈtʃekpɔɪnt] der Kontrollpunkt
cheese [tʃiːz] der Käse 5 (148/149)
°**chess** [tʃes] das Schach

chicken [ˈtʃɪkɪn] das Huhn; das (Brat-) Hähnchen 5 (159)
°**chicken stock** [ˈtʃɪkɪn stɒk] die Hühnerbrühe
°**child** [tʃaɪld], *pl* **children** das Kind
°**children** [tʃɪldrən] *Plural von* **child**
°**chill** [tʃɪl] *(infml)* relaxen, sich ausruhen
China [ˈtʃaɪnə] China 5 (160)
Chinese [tʃaɪˈni:z]:
1. chinesisch; Chinesisch 5 (160)
2. **the Chinese** die Chinesen 5 (160)
chips *(pl)* [tʃɪps] die Pommes frites 4 (116/117) **fish and chips** der Fisch mit Pommes frites 4 (116/117)
chocolate [ˈtʃɒklət] die Schokolade 2 (60) **hot chocolate** der Kakao, die heiße (Trink-)Schokolade 4 (128)
choose [tʃu:z] (aus)wählen 3 (87)
Christmas [ˈkrɪsməs] (das) Weihnachten 5 (148/149)
Christmas Day [krɪsməs ˈdeɪ] der 1. Weihnachtstag (25. 12.) 5 (148/149)
cinema [ˈsɪnəmə] das Kino 4 (116/117) **at the cinema** im Kino 4 (116/117)
circle [ˈsɜ:kl] der Kreis 2 (50/51)
circus [ˈsɜ:kəs] der Zirkus 5 (150)
city [ˈsɪti] die City, die (Groß-) Stadt 3 (90)
°**clap** [klæp] klatschen
class [klɑ:s] die Klasse; der Unterricht; der Kurs (10/11) **in class** im Unterricht (10/11)
class teacher [ˈklɑ:s ti:tʃə] der Klassenlehrer, die Klassenlehrerin 1 (22)
°**classmate** [ˈklɑ:smeɪt] der Mitschüler, die Mitschülerin
classroom [ˈklɑ:sru:m] das Klassenzimmer 1 (23)
clean [kli:n]:
1. sauber 4 (118)
°**get clean** sauber werden
2. sauber machen, putzen 4 (118)
clean sth. up etwas aufräumen, sauber machen 4 (130)
clean-up [ˈkli:n ʌp] das Säubern, das Saubermachen 4 (130)
clean-up day [ˈkli:n ʌp deɪ] der Dreck-weg-Tag *(Aktionstag zum Müllsammeln)* 4 (130)
cleaner [ˈkli:nə] die Reinigungskraft 3 (100)
clear [klɪə] klar, deutlich 3 (103)
clearly [ˈklɪəli]: **speak clearly** deutlich sprechen 3 (103)
clever [ˈklevə] schlau, klug (10/11)
clock [klɒk] die (Wand-, Stand-, Turm-)Uhr 3 (86)
close [kləʊz] schließen, zumachen (17)
closed [kləʊzd] geschlossen (17)
clothes *(pl)* [kləʊðz] die Kleidung, die Kleidungsstücke 2 (60)
clothes swap [ˈkləʊðz swɒp] der Kleidertausch, die Kleidertauschparty 4 (128)
clotted cream [klɒtɪd ˈkri:m] die besonders dicke Sahne, der Streichrahm 5 (148/149)
cloud [klaʊd] die Wolke 4 (126) **have your head in the clouds** in Gedanken verloren / unrealistisch sein 4 (129)
cloudy [ˈklaʊdi]:
1. wolkig, bewölkt 4 (126)
°2. trüb, milchig
club [klʌb] der Klub, der Verein 1 (31) **join a club** bei einer AG mitmachen, in einen Klub eintreten 3 (90) **school club** die AG *(in der Schule)* 1 (31)
cocoa [ˈkəʊkəʊ] der Kakao 5 (158)
code [kəʊd]:
1. programmieren *(Computer)*; kodieren 1 (18/19)
2. der Code 1 (18/19)
3. die Vorwahl(nummer) 1 (18/19)
coding [ˈkəʊdɪŋ] das Programmieren 1 (18/19)
coffee [ˈkɒfi] der Kaffee 5 (160)
cola [ˈkəʊlə] die Cola 3 (102)
cold [kəʊld]:
1. kalt 4 (126)
be cold frieren 4 (126)
2. die Kälte 4 (126)
3. die Erkältung 4 (126)
have a cold erkältet sein 4 (126)
collect [kəˈlekt]:
1. (ein)sammeln 3 (102)
°2. (ab)holen
colour [ˈkʌlə] die Farbe (10/11) **What colour is ...?** Welche Farbe hat ...? (10/11)
°**colourful** [ˈkʌləfl] farbig, bunt
come [kʌm] (mit)kommen 3 (84/85) **come rain or shine** bei jedem Wetter; was auch (immer) geschieht 4 (129)
comic [ˈkɒmɪk] der Comic 3 (90)
°**comment on sth.** [ˈkɒment] etwas kommentieren
°**compare** [kəmˈpeə] vergleichen
competition [kɒmpəˈtɪʃn] der Wettbewerb 3 (87)
°**complete** [kəmˈpli:t] vervollständigen
computer [kəmˈpju:tə] der Computer 1 (28)
computing [kəmˈpju:tɪŋ] die Informatik 1 (26)
°**concert** [ˈkɒnsət] das Konzert
console [kənˈsəʊl] die Konsole 3 (100)
continue [kənˈtɪnju:] fortfahren, weitermachen; (sich) fortsetzen, weitergehen 4 (134) **continue to do sth.** etwas weiterhin tun, (mit) etwas weitermachen, fortfahren 4 (134)
°**conversation** [kɒnvəˈseɪʃn] das Gespräch
cook [kʊk]:
1. der Koch, die Köchin 1 (18/19)
2. kochen 1 (18/19)
cooking [ˈkʊkɪŋ]:
1. das Kochen 1 (18/19)
2. das *(gekochte)* Essen 4 (118)
cool [ku:l] cool (15)
°**copy** [ˈkɒpi] kopieren, abschreiben
cornflake crumbs *(pl)* [ˈkɔ:nfleɪk krʌmz] die zerbröselten Cornflakes 5 (161)
cornflakes *(pl)* [ˈkɔ:nfleɪks] die Cornflakes 5 (161)
°**correct** [kəˈrekt]:
1. korrekt
2. korrigieren
corridor [ˈkɒrɪdɔ:] der Korridor 1 (28)
cost [kɒst]:
1. die Kosten; der Preis 4 (127)
2. kosten 4 (127)
cottage [ˈkɒtɪdʒ] das Häuschen, das Cottage *(kleines Haus, meist auf dem Land)* 2 (59)
°**count** [kaʊnt] zählen
country [ˈkʌntri] das Land, *(auch:)* die ländliche Gegend 3 (89)
course [ˈkɔ:s]:
1. **main course** das Hauptgericht 5 (160)
°2. der Kurs(us)
cousin [ˈkʌzn] der Cousin, die Cousine 2 (50/51)
crack [kræk] lösen *(z.B. Problem)*, knacken *(z.B. Code)* 3 (97)
crafts *(pl)* [krɑ:fts] das Kunsthandwerk, das Basteln 4 (120)
cream [kri:m] die Sahne 5 (148/149)
°**creative commons** [krieɪtɪv ˈkɒmənz] „das schöpferische Gemeingut" *(gemeinnützige Organisation, die das einfache Verbreiten von Nutzungsrechten zum Ziel hat)*
cricket [ˈkrɪkɪt]:
1. das Kricket *(Mannschaftssportart)* 3 (90)
2. die Grille *(Insekt)* 3 (97)
°**cross** [krɒs] mit einem Kreuz versehen **cross sth. out** etwas durchstreichen
crumb [krʌm] die Flocke, der Krümel 5 (161) **cornflake crumbs** *(pl)* die zerbröselten Cornflakes 5 (161)
°**cry** [kraɪ] rufen, schreien; weinen
culture [ˈkʌltʃə] die Kultur 5 (160)
curry [ˈkʌri] das Curry *(Gewürz und auch Gericht)* 5 (166)
cushion [ˈkʊʃn] das Kissen 2 (60)
custard [ˈkʌstəd] der Custard *(Vanillesoße)* 5 (148/149)
cut [kʌt]:
1. der Schnitt 5 (161)
2. schneiden 5 (161)
cut sth. out etwas ausschneiden 5 (161)
cute [kju:t] niedlich, süß 2 (55)
cycle [ˈsaɪkl] Rad fahren 3 (90)
cycling [ˈsaɪklɪŋ] das Radfahren 3 (90)

D

dad [dæd] der Papa, der Vati (12)
°**daily** [ˈdeɪli] täglich
dance [dɑ:ns]:
1. tanzen (15)
2. der Tanz (15)
do a dance einen Tanz tanzen (15)

dancer [ˈdɑːnsə] der Tänzer, die Tänzerin (15)
dancing [ˈdɑːnsɪŋ] das Tanzen (15)
date [deɪt] das Datum 5(151) **date of birth** das Geburtsdatum 5(151)
daughter [ˈdɔːtə] die Tochter 2(50/51)
day [deɪ] der Tag 1(25) **work long days** lange arbeiten, lange Arbeitstage haben 3(87)
dead [ded] tot 4(131) °**My phone is dead.** Mein Telefon-Akku ist leer.
Dear … [dɪə] Liebe/r … 1(25)
December [dɪˈsembə] der Dezember 5(150)
°**decide** [dɪˈsaɪd] beschließen, sich entscheiden
decorate [ˈdekəreɪt] dekorieren, schmücken 5(158)
decoration [dekəˈreɪʃn] die Dekoration, der Schmuck, die Verzierung 5(158)
degree (°) [dɪˈgriː] das/der Grad 4(127)
delicious [dɪˈlɪʃəs] köstlich, lecker 5(160)
describe [dɪˈskraɪb] beschreiben 2(59)
description [dɪˈskrɪpʃn] die Beschreibung 2(59)
design [dɪˈzaɪn]:
1. die Gestaltung, das Design 1(26)
2. entwerfen, gestalten 3(97)
design and technology [dɪzaɪn ən tekˈnɒlədʒi] das Werken, der Werkunterricht 1(26)
desk [desk] der Schreibtisch 1(21)
dessert [dɪˈzɜːt] die Nachspeise, das Dessert 5(148/149) **for dessert** zum/als Nachtisch 5(148/149)
detached home/house [dɪˈtætʃt] das frei stehende Haus 2(59)
°**dialogue** [ˈdaɪəlɒg] der Dialog
°**diary** [ˈdaɪəri] das Tagebuch; der Kalender
°**dice** [daɪs], *pl* **dice** der Würfel **throw the dice** würfeln
°**dictionary** [ˈdɪkʃənri] das Wörterbuch, das *(alphabetische)* Wörterverzeichnis
difference [ˈdɪfrəns] der Unterschied 1(22)
different (to) [ˈdɪfrənt] verschieden; anders (als) 1(22)
difficult [ˈdɪfɪkəlt] schwierig, schwer 1(37)
dig [dɪg] graben 4(131)
°**digital** [ˈdɪdʒɪtl] digital
dining room [ˈdaɪnɪŋ ruːm] das Esszimmer 2(57)
dinner [ˈdɪnə] das Abendessen 2(65) **for dinner** zum Abendessen 2(65)
dirty [ˈdɜːti] schmutzig 4(118)
°**discuss** [dɪˈskʌs] diskutieren
dish [dɪʃ]:
1. die Schüssel, die Schale 5(148/149)
2. das Gericht *(Mahlzeit)* 5(148/149) **main dish** das Hauptgericht 5(160)
do [duː] machen, tun (16) **do your homework** Hausaufgaben machen 2(54) °**do sport(s)** Sport treiben
dog [dɒg] der Hund (12) **rain cats and dogs** stark regnen 4(129)
done [dʌn]: **Well done.** Gut gemacht! 3(99)
door [dɔː] die Tür 2(61)
°**doorbell** [ˈdɔːbel] die (Tür-)Klingel
°**double** [ˈdʌbl] doppelt, Doppel-
dough [dəʊ] der Teig 5(161)
down [daʊn] hinunter, herunter 4(126)
°**down there** [daʊn ˈðeə] dort runter, dort hinunter; dort unten
drama [ˈdrɑːmə] das Schauspiel, die darstellende Kunst 3(90)
draw [drɔː] zeichnen (15)
drawing [ˈdrɔːɪŋ]:
1. die Zeichnung (15)
2. das Zeichnen (15)
dream [driːm]:
1. der Traum 2(55)
2. **dream (of/about sth.)** träumen (von etwas) 2(55)
dressed [drest]: **get dressed** sich anziehen 3(87)
drink [drɪŋk]:
1. das Getränk (12)
2. trinken (12)
drone [drəʊn] die Drohne 5(154)
duke [djuːk] der Herzog 4(116/117)

E

each [iːtʃ] jede(r, s) (einzelne), jeweils 2(56)
°**early** [ˈɜːli] früh
°**easy** [ˈiːzi] einfach, leicht
eat [iːt] essen; fressen (12)
egg [eg] das Ei 5(158)
eight [eɪt] acht (10/11)
eighteen [eɪˈtiːn] achtzehn 2(68)
eighty [ˈeɪti] achtzig 2(68)
electric [ɪˈlektrɪk] elektrisch, Elektro- 2(65)
elephant [ˈelɪfənt] der Elefant (14)
eleven [ɪˈlevən] elf (10/11)
else [els]: **What else?** Was sonst noch? 4(120)
end [end]:
1. enden; beenden 3(86)
2. das Ende, der Schluss 3(86) **at the end (of)** am Ende (von) 3(86) **in the end** schließlich; zum Schluss 3(86)
°**ending** [ˈendɪŋ] das Ende *(Satz, Text)*
England [ˈɪŋglənd] England 1(21)
English [ˈɪŋglɪʃ] das Englisch; englisch 1(21)
enjoy [ɪnˈdʒɔɪ] genießen 5(148/149) **enjoy doing sth.** es genießen, etwas zu tun 5(148/149) **Enjoy!** Viel Vergnügen! / Guten Appetit! 5(148/149)
enough [ɪˈnʌf] genug 2(64)
°**erm** [ɜːm] äh *(Verlegenheitslaut)*
°**especially** [ɪˈspeʃəli] insbesondere
estate [ɪˈsteɪt] die Wohnsiedlung; das Gewerbegebiet 4(118)
euro [ˈjʊərəʊ], *pl* **euros** der Euro 3(100)
°**even** [ˈiːvn] sogar, selbst
evening [ˈiːvnɪŋ] der Abend 3(86) **in the evening** abends, am Abend 3(86)
ever [ˈevə]: **the best son ever** der beste Sohn überhaupt / der beste Sohn, den man sich wünschen kann 3(87)
every [ˈevri] jede(r, s) 3(90) **every 30 minutes** alle 30 Minuten 3(90)
everybody [ˈevribɒdi] jeder; alle 3(89) **Hello everybody!** Hallo allerseits! 3(89)
everyone [ˈevriwʌn] jeder, alle 4(131)
°**everything** [ˈevriθɪŋ] alles
everywhere [ˈevriweə] überall 4(124)
example [ɪgˈzɑːmpl] das Beispiel 3(103) **for example** zum Beispiel 3(103)
exciting [ɪkˈsaɪtɪŋ] aufregend 3(90)
Excuse me, … [ɪksˈkjuːz miː] Entschuldigung, … / Entschuldigen Sie, … 4(124)
exercise [ˈeksəsaɪz] die Übung, die Aufgabe 1(21)
exercise book [ˈeksəsaɪz bʊk] das Schulheft, das Übungsheft 1(21)
expensive [ɪkˈspensɪv] teuer 2(64)
explain sth. to sb. [ɪkˈspleɪn] jm. etwas erklären 3(99)
°**explanation** [ekspləˈneɪʃn] die Erklärung
°**eye** [aɪ] das Auge

F

face [feɪs] das Gesicht 5(163)
°**fact** [fækt] die Tatsache
°**fall down** [fɔːl ˈdaʊn] hinfallen
false [fɔːls] falsch, unrichtig 5(159)
family [ˈfæməli] die Familie 2(50/51)
family name [ˈfæməli neɪm] der Familienname, der Nachname 2(68)
fan [fæn] der Fan 2(53)
°**far** [fɑː] weit (entfernt)
fast [fɑːst] schnell 2(55)
°**father** [ˈfɑːðə] der Vater
favourite [ˈfeɪvərɪt]:
1. Lieblings- (14)
2. der Liebling, der Favorit, die Favoritin (14)
February [ˈfebruəri] der Februar 5(150)
°**feed** [fiːd] **Don't feed the seagulls.** Bitte nicht die Möwen füttern.
feedback *(no pl)* [ˈfiːdbæk] das Feedback *(Rückmeldung)* 3(103)
feel [fiːl] fühlen; sich fühlen 3(91) **feel sorry for sb.** Mitleid haben mit jm. 3(98)
°**feeling** [ˈfiːlɪŋ] das Gefühl
°**few** [fjuː]: **a few** ein paar, einige
field [fiːld]:
1. das Feld; die Weide; die Wiese 4(118) **in the field** auf der Weide 4(118)
2. das Spielfeld, der Platz *(im Sport, z.B. Fußballplatz)* 3(97) **on the field** auf dem Spielfeld, auf dem Platz 3(97)
fifteen [fɪfˈtiːn] fünfzehn 2(68)

fifty [ˈfɪfti] fünfzig 2 (68)
file [faɪl] die Datei; der Ordner, die Liste 1 (36)
film [fɪlm] der Film (16)
finally [ˈfaɪnəli] schließlich, endlich 4 (134)
find [faɪnd] finden 2 (54) **find out (about)** herausfinden; sich informieren (über) 3 (99)
fine [faɪn]: **I'm fine.** Mir geht es gut. (13)
finger [ˈfɪŋgə] der Finger 5 (161)
°finish [ˈfɪnɪʃ]:
1. das Ende, das Ziel
2. enden; beenden, zu Ende machen
°firework [ˈfaɪəwɜːk] der Feuerwerkskörper **fireworks** *(pl)* das Feuerwerk
first [fɜːst]:
1. erste(r, s) 1 (33)
2. zuerst, als Erstes 1 (33)
at first zuerst, am Anfang 1 (33)
first name [ˈfɜːst neɪm] der Vorname 2 (68)
fish [fɪʃ] der Fisch (14)
fish and chip shop [fɪʃ ən ˈtʃɪp ʃɒp] *die Imbissstube, die Fisch mit Pommes frites verkauft* 4 (124)
five [faɪv] fünf (10/11)
flat [flæt] die Wohnung 2 (56)
floor [flɔː]:
1. der Fußboden 2 (56)
2. die Etage, der Stock, das Stockwerk 2 (56)
flour [ˈflaʊə] das Mehl 5 (158)
fly [flaɪ] fliegen 2 (54)
folder [ˈfəʊldə] die Mappe, der Ordner 1 (21)
°follow [ˈfɒləʊ] (ver)folgen
food [fuːd] das Essen, das Lebensmittel; das Futter 1 (29)
football [ˈfʊtbɔːl] der Fußball (10/11)
for [fɔː] für (17) **for 30 seconds** für 30 Sekunden, 30 Sekunden lang 4 (126) **What's for homework?** Was haben wir als Hausaufgabe(n) auf? 2 (54)
forget [fəˈget] vergessen 4 (131) **Don't forget.** Vergiss (es) nicht. / Denk dran! 4 (131)
fork [fɔːk] die Gabel 5 (158)
°form [fɔːm] das Formular
°formula [ˈfɔːmjələ] die Formel
forty [ˈfɔːti] vierzig 2 (68)
°found [faʊnd]: **they found** sie fanden / sie haben gefunden
four [fɔː] vier (10/11)
fourteen [fɔːˈtiːn] vierzehn (10/11)
free [friː]:
1. kostenlos 1 (32)
2. frei 1 (32)
free time die Freizeit, die freie Zeit 1 (32) **Are you free after school?** Hast du nach der Schule Zeit? 1 (32)
freeze [friːz] (ge)frieren; erstarren 3 (100)
freeze-frame [ˈfriːz freɪm] das Standbild *(Film)* 3 (100)
French [frentʃ] Französisch; französisch 1 (26)
Friday [ˈfraɪdeɪ], [ˈfraɪdi] der Freitag 1 (25)
°fridge [frɪdʒ] der Kühlschrank
fried [fraɪd] frittiert, gebraten 5 (159)
friend [frend] der Freund, die Freundin 1 (20)
friendly [ˈfrendli] freundlich, nett 1 (31)
from [frɒm] von, aus (10/11) **Where are you from?** Wo kommst du her? (10/11)
front [frʌnt]: **in front of** vor 2 (60)
fruit [fruːt] das Obst 5 (148/149)
fry [fraɪ] braten; frittieren 5 (159)
°frying pan [ˈfraɪɪŋ pæn] die Bratpfanne
fun [fʌn] der Spaß 1 (25) **be fun** Spaß machen; lustig sein 1 (25) **have fun** Spaß haben 1 (25)
funny [ˈfʌni]:
1. seltsam 2 (64)
2. witzig, lustig 2 (64)
What's funny about ...? Was ist lustig an ...? 2 (64)
furniture [ˈfɜːnɪtʃə] die Möbel(stücke) 4 (131)
°further [ˈfɜːðə] weiter (entfernt)
°furthest [ˈfɜːðəst] am weitesten (entfernt)
°fuss [fʌs]: **make a fuss (of/over)** Theater/Wirbel machen (wegen)

G

°gallery [ˈgæləri] die Galerie
game [geɪm] das Spiel 2 (65)
gaming [ˈgeɪmɪŋ] das Gaming *(Spielen am Computer)* 3 (96)
garage [ˈgærɑːʒ] die Garage 2 (56)
garden [ˈgɑːdn] der Garten 2 (56)
garlic [ˈgɑːlɪk] der Knoblauch 5 (161)
gate [geɪt] das Tor, das Gatter 1 (31)
°gave [geɪv]: **she gave** sie gab, sie hat gegeben
geography [dʒiˈɒgrəfi] die Geografie, die Erdkunde 1 (26)
German [ˈdʒɜːmən] deutsch; Deutsch; der/die Deutsche 1 (27)
Germany [ˈdʒɜːməni] Deutschland 1 (27)
get [get]:
1. bekommen 1 (29)
get sth. *(sich etwas)* holen/besorgen 1 (29)
2. werden 4 (124)
get dressed sich anziehen 3 (87) **get up** aufstehen 3 (87) **get warm** warm werden 4 (124) **°get ready** sich fertig machen
girl [gɜːl] das Mädchen 1 (20)
give [gɪv] geben 1 (31)
°glad [glæd]: **I'm glad** ich bin froh
glass [glɑːs] das Glas 5 (161) **a glass of milk** ein Glas Milch 5 (161)
°glove [glʌv] der Handschuh
glue [gluː] der Kleber, der Klebstoff 1 (21)
glue stick [ˈgluː stɪk] der Klebestift 1 (21)
go [gəʊ]:
1. gehen; fahren 1 (22)
go up aufgehen *(Sonne)*; hochgehen; (an)steigen 4 (129) **I must go.** Ich muss Schluss machen. *(am Telefon/Briefschluss)* 5 (152) **°go out** rausgehen, weggehen; ausgehen
2. **go green** grün/umweltfreundlich werden 4 (132)
goat [gəʊt] die Ziege 1 (31)
gold [gəʊld]:
1. das Gold (15)
2. goldfarben (15)
good [gʊd]:
1. brav 1 (32)
2. gut (13)
be good at sth. gut in etwas sein 5 (163) **be good with ...** gut umgehen können mit ... 1 (33)
Goodbye. [gʊdˈbaɪ] Auf Wiedersehen! (10/11)
gram (g) [græm] das Gramm 5 (158)
°granddaughter [ˈgrændɔːtə] die Enkelin
grandma [ˈgrænmɑː] die Oma 1 (30)
grandpa [ˈgrænpɑː] der Opa 1 (30)
°grandparents *(pl)* [ˈgrænpeərənts] die Großeltern
°grass [grɑːs] das Gras; der Rasen
great [greɪt] großartig, toll 1 (20)
Great Britain [greɪt ˈbrɪtn] Großbritannien 1 (20)
green [griːn]:
1. grün (10/11)
2. umweltbewusst 4 (132)
go green grün/umweltfreundlich werden 4 (132)
greet [griːt] begrüßen 4 (134)
greeting [ˈgriːtɪŋ] die Begrüßung; der Gruß 4 (134)
grey [greɪ] grau (10/11)
ground [graʊnd] der (Erd-)Boden 2 (56)
ground floor [graʊnd ˈflɔː] das Erdgeschoss 2 (56)
group [gruːp]:
1. die Gruppe 3 (102)
2. gruppieren 3 (102)
guess [ges]:
1. die Vermutung 4 (130)
Make/Have/Take a guess! Rate mal! 4 (130)
2. (er)raten 4 (130)
Guess what! Stell dir / Stellt euch (mal) vor! 4 (130) **I guess** ich glaube, ich nehme an 4 (130)
guide [gaɪd]:
1. führen, leiten 4 (124)
2. **(tour) guide** der Reiseleiter, die Reiseleiterin / der Fremdenführer, die Fremdenführerin 4 (124)
guide dog [ˈgaɪd dɒg] der Blindenhund 4 (124)
guitar [gɪˈtɑː] die Gitarre (15)
guys *(pl)* [gaɪz] Leute *(Anrede)* 3 (98)

H

°had [hæd]: we had wir hatten; wir haben gehabt
°hair [heə] das Haar, die Haare
hall [hɔ:l]:
1. der Flur, die Diele 1(28)
2. die Halle, der Saal 1(28)
sports hall die Sporthalle 1(28)
°Halloween [hæləʊ'i:n] (das) Halloween *(der Abend des 31. Oktober)*
ham [hæm] der Schinken 5(155)
hamster ['hæmstə] der Hamster 2(52)
hand [hænd] die Hand (17) put your hand up / put up your hand sich melden, aufzeigen (17)
hang out [hæŋ 'aʊt] rumhängen, abhängen 3(96)
happen (to sb.) ['hæpən] (jm.) geschehen, passieren 3(99)
happy ['hæpi] glücklich, froh 1(20) Happy birthday! Herzlichen Glückwunsch zum Geburtstag! 5(148/149)
hard [hɑ:d] schwer, schwierig; hart 1(27)
has [hæz], [həz]: he/she/it has er/sie/es hat 1(31)
hat [hæt] der Hut, die Mütze (16)
hate [heɪt]:
1. hassen 3(98)
2. der Hass 3(98)
have [hæv] haben 1(20)
he [hi:] er 1(24) he's (= he is) er ist 1(24)
head [hed] der Kopf 4(124) have your head in the clouds in Gedanken verloren / unrealistisch sein 4(129)
heading ['hedɪŋ] die Überschrift 3(99)
°headline ['hedlaɪn] die Überschrift
headphones *(pl)* ['hedfəʊnz] der Kopfhörer 2(65)
health [helθ] die Gesundheit 5(148/149)
healthy ['helθi] gesund 5(148/149)
hear [hɪə] hören 4(116/117)
heat [hi:t]:
1. die Hitze, die Wärme 5(161)
2. erwärmen, erhitzen 5(161)
Hello. [hə'ləʊ] Hallo. (10/11) Hello everybody! Hallo allerseits! 3(89)
help [help]:
1. helfen 1(23)
2. die Hilfe 1(23)
helpful ['helpfl] hilfsbereit; hilfreich, nützlich 1(32)
her [hɜ:]: 1. sie; ihr 3(98)
2. her friends ihre Freunde/Freundinnen 1(33)
here [hɪə] hier; hierher (12) Here you are. Bitte schön. / Hier, bitte. 1(23)
Hi. [haɪ] Hallo. (10/11)
°high [haɪ] hoch
highlight ['haɪlaɪt]:
1. das Highlight *(Höhepunkt)* 3(103)
2. hervorheben, markieren, unterstreichen 3(103)
hike [haɪk] wandern 3(90)
hiking ['haɪkɪŋ] das Wandern 3(90)
him [hɪm] ihm, ihn 1(33)
his friends [hɪz] seine Freunde/Freundinnen 1(33)
history ['hɪstri] die Geschichte *(vergangene Zeiten)* 1(26)
hobby ['hɒbi] das Hobby (15)
hockey ['hɒki] das Hockey 3(90)
°hold [həʊld] halten hold sth. up etwas hochhalten
°hole [həʊl] das Loch
holiday ['hɒlədeɪ] der Urlaub (12) holidays die Ferien (12) on holiday im/in den Urlaub (12)
home [həʊm]:
1. das Heim, das Zuhause 2(50/51) at home zu Hause 2(50/51)
2. nach Hause 2(50/51) go home nach Hause gehen 2(50/51)
homework ['həʊmwɜ:k] die Hausaufgabe(n) 2(54) do your homework Hausaufgaben machen 2(54) What's for homework? Was haben wir als Hausaufgabe(n) auf? 2(54)
honey ['hʌni] der Honig 5(160)
°hope [həʊp] hoffen
horrible ['hɒrəbl] schrecklich 1(20)
horse [hɔ:s] das Pferd (14)
°horseshoe ['hɔ:sʃu:] das Hufeisen
hospital ['hɒspɪtl] das Krankenhaus 4(122)
hot [hɒt] heiß, warm 4(128)
hot chocolate [hɒt 'tʃɒklət] der Kakao, die heiße (Trink-)Schokolade 4(128)
hot meal [hɒt 'mi:l] die warme Mahlzeit 5(161)
hour ['aʊə] die Stunde 3(86) per hour pro Stunde 4(116/117)
house [haʊs] das Haus 2(52)
how [haʊ] wie (10/11) How are you? Wie geht's? / Wie geht es dir/euch/Ihnen? (13) how to do sth. wie man etwas tut / tun kann / tun soll 3(90)
°hug (sb.) [hʌg] (jn.) umarmen
hundred ['hʌndrəd]: a/one hundred (ein)hundert 2(68)
hungry ['hʌŋgri] hungrig (10/11) I'm hungry. Ich habe Hunger. (10/11)
husband ['hʌzbənd] der (Ehe-)Mann 3(87)

I

I [aɪ] ich (10/11) I'm (= I am) ich bin (10/11)
ice cream ['aɪs kri:m] das (Speise-)Eis 4(125)
ice rink ['aɪs rɪŋk] die Schlittschuhbahn 4(122)
icing ['aɪsɪŋ] die Glasur, der Zuckerguss 5(158)
icing sugar ['aɪsɪŋ ʃʊgə] der Puderzucker 5(158)
idea [aɪ'dɪə] die Idee 2(66)
if [ɪf]:
1. wenn, falls 2(54) What if? Was wäre, wenn? 2(54)
2. ob 2(54)
ill [ɪl] krank 3(87)
illness ['ɪlnəs] die Krankheit 3(87)
important [ɪm'pɔ:tnt] wichtig 5(160)
in [ɪn]:
1. in; auf (12) in English auf Englisch 1(21) in the afternoon nachmittags, am Nachmittag 3(86) in the country auf dem Land 3(89) in the evening abends, am Abend 3(86) in the field auf der Weide 4(118) in the morning morgens, am Morgen 3(86) in the photo auf dem Foto (15) in the picture auf dem Bild (12) in town in der Stadt 4(118) °in the sky am Himmel
°2. herein; hinein °Come in! Kommen Sie herein!
India ['ɪndiə] Indien 5(148/149)
Indian ['ɪndiən]:
1. indisch 5(148/149)
2. der Inder, die Inderin 5(148/149)
information [ɪnfə'meɪʃn] die Information(en) 4(123)
°ingredient [ɪn'gri:diənt] die Zutat
inside [ɪn'saɪd]:
1. (dr)innen; nach (dr)innen 4(126)
2. innerhalb (von) 4(126)
instruction [ɪn'strʌkʃn] die Anweisung 5(167)
interesting ['ɪntrəstɪŋ] interessant 2(55)
internet ['ɪntənet] das Internet 2(69)
°interview ['ɪntəvju:] befragen, interviewen
into ['ɪntu], ['ɪntə] in (... hinein) 4(118)
introduction [ɪntrə'dʌkʃn] die Einführung, die Einleitung 5(167)
invitation (to) [ɪnvɪ'teɪʃn] die Einladung (zu, nach) 5(150)
invite (to) [ɪn'vaɪt] einladen (zu, nach) 5(150)
is [ɪz] *(er/sie/es)* ist (10/11) he isn't (= is not) er ist nicht 1(24)
island ['aɪlənd] die Insel 4(129)
it [ɪt] es *(bei Sachen und Tieren auch: er; sie)* (10/11) it's (= it is) es ist (10/11)
its [ɪts] sein/seine, ihr/ihre *(besitzanzeigend: Dinge und Tiere)* 2(63)

J

jam [dʒæm] die Marmelade 5(159)
January ['dʒænjuəri] der Januar 5(150)
jelly ['dʒeli] das Gelee; der Wackelpudding 5(148/149)
°jewellery ['dʒu:əlri] der Schmuck jewellery making Schmuck herstellen *(als Hobby)*
jigsaw (puzzle) ['dʒɪgsɔ:] das Puzzle 3(102)
join sb./sth. [dʒɔɪn] sich jm. anschließen; bei etwas mitmachen 3(90) join a club bei einer AG mitmachen, in einen Klub eintreten 3(90)
journey ['dʒɜ:ni] die Reise, die Fahrt; der Weg 3(84/85)
juggle ['dʒʌgl] jonglieren 5(152)

July [dʒu'laɪ] der Juli 5(150)
June [dʒu:n] der Juni 5(150)
just [dʒʌst] nur, bloß; einfach 5(162)

K

°kangaroo [kæŋgə'ru:] das Känguru
karaoke [kæri'əʊki] das Karaoke 5(153)
kebab [kɪ'bæb] der Kebab 5(152)
°keep [ki:p] behalten; halten **keep sb. cool** jn. kühl halten *(bei Hitze)*
°key ring [ki: rɪŋ] das Schlüsselbund, der Schlüsselring
°keyword ['ki:wɜ:d] das Stichwort, das Schlagwort
°kick [kɪk] treten; *(Sport)* schießen
kid [kɪd] das Kind, der/die Jugendliche 3(87)
kilometre (km) ['kɪləmi:tə] der Kilometer 4(116/117)
kind [kaɪnd] freundlich, nett 1(31)
kind (of) [kaɪnd] die Art (von), die Sorte (von) 5(155)
Kingdom ['kɪŋdəm]: **the United Kingdom (the UK)** das Vereinigte Königreich 3(86)
kiosk ['ki:ɒsk] der Kiosk, die Verkaufsbude 4(127)
°kiss [kɪs] (sich) küssen
kitchen ['kɪtʃɪn] die Küche 2(57)
knife [naɪf], *pl* **knives** das Messer 5(158)
knives [naɪvz] *Plural von* **knife**
know [nəʊ] wissen; kennen 1(20)

L

lab [læb] *siehe* **laboratory**
laboratory [lə'bɒrətri], *infml auch* **lab** das Labor 1(27)
°lamb [læm] das Lamm(fleisch)
lamp [læmp] die Lampe 2(56)
language ['læŋgwɪdʒ] die Sprache 3(102)
°last [lɑ:st] letzte(r, s)
late [leɪt] (zu) spät 1(22) **I'm late.** Ich habe mich verspätet. 1(22)
later ['leɪtə] später 2(64) **Speak later.** Tschüs. / Bis später. 2(64)
°laugh (at) [lɑ:f] lachen (über)
°leap year ['li:p jɪə] das Schaltjahr
learn [lɜ:n] lernen 1(36)
°least [li:st]: **at least** wenigstens, zumindest
°leave sb./sth. [li:v] lassen; jn./etwas zurücklassen
°left [left] links **on the left** auf der linken Seite
lemon ['lemən] die Zitrone 5(155)
lemonade [lemə'neɪd] die Limonade 5(155)
lesson ['lesn] die (Unterrichts-)Stunde 1(24)
let [let] lassen 1(22) **let's (= let us)** lass(t) uns 1(22)
letter ['letə]:
1. der Brief 3(87)
2. der Buchstabe 3(87)

library ['laɪbrəri] die Bücherei, die Bibliothek 1(30)
°lick [lɪk] (ab)lecken
lie [laɪ] liegen 5(153)
°life skills *(pl)* ['laɪf skɪlz] die Alltagskompetenzen, die lebenswichtigen Fertigkeiten
light [laɪt] das Licht; die Lampe 3(103) **car light** der Autoscheinwerfer 3(103)
like [laɪk] mögen (10/11) **I'd (= I would) like ...** Ich hätte gern ... / Ich möchte ... 3(94) **I'd (= I would) like to meet ....** Ich würde mich gerne mit ... treffen. 3(94) **Would you like ...?** Möchtest du ...? 3(94) **°I like to be ...** Ich bin gerne ...
like [laɪk] wie; wie zum Beispiel 4(120) **like this** so, auf diese Art 2(68) **a story like this** so/solch eine Geschichte 2(68) **It looks like rain.** Es sieht nach Regen aus. 4(129) **What does it look like?** Wie sieht es aus? 4(129) **What's ... like?** Wie ist ...? / Wie sieht ... aus? 4(120)
line [laɪn]:
1. die Reihe 3(88)
2. die Zeile 3(88)
lion ['laɪən] der Löwe (14)
list [lɪst]:
1. die Liste 5(155)
2. (auf)listen 5(155)
listen (to) ['lɪsn] zuhören; (sich etwas) anhören (15)
little ['lɪtl]:
1. klein 2(59)
2. **a little** ein wenig, ein bisschen 5(162)
live [lɪv] leben, wohnen 2(58)
living room ['lɪvɪŋ ru:m] das Wohnzimmer 2(57)
lizard ['lɪzəd] die Eidechse 2(55)
long [lɒŋ] lang 2(66) **a long time** lange 2(66) **work long days** lange arbeiten, lange Arbeitstage haben 3(87)
look [lʊk]:
1. aussehen 4(129)
It looks like rain. Es sieht nach Regen aus. 4(129)
2. sehen, schauen (17)
look after sich kümmern um; aufpassen auf 4(118) **look at sth.** sich etwas anschauen (17)
look sth. up etwas nachschlagen, nachschauen 3(102) **°look for** suchen; Ausschau halten nach
°Look out! Vorsicht! / Pass(t) auf!
lost [lɒst]: **Are you lost?** Hast du dich verlaufen/verirrt? 2(52) **be lost** sich verlaufen/verirrt haben 2(52) **get lost** sich verlaufen/verirren 2(52)
lot [lɒt]:
1. **a lot (of) / lots (of)** viel/e 2(52)
2. **a lot** sehr 2(52)
loud [laʊd] laut 1(34)
loudly ['laʊdli]: **speak loudly** laut sprechen 2(64)

love [lʌv]:
1. der Liebling 2(65)
2. die Liebe (15)
3. lieben, sehr mögen (15)
I'd (= I would) love ... Ich hätte liebend gern ... / Ich möchte liebend gern... 3(94) **I'd (= I would) love to meet ....** Ich würde mich liebend gerne mit ... treffen. 3(94)
lucky ['lʌki] Glücks-, glücklich 1(25)
lucky number die Glückszahl 1(25)
be lucky Glück haben 1(25)
lunch [lʌntʃ] das Mittagessen 1(26) **at lunch** beim Mittagessen 1(26) **What's for lunch?** Was gibt es zum Mittagessen? 1(26)
lunchtime ['lʌntʃtaɪm] die Mittagszeit 3(86) **at lunchtime** zur Mittagszeit 3(86)

M

magic ['mædʒɪk]:
1. magisch 5(154)
2. die Zauberei 5(154)
do magic zaubern 5(154)
magic set ['mædʒɪk set] der Zauberkasten 5(154)
magic trick ['mædʒɪk trɪk] der Zaubertrick 5(154)
main [meɪn] Haupt-, wichtigste(r, s) 5(160) **main course/dish** das Hauptgericht 5(160)
make [meɪk] machen, herstellen 1(37)
man [mæn], *pl* **men** der Man 4(126)
many ['meni] viele 4(121) **how many?** wie viele? 4(121)
map [mæp] die Landkarte, der Stadtplan 1(28)
March [mɑ:tʃ] der März 5(150)
marina [mə'ri:nə] der Jachthafen 4(116/117)
market ['mɑ:kɪt] der Markt 4(122)
married (to) ['mærid] verheiratet (mit) 2(50/51)
marry ['mæri] heiraten 2(50/51)
°match [mætʃ]:
1. (passend) zusammenfügen
match to zuordnen
2. das Gegenstück, das (zusammenpassende) Paar
be a good match for (gut) passen zu
match [mætʃ] das Spiel, der Wettkampf 3(91)
°material [mə'tɪəriəl] das Material; der Stoff
maths [mæθs] die Mathe(matik) 1(26)
°mattar paneer [mʌtr pʌ'nɪə] das Mattar Paneer *(nordindisches Gericht)*
May [meɪ] der Mai 5(150)
maybe ['meɪbi] vielleicht 1(28)
me [mi:] mich; mir (14) **Me, too.** Ich auch. (14) **It's me.** Ich bin's. (14) **Not me!** Ich nicht! (= Ich bin/war/habe/... es/das nicht!) (14)
meal [mi:l] die Mahlzeit, das Essen 5(161) **hot meal** die warme Mahlzeit 5(161)

mean [miːn]:
1. gemein, fies 1 (32)
2. bedeuten 4 (132)
3. meinen *(sagen wollen)* 4 (132)

meaning [ˈmiːnɪŋ] die Bedeutung 4 (132)
meat [miːt] das Fleisch 5 (148/149)
°mediation [miːdiˈeɪʃn] die Vermittlung, die Sprachmittlung
meet [miːt] kennenlernen; (sich) treffen (10/11) **Nice to meet you.** Freut mich, dich/euch/Sie kennenzulernen. (10/11)
melon [ˈmelən] die Melone 5 (155)
°meme [miːm] das Internet-Mem, das Internetphänomen
men [men] *Plural von* **man**
menu [ˈmenjuː] die Speisekarte 5 (155)
mess [mes] das Chaos, die Unordnung 2 (52)
message [ˈmesɪdʒ]:
1. die Botschaft, die Aussage 1 (25)
2. die Nachricht, die Mitteilung 1 (25)
3. **message (sb.)** (sb.) (jm.) Nachrichten schicken, Nachrichten austauschen (mit jm.) 1 (25)

messy [ˈmesi] unordentlich 2 (52)
metre [ˈmiːtə] der Meter 4 (116/117)
mice [maɪs] *Plural von* **mouse**
°middle [ˈmɪdl] die Mitte
midnight [ˈmɪdnaɪt] die Mitternacht 3 (86)
mile [maɪl] die Meile *(ca. 1,6 km)* 4 (116/117)
miles per hour (mph) [maɪlz pər ˈaʊə] Meilen pro Stunde 4 (116/117) **at 30 miles per hour** mit 30 Meilen pro Stunde 4 (116/117)
milk [mɪlk] die Milch 5 (158)
millilitre (ml) [ˈmɪliliːtə] der Milliliter 5 (158)
°mime [maɪm] vorspielen, pantomimisch darstellen
mind map [ˈmaɪnd mæp] die Gedankenkarte, das Wörternetz, die Mindmap 1 (36)
mini [ˈmɪni] Mini- 5 (154)
mini-drone [mɪnɪ ˈdrəʊn] die Minidrohne 5 (154)
minute [ˈmɪnɪt] die Minute 1 (24)
mirror [ˈmɪrə] der Spiegel 2 (60)
°miss [mɪs] verpassen, versäumen, auslassen
missing [ˈmɪsɪŋ] vermisst 2 (54) **°the missing words** die fehlenden Wörter
°mistake [mɪˈsteɪk] der Fehler
mix [mɪks] (ver)mischen 5 (158) **°mix up** *(Spielkarten)* mischen
mixture [ˈmɪkstʃə] die Mischung 5 (158)
mobile phone [məʊbaɪl ˈfəʊn] das Handy, das Telefon (15)
modern [ˈmɒdn] modern 2 (58)
moment [ˈməʊmənt] der Moment 4 (129) **at the moment** im Moment, zurzeit 4 (129) **have a moment in the sun** kurz im Mittelpunkt stehen 4 (129)
Monday [ˈmʌndeɪ], [ˈmʌndi] der Montag 1 (25)
money [ˈmʌni] das Geld 3 (99)
monkey [ˈmʌŋki] der Affe (14)
month [mʌnθ] der Monat 3 (90)
more [mɔː] mehr, weitere 4 (127) **three more** noch drei, drei weitere 4 (127)
morning [ˈmɔːnɪŋ] der Morgen 3 (86) **in the morning** morgens, am Morgen 3 (86)
most [məʊst]: **the most ...** die meisten ...; am meisten 1 (31) **°most important** der/die/das wichtigste; am wichtigsten
mouse [maʊs], *pl* **mice** die Maus 4 (131)
move [muːv] (sich) bewegen 1 (32)
Mr Lee [ˈmɪstə] Herr Lee 1 (22)
Mrs Lee [ˈmɪsɪz] Frau Lee *(Anrede für verheiratete Frauen)* 1 (22)
Ms Lee [mɪz] Frau Lee 1 (22)
much [mʌtʃ] viel; sehr 3 (99) **Thank you very much.** Vielen Dank. / Danke vielmals. 3 (99)
mum [mʌm] die Mama/Mutti (12)
museum [mjuˈziːəm] das Museum 4 (122)
music [ˈmjuːzɪk] die Musik (15)
must [mʌst] müssen 5 (152) **I must go.** Ich muss Schluss machen. *(am Telefon/Briefschluss)* 5 (152)
my [maɪ] mein/e (14)

N

name [neɪm] der Name (10/11) **first name** der Vorname 2 (68) **What's your name?** Wie heißt du? (10/11)
near [nɪə] nahe (bei), in der Nähe von 1 (28)
°nectarine [ˈnektəriːn] die Nektarine
need [niːd] brauchen 4 (127) **need to do sth.** etwas tun müssen 4 (127)
neighbour [ˈneɪbə] der Nachbar, die Nachbarin 2 (50/51)
neighbourhood [ˈneɪbəhʊd] die Nachbarschaft, die Gegend, das Viertel 2 (50/51)
never [ˈnevə] nie, niemals 3 (91)
new [njuː] neu (15)
news [njuːz] die Nachrichten 3 (99)
newspaper [ˈnjuːspeɪpə] die (Tages-) Zeitung 3 (87)
next [nekst]:
1. nächste(r, s) 1 (34) **the next day** am nächsten Tag 1 (34)
2. **Next ...** Als Nächstes ... 4 (131)

next to [ˈnekst tə] neben 2 (60)
nice [naɪs] nett, schön (10/11) **Nice to meet you.** Freut mich, dich/euch/Sie kennenzulernen. (10/11)
Nigeria [naɪˈdʒɪəriə] Nigeria 5 (160)
Nigerian [naɪˈdʒɪəriən]:
1. nigerianisch 5 (160)
2. der Nigerianer, die Nigerianerin 5 (160)

night [naɪt] die Nacht 1 (25) **at night** nachts, in der Nacht 1 (25)
nine [naɪn] neun (10/11)
nineteen [naɪnˈtiːn] neunzehn 2 (68)
ninety [ˈnaɪnti] neunzig 2 (68)
no [nəʊ]:
1. nein 1 (22)
2. kein, keine; verboten 2 (56)

noise [nɔɪz] das Geräusch; der Lärm 2 (66)
noodles *(pl)* [nuːdlz] die Nudeln 5 (160)
noon [nuːn] der Mittag; 12 Uhr mittags 3 (86)
north [nɔːθ] der Norden; nördlich; Nord- 4 (116/117)
not [nɒt] nicht (13) **I'm not a boy.** Ich bin kein Junge. (13)
note [nəʊt] die Notiz; der kurze Brief 4 (119) **make notes** (sich) Notizen machen *(zur Vorbereitung)* 4 (119)
notice [ˈnəʊtɪs]:
1. (be)merken 4 (131)
2. der Anschlag, die Bekanntmachung *(an einem Schwarzen Brett)* 4 (131)

November [nəʊˈvembə] der November 5 (150)
now [naʊ] nun, jetzt 1 (22)
number [ˈnʌmbə] die Zahl, die Ziffer, die Nummer (10/11)

O

o'clock [əˈklɒk]: **at 8 o'clock** um 8 Uhr 3 (86)
October [ɒkˈtəʊbə] der Oktober 5 (150)
°odd word out [ɒd wɜːd ˈaʊt] das Wort, das nicht zu den anderen passt
of [ɒv], [əv] von (16) **a glass of milk** ein Glas Milch 5 (161) **bags of rubbish** Tüten/Säcke (mit/voller) Müll 4 (131) **the first of April (1st April)** der erste April 5 (151)
of course [əv ˈkɔːs] natürlich, selbstverständlich 2 (64)
office [ˈɒfɪs] das Büro 2 (57)
often [ˈɒfn], [ˈɒftən] oft 1 (20)
oh [əʊ] Null *(im gesprochenen Englisch)* 2 (68)
oil [ɔɪl] das Öl 5 (158)
OK [əʊˈkeɪ]: **I'm OK.** Es geht mir gut. (13) **That's OK.** Schon gut. / Kein Problem. 2 (65)
old [əʊld] alt (10/11) **How old are you?** Wie alt bist du? (10/11)
on [ɒn] auf 1 (25) **on holiday** im/in den Urlaub (12) **on Monday** am Montag 1 (25) **on Mondays** an jedem Montag, montags 1 (25) **on my birthday** an meinem Geburtstag 5 (148/149) **on the beach** am Strand 1 (32) **on the bus** im Bus 3 (84/85) **on the field** auf dem Spielfeld, auf dem Platz 3 (97) **on the phone** am Telefon 2 (66)

one [wʌn]:
1. eins (10/11)
°2. **a dream one** einer/eine/eins aus dem Traum

onion [ˈʌnjən] die Zwiebel 5 (160)
online [ɒnˈlaɪn] online, Online- 1 (31)
only [ˈəʊnli]:
1. nur, bloß 2 (53)
2. erst 2 (53)
°3. **the only thing** das Einzige

open [ˈəʊpən]:
1. öffnen; aufschlagen *(Buch)* (17)
2. offen, geöffnet (17)

opinion (of) [əˈpɪnjən] die Meinung (zu/bezüglich) 1 (34) **in my opinion** meiner Meinung nach 1 (34)
°**opposite** [ˈɒpəzɪt] das Gegenteil
or [ɔː] oder; sonst 1 (31)
orange [ˈɒrɪndʒ]:
1. orange(farben) (10/11)
2. die Orange (10/11)

°**order** [ˈɔːdə] die Reihenfolge **put in the right order** in die richtige Reihenfolge bringen
°**organize** [ˈɔːgənaɪz] organisieren
other [ˈʌðə] andere(r, s) (12) **the others** die anderen (12)
our [ˈaʊə] unser/e 1 (28)
°**out of** [aʊt] aus ... (heraus/hinaus)
outside [aʊtˈsaɪd]:
1. draußen; nach draußen 4 (126)
2. außerhalb (von) 4 (126)

oven [ˈʌvn] der Backofen 5 (158)
over [ˈəʊvə] über; mehr als 2 (60) **over here** hier herüber; hier drüben 4 (131) **over there** da drüben, dort drüben 4 (131) °**over the sea** über dem Meer °**run over** rüberrennen
own [əʊn]: **your own room** dein/ein eigenes Zimmer 2 (63)
°**owner** [ˈəʊnə] der Besitzer, die Besitzerin

P

packet [ˈpækɪt] die Packung, das Päckchen 5 (155)
°**pad thai** [pæd ˈtaɪ] das Pad Thai *(thailändisches Nudelgericht)*
page (= p.) [peɪdʒ] die (Buch-/Heft-) Seite 1 (23)
°**pair** [peə] das Paar
palace [ˈpæləs] der Palast, das Schloss 4 (116/117)
°**pan** [pæn] die Pfanne
paper [ˈpeɪpə]:
1. die (Tages-)Zeitung 3 (87)
2. das Papier 3 (87)

piece of paper das Stück Papier, der Zettel 5 (156)
°**paragraph** [ˈpærəgrɑːf] der (Text-)Abschnitt
°**parallel** [ˈpærəlel] parallel, Parallel-
parents *(pl)* [ˈpeərənts] die Eltern 2 (64)
park [pɑːk] der Park 3 (88)
°**parking** [ˈpɑːkɪŋ]: **No parking.** Parken verboten.
parkour [pɑːˈkʊə] der Parkour *(akrobatischer Hindernislauf in der Stadt)* 1 (18/19)
parrot [ˈpærət] der Papagei (14)
part (of) [pɑːt] der Teil (von) 2 (65)
partner [ˈpɑːtnə] der Partner, die Partnerin 1 (36)
party [ˈpɑːti] die Party 3 (100)
passive [ˈpæsɪv] passiv 2 (55)
°**past** [pɑːst] die Vergangenheit
pasta [ˈpæstə] die Pasta *(italienische Bezeichnung für Teigwaren)* 5 (155)
pay (for sth.) [peɪ] zahlen; (etwas) bezahlen 3 (100)
PE (= physical education) [piː ˈiː] der (Schul-)Sport 1 (26)
pea [piː] die Erbse 5 (148/149)
pen [pen] der Kugelschreiber, der Stift; der Füller 1 (21)
pence [pens] *Plural von* **penny**
pencil [ˈpensl] der Bleistift 1 (21)
pencil case [ˈpensl keɪs] das Federmäppchen 1 (21)
pencil sharpener [ˈpensl ʃɑːpnə] der Bleistift(an)spitzer 1 (21)
penny (p) [ˈpeni], *pl* **pence** der Penny *(kleinste britische Münze)* 3 (100)
people *(pl)* [ˈpiːpl] die Leute, die Menschen 1 (24)
pepper [ˈpepə]:
1. der Pfeffer 5 (160)
2. die Paprika, die Peperoni 5 (160)

per [pɜː], [pə] pro 4 (116/117) **miles per hour (mph)** Meilen pro Stunde 4 (116/117)
perfect [ˈpɜːfɪkt] perfekt 2 (64)
perfectly (still) [ˈpɜːfɪktli] ganz/völlig (still) 2 (64)
person [ˈpɜːsn] die Person 2 (62)
pet [pet] das (Haus-)Tier 2 (52)
phone [fəʊn]:
1. anrufen; telefonieren (15)
2. das Handy, das Telefon (15)

by phone per Telefon / telefonisch 5 (150) **on the phone** am Telefon 2 (66)
phone call [ˈfəʊn kɔːl] der (Telefon-) Anruf 2 (54)
phone number [ˈfəʊn nʌmbə] die Telefonnummer (15)
photo [ˈfəʊtəʊ] das Foto (15) **in the photo** auf dem Foto (15) **take photos** Fotos machen (15)
photographer [fəˈtɒgrəfə] der Fotograf, die Fotografin 2 (69)
phrase [freɪz] der Ausdruck, die (Rede-)Wendung 4 (134)
physical education (PE) [fɪzɪkl edʒuˈkeɪʃn] der (Schul-)Sport 1 (26)
picnic [ˈpɪknɪk] das Picknick 4 (116/117) **have a picnic** ein Picknick machen 4 (116/117)
picture [ˈpɪktʃə] das Bild (12)
piece [piːs] das Stück, der/das Teil 5 (156) **piece of paper** das Stück Papier 5 (156)
pier [pɪə] der Pier, die Seebrücke 4 (116/117)
pink [pɪŋk] rosa (10/11)
place [pleɪs] der Ort, der Platz 1 (28) **in this place** an diesem Ort 1 (28)
°**placemat** [ˈpleɪsmæt] das Platzdeckchen
plan [plæn]:
1. der Plan 3 (95)
2. planen 3 (95)

plan to do sth. planen, etwas zu tun 3 (95)
°**plantain** [ˈplæntɪn] die Kochbanane
°**plate** [pleɪt] der Teller
play [pleɪ]:
1. spielen (15)
°2. das Theaterstück

°**played** [pleɪd]: **we played** wir spielten, wir haben gespielt
player [ˈpleɪə] der Spieler, die Spielerin (15)
playground [ˈpleɪgraʊnd] der Schulhof; der Spielplatz 1 (30)
playing card [ˈpleɪɪŋ kɑːd] die Spielkarte 3 (102)
playlist [ˈpleɪlɪst] die Playlist 5 (157)
please [pliːz] bitte (17)
p.m. [piːˈem]: **4 p.m.** 4 Uhr nachmittags, 16 Uhr 3 (86) **9 p.m.** 9 Uhr abends, 21 Uhr 3 (86)
°**pocket** [ˈpɒkɪt] die Tasche *(an Kleidungsstücken)*
°**poem** [ˈpəʊɪm] das Gedicht
point [pɔɪnt]:
1. der Punkt 4 (116/117)
2. das Komma *(Dezimalzeichen)* 4 (116/117)

1.6 (one point six) 1,6 (eins Komma sechs) 4 (116/117)
°**point (at/to)** [pɔɪnt] zeigen (auf)
°**police** *(pl)* [pəˈliːs] die Polizei
°**police car** [pəˈliːs kɑː] das Polizeiauto
°**police officer** [pəˈliːs ɒfɪsə] der Polizeibeamte, die Polizeibeamtin
°**policewoman** [pəˈliːswʊmən], *pl* **policewomen** die Polizistin
°**policewomen** [pəˈliːswɪmɪn] *Plural von* **policewoman**
polite [pəˈlaɪt] höflich 2 (53)
pool [puːl] das Pool(billiard) 4 (120)
°**Poor dog!** [pʊə ˈdɒg] Der arme Hund!
pop (music) [ˈpɒp mjuːzɪk] der Pop, die Popmusik 3 (97)
popcorn [ˈpɒpkɔːn] das Popcorn 4 (135)
popular [ˈpɒpjələ] beliebt, populär 3 (97)
post [pəʊst]:
1. der Post *(Teil eines Blogs)* 4 (121)
2. posten *(im Internet veröffentlichen)* 4 (121)

poster [ˈpəʊstə] das Poster 1 (37)
potato [pəˈteɪtəʊ], *pl* **potatoes** die Kartoffel 5 (161)
pound (£) [paʊnd] das Pfund *(britische Währung)* 3 (100)
powder [ˈpaʊdə] das Pulver 5 (158)
practice [ˈpræktɪs] die Übung(en) 4 (116/117)
practise [ˈpræktɪs] üben 4 (116/117)
preheat (the oven to ...) [priːˈhiːt] (den Backofen) vorheizen (auf) 5 (161)

present ['preznt] das Geschenk 5 (154)
present sth. (to sb.) [prɪ'zent] (jm.) etwas präsentieren, vorstellen 2 (69)
presentation [prezn'teɪʃn] das Referat, die Präsentation 2 (69) **give a presentation** ein Referat halten 2 (69)
prize [praɪz] der Preis, der Gewinn 3 (98)
problem ['prɒbləm] das Problem 2 (64)
°**profile** ['prəʊfaɪl] das Profil; die Beschreibung, das Portrait
project ['prɒdʒekt] das Projekt 3 (89)
°**puppet** ['pʌpɪt] die Puppe *(Handpuppe, Marionette)*
purple ['pɜːpl] violett, lila (10/11)
put [pʊt] *(etwas wohin)* tun, legen, stellen, stecken (15) **put sth. up** etwas aufhängen *(an der Wand)* 4 (131) **put your hand up / put up your hand** sich melden, aufzeigen (17) °**put in the right order** in die richtige Reihenfolge bringen
puzzle ['pʌzl] das Rätsel 3 (102)

Q

question ['kwestʃən] die Frage 1 (23) **ask a question** eine Frage stellen 1 (23)
°**questionnaire** [kwestʃə'neə] der Fragebogen
°**quick** [kwɪk] schnell
°**quicker** ['kwɪkə] schneller
quiet ['kwaɪət] ruhig, still, leise (17)
quite [kwaɪt] ziemlich, ganz 2 (55)
quiz [kwɪz], *pl* **quizzes** das Quiz, das Ratespiel; der Test 3 (97) **do a quiz** ein Quiz / ein Ratespiel / einen Test machen 3 (97)
quizzes ['kwɪzɪz] *Plural von* **quiz**

R

rabbit ['ræbɪt] das Kaninchen 2 (52)
°**race** [reɪs]:
1. Rennen fahren; um die Wette laufen/reiten/...
2. das (Wett-)Rennen
do a race ein Rennen veranstalten
rain [reɪn]:
1. der Regen 4 (126)
come rain or shine bei jedem Wetter; was auch (immer) geschieht 4 (129)
2. regnen 4 (126)
rain cats and dogs stark regnen 4 (129)
rainy ['reɪni] regnerisch 4 (126)
rare [reə] selten *(Adj.)* 3 (91)
rarely ['reəli] selten *(Adv.)* 3 (91)
°**reaction (to)** [ri'ækʃn] die Reaktion (auf)
read [riːd] lesen (15)
reader ['riːdə] der Leser, die Leserin (15)
ready ['redi] fertig, bereit (17)
°**Ready, steady, go!** Auf die Plätze, fertig, los! °**get ready** sich fertig machen
°**real** [rɪəl] echt, wirklich
really ['riːəli], ['rɪəli] wirklich 1 (28)
reason ['riːzn] der Grund, die Begründung 5 (148/149) **for this reason** aus diesem Grund 5 (148/149)
°**reception** [rɪ'sepʃn] der Empfang *(auch beim Telefon)*; die Rezeption
in reception an der Rezeption
recipe ['resəpi] das (Koch-)Rezept 5 (148/149)
recipe book ['resəpi bʊk] das Kochbuch 5 (148/149)
record [rɪ'kɔːd] aufnehmen, aufzeichnen 3 (103)
red [red] rot (10/11)
registration [redʒɪ'streɪʃn] *die Anwesenheitskontrolle und Ankündigung aktueller Ereignisse vor dem Unterricht* 1 (26)
°**relax** [rɪ'læks] sich entspannen
religion [rɪ'lɪdʒən] die Religion 5 (148/149)
religious [rɪ'lɪdʒəs] religiös 5 (148/149)
remember [rɪ'membə]:
1. daran denken, nicht vergessen (12)
remember to do sth. daran denken, etwas zu tun (12)
2. sich erinnern an (12)
remember doing sth. sich daran erinnern, etwas getan zu haben (12)
°**repeat** [rɪ'piːt] wiederholen **Repeat after me: ....** Sprich mir nach: ....
research [rɪ'sɜːtʃ]:
1. erforschen, untersuchen, recherchieren 5 (167)
2. die Forschung(en), die Recherche(n) 5 (167)
do research recherchieren 5 (167)
rest [rest]:
1. ruhen; sich ausruhen 5 (152)
2. die Ruhe, die Pause, die Erholung 5 (152)
take a rest Pause machen 5 (152)
restaurant ['restrɒnt] das Restaurant 5 (148/149)
°**review** [rɪ'vjuː] der Bericht, die Rezension *(kritische Besprechung)*
°**rhyme** [raɪm] (sich) reimen
°**rhythm** ['rɪðəm] der Rhythmus
rice [raɪs] der Reis 5 (148/149)
°**ride** [raɪd] die Fahrt; das Fahrgeschäft *(auf Volksfesten, in Vergnügungsparks)*
ride (a bike) [raɪd] (mit dem Fahrrad) fahren 4 (135)
right [raɪt]:
1. richtig (10/11)
be right Recht haben 1 (24)
°2. rechts
°**on the right** auf der rechten Seite °**to the right** nach rechts
°3. **right by the sea** direkt am Meer
ring [rɪŋ] der Ring 4 (131) **wedding ring** der Ehering 4 (131)
robot ['rəʊbɒt] der Roboter 2 (60)
°**rock** [rɒk]:
1. die Zuckerstange
2. der Fels(en)
°**role** [rəʊl] die Rolle *(Film, Theater)*
°**role-play** ['rəʊlpleɪ] das Rollenspiel
roll (out) [rəʊl] rollen; ausrollen *(Teig)* 5 (161)
room [ruːm] der Raum, das Zimmer 1 (24)
°**rose** [rəʊz] die Rose
round [raʊnd]:
1. rund 5 (159)
2. die Runde 5 (159)
3. **round ...** um (... herum), in ... umher 5 (159)
°**routine** [ruː'tiːn] die Routine, der (Tages-/Übungs-)Ablauf
°**RSVP** [ɑːr es viː 'pi] u.A.w.g. (um Antwort wird gebeten)
rubber ['rʌbə] das Radiergummi 1 (21)
rubbish ['rʌbɪʃ] der (Haus-)Müll, der Abfall 4 (118)
rucksack ['rʌksæk] der Rucksack (15)
rude [ruːd] unhöflich, frech 2 (65)
°**rule** [ruːl] die Regel
ruler ['ruːlə] das Lineal 1 (21)
run [rʌn] rennen, laufen 3 (90) °**run for sth.** hinter etwas herlaufen °**run over** hinüber-/herüberrennen
running ['rʌnɪŋ] das Laufen *(Sport)* 3 (90)
Russia ['rʌʃə] Russland 4 (126)
Russian ['rʌʃn]:
1. russisch, Russisch 4 (126)
2. der Russe, die Russin 4 (126)

S

sad [sæd] traurig 1 (32)
salad ['sæləd] der Salat *(als Gericht oder Beilage)* 5 (155)
salt [sɔːlt] das Salz 5 (158)
same [seɪm]: **the same** gleich; derselbe/dieselbe/dasselbe; dieselben 1 (20)
sandwich ['sænwɪtʃ], ['sænwɪdʒ] das Sandwich (10/11)
Saturday ['sætədeɪ], ['sætədi] der Samstag 1 (25)
sauce [sɔːs] die Soße 5 (148/149)
sausage ['sɒsɪdʒ] das (Brat-, Bock-) Würstchen, die Wurst 5 (150)
savoury ['seɪvəri] herzhaft, salzig 5 (159)
°**saw** [sɔː]: **I saw** ich sah; ich habe gesehen
say [seɪ] sagen 1 (22)
scared [skeəd]: **be scared (of)** Angst haben (vor) 1 (20)
scene [siːn] die Szene 4 (132)
school [skuːl] die Schule (17)
at school in der Schule 1 (18/19)
school club ['skuːl klʌb] die AG *(in der Schule)* 1 (31)
school uniform [skuːl 'juːnɪfɔːm] die Schuluniform 1 (20)
science ['saɪəns] die Naturwissenschaft 1 (26)
scone [skɒn] *das Milchbrötchen, leicht süß, oft mit Rosinen* 5 (159)
scooter ['skuːtə] der (Tret-)Roller (15)
sea [siː] das Meer, die See 3 (90) **by the sea** am Meer, an der See 3 (90)

seagull ['si:gʌl] die Möwe (10/11)
season ['si:zn] die Jahreszeit; die Saison 5 (150)
second ['sekənd]:
1. die Sekunde 4 (126)
2. **(2nd)** zweite(r, s) 3 (102)
secondary school ['sekəndri sku:l] die weiterführende Schule 1 (22)
secret ['si:krət]:
1. geheim 3 (93)
2. das Geheimnis 3 (93)
see [si:] sehen (12) **See you soon.** Bis bald! 1 (25) **See you.** Bis dann. / Tschüs. 1 (25)
°**sell** [sel] verkaufen
semi-detached home/house [semi dɪ'tætʃt] die Doppelhaushälfte 2 (59)
send [send] senden, schicken 3 (98)
sentence ['sentəns] der Satz 3 (93)
°**sentence starter** ['sentəns stɑ:tə] der Satzanfang
September [sep'tembə] der September 5 (150)
seven ['sevn] sieben (10/11)
seventeen [sevn'ti:n] siebzehn 2 (68)
seventy ['sevnti] siebzig 2 (68)
°**several** ['sevrəl] mehrere, einige
shame [ʃeɪm]: **a shame** schade; eine Schande 3 (94)
share [ʃeə]:
1. der (An-)Teil 3 (103)
2. teilen 3 (103)
sharpener ['ʃɑ:pnə] der Anspitzer 1 (21)
she [ʃi:] sie *(weibliche Person)* 1 (24)
she's (= she is) sie ist 1 (24)
shelf [ʃelf], *pl* **shelves** das Regal(brett) 2 (60)
shelves [ʃelvz] *Plural von* **shelf**
shine [ʃaɪn]:
1. scheinen *(Sonne)*; strahlen, glänzen 4 (129)
2. der Sonnenschein; der Glanz 4 (129)
come rain or shine bei jedem Wetter; was auch (immer) geschieht 4 (129)
shirt [ʃɜ:t] das Hemd 1 (31)
shoe [ʃu:] der Schuh 1 (31)
shop [ʃɒp] der Laden, das Geschäft 1 (31)
shopping ['ʃɒpɪŋ] das Einkaufen; die Einkäufe 3 (88) **do the shopping** die Einkäufe erledigen, einkaufen gehen 3 (88) **go shopping** einkaufen gehen 3 (88)
shopping centre ['ʃɒpɪŋ sentə] das Einkaufszentrum 4 (122)
shopping list ['ʃɒpɪŋ lɪst] die Einkaufsliste 5 (155)
short [ʃɔ:t] kurz; klein *(Person; Körpergröße)* 3 (84/85)
°**shout** [ʃaʊt] rufen
show [ʃəʊ]:
1. die Show, die Aufführung; die Ausstellung 1 (29)
2. zeigen 3 (98)
shower ['ʃaʊə] die Dusche 3 (87) **have a shower** (sich) duschen 3 (87)
°**side** [saɪd] die Seite

°**sight** [saɪt] die Sehenswürdigkeit
°**sign** [saɪn] das Schild; das Zeichen
silver ['sɪlvə]:
1. das Silber (15)
2. silberfarben (15)
sing [sɪŋ] singen (16)
singer ['sɪŋə] der Sänger, die Sängerin (16)
singing ['sɪŋɪŋ] das Singen (16)
sister ['sɪstə] die Schwester 2 (50/51)
sit [sɪt] sitzen (17) **sit down** sich hinsetzen (17)
six [sɪks] sechs (10/11)
sixteen [sɪks'ti:n] sechzehn 2 (68)
sixty ['sɪksti] sechzig 2 (68)
°**size** [saɪz] die Größe
skateboard ['skeɪtbɔ:d]:
1. das Skateboard 3 (95)
2. Skateboard fahren 3 (95)
skateboarding ['skeɪtbɔ:dɪŋ] das Skateboardfahren 3 (95)
skatepark ['skeɪtpɑ:k] der Skatepark 3 (95)
°**skating** ['skeɪtɪŋ] das Schlittschuhlaufen; das (Inline-)Skaten
skill [skɪl]:
1. die Fähigkeit, die Fertigkeit 4 (116/117)
°**life skills** *(pl)* die Alltagskompetenzen, die lebenswichtigen Fertigkeiten
°2. die Lern- und Arbeitstechnik
°**study skills** *(pl)* die Lerntechniken
skirt [skɜ:t] der Rock 1 (31)
°**sky** [skaɪ] der Himmel **in the sky** am Himmel
sleep [sli:p]:
1. der Schlaf 5 (152)
2. schlafen 5 (152)
°**sleep in** ausschlafen
°**slide** [slaɪd] das Dia; die Folie *(Präsentationssoftware)*
slide show ['slaɪd ʃəʊ] die Slideshow, die Bildschirmpräsentation 4 (134)
slow [sləʊ] langsam 1 (32)
small [smɔ:l] klein (15)
small talk ['smɔ:l tɔ:k] der/das Small Talk *(oberflächliche, leichte Konversation)* 4 (129)
smart [smɑ:t]:
1. schick 5 (154)
2. intelligent, clever 5 (154)
smell [smel]:
1. der Geruch; der Gestank 4 (118)
2. riechen; schlecht riechen 4 (118)
smile [smaɪl]:
1. das Lächeln 5 (163)
2. lächeln 5 (163)
smile at sb. jn. anlächeln 5 (163)
°**smooth** [smu:ð] gleichmäßig, glatt
snack [snæk] der Snack, die kleine Mahlzeit 1 (31)
snake [sneɪk] die Schlange (14)
snow [snəʊ]:
1. der Schnee 4 (126)
2. schneien 4 (126)
snowy ['snəʊi] schneebedeckt; verschneit 4 (126)

so [səʊ]:
1. so (13)
so good so gut (13)
2. also, daher 2 (52)
3. **so (that)** sodass 4 (131)
sock [sɒk] die Socke 1 (31)
sofa ['səʊfə] das Sofa 2 (60)
software ['sɒftweə] die Software 3 (87)
solution (to a problem) [sə'lu:ʃn] die Lösung (eines Problems) 2 (66)
some [sʌm], [səm] einige, ein paar; etwas, ein wenig 1 (32)
somebody ['sʌmbədi] jemand 4 (131)
someone ['sʌmwʌn] jemand 4 (131)
something ['sʌmθɪŋ] etwas 4 (124)
sometimes ['sʌmtaɪmz] manchmal 3 (91)
son [sʌn] der Sohn 2 (50/51)
song [sɒŋ] das Lied (13)
soon [su:n] bald 1 (24)
sorry ['sɒri]: **Sorry. / I'm sorry.** Tut mir leid. / Entschuldigung. (16) **be/feel sorry for sb.** Mitleid haben mit jm. 3 (98) **I'm / I feel sorry for him.** Er tut mir leid. 3 (98)
sound [saʊnd]:
1. das Geräusch; der Klang, der Laut 3 (95)
2. klingen *(sich … anhören)* 3 (95)
°**south** [saʊθ] südlich; Süd-
spaghetti [spə'geti] die Spaghetti 5 (166)
speak (to) [spi:k] sprechen (mit) 2 (64) **Speak later.** Tschüs. / Bis später. 2 (64)
speaking ['spi:kɪŋ] das Sprechen 2 (64)
special ['speʃl] besondere(r, s) 2 (55)
°**speech** [spi:tʃ] die Rede, die Ansprache
speech bubble ['spi:tʃ bʌbl] die Sprechblase 3 (103)
spell [spel] buchstabieren 2 (68)
spelling ['spelɪŋ] die Schreibweise, die Rechtschreibung 2 (68)
spice [spaɪs] das Gewürz 5 (148/149)
spicy ['spaɪsi] würzig 5 (148/149)
spoon [spu:n] der Löffel 5 (158)
sport [spɔ:t] der Sport; die Sportart (15) °**do sport(s)** Sport treiben
sports hall ['spɔ:ts hɔ:l] die Sporthalle 1 (28)
spring [sprɪŋ] der Frühling 5 (150)
stadium ['steɪdiəm] das Stadion 4 (122)
stand [stænd] stehen; sich (hin)stellen (17) **stand up** aufstehen (17)
star [stɑ:] der (Film-/Pop-)Star 1 (32)
stare [steə]:
1. das Starren, der starre Blick 3 (98)
2. **stare (at)** (an)starren 3 (98)
start [stɑ:t]:
1. der Anfang, der Start 1 (22)
2. beginnen, anfangen (mit) 1 (22)
°**statement** ['steɪtmənt] der Aussage(satz)

station ['steɪʃn] der Bahnhof 4 (122)
°stay [steɪ] bleiben; übernachten
°steady [redi stedi 'gəʊ]: **Ready, steady, go!** Auf die Plätze, fertig, los!
step [step] die Stufe; der Schritt 1 (37)
stepbrother ['stepbrʌðə] der Stiefbruder 2 (50/51)
stepdad ['stepdæd] der Stiefvater 2 (50/51)
stepdaughter ['stepdɔːtə] die Stieftochter 2 (50/51)
stepfather ['stepfɑːθə] der Stiefvater 2 (50/51)
stepmother ['stepmʌθə] die Stiefmutter 2 (50/51)
stepmum ['stepmʌm] die Stiefmutter 2 (50/51)
stepsister ['stepsɪstə] die Stiefschwester 2 (50/51)
stepson ['stepsʌn] der Stiefsohn 2 (50/51)
still [stɪl]:
1. (immer) noch; trotzdem 1 (33)
°2. still, ruhig
stir [stɜː] (um)rühren 5 (160)
stir-fry ['stɜː fraɪ]:
1. *das Gericht aus kurz angebratenen Zutaten, z.B. kleinen Stücken Fleisch, Fisch und/oder Gemüse* 5 (160)
2. (Gemüse- oder Fleischstücke) unter Rühren scharf anbraten 5 (160)
stop [stɒp]:
1. (an)halten; stoppen; aufhören (mit) 4 (127)
2. der Halt, der Haltepunkt; die Unterbrechung 4 (127)
bus stop die Bushaltestelle 4 (127)
story ['stɔːri] die Geschichte *(Erzählung)* 1 (32)
strawberry ['strɔːbəri] die Erdbeere 5 (148/149)
street [striːt] die Straße *(in Ortschaften)* 2 (58) **in the street** auf der Straße 2 (58) **on a quiet street** an einer ruhigen Straße 2 (58)
street dance ['striːt dɑːns] der Streetdance *(Tanzstil)* 2 (58)
street music ['striːt mjuːzɪk] die Straßenmusik 2 (58)
stressed [strest] gestresst 3 (91)
°strong [strɒŋ] stark
student ['stjuːdnt] der Schüler, die Schülerin; der Student, die Studentin 1 (18/19)
°study ['stʌdi] lernen *(auch z.B. für Prüfungen)*
°study skills *(pl)* ['stʌdi skɪlz] die Lerntechniken
subject ['sʌbdʒɪkt] das (Schul-)Fach 1 (26)
sugar ['ʃʊgə] der Zucker 5 (155)
summer ['sʌmə] der Sommer 4 (124)
sun [sʌn] die Sonne 2 (58) **have a moment in the sun** kurz im Mittelpunkt stehen 4 (129)
Sunday ['sʌndeɪ], ['sʌndi] der Sonntag 1 (25)
°sunglasses *(pl)* ['sʌnglɑːsɪz] die Sonnenbrille

sunny ['sʌni] sonnig 2 (58) **It's sunny.** Die Sonne scheint. 2 (58)
super ['suːpə] super 3 (103)
superhero ['suːpəhɪərəʊ], *pl* **superheroes** der Superheld, die Superheldin 3 (103) **super** ['suːpə] super
supermarket ['suːpəmɑːkɪt] der Supermarkt 4 (122)
sure [ʃʊə], [ʃɔː] sicher 5 (154)
surprised [sə'praɪzd] überrascht 3 (98)
swap [swɒp]:
1. tauschen 4 (128)
2. der Tausch 4 (128)
clothes swap der Kleidertausch, die Kleidertauschparty 4 (128)
sweatshirt ['swetʃɜːt] das Sweatshirt 5 (154)
sweet [swiːt]:
1. süß 2 (63)
2. das Bonbon 2 (63)
sweets *(pl)* die Süßigkeiten 2 (63)
swim [swɪm] schwimmen (15)
swimmer ['swɪmə] der Schwimmer, die Schwimmerin (15)
swimming ['swɪmɪŋ] das Schwimmen (15)

T

T-shirt ['tiː ʃɜːt] das T-Shirt 5 (153)
°Ta-dah! [tʌ'dɑː] Tada! / Siehe da!
table ['teɪbl]:
1. der Tisch 2 (60)
°2. die Tabelle
table tennis ['teɪbl tenɪs] das Tischtennis 3 (90)
tablespoon ['teɪblspuːn] der Esslöffel 5 (158)
°tail [teɪl] der Schwanz
take [teɪk]:
1. (mit)nehmen; bringen 1 (22)
take photos Fotos machen (15)
2. dauern, *(Zeit)* brauchen, in Anspruch nehmen 3 (87)
talk [tɔːk]:
1. das Gespräch; die Rede, der Vortrag 1 (22)
2. **talk (to)** sprechen, reden (mit) 1 (22)
talk about sprechen, reden über 1 (22)
°tall [tɔːl] groß *(Person; Körpergröße)*
°tamarind ['tæmərɪnd] die Tamarinde
task [tɑːsk] die Aufgabe 3 (103)
do a task eine Aufgabe machen/erledigen 3 (103)
taste [teɪst]:
1. schmecken; kosten, probieren 5 (159)
2. der Geschmack 5 (159)
tasty ['teɪsti] schmackhaft, lecker 5 (159)
tea [tiː] der Tee 5 (160)
teach [tiːtʃ] lehren, unterrichten 5 (152) **teach sb. to do sth.** jm. beibringen, etwas zu tun 5 (152)
teacher ['tiːtʃə] der Lehrer, die Lehrerin 1 (22)

team [tiːm] das Team, die Mannschaft 3 (97)
°tear [tɪə] die Träne
teaspoon ['tiːspuːn] der Teelöffel 5 (158)
tech [tek] *siehe* **technology**
technology [tek'nɒlədʒi], *infml auch* **tech** die Technik, der Technikunterricht; die Technologie 1 (26)
teeth [tiːθ] *Plural von* **tooth**
brush your teeth (sich) die Zähne putzen 3 (89)
tell [tel] erzählen, sagen 2 (58)
ten [ten] zehn (10/11)
°ten thousand [ten 'θaʊznd] zehntausend (10000)
tennis ['tenɪs] das Tennis 3 (90)
terraced home/house ['terəst] das Reihenhaus 2 (59)
terrarium [te'reəriəm] das Terrarium 2 (63)
terrible ['terəbl] schrecklich, fürchterlich 4 (129)
test [test]:
1. der Test; die Klassenarbeit 1 (36)
2. testen 1 (36)
text [tekst]:
1. der Text 3 (99)
2. **text (message)** die SMS 3 (99)
3. **text sb.** jm. eine SMS schicken 3 (99)
°than [ðən]: **more than 100** mehr als 100
thank you ['θæŋk juː] danke (schön) (10/11) **Thank you very much.** Vielen Dank. / Danke vielmals. 3 (99)
thanks [θæŋks] danke (schön) (10/11)
that [ðæt]:
1. das (dort) (16)
that's (= that is) das (da) ist (16)
°That's where I like to be. Dort / Genau dort bin ich gerne.
2. dass 1 (33)
I'm happy that ... Ich bin froh, dass ... 1 (33) **so that** sodass 4 (131)
3. der, die, das *(Relativpronomen)* 4 (122)
the [ðə] der, die, das (10/11)
theatre ['θɪətə] das Theater 1 (30)
their [ðeə]:
1. ihr/e *(Plural)* 2 (59)
°2. sein/e; ihr/e *(gender-neutral)*
them [ðem], [ðəm] sie, ihnen 1 (32)
°theme [θiːm] das Thema
then [ðen] dann, danach 1 (32)
there [ðeə] da, dort; dahin, dorthin (14) **there are** es sind ... / es gibt ... (14) **there's (= there is)** es ist ... / es gibt ... (14)
these [ðiːz] diese (hier) 1 (33) **These are my friends.** Das hier sind meine Freunde/Freundinnen. 1 (33)
they [ðeɪ] sie *(Plural)* 1 (24) **they're (= they are)** sie sind 1 (24)
thing [θɪŋ] das Ding, die Sache (12)
think [θɪŋk] denken, meinen, glauben 1 (24) **think about** nachdenken über 3 (103) **I think ...** Ich denke/meine/glaube/finde, ... 1 (24)

third (3rd) [θɜːd] dritte(r, s) 5 (150)
thirteen [θɜːˈtiːn] dreizehn (10/11)
thirty [ˈθɜːti] dreißig 2 (68)
this [ðɪs] dies; diese(r, s) (15)
those [ðəʊz] die dort, jene (dort) 1 (32)
°thousand [ˈθaʊznd] tausend
three [θriː] drei (10/11)
°through [θruː] durch
°throw [θrəʊ] werfen
Thursday [ˈθɜːzdeɪ], [ˈθɜːzdi] der Donnerstag 1 (25)
°tick [tɪk] ankreuzen, abhaken
ticket [ˈtɪkɪt] die Eintrittskarte, die Fahrkarte, das Ticket 3 (99)
tidy [ˈtaɪdi]:
1. ordentlich 2 (61)
2. aufräumen 2 (61)
tie [taɪ] die Krawatte 1 (20)
°till [tɪl] bis
time [taɪm] die Zeit; die Uhrzeit 1 (20) **What time is it?** Wie spät ist es? 3 (86) **What time?** Um wie viel Uhr? 3 (86) **What's the time?** Wie spät ist es? 3 (86)
timetable [ˈtaɪmteɪbl] der Stundenplan 1 (24)
tip [tɪp] der Tipp 4 (127)
tired [ˈtaɪəd] müde 1 (20)
title [ˈtaɪtl] der Titel, die Überschrift 4 (134)
to [tu], [tə]:
1. zu, nach 1 (22)
different to you anders als du 1 (22) **the answer to the question** die Antwort auf die Frage 1 (23) **°an email to / (to) write to** eine E-mail an / schreiben an
2. bis 1 (36)
(from) A to Z (von) A bis Z 1 (36)
3. (um) zu (12)
how to do sth. wie man etwas tut / tun kann / tun soll 3 (90) **things to eat** Dinge zum Essen (12)
°toad [təʊd] die Kröte
today [təˈdeɪ] heute 1 (29) **today's letter** der Brief von heute 1 (29)
together [təˈgeðə] zusammen 4 (131)
toilet [ˈtɔɪlət] die Toilette 1 (22)
tomato [təˈmɑːtəʊ], *pl* **tomatoes** die Tomate 5 (148/149)
°tomato paste [təˈmɑːtəʊ peɪst] das Tomatenmark
tomato sauce [təˈmɑːtəʊ sɔːs] die Tomatensoße 5 (148/149)
°tomorrow [təˈmɒrəʊ] morgen
°tonight [təˈnaɪt] heute Abend, heute Nacht
too [tuː]:
1. auch (10/11)
from York too auch aus York (10/11)
2. **too slow** zu langsam 1 (32)
tooth [tuːθ], *pl* **teeth** der Zahn 3 (89)
top [tɒp] die Spitze, das obere Ende 2 (56) **the top six films** die sechs besten Filme (16)
top floor [tɒp ˈflɔː] das Dach-/Obergeschoss, das oberste Stockwerk, die oberste Etage 2 (56)
topic [ˈtɒpɪk] das Thema 4 (135)
tour (of) [tʊə] die Tour, die Reise, der Rundgang / die Rundfahrt 2 (57)
tour guide [ˈtʊə gaɪd] der Reiseleiter, die Reiseleiterin / der Fremdenführer, die Fremdenführerin 4 (124)
tourist [ˈtʊərɪst] der Tourist, die Touristin 4 (126)
°tower [ˈtaʊə] der Turm
town [taʊn] die Stadt 4 (118)
town centre [taʊn ˈsentə] das Stadtzentrum 4 (118)
toy [tɔɪ] das Spielzeug 4 (132)
tradition [trəˈdɪʃn] die Tradition 5 (160)
traditional [trəˈdɪʃənl] traditionell 5 (160)
train [treɪn] der Zug, die Eisenbahn 3 (84/85)
train station [ˈtreɪn steɪʃn] der Bahnhof 4 (122)
trainer [ˈtreɪnə] der Trainer, die Trainerin 3 (100)
training [ˈtreɪnɪŋ] das Training 3 (87)
trampoline [ˈtræmpəliːn] das Trampolin 3 (90)
trampolining [ˈtræmpəliːnɪŋ] das Trampolinspringen/-turnen 3 (90)
°transport *(no pl)* [ˈtrænspɔːt] das Fortbewegungsmittel
travel [ˈtrævl]:
1. das Reisen 4 (126)
2. reisen, fahren 4 (126)
tree [triː] der Baum 2 (56)
trick [trɪk] der Trick, das Kunststück 5 (154)
trifle [ˈtraɪfl] das Trifle *(britischer Nachtisch)* 5 (148/149)
°trip [trɪp]: **take a trip** eine Reise machen
trouble [ˈtrʌbl] der Ärger, die Schwierigkeiten 1 (32) **be in trouble** Ärger haben, in Schwierigkeiten sein 1 (32)
trousers *(pl)* [ˈtraʊzəz] die Hose 1 (31)
true [truː] wahr, richtig 5 (159)
°try [traɪ] versuchen, (aus)probieren **try sth. out** etwas ausprobieren **try to do sth.** versuchen, etwas zu tun
Tuesday [ˈtjuːzdeɪ], [ˈtjuːzdi] der Dienstag 1 (25)
turn [tɜːn] (sich) (um)drehen 4 (127) **Turn it upside down.** Dreh/Stell es auf den Kopf. 4 (127) **turn sth. (over)** etwas umdrehen 4 (127)
turn [tɜːn]: **it is sb.'s turn (to do sth.)** jd. ist dran / an der Reihe (etwas zu tun) 5 (163) **take turns / take it in turns (to do sth)** sich abwechseln; sich dabei abwechseln, etwas zu tun 5 (163) **When is (it) my turn (to do sth.)?** Wann bin ich dran / an der Reihe (etwas zu tun)? 5 (163)
TV [tiːˈviː] der Fernseher; das Fernsehen 3 (87)
twelfth (12th) [twelfθ] zwölfte(r, s) 5 (150)
twelve [twelv] zwölf (10/11)
twenty [ˈtwenti] zwanzig 2 (68)
two [tuː] zwei (10/11)
°type (of) [taɪp] die Art, die Sorte

U

°Ugh! [ɜː] Bah!
UK (= United Kingdom) [juː ˈkeɪ] das Vereinigte Königreich 3 (86)
umbrella [ʌmˈbrelə] der (Regen-)Schirm 4 (129)
°umbrella word [ʌmˈbrelə wɜːd] der Oberbegriff, der Sammelbegriff
uncle [ˈʌŋkl] der Onkel 2 (50/51)
under [ˈʌndə] unter 2 (60)
understand [ʌndəˈstænd] verstehen 1 (23)
unfriendly [ʌnˈfrendli] unfreundlich 4 (118)
uniform [ˈjuːnɪfɔːm] die Uniform 1 (20) **(school) uniform** die (Schul-)Uniform 1 (20)
unit [ˈjuːnɪt] die Unit *(Lerneinheit)* 1 (18/19)
United Kingdom (UK) [junaɪtɪd ˈkɪŋdəm] das Vereinigte Königreich 3 (86)
°until [ənˈtɪl] bis *(zeitlich)*
up [ʌp] hinauf, hoch 4 (126)
upside down [ʌpsaɪd ˈdaʊn] verkehrt herum, auf dem Kopf 4 (127)
us [ʌs], [əs] uns 1 (22)
use [juːz] benutzen, verwenden 1 (23)
useful [ˈjuːsfl] nützlich, hilfreich 1 (37)
user [ˈjuːzə] der (Be-)Nutzer, die (Be-)Nutzerin 1 (23)
usually [ˈjuːʒuəli] normalerweise, meistens 5 (148/149)

V

vanilla [vəˈnɪlə] die Vanille 5 (158)
vegan [ˈviːgən]:
1. vegan 5 (148/149)
2. der Veganer, die Veganerin 5 (148/149)
vegetables *(pl)* [ˈvedʒtəblz] das/die Gemüse 5 (148/149)
vegetarian [vedʒəˈteəriən], *infml auch* **veggie**:
1. vegetarisch 5 (148/149)
2. der/die Vegetarier/in 5 (148/149)
veggie [ˈvedʒi] *siehe* **vegetarian**
°verse [vɜːs] die Strophe *(Lied)*
°version [ˈvɜːʃn] die Version
very [ˈveri] sehr 1 (30)
vet [vet] der Tierarzt, die Tierärztin 2 (52)
video [ˈvɪdiəʊ] das Video; Video- 2 (65)
view [vjuː]:
1. der (An-)Blick, die (Aus-)Sicht 4 (126)
2. **view sth.** etwas anschauen 4 (126)
°viewing [ˈvjuːɪŋ] das Fernsehen, das Betrachten *(von DVDs, Filmen usw.)*
village [ˈvɪlɪdʒ] das Dorf 4 (121)
visit [ˈvɪzɪt]:
1. besuchen 4 (123)
2. der Besuch 4 (123)
visitor [ˈvɪzɪtə] der Besucher, die Besucherin; der Gast 4 (123)

visitor information centre [vɪzɪtər ɪnfəˈmeɪʃn sentə] die Touristeninformation, das Fremdenverkehrsbüro 4(123)
vocab [ˈvəʊkæb] *siehe* **vocabulary**
vocabulary [vəˈkæbjələri] *infml auch* **vocab** der Wortschatz, das Vokabular; das Vokabelverzeichnis 1(36)

W

°wag [wæg] wedeln (mit)
°wait (for) [weɪt] warten (auf)
walk [wɔːk]:
1. der Spaziergang 1(18/19)
2. (zu Fuß) gehen, wandern 1(18/19)
°walk around umhergehen
walking [ˈwɔːkɪŋ] das Wandern 1(18/19)
wall [wɔːl] die Wand, die Mauer 2(63) **on the wall** an die Wand; an der Wand 2(63)
want [wɒnt] wollen 2(55) **want to do sth.** etwas tun wollen 2(55) **°I want your party to be fun for you.** Ich will/möchte, dass dir deine Party Spaß macht.
wardrobe [ˈwɔːdrəʊb] der Kleiderschrank 2(60)
warm [wɔːm] warm 4(124)
°was [wɒz], [wəz]: **it was** es war
watch (sth.) [wɒtʃ] (sich etwas) anschauen; (etwas) beobachten 3(87)
water [ˈwɔːtə] das Wasser 5(155)
watermelon [ˈmelən] die Wassermelone 5(155)
wave [weɪv]:
1. **wave (to sb.)** (jm. zu)winken 5(162)
2. das Winken 5(162)
give sb. a wave jm. zuwinken 5(162)
way [weɪ]:
1. der Weg 1(36)
2. die Art und Weise 1(36)
(in) this way auf diese Art/Weise 1(36) **in different ways** unterschiedlich *(Adv.)*, auf unterschiedliche Art/Weise 1(36)
we [wiː] wir 1(24) **we're (= we are)** wir sind 1(24)
wear [weə] tragen, anhaben *(Kleidung)* 1(31)
weather [ˈweðə] das Wetter, die Witterung 4(126)
website [ˈwebsaɪt] die Website 1(29)
wedding [ˈwedɪŋ] die Hochzeit 4(131)
wedding present [ˈwedɪŋ preznt] das Hochzeitsgeschenk 4(131)
wedding ring [ˈwedɪŋ rɪŋ] der Ehering 4(131)
Wednesday [ˈwenzdeɪ], [ˈwenzdi] der Mittwoch 1(25)
week [wiːk] die Woche 1(25)
weekday [ˈwiːkdeɪ] der Werktag, der Wochentag 3(86)
weekend [wiːkˈend] das Wochenende 2(52) **at the weekend** am Wochenende 2(52)
weird [wɪəd] seltsam, komisch 1(32)
welcome [ˈwelkəm]:
1. **Welcome to ...** Willkommen in/an ... 4(125)
2. **You're welcome.** Bitte, gern geschehen. / Nichts zu danken. 1(23)
well [wel]:
1. gut *(Adv.)* 3(99)
Well done. Gut gemacht! 3(99)
2. **Well, ...** Nun, .../ Also, .../ Na ja, ... 4(130)
what [wɒt]:
1. was (10/11)
2. welche(r, s) 1(23)
What about a ... ? Wie wäre es mit einer/einem ... ? 5(154) **What about you?** Und du? / Was ist mit dir? (10/11) **What's your name?** Wie heißt du? (10/11)
wheelchair [ˈwiːltʃeə] der Rollstuhl 3(87)
when [wen]:
1. wann 2(54)
2. wenn *(zeitlich)* 2(54)
where [weə] wo; wohin (10/11)
Where are you from? Wo kommst du her? (10/11)
which [wɪtʃ] welche(r, s) 3(90) **Which clubs ...?** Welche AGs ...? 3(90)
°while [waɪl] während
whipped cream [wɪpt ˈkriːm] die Schlagsahne, die geschlagene Sahne 5(148/149)
°whisper [ˈwɪspə] flüstern
white [waɪt] weiß (10/11)
who [huː] wer 1(32)
°whole [həʊl] ganze(r, s)
why [waɪ] warum 3(87) **°the reason why ...** der Grund dafür, dass ...
wife [waɪf], *pl* **wives** die (Ehe-)Frau 3(87)
win [wɪn] gewinnen 3(87)
wind [wɪnd] der Wind 4(126)
window [ˈwɪndəʊ] das Fenster 1(22)
windsurfing [wɪndsɜːfɪŋ] das Windsurfing 3(90)
windy [ˈwɪndi] windig 4(126)
winner [ˈwɪnə] der Gewinner, die Gewinnerin / der Sieger, die Siegerin 3(87)
winter [ˈwɪntə] der Winter 4(124)
with [wɪð]:
1. mit (15)
2. bei (15)
with me/us/... bei mir/uns/... (15)
wives [waɪvz] *Plural von* **wife**
wok [wɒk] der Wok *(chinesischer Kochtopf)* 5(167)
woman [ˈwʊmən], *pl* **women** die Frau 4(126)
women [ˈwɪmɪn] *Plural von* **woman**
°wonderful [ˈwʌndəfl] wunderbar
word [wɜːd] das Wort 1(36)
°wordbank [ˈwɜːdbæŋk] die Wortbank *(Wörtersammlung zu einem Thema)*
work [wɜːk]:
1. funktionieren 2(52)
2. arbeiten 2(52)
work long days lange arbeiten, lange Arbeitstage haben 3(87)
3. die Arbeit 2(52)
at work bei der Arbeit, am Arbeitsplatz 2(52)
°workbook [ˈwɜːkbʊk] das Arbeitsheft
worried (about) [ˈwʌrid] beunruhigt, besorgt (wegen) 5(163)
worry [ˈwʌri]:
1. die Sorge 5(163)
2. **worry (about)** sich Sorgen machen (wegen, um) 5(163)
Don't worry. Mach dir keine Sorgen. 5(163)
would [wʊd]: **Would you like ...?** Möchtest du ...? 3(94) **I'd (= I would) like/love ...** Ich hätte (liebend) gern ... / Ich möchte (liebend gern)... 3(94) **I'd (= I would) love/like to meet ....** Ich würde mich (liebend) gerne mit ... treffen. 3(94)
write [raɪt] schreiben 2(68) **°write it down** es aufschreiben
wrong [rɒŋ] falsch (10/11) **be wrong** Unrecht haben 1(24) **°What's wrong with Zane?** Was ist mit Zane los? **°What's wrong?** Was ist los? / Was/Wo ist das Problem?

Y

°yeah [jeə] *(infml)* ja
year [jɪə] das Jahr; der Jahrgang (10/11) **°leap year** das Schaltjahr
yellow [ˈjeləʊ] gelb (10/11)
yes [jes] ja 1(22)
°yesterday [ˈjestədeɪ] gestern
yoga [ˈjəʊgə] das Yoga 1(18/19)
you [juː] du; dich; dir; ihr; euch; Sie; Ihnen (10/11)
°young [jʌŋ] jung
your [jɔː], [jə] dein/e; euer/eure; Ihr/e (10/11)
yours [jɔːz] deine, deiner, deins; eurer, eure, eures; Ihrer, Ihre, Ihres 1(25)
°yourself [jəˈself] du/dir/dich (selbst)
youth [juːθ] die Jugend; der Jugendliche 4(118)
youth centre [ˈjuːθ sentə] das Jugendzentrum 4(118)
°Yuck! [jʌk] Igitt!
°yum [jʌm] *(infml)* lecker

Z

zero [ˈzɪərəʊ], *pl* **zeros** die Null, die Nullen 2(68)
zoo [zuː] der Zoo 4(135)

Das *German-English Dictionary* enthält den **Lernwortschatz** deines Schulbuchs. Es kann dir eine erste Hilfe sein, wenn du vergessen hast, wie etwas auf Englisch heißt.
Wenn du wissen möchtest, wo das englische Wort zum ersten Mal in deinem Schulbuch vorkommt, dann kannst du im *English-German Dictionary* (Seiten 283–296) nachschlagen.

Es werden folgende **Abkürzungen und Symbole** verwendet:

infml = *informal* (umgangssprachlich)
sb. = *somebody* (jemand)
jd. = jemand jm. = jemandem
pl = *plural* (Mehrzahl)
sth. = *something* (etwas)
jn. = jemanden

A

Abend evening [ˈiːvnɪŋ] **am Abend** in the evening
Abendessen dinner [ˈdɪnə] **zum Abendessen** for dinner
abends in the evening [ˈiːvnɪŋ] **9 Uhr abends** *(21 Uhr)* 9 p.m. [piːˈem]
aber but [bʌt], [bət]
abhängen, rumhängen hang out [hæŋ ˈaʊt]
A bis Z: (von) A bis Z (from) A to Z [eɪ tu zed]
Abfall rubbish [ˈrʌbɪʃ]
abwechseln: sich abwechseln take turns [tɜːn] **sich dabei abwechseln, etwas zu tun** take it in turns (to do sth.)
acht eight [eɪt]
achtzehn eighteen [eɪˈtiːn]
achtzig eighty [ˈeɪti]
addieren add [æd]
Adresse address [əˈdres]
Affe monkey [ˈmʌŋki]
AG *(in der Schule)* school club [skuːl klʌb]
aktiv active [ˈæktɪv]
Aktivität activity [ækˈtɪvəti]
albern stupid [ˈstjuːpɪd]
alle(s) all [ɔːl] **alle 30 Minuten** every 30 minutes [ˈevri]
allein alone [əˈləʊn]
allergisch (gegen) allergic (to) [əˈlɜːdʒɪk]
Alphabet alphabet [ˈælfəbet]
also so [səʊ] **Also, ...** Well, ... [wel]
alt old [əʊld] **Wie alt bist du?** How old are you?
am: am Anfang at first [æt], [ət] **am Arbeitsplatz** at work **am besten** best [best] **am Ende (von)** at the end (of) **am größten** biggest [ˈbɪgɪst] **am Meer** by the sea [baɪ] **am Montag** on Monday [ɒn] **am Morgen** in the morning [ɪn] **am Nachmittag** in the afternoon **am nächsten Tag** the next day **am oberen Ende (von)** at the top (of) **am Strand** on the beach **am Telefon** on the phone **am Wochenende** at the weekend
an at [æt], [ət]
Anblick, (Aus-)Blick, Aussicht view [vjuː]
anbraten: *(Gemüse- oder Fleischstücke)* **unter Rühren scharf anbraten** stir-fry [ˈstɜː fraɪ]
andere(r, s) other [ˈʌðə] **die anderen** the other **ein/e andere(r, s)** another [əˈnʌðə]
anders different [ˈdɪfrənt]
Anfang start [stɑːt] **am Anfang** at first [æt], [ət]
anfangen (mit) start [stɑːt]
Angst: Angst haben be scared (of) [skeəd]
anhaben *(Kleidung)* wear [weə]
anhalten stop [stɒp]
anhören: sich etwas anhören listen to sth. [ˈlɪsn]
anlächeln: jn. anlächeln smile at sb. [smaɪl]
Anruf (phone) call [ˈfəʊn kɔːl]
anrufen call [kɔːl]; phone [fəʊn]
anschauen: etwas/jn. anschauen look at sth./sb. [lʊk] **sich etwas anschauen** watch sth. [wɒtʃ]
Anspitzer sharpener [ˈʃɑːpnə]
Anteil share [ʃeə]
Antwort answer [ˈɑːnsə] **Antwort auf die Frage** the answer to the question
antworten answer [ˈɑːnsə]
Anweisung instruction [ɪnˈstrʌkʃn]
anziehen: sich anziehen get dressed [drest]
App app [æp]
Appetit: Guten Appetit! Enjoy! [ɪnˈdʒɔɪ]
April April [ˈeɪprəl]
Arbeit work [wɜːk] **bei der Arbeit, am Arbeitsplatz** at work
arbeiten work [wɜːk] **lange arbeiten** work long days [lɒŋ]
Ärger trouble [ˈtrʌbl] **Ärger kriegen** be in trouble
Art way [weɪ] **auf diese Art** (in) this way, like this [laɪk] **auf unterschiedliche Art** in different ways **eine Art (von)...** a kind (of) ... [kaɪnd], sort (of) [sɔːt]
Artikel article [ˈɑːtɪkl]
auch also [ˈɔːlsəʊ]; too [tuː] **auch aus Berlin** from Berlin too
auf at [æt], [ət]; in [ɪn]; on [ɒn] **auf dem Bild, auf dem Foto** in the picture **auf dem Kopf** upside down [ʌpsaɪd ˈdaʊn] **auf dem Land** in the country **auf der Weide** in the field **auf English** in English **Auf Wiedersehen!** Goodbye. [gʊdˈbaɪ]
Aufführung show [ʃəʊ]
Aufgabe exercise [ˈeksəsaɪz]
aufhören (mit) stop [stɒp]
auflisten list [lɪst]
aufpassen auf look after [lʊk]
aufräumen tidy [ˈtaɪdi] **etwas aufräumen** clean sth. up [kliːn]
aufschlagen *(Buch)* open [ˈəʊpən] **Schlagt eure Bücher auf Seite 10 auf.** Open your books at page 10.
aufstehen *(aus dem Bett)* get up [get ˈʌp]; *(sich hinstellen)* stand up [stænd ˈʌp]
August August [ɔːˈgʌst]
aus from [frɒm]
Ausdruck phrase [freɪz]
ausschneiden: etwas ausschneiden cut sth. out [kʌt]
ausruhen: sich ausruhen relax [rɪˈlæks]
aussehen look [lʊk]
außerhalb (von) outside [ˌaʊtˈsaɪd]
Ausstellung show [ʃəʊ]
auswählen choose [tʃuːz]
Auto car [kɑː]
Autoscheinwerfer car light [ˈkɑː laɪt]

B

backen bake [beɪk]
Backofen oven [ˈʌvn]
Backpulver baking powder [ˈbeɪkɪŋ paʊdə]
Bad(ezimmer) bathroom [ˈbɑːθruːm]
Badminton badminton [ˈbædmɪntən]
Bahnhof (train) station [ˈtreɪn steɪʃn]
bald soon [suːn]
Balkon balcony [ˈbælkəni]
Ball ball [bɔːl]
Ballon balloon [bəˈluːn]
Banane banana [bəˈnɑːnə]
Band band [bænd]
Basketball basketball [ˈbɑːskɪtbɔːl]
Basteln crafts *(pl)* [krɑːfts]
Baum tree [triː]
beantworten answer [ˈɑːnsə]
bedeuten mean [miːn]
Bedeutung meaning [ˈmiːnɪŋ]
beenden end [end]
beginnen start [stɑːt]
begrüßen greet [griːt]
Behälter case [keɪs]
bei at [æt], [ət]; with [wɪð] **bei der Arbeit** at work **bei ihrer Mutter (zu Hause/daheim)** at her mum's (house)
beibringen: jm. beibringen, etwas zu tun teach sb. to do sth. [tiːtʃ]
Beispiel example [ɪgˈzɑːmpl] **zum Beispiel** for example **wie zum Beispiel** like [laɪk]

bekommen get [get]
belebt busy ['bɪzi]
bellen: (jn. an)bellen bark (at sb.) [bɑ:k]
benutzen use [ju:z]
Benutzer/in user ['ju:zə]
beobachten: (etwas) beobachten watch (sth.) [wɒtʃ]
bereit ready ['redi]
beschäftigt: (viel) beschäftigt busy ['bɪzi] **du bist beschäftigt** you're busy
beschreiben describe [dɪ'skraɪb]
Beschreibung description [dɪ'skrɪpʃn]
besondere(r, s) special ['speʃl]
besorgen: (sich etwas) besorgen get sth. [get]
beste(r, s) best [best] **der beste Sohn überhaupt / der beste Sohn, den man sich wünschen kann** the best son ever ['evə]
Besuch visit ['vɪzɪt]
besuchen visit ['vɪzɪt]
Besucher/in visitor ['vɪzɪtə]
Bett bed [bed] **ins Bett gehen** go to bed
beunruhigt/besorgt (wegen) worried ['wʌrid]
bevor before [bɪ'fɔ:] **bevor du liest** before you read
bewegen: sich bewegen move [mu:v]
bewölkt cloudy ['klaʊdi]
Bibliothek library ['laɪbrəri]
Bild picture ['pɪktʃə] **auf dem Bild** in the picture [ɪn]
Bildschirmpräsentation slide show ['slaɪd ʃəʊ]
Biologie biology [baɪ'ɒlədʒi]
bis to [tu], [tə] **Bis bald!** See you soon. ['si: ju], ['si: jə] **Bis dann.** See you. **Bis später.** Speak later. ['leɪtə]
bisschen: ein bisschen a little ['lɪtl]
bitte please [pli:z] **Bitte schön. / Hier, bitte.** Here you are. [hɪə ju 'ɑ:] **Bitte, gern geschehen.** You're welcome. ['welkəm]
bitten: jn. bitten, etwas zu tun ask sb. to do sth. [ɑ:sk] **jn. um etwas bitten** ask sb. for sth.
blau blue [blu:]
Blazer *(das Jackett, oft Teil der Schuluniform)* blazer ['bleɪzə]
Bleistift pencil ['pensl]
Bleistift(an)spitzer pencil sharpener ['pensl ʃɑ:pnə]
Blindenhund guide dog ['gaɪd dɒg]
blöd stupid ['stju:pɪd]
bloß just [dʒʌst]; only ['əʊnli]
Bockwurst sausage ['sɒsɪdʒ]
Boden ground [graʊnd]
Bonbon sweet [swi:t]
Bowling bowling ['bəʊlɪŋ]
Boxen boxing ['bɒksɪŋ]
boxen box [bɒks]
braten fry [fraɪ] **gebraten** fried [fraɪd]
Brathähnchen chicken ['tʃɪkɪn]
Bratwurst sausage ['sɒsɪdʒ]
brauchen need [ni:d]; *(Zeit)* take [teɪk]
braun brown [braʊn]
brav good [gʊd]
Brief letter ['letə] **der kurze Brief** note [nəʊt]
bringen bring [brɪŋ]; take [teɪk]
britisch British ['brɪtɪʃ]
Brot bread [bred]
Browser *(Computerprogramm zum Finden und Lesen von Websites)* browser ['braʊzə]
Bruder brother ['brʌðə]
Buch book [bʊk]
Buchseite page (p.) [peɪdʒ]
Bücherei library ['laɪbrəri]
Buchstabe letter ['letə]
buchstabieren spell [spel]
Bürste brush [brʌʃ]
bürsten brush [brʌʃ]
Bus bus [bʌs] **im Bus** on the bus **mit dem Bus** by bus
Bushaltestelle bus stop ['bʌs stɒp]
Butter butter ['bʌtə]

C

Café cafe ['kæfeɪ]
Cent cent [sent]
Chaos mess [mes]
clever smart [smɑ:t]
Code code [kəʊd]
codieren code [kəʊd]
Cola cola ['kəʊlə]
Comic comic ['kɒmɪk]
Computer computer [kəm'pju:tə]
cool cool [ku:l]
Cousin/e cousin ['kʌzn]
Cricket *(Mannschaftssportart)* cricket ['krɪkɪt]
Curry *(Gewürz und auch Gericht)* curry ['kʌri]
Custard *(Vanillesoße)* custard ['kʌstəd]

D

da there [ðeə] **da drüben** over there
Dachgeschoss top floor [tɒp 'flɔ:]
daher so [səʊ]
dahin there [ðeə]
damit so that [səʊ ðæt]
danach then [ðen]
Dank: Vielen Dank. Thank you very much. ['θæŋk ju:]
Danke (schön). Thank you. ['θæŋk ju:]; thanks [θæŋks] **Danke vielmals.** Thank you very much. [mʌtʃ]
danken: Nichts zu danken. You're welcome. ['welkʌm]
dann then [ðen]
das
1. *(Artikel)* the [ðə]
2. *(Relativpronomen)* that [ðæt]
das (dort) that [ðæt] **das (da)** that's (= that is)
dass that [ðæt]
Ich bin froh, dass I'm happy that ...
dasselbe the same [seɪm]
Datei file [faɪl]
Datum date [deɪt] **Geburtsdatum** date of birth ['bɜ:θdeɪ]
dauern take [teɪk]
dein/e your [jɔ:], [jə]
deine/deiner/deins yours [jɔ:z]
dekorieren decorate ['dekəreɪt]
denken think [θɪŋk] **daran denken (etwas zu tun)** remember (to do sth.) [rɪ'membə] **Ich denke, ...** I think ...
der
1. *(Artikel)* the [ðə]
2. *(Relativpronomen)* that [ðæt]
derselbe the same [seɪm]
Design design [dɪ'zaɪn]
Dessert dessert [dɪ'zɜ:t]
deutlich clear [klɪə] **deutlich sprechen** speak clearly [spi:k 'klɪəli]
Deutsch; deutsch German ['dʒɜ:mən]
Deutsche German ['dʒɜ:mən]
Deutschland Germany ['dʒɜ:məni]
Dezember December [dɪ'sembə]
die
1. *(Artikel)* the [ðə]
2. *(Relativpronomen)* that [ðæt]
die dort those [ðəʊz]
Diele hall [hɔ:l]
Dienstag Tuesday ['tju:zdeɪ]
diese (hier) these [ði:z]
diese(r, s) this [ðɪs]
dieselbe(n) the same [seɪm]
Ding thing [θɪŋ] **Dinge, die Menschen gebrauchen/benutzen können** things that people can use **Dinge zum Essen** things to eat
Donnerstag Thursday ['θɜ:zdeɪ]
Dorf village ['vɪlɪdʒ]
dort there [ðeə] **dort drüben** over there ['əʊvə]
dorthin there [ðeə]
dran: jd. ist dran it is sb.'s turn [tɜ:n] **Wann bin ich dran (etwas zu tun)?** When is (it) my turn (to do sth.)?
draußen; nach draußen outside [aʊt'saɪd]
Dreck-weg-Tag *(Aktionstag zum Müllsammeln)* clean-up day ['kli:n ʌp deɪ]
drehen turn [tɜ:n] **Dreh etwas auf den Kopf.** Turn it upside down. [ʌpsaɪd 'daʊn] **etwas umdrehen** turn sth. (over)
drei three [θri:]
dreißig thirty ['θɜ:ti]
dreizehn thirteen [θɜ:'ti:n]
drinnen; nach drinnen inside [ɪn'saɪd]
dritte(r, s) third (3rd) [θɜ:d]
Drohne drone [drəʊn]
du you [ju:] **du bist** you're (= you are) [jɔ:] **du bist beschäftigt** you're busy ['bɪzi]
dumm stupid ['stju:pɪd]
Dusche shower ['ʃaʊə]
duschen: (sich) duschen have a shower ['ʃaʊə]

E

Ehemann husband [ˈhʌzbənd]
Ei egg [eg]
Eidechse lizard [ˈlɪzəd]
eigene(r, s): mein/ein eigenes Zimmer my own room [əʊn]
Eimer *(Mülleimer)* bin [bɪn]
ein(e) *(Artikel)* a [ə]; *(vor Vokalen)* an [ən] **ein paar** some [sʌm], [səm] **ein wenig** some; a little [ˈlɪtl] **noch ein(e)** another [əˈnʌðə]
einfach just [dʒʌst]
Einführung introduction [ɪntrəˈdʌkʃn]
einige some [sʌm], [səm]
Einkäufe shopping [ˈʃɒpɪŋ] **Einkäufe erledigen** do the shopping, be at the shops [ʃɒp]
Einkaufen shopping [ˈʃɒpɪŋ]
einkaufen gehen do the shopping [ˈʃɒpɪŋ]; go shopping
Einkaufsliste shopping list [ˈʃɒpɪŋ lɪst]
Einkaufszentrum shopping centre [ˈʃɒpɪŋ sentə]
Einladung (zu, nach) invitation (to) [ˌɪnvɪˈteɪʃn]
Einleitung introduction [ɪntrəˈdʌkʃn]
einmal: noch einmal again [əˈgen]
eins one [wʌn]
einsammeln collect [kəˈlekt]
Eintrittskarte ticket [ˈtɪkɪt]
Eisenbahn train [treɪn]
Elefant elephant [ˈelɪfənt]
elektrisch, Elektro- electric [ɪˈlektrɪk]
elf eleven [ɪˈlevən]
Eltern parents *(pl)* [ˈpeərənts]
Ende end [end] **das obere Ende** top [tɒp] **am oberen Ende** at the top (of)
enden end [end]
England England [ˈɪŋglənd]
Englisch; englisch English [ˈɪŋglɪʃ] **auf Englisch** in English [ɪn]
Enkel grandson [ˈgrænsʌn]
Enkelin granddaughter [ˈgrændɔːtə]
Entschuldigung. Sorry / I'm sorry. [ˈsɒri] **Entschuldigung, ... / Entschuldigen Sie, ...** Excuse me, ... [ɪkˈskjuːz miː]
entspannen: sich entspannen relax [rɪˈlæks]
er he [hiː] **er ist** he's (= he is) **er ist nicht** he isn't (= is not)
Erbse pea [piː]
Erdbeere strawberry [ˈstrɔːbəri]
Erdboden ground [graʊnd]
Erdgeschoss ground floor [graʊnd ˈflɔː]
Erdkunde geography [dʒiˈɒgrəfi]
erforschen research [rɪˈsɜːtʃ]
Erholung rest [rest]
erinnern: sich erinnern an remember [rɪˈmembə] **sich daran erinnern, etwas getan zu haben** remember doing sth.
erklären: jm. etwas erklären explain sth. to sb. [ɪkˈspleɪn]
erst only [ˈəʊnli]
erstaunlich amazing [əˈmeɪzɪŋ]
erste(r, s) first [fɜːst] **als Erstes** first
erwärmen heat [hiːt]
erzählen tell [tel]
es it [ɪt] **es ist** *(bei Sachen und Tieren auch: er ist; sie ist)* it's (= it is) **es ist ... / es gibt ...** there's [ðeəz] **es sind ... / es gibt ...** there are [ˈðeər ɑː]
Essen cooking [ˈkʊkɪŋ]; food [fuːd]; meal [miːl]
essen eat [iːt] **Dinge zum Essen** things to eat
Esslöffel tablespoon [ˈteɪblspuːn]
Esszimmer dining room [ˈdaɪnɪŋ ruːm]
Etage floor [flɔː] **die oberste Etage** top floor [tɒp ˈflɔː]
Etui case [keɪs]
etwas some [sʌm], [səm]; something [ˈsʌmθɪŋ]
euer/eure your [jɔː], [jə]
eure/eurer/eures yours [jɔːz]
Euro euro, *pl* euros [ˈjʊərəʊ]

F

Fach subject [ˈsʌbdʒɪkt]
Fähigkeit skill [skɪl]
fahren go [gəʊ]; travel [ˈtrævl] **mit dem Fahrrad fahren** ride a bike [raɪd] **Rad fahren** cycle [ˈsaɪkl] **Skateboard fahren** skateboard [ˈskeɪtbɔːd]
Fahrkarte ticket [ˈtɪkɪt]
Fahrrad bike [baɪk]
Fahrt journey [ˈdʒɜːni]
Fakt fact [fækt]
falls if [ɪf]
falsch wrong [rɒŋ]
Familie family [ˈfæməli]
Familienname family name [ˈfæməli neɪm]
Fan fan [fæn]
Farbe colour [ˈkʌlə] **Welche Farbe hat ...?** What colour is ...?
Favorit/in favourite [ˈfeɪvərɪt]
Februar February [ˈfebruəri]
Federball badminton [ˈbædmɪntən]
Federmäppchen pencil case [ˈpensl keɪs]
Feedback *(Rückmeldung)* feedback *(no pl)* [ˈfiːdbæk]
Feier ceremony [ˈserəməni]
Feld field [fiːld]
Fenster window [ˈwɪndəʊ]
Ferien holidays *(pl)* [ˈhɒlədeɪz]
Fernsehen, Fernseher TV [ˌtiːˈviː]
fertig ready [ˈredi]
Fertigkeit skill [skɪl]
fies mean [miːn]
Film film [fɪlm] **die sechs besten Filme** the top six films [tɒp]
Filmstar star [stɑː]
finden find [faɪnd] **Ich finde, ...** I think ... [θɪŋk]
Finger finger [ˈfɪŋgə]
Fisch fish, *pl* fish [fɪʃ] **Fisch mit Pommes frites** fish and chips [fɪʃ ən ˈtʃɪps] **Imbissstube, die Fisch mit Pommes frites verkauft** fish and chip shop [ʃɒp]
Fleisch meat [miːt]
fliegen fly [flaɪ]
Flur hall [hɔːl]
Forschungen research [rɪˈsɜːtʃ]
fort away [əˈweɪ]
fortfahren continue [kənˈtɪnjuː] **etwas fortfahren** continue to do sth. [duː]
fortsetzen: (sich) fortsetzen continue [kənˈtɪnjuː]
Foto photo [ˈfəʊtəʊ] **auf dem Foto** in the photo **ein Foto machen** take a photo
Fotograf/in photographer [fəˈtɒgrəfə]
Frage question [kwestʃən] **Antwort auf die Frage** the answer to the question [ˈɑːnsə] **eine Frage stellen** ask a question **Habt ihr / Hast du (irgendwelche) Fragen?** Do you have any questions?
fragen ask [ɑːsk]
Frau woman, *pl* women [ˈwʊmən], [ˈwɪmɪn] **Frau Lee** *(Anrede für verheiratete Frauen)* Mrs Lee [ˈmɪsɪz] *(allgemeine Anrede für Frauen)* Ms Lee [mɪz]
frech rude [ruːd]
frei free [friː] **freie Zeit** free time [taɪm]
Freitag Friday [ˈfraɪdeɪ], [ˈfraɪdi]
Freizeit free time [ˈfriː taɪm]
Fremdenverkehrsbüro tourist information centre [tʊərɪst ɪnfəˈmeɪʃn sentə]
fressen eat [iːt]
freuen: Freut mich, dich/euch/ Sie kennenzulernen. Nice to meet you. [naɪs]
Freund/in friend [ˈfrend] **Das hier sind meine Freunde/Freundinnen.** These are my friends. [ðiːz] **ihre Freunde/Freundinnen** her friends [hɜː], [hə] **seine Freunde/ Freundinnen** his friends [hɪz]
freundlich friendly [ˈfrendli]; kind [kaɪnd]
frieren be cold [kəʊld]
frittieren fry [fraɪ] **frittiert** fried [fraɪd]
froh happy [ˈhæpi]
Frühling spring [sprɪŋ]
Frühstück breakfast [ˈbrekfəst]
fühlen: sich fühlen feel [fiːl]
Füller pen [pen]
für for [fɔː] **für 30 Sekunden** for 30 seconds
fünf five [faɪv]
fünfzehn fifteen [fɪfˈtiːn]
fünfzig fifty [ˈfɪfti]
Fußball football [ˈfʊtbɔːl]
Fußboden floor [flɔː]
Futter food [fuːd]

G

ganz quite [kwaɪt] **ganz (still)** perfectly (still) [ˈpɜːfɪktli]
Garage garage [ˈgærɑːʒ]
Garten garden [ˈgɑːdn]
Gast visitor [ˈvɪzɪtə]

Gebäude building [ˈbɪldɪŋ]
geben give [gɪv] **es gibt ...** there's (= there is) ... [ðeəz]; there are ... [ˈðeər ɑː] **es gibt keine ...** there aren't any ... [ˈeni] **Was gibt es zum Mittagessen?** What's for lunch? [lʌntʃ]
Geburtstag birthday [ˈbɜːθdeɪ] **an meinem Geburtstag** on my birthday **Geburtsdatum** date of birth [deɪt] **Herzlichen Glückwunsch zum Geburtstag!** Happy birthday! [ˈhæpi] **Ich habe im April Geburtstag.** My birthday is in April. **Wann hast du Geburtstag?** When's your birthday?
Gedankenkarte mind map [ˈmaɪnd mæp]
Gegend: ländliche Gegend country [ˈkʌntri]
geheim secret [ˈsiːkrət]
Geheimnis secret [ˈsiːkrət]
gehen go [gəʊ] **ins Bett gehen** go to bed [bed] **nach Hause gehen** go home [həʊm] **Wie geht's? / Wie geht es dir / euch / Ihnen?** How are you? [haʊ] **(zu Fuß) gehen** walk [wɔːk]
gelb yellow [ˈjeləʊ]
Geld money [ˈmʌni]
Gelee jelly [ˈdʒeli]
gemein mean [miːn]
Gemüse vegetables *(pl)* [ˈvedʒtəblz]
genießen enjoy [ɪnˈdʒɔɪ] **es genießen, etwas zu tun** enjoy doing sth.
Geografie geography [dʒiˈɒgrəfi]
Geräusch noise [nɔɪz]
Gericht *(Mahlzeit)* dish [dɪʃ] *das Gericht aus unter Rühren kurz angebratenen Zutaten, z. B. kleine Stücke Fleisch, Fisch und/oder Gemüse* stir-fry [ˈstɜː fraɪ]
gern: ich hätte gern ... I'd (= I would like ... [laɪk] **Ich hätte liebend gern ... / Ich möchte liebend gern...** I'd (= I would) love ... [lʌv] **Ich würde mich (liebend) gerne mit ... treffen.** I'd (= I would) like/love to meet ...
Geruch smell [smel]
Geschäft shop [ʃɒp]
geschehen: (jm.) geschehen happen (to sb.) [ˈhæpən] **Bitte, gern geschehen.** You're welcome. [ˈwelkʌm]
Geschenk present [ˈpreznt]
Geschichte *(Erzählung)* story [ˈstɔːri]; *(vergangene Zeiten)* history [ˈhɪstri] **so/solch eine Geschichte** a story like this [laɪk]
Gespräch talk [tɔːk]
Gestaltung design [dɪˈzaɪn]
Gestank smell [smel]
gesund healthy [ˈhelθi]
Gesundheit health [helθ]
Getränk drink [drɪŋk]
Gewerbegebiet estate [ɪˈsteɪt]
Gewinn prize [praɪz]
gewinnen win [wɪn]
Gewinner/in winner [ˈwɪnə] **als Gewinner/in** as the winner
Gewürz spice [spaɪs]
Gitarre guitar [gɪˈtɑː]
Glas glass [glɑːs]
Glasur icing [ˈaɪsɪŋ]
glauben think [θɪŋk] **Ich glaube, ...** I think ...
gleich the same [seɪm]
Glück: Glücks-, lucky [ˈlʌki] **Glück haben** be lucky
glücklich happy [ˈhæpi]; lucky [ˈlʌki]
Glückszahl lucky number [lʌki ˈnʌmbə]
Gold gold [gəʊld]
goldfarben gold [gəʊld]
graben dig [dɪg]
Gramm gram (g) [græm]
Grad degree [dɪˈgriː]
grau grey [greɪ]
Grillen barbecue [ˈbɑːbɪkjuː]
Grillfest barbecue [ˈbɑːbɪkjuː]
groß big [bɪg] **der/die/das größte, am größten** biggest
großartig amazing [əˈmeɪzɪŋ]; great [greɪt]
Großbritannien (Great) Britain [ˈbrɪtn]
Großeltern grandparents *(pl)* [ˈgrænpeərənts]
Großstadt city [ˈsɪti]
grün green [griːn] **grün/ umweltfreundlich werden** go green [gəʊ]
Gruppe group [gruːp]
gut good [gʊd]; *(Adv.)* well [wel] **Es geht mir gut.** I'm OK. [əʊˈkeɪ] **etwas gut können; gut in etwas sein** be good at sth. / at doing sth. **Guten Appetit! Enjoy!** [ɪnˈdʒɔɪ] **Gut gemacht.** Well done. [dʌn] **gut umgehen können mit ...** be good with ... **Mir geht es gut.** I'm fine. [faɪn] **so gut** so good [səʊ]

H

haben have [hæv] **er/sie/es hat** he/she/it has [hæz], [həz]
Hähnchen chicken [ˈtʃɪkɪn]
Halle hall [hɔːl]
Hallo. Hello. [həˈləʊ]; Hi. [haɪ] **Hallo allerseits!** Hello everybody! [ˈevribɒdi]
halten stop [stɒp]
Hamburger *(Frikadelle)* burger [ˈbɜːgə]
Hamster hamster [ˈhæmstə]
Hand hand [hænd] **Hand / Hände hochstrecken** put your hand / hands up [pʊt]
Handy phone [fəʊn]
hart hard [hɑːd]
Hass hate [heɪt]
hassen hate [heɪt]
Haupt- main [meɪn]
Hauptgericht main course [ˈkɔːs]; main dish [dɪʃ]
Haus house [haʊs] **nach Hause gehen** go home [həʊm] **im Haus** inside the house [ɪnˈsaɪd] **wieder zu Hause** back at home [bæk] **zu Hause** at home
Hausaufgabe(n) homework [ˈhəʊmwɜːk] **Hausaufgaben machen** do your homework **Was haben wir als Hausaufgabe(n) auf?** What's for homework? [wɒts fɔː]
Hausmüll rubbish [ˈrʌbɪʃ]
Haustier pet [pet]
heben lift [lɪft]
Heftseite page (p.) [peɪdʒ]
Heim home [həʊm]
heiß hot [hɒt] **heiße (Trink-) Schokolode** hot chocolate [ˈtʃɒklət]
heißen: Wie heißt du? What's your name? [wɒts jɔː ˈneɪm]
hektisch busy [ˈbɪzi]
helfen help [help]
herausfinden find out (about) [ˌfaɪnd ˈaʊt]
Herbst autumn [ˈɔːtəm]
Herr Lee Mr Lee [ˈmɪstə]
herstellen make [meɪk]
herunter down [daʊn]
hervorheben highlight [ˈhaɪlaɪt]
Herzog duke [djuːk]
heute today [təˈdeɪ]
hier here [hɪə] **Hier, bitte.** Here you are. **hier herüber; hier drüben** over here [ˈəʊvə]
hierher here [hɪə]
Highlight *(Höhepunkt)* highlight [ˈhaɪlaɪt]
Hilfe help [help]
hilfreich helpful [ˈhelpfl]; useful [ˈjuːsfl]
hilfsbereit helpful [ˈhelpfl]
hinauf up [ʌp]
hinsetzen: sich hinsetzen sit down [sɪt ˈdaʊn]
hinter behind [bɪˈhaɪnd]
hinunter down [daʊn]
hinzufügen add [æd]
Hitze heat [hiːt]
Hobby hobby [ˈhɒbi]
hoch up [ʌp]
Hockey hockey [ˈhɒki]
höflich polite [pəˈlaɪt]
holen: (sich etwas) holen get sth. [get]
Honig honey [ˈhʌni]
hören hear [hɪə]
Hotdog *(heißes Würstchen in einem Brötchen)* hot dog [ˈhɒt dɒg]
Huhn chicken [ˈtʃɪkɪn]
Hund dog [dɒg]
Hunger: Ich habe Hunger. I'm hungry. [ˈhʌŋgri]
hungrig hungry [ˈhʌŋgri]
Hut hat [hæt]

I

ich I [aɪ] **Ich bin** I'm (= I am) [æm] **Ich bin's.** It's me. **Ich nicht!** *(= Ich bin/war/habe/... es/das nicht!)* Not me! [nɒt]

Idee idea [aɪˈdɪə]
ihm, ihn him [hɪm]
Ihnen *(höfliche Anrede)* you [juː]
ihnen them [ðem], [ðəm]
ihr *(Plural von „du")* you [juː] **ihr seid** you're (= you are) [ɑː]
Ihr/e ... *(besitzanzeigend zur höflichen Anrede „Sie")* your [jɔː], [jə]
ihr/e ... *(vor Nomen; besitzanzeigend)*
1. (zu „she") her ... [hɜː, hə]
2. *(zu „it")* its ... [ɪts]
3. (zu „they") their ... [ðeə]
Ihre/Ihrer/Ihres yours [jɔːz]
immer always [ˈɔːlweɪz]
immer noch still [stɪl]
in at [æt], [ət]; in [ɪn] **in den Urlaub** on holiday [ˈhɒlədeɪ] **in der Nähe von** near [nɪə] **in der Schule** at school [skuːl] **in der Stadt** in town [taʊn]
Indien India [ˈɪndiə]
Informatik computing [kəmˈpjuːtɪŋ]
Information information [ɪnfəˈmeɪʃn]
informieren: sich informieren (über) find out (about) [ˌfaɪnd ˈaʊt]
innen; nach innen inside [ɪnˈsaɪd]
innerhalb (von) inside [ˌɪnˈsaɪd]
intelligent smart [smɑːt]
interessant interesting [ˈɪntrəstɪŋ]
Internet internet [ˈɪntənet]

J

Ja. Yes. [jes] **Na ja, ...** Well, ... [wel]
Jachthafen marina [məˈriːnə]
Jahr year [jɪə] **Ich bin elf Jahre alt.** I'm eleven years old. [jɪəz]
Jahreszeit season [ˈsiːzn]
Jahrgang year [jɪə]
Januar January [ˈdʒænjuəri]
jede(r, s) every [ˈevri] **jede(r, s) einzelne** each [iːtʃ]
jeder everybody [ˈevribɒdi]
jemand somebody [ˈsʌmbədi]; someone [ˈsʌmwʌn]
jene (dort) those [ðəʊz]
jetzt now [naʊ]
jeweils each [iːtʃ]
jonglieren juggle [ˈdʒʌgl]
Jugend youth [juːθ]
Jugendliche kid [kɪd]; youth [juːθ]
Jugendzentrum youth centre [ˈjuːθ sentə]
Juli July [dʒuˈlaɪ]
Junge boy [bɔɪ] **Ich bin kein Junge.** I'm not a boy. [nɒt]
Juni June [dʒuːn]

K

Kaffee coffee [ˈkɒfi]
Kakao cocoa [ˈkəʊkəʊ]; hot chocolate [hɒt ˈtʃɒklət]
kalt cold [kəʊld] **kalt werden** get cold [get]
Kälte cold [kəʊld]
Kaninchen rabbit [ˈræbɪt]
Kantine canteen [kænˈtiːn]
Kappe cap [kæp]
Karaoke karaoke [kæriˈəʊki]
Karotte carrot [ˈkærət]
Karte card [kɑːd]
Kartoffel potato, *pl* potatoes [pəˈteɪtəʊ]
Käse cheese [tʃiːz]
Kasten case [keɪs]
Katze cat [kæt]
kaufen buy [baɪ]
Kebab kebab [kɪˈbæb]
Kegeln bowling [ˈbəʊlɪŋ]
kein/e no [nəʊ] **es gibt keine ...** there aren't any [ˈeni]
kennen know [nəʊ]
kennenlernen meet [miːt] **Freut mich, dich/euch/Sie kennenzulernen.** Nice to meet you. [naɪs]
Kette chain [tʃeɪn]
Kilometer kilometre (km) [ˈkɪləmiːtə]
Kind kid [kɪd]
Kino cinema [ˈsɪnəmə] **im Kino** at the cinema
Kiosk kiosk [ˈkiːɒsk]
Kissen cushion [ˈkʊʃn]
klar clear [klɪə]
Klasse class [klɑːs]
Klassenarbeit test [test]
Klassenlehrer/in class teacher [ˈklɑːs tiːtʃə]
Klassenzimmer classroom [ˈklɑːsruːm]
Kleber glue [gluː]
Klebestift glue stick [ˈgluː stɪk]
Klebstoff glue [gluː]
Kleiderschrank wardrobe [ˈwɔːdrəʊb]
Kleidertausch(party) clothes swap [ˈkləʊðz swɒp]
Kleidung clothes *(pl)* [kləʊðz]
Kleidungsstücke clothes *(pl)* [kləʊðz]
klein little [ˈlɪtl]; short [ʃɔːt]; small [smɔːl] **kleine Mahlzeit** snack [snæk]
Klub club [klʌb]
klug clever [ˈklevə]
Koch, Köchin cook [kʊk]
Kochbuch recipe book [ˈresəpi]
kochen cook [kʊk]; *(in Wasser)* boil [bɔɪl]
Kochen cooking [ˈkʊkɪŋ]
Kochrezept recipe [ˈresəpi]
komisch weird [wɪəd]
Komma *(Dezimalzeichen)* point [pɔɪnt] **1,6 (eins Komma sechs)** 1.6 (one point six)
kommen come [kʌm] **Wo kommst du her?** Where are you from?
können can [kæn], [kən] **etwas gut können** be good at sth. / at doing sth. [æt], [ət] **gut umgehen können mit ...** be good at ... [gʊd] **Ich kann ... sehen.** I can see ... **Ich kann ... nicht sehen.** I can't (= cannot) see ... [kɑːnt]
Konsole console [kənˈsəʊl]
Kontrolle check [tʃek]
kontrollieren check [tʃek]
Kopf head [hed] **Dreh/Stell es auf den Kopf.** Turn it upside down. [ʌpsaɪd ˈdaʊn]
Kopfhörer headphones *(pl)* [ˈhedfəʊnz]
Korridor corridor [ˈkɒrɪdɔː]
Kosten cost [kɒst]
kosten cost [kɒst]
kostenlos free [friː]
köstlich delicious [dɪˈlɪʃəs]
krank ill [ɪl]
Krankenhaus hospital [ˈhɒspɪtl]
Krankheit illness [ˈɪlnəs]
Krawatte tie [taɪ]
Kreis circle [ˈsɜːkl]
Küche kitchen [ˈkɪtʃɪn]
Kuchen cake [keɪk]
Kugelschreiber pen [pen]
Kultur culture [ˈkʌltʃə]
kümmern: sich kümmern um look after [lʊk]
Kunst art [ɑːt] **darstellende Kunst** drama [ˈdrɑːmə]
Kunsthandwerk crafts *(pl)* [krɑːfts]
Kunststück trick [trɪk]
Kurs class [klɑːs]
kurz short [ʃɔːt]

L

Lächeln smile [smaɪl]
lächeln smile [smaɪl]
Laden shop [ʃɒp]
Lampe lamp [læmp]; light [laɪt]
Land country [ˈkʌntri] **auf dem Land** in the country
Landkarte map [mæp]
lang(e) long [lɒŋ] **30 Sekunden lang** for 30 seconds [fɔː] **(für) eine lange Zeit** (for) a long time [taɪm] **lange arbeiten, lange Arbeitstage haben** work long days [wɜːk]
langsam slow [sləʊ] **zu langsam** too slow [tuː]
langweilig boring [ˈbɔːrɪŋ]
Lärm noise [nɔɪz]
lassen: lass(t) uns let's (= let us) [lets]
Laufen *(Sport)* running [ˈrʌnɪŋ]
laut loud [laʊd] **lauter sprechen** speak more loudly [mɔː]
leben live [lɪv]
Lebensmittel food [fuːd]
lecker delicious [dɪˈlɪʃəs]
legen: (etwas wohin) legen put [pʊt]
lehren teach [tiːtʃ]
Lehrer/in teacher [ˈtiːtʃə]
leidtun: Er tut mir leid. I'm / I feel sorry for him. [ˈsɒri]
leise quiet [ˈkwaɪət]
lernen learn [lɜːn]
lesen read [riːd]
Leser/in reader [ˈriːdə]
Leute people *(pl)* [ˈpiːpl]; *(Anrede)* guys *(pl)* [gaɪz]
Licht light [laɪt]
Liebe love [lʌv]
Liebe/r ... Dear ... [dɪə]
lieben love [lʌv] **Ich hätte liebend gern ... / Ich möchte liebend gern ...** I'd (= I would) love ... **Ich würde mich liebend gerne mit ... treffen.** I'd (= I would) love to meet ... [miːt]

Liebling favourite [ˈfeɪvərɪt]; love [lʌv]
Lieblings- favourite [ˈfeɪvərɪt]
Lied song [sɒŋ]
liegen lie [laɪ]
lila purple [ˈpɜːpl]
Limonade lemonade [leməˈneɪd]
Lineal ruler [ˈruːlə]
Liste file [faɪl]; list [lɪst]
listen list [lɪst]
Löffel spoon [spuːn]
Lösung (eines Problems) solution (to a problem) [əˈluːʃn]
Löwe lion [ˈlaɪən]
lustig (be) funny [ˈfʌni] **Was ist lustig an ...?** What's funny about ...?

M

machen do [duː]; make [meɪk]
Mädchen girl [gɜːl]
magisch magical [ˈmædʒɪkl]
Mahlzeit meal [miːl] **kleine Mahlzeit** snack [snæk] **warme Mahlzeit** hot meal [hɒt]
Mai May [meɪ]
Mama mum [mʌm]
manchmal sometimes [ˈsʌmtaɪmz]
markieren highlight [ˈhaɪlaɪt]
Markt market [ˈmɑːkɪt]
März March [mɑːtʃ]
Mathe(matik) maths [mæθs]
Mauer wall [wɔːl]
Maus mouse, *pl* mice [maʊs], [maɪs]
Meer sea [siː] **am Meer** by the sea
Mehl flour [ˈflaʊə]
mehr more [mɔː] **mehr als 50** over 50 [ˈəʊvə]
Meile *(ca. 1,6 km)* mile [maɪl] **mit 30 Meilen pro Stunde** at 30 miles per hour [pər ˈaʊə] **Meilen pro Stunde** miles per hour (mph)
mein/e my [maɪ]
meinen *(sagen wollen)* mean [miːn]; *(denken, glauben)* think [θɪŋk] **Ich meine, ...** I think ...
meiste(r, s): die meisten Schulen most schools [məʊst]
meistens usually [ˈjuːʒuəli]
Melone melon [ˈmelən]
Mensa canteen [kænˈtiːn]
Menschen people *(pl)* [ˈpiːpl]
Messer knife, *pl* knives [naɪf], [naɪvz]
Meinung opinion [əˈpɪnjən] **meiner Meinung nach** in my opinion
Meter metre [ˈmiːtə]
mich me [miː]
Milch milk [mɪlk]
Millimeter millilitre (ml) [ˈmɪliliːtə]
Mindmap mind map [ˈmaɪnd mæp]
Mini- mini [ˈmɪni]
Minidrohne mini-drone [mɪnɪ ˈdrəʊn]
Minute minute [ˈmɪnɪt]
mir me [miː]
mischen mix [mɪks]
Mischung mixture [ˈmɪkstʃə]
mit with [wɪð]
mitbringen bring [brɪŋ]
mitkommen come [kʌm]
Mitleid: Mitleid haben mit jm. be/feel sorry for sb. [ˈsɒri]
mitnehmen take [teɪk]
Mittag / 12 Uhr mittags noon [nuːn]
Mittagessen lunch [lʌntʃ] **Was gibt es zum Mittagessen?** What's for lunch?
Mittagszeit lunchtime [ˈlʌntʃtaɪm] **zur Mittagszeit** at lunchtime
Mitte centre [ˈsentə]
Mitteilung message [ˈmesɪdʒ]
Mitternacht midnight [ˈmɪdnaɪt]
Mittwoch Wednesday [ˈwenzdeɪ], [ˈwenzdi]
mobben bully [ˈbʊli]
Mobber/in bully [ˈbʊli]
möchten: Ich möchte ... I'd (= I would) like ... [laɪk]
modern modern [ˈmɒdn]
mögen like [laɪk] **sehr mögen** love [lʌv]
Möhre carrot [ˈkærət]
Moment moment [ˈməʊmənt] **in diesem Moment** at the moment
Monat month [mʌnθ]
Montag Monday [ˈmʌndeɪ], [ˈmʌndi] **an jedem Montag** on Mondays
montags on Mondays [ˈmʌndeɪ], [ˈmʌndi]
Morgen morning [ˈmɔːnɪŋ] **am Morgen** in the morning
morgens in the morning [ˈmɔːnɪŋ] **4 Uhr (früh) morgens** 4 a.m. [eɪˈem]
Möwe seagull [ˈsiːgʌl]
müde tired [ˈtaɪəd]
Museum museum [mjuˈziːəm]
Musik music [ˈmjuːzɪk]
Musikgruppe band [bænd]
müssen must [mʌst] **etwas tun müssen** need to do sth. [niːd] **Ich muss Schluss machen.** *(am Telefon/ Briefschluss)* I must go.
Müll rubbish [ˈrʌbɪʃ] **Tüten/Säcke voller Müll** bags of rubbish [bægz]
Mülleimer bin [bɪn]
mutig brave [breɪv]
Mutti mum [mʌm]
Mütze cap [kæp]; hat [hæt]

N

na: Na ja, ... Well, ... [wel]
nach
1. *(örtlich)* to [tu], [tə] **nach draußen** outside [ˌaʊtˈsaɪd] **nach (dr)innen** inside [ˌɪnˈsaɪd]
2. *(zeitlich)* after [ˈɑːftə] **nach der Schule** after school

Nachbar/in neighbour [ˈneɪbə]
nachdem: nachdem du liest after you read [ˈɑːftə]
Nachmittag afternoon [ˌɑːftəˈnuːn] **am Nachmittag** in the afternoon
nachmittags in the afternoon [ɑːftəˈnuːn] **4 Uhr nachmittags** *(16 Uhr)* 4 p.m. [piːˈem]
Nachname family name [ˈfæməli neɪm]
Nachricht message [ˈmesɪdʒ]
Nachrichten news [njuːz]
nachschauen look sth. up [lʊk ˈʌp]
nachschlagen: etwas nachschlagen look sth. up [lʊk ˈʌp]
nächste(r, s) next [nekst] **Als nächstes ...** Next ...
Nachtisch dessert [dɪˈzɜːt] **zum/als Nachtisch** for dessert
nahe (bei) near [nɪə]
Nähe: in der Nähe von near [nɪə]
Name name [neɪm]
natürlich of course [əv ˈkɔːs]
Naturwissenschaft science [ˈsaɪəns]
neben next to [ˈnekst tə]
nehmen, in Anspruch nehmen take [teɪk]
nein no [nəʊ]
nennen call [kɔːl]
nett friendly [ˈfrendli]; kind [kaɪnd]; nice [naɪs]
neu new [njuː]
neun nine [naɪn]
neunzehn nineteen [naɪnˈtiːn]
neunzig ninety [ˈnaɪnti]
nicht not [nɒt]
nie never [ˈnevə]
niedlich cute [kjuːt]
niemals never [ˈnevə]
noch: (immer) noch still [stɪl] **noch drei** three more [mɔː] **noch ein/e** another [əˈnʌðə] **noch einmal** again [əˈgen]
Norden north [nɔːθ]
nördlich; Nord- north [nɔːθ]
Nordosten; nordöstlich north-east [nɔːθˈiːst]
Nordwesten; nordwestlich northwest [nɔːθˈwest]
normalerweise usually [ˈjuːʒuəli]
Notiz note [nəʊt]
Notizen: (sich) Notizen machen *(zur Vorbereitung)* make notes
November November [nəʊˈvembə]
Nudeln noodles *(pl)* [nuːdlz]
Null *(im gesprochenen Englisch)* oh [əʊ]
Nummer number [ˈnʌmbə]
nun now [naʊ] **Nun, ...** Well, ... [wel]
nur just [dʒʌst]; only [ˈəʊnli] **Es sind nur wir.** It's just us.
Nutzer/in user [ˈjuːzə]
nützlich helpful [ˈhelpfl]; useful [ˈjuːsfl]

O

ob if [ɪf]
oben at the top (of) [tɒp]
Obergeschoss top floor [tɒp ˈflɔː]
Obst fruit [fruːt]
oder or [ɔː]
öffnen open [ˈəʊpən]
oft often [ˈɒfn], [ˈɒftən]
Oktober October [ɒkˈtəʊbə]
Öl oil [ɔɪl]
Oma grandma [ˈgrænmɑː]
Onkel uncle [ˈʌŋkl]
online; Online- online [ˌɒnˈlaɪn]

Opa grandpa [ˈɡrænpɑː]
orange orange [ˈɒrɪndʒ]
Orange orange [ˈɒrɪndʒ]
ordentlich tidy [ˈtaɪdi]
Ordner file [faɪl]
Ort place [pleɪs]

P

paar: ein paar some [sʌm], [səm]
Päckchen packet [ˈpækɪt]
Packung packet [ˈpækɪt]
Palast palace [ˈpæləs]
Papa dad [dæd]
Papagei parrot [ˈpærət]
Papier paper [ˈpeɪpə] **Stück Papier** piece of paper [piːs]
Paprika pepper [ˈpepə]
Park park [pɑːk]
Parkour *(akrobatischer Hindernislauf in der Stadt)* parkour [pɑːˈkʊə]
Partner/in partner [ˈpɑːtnə]
Party party [ˈpɑːti]
passieren happen (to sb.) [ˈhæpən]
passiv passive [ˈpæsɪv]
Pasta *(italienische Bezeichnung für Teigwaren)* pasta [ˈpæstə]
Pause break [breɪk]; rest [rest] **Pause machen** take a rest [teɪk]
Penny *(kleinste britische Münze)* penny (p), *pl* pence [ˈpeni], [pens]
Peperoni pepper [ˈpepə]
perfekt perfect [ˈpɜːfɪkt]
Person person [ˈpɜːsn]
Pfeffer pepper [ˈpepə]
Pferd horse [hɔːs]
Pfund *(britische Währung)* pound (£) [paʊnd]
Picknick picnic [ˈpɪknɪk] **ein Picknich machen** have a picnic [hæv]
Pier pier [pɪə]
Plan plan [plæn]
planen plan [plæn] **planen, etwas zu tun** plan to do sth. [duː]
Platz place [pleɪs]
Playlist playlist [ˈpleɪlɪst]
Pommes frites chips *(pl)* [tʃɪps] **Fisch mit Pommes frites** fish and chips [fɪʃ ən ˈtʃɪps] **Imbissstube, die Fisch mit Pommes frites verkauft** fish and chip shop [ʃɒp]
Pool(billiard) pool [puːl]
Pop(musik) pop (music) [ˈpɒp mjuːzɪk]
Popcorn popcorn [ˈpɒpkɔːn]
Popstar star [stɑː]
Post *(Teil eines Blogs)* post [pəʊst]
posten *(im Internet veröffentlichen)* post [pəʊst]
Poster poster [ˈpəʊstə]
Präsentation presentation [preznˈteɪʃn]
präsentieren: (jm.) etwas präsentieren present sth. (to sb.) [prɪˈzent]
Preis *(Kosten)* cost [kɒst]; *(Gewinn)* prize [praɪz]
Preisverleihung prize ceremony [ˈpraɪz serəməni]
pro per [pɜː], [pə] **Meilen pro Stunde** miles per hour (mph) [maɪlz] **pro Stunde** per hour [ˈaʊə]
Problem problem [ˈprɒbləm]
Programmieren coding [ˈkəʊdɪŋ]
programmieren *(Computer)* code [kəʊd]
Projekt project [ˈprɒdʒekt]
prüfen check [tʃek]
Prüfung check [tʃek]
Puderzucker icing sugar [ˈaɪsɪŋ ʃʊɡə]
Pulver powder [ˈpaʊdə]
putzen clean [kliːn] **(sich) die/deine Zähne putzen** brush your teeth [brʌʃ]
Puzzle jigsaw (puzzle) [ˈdʒɪɡsɔː]

Q

Quiz quiz, *pl* quizzes [kwɪz], [ˈkwɪzɪz] **ein Quiz machen** do a quiz [duː]

R

Rad: Rad fahren cycle [ˈsaɪkl]
Radfahren cycling [ˈsaɪklɪŋ]
Radiergummi rubber [ˈrʌbə]
Ratespiel quiz, *pl* quizzes [kwɪz], [ˈkwɪzɪz] **Ratespiel machen** do a quiz [duː]
Rätsel puzzle [ˈpʌzl]
Raum room [ruːm]
Recherche(n) research [rɪˈsɜːtʃ]
recherchieren (do) research [rɪˈsɜːtʃ]
Recht: Recht haben be right [raɪt]
Rechtschreibung spelling [ˈspelɪŋ]
Rede talk [tɔːk]
reden (mit) talk (to) [tɔːk] **reden über** talk about [əˈbaʊt]
Redewendung phrase [freɪz]
Referat presentation [preznˈteɪʃn] **ein Referat halten** give a presentation [ɡɪv]
Regal shelf, *pl* shelves [ʃelf], [ʃelvz]
Regen rain [reɪn]
regen rain [reɪn]
regnerisch rainy [ˈreɪni]
Reihe line [laɪn]; turn [tɜːn] **Wann bin ich an der Reihe (etwas zu tun)?** When is (it) my turn (to do sth.)?
Reinigungskraft cleaner [ˈkliːnə]
Reis rice [raɪs]
Reise journey [ˈdʒɜːni]; tour [tʊə]
Reisen travel [ˈtrævl]
reisen travel [ˈtrævl]
Restaurant restaurant [ˈrestrɒnt]
Rezept recipe [ˈresəpi]
richtig correct [kəˈrekt]; right [raɪt]; true [truː]
riechen; schlecht riechen smell [smel]
Ring ring [rɪŋ]
Roboter robot [ˈrəʊbɒt]
Rock skirt [skɜːt]
Roller scooter [ˈskuːtə]
Rollstuhl wheelchair [ˈwiːltʃeə]
rosa pink [pɪŋk]
Rucksack rucksack [ˈrʌksæk]
Ruf call [kɔːl]
Ruhe rest [rest]
ruhen rest [rest]
ruhig quiet [ˈkwaɪət]
rühren stir [stɜː]
rumhängen, abhängen hang out [hæŋ ˈaʊt]
Rundfahrt (durch) tour (of) [tʊə]
Rundgang (durch) tour (of) [tʊə]

S

Saal hall [hɔːl]
Sache thing [θɪŋ]
Sack: Säcke voller Müll bags of rubbish [bæɡz]
sagen say [seɪ]; tell [tel]
Saison season [ˈsiːzn]
Salat *(als Gericht oder Beilage)* salad [ˈsæləd]
Salz salt [sɔːlt]
sammeln collect [kəˈlekt]
Samstag Saturday [ˈsætədeɪ], [ˈsætədi]
Sandwich sandwich [ˈsænwɪtʃ], [ˈsænwɪdʒ]
Sänger/in singer [ˈsɪŋə]
Satz sentence [ˈsentəns]
sauber clean [kliːn]
sauber machen clean (sth. up) [kliːn]
Saubermachen clean-up [ˈkliːn ʌp]
Säubern clean-up [ˈkliːn ʌp]
schade a shame [ʃeɪm]
Schande a shame [ʃeɪm]
schauen look [lʊk]
Schauspiel drama [ˈdrɑːmə]
schick smart [smɑːt]
schicken send [send]
Schinken ham [hæm]
Schirmmütze cap [kæp]
Schlaf sleep [sliːp]
schlafen be asleep [əˈsliːp]; sleep [sliːp]
Schlafzimmer bedroom [ˈbedruːm]
Schlange snake [sneɪk]
schlau clever [ˈklevə]
schlecht bad [bæd]
schließen close [kləʊz]
schließlich in the end [end]
schlimm bad [bæd]
Schlittschuhbahn ice rink [ˈaɪs rɪŋk]
Schloss palace [ˈpæləs]
Schluss end [end] **Ich muss Schluss machen.** *(am Telefon/ Briefschluss)* I must go. [mʌst ɡəʊ] **zum Schluss** in the end
schmücken decorate [ˈdekəreɪt]
schmutzig dirty [ˈdɜːti]
Schnee snow [snəʊ]
schneebedeckt snowy [ˈsnəʊi]
schneien snow [snəʊ]
Schokolade chocolate [ˈtʃɒklət] **heiße (Trink-)Schokolade** hot chocolate [hɒt]
schon already [ɔːlˈredi]
schön nice [naɪs]
schrecklich horrible [ˈhɒrəbl]
schreiben write [raɪt]
Schreibtisch desk [desk]
Schreibweise spelling [ˈspelɪŋ]
Schritt step [step]
Schuh shoe [ʃuː]

Schule school [sku:l] **Hast du nach der Schule Zeit?** Are you free after school? **in der Schule** at school **nach der Schule** after school **weiterführende Schule** secondary school ['sekəndri]
Schüler/in student ['stju:dnt]
Schulfach subject ['sʌbdʒɪkt]
Schulheft exercise book ['eksəsaɪz bʊk]
Schulmensa canteen [kæn'ti:n]
Schulsport PE (= physical education) [pi:'i:], [fɪzɪkl edʒu'keɪʃn]
Schuluniform school uniform [sku:l 'ju:nɪfɔ:m]
Schulversammlung assembly [ə'sembli]
schwarz black [blæk]
schwer difficult ['dɪfɪkəlt]; hard [hɑ:d]
Schwester sister ['sɪstə]
schwierig difficult ['dɪfɪkəlt]; hard [hɑ:d]
Schwierigkeiten trouble ['trʌbl] **in Schwierigkeiten sein** be in trouble
Schwimmen swimming ['swɪmɪŋ]
schwimmen swim [swɪm]
Schwimmer/in swimmer ['swɪmə]
sechs six [sɪks]
sechzehn sixteen [sɪks'ti:n]
sechzig sixty ['sɪksti]
See *(Meer)* sea [si:] **an der See** by the sea [baɪ]
Seebrücke pier [pɪə]
sehen look [lʊk]; see [si:]
sehr lot [lɒt]; much [mʌtʃ]; very ['veri]
sein be [bi:] **bist, sind, seid** are [ɑ:] *(er/sie/es)* **ist** is [ɪz]
sein/e its [ɪts]
Seite page (p.) [peɪdʒ]
Sekunde second ['sekənd] **für 30 Sekunden** for 30 seconds [fɔ:]
selbstverständlich of course [əv 'kɔ:s]
selten *(Adj.)* rare [reə]; *(Adv.)* rarely ['reəli]
seltsam funny ['fʌni]; weird [wɪəd]
senden send [send]
September September [sep'tembə]
Show show [ʃəʊ]
sicher sure [ʃʊə], [ʃɔ:]
Sie *(höfliche Anrede)* you [ju:] **Sie sind** you're (= you are)
sie
1. *(weibliche Person)* her [hɜ:], [hə]; she [ʃi:] **sie ist** she's (= she is)
2. *(bei Dingen und Tieren)* it [ɪt]
3. *(Plural)* them [ðem], [ðəm]; they [ðeɪ] **sie sind** they're (= they are) **sie sind nicht** they aren't

sieben seven ['sevn]
siebzehn seventeen [sevn'ti:n]
siebzig seventy ['sevnti]
sieden boil [bɔɪl]
Sieger/in winner ['wɪnə]
Silber silver ['sɪlvə]
silberfarben silver ['sɪlvə]
Singen singing ['sɪŋɪŋ]
singen sing [sɪŋ]
sitzen sit [sɪt]
Skateboard (fahren) skateboard ['skeɪtbɔ:d]
Skateboardfahren skateboarding ['skeɪtbɔ:dɪŋ]
Skatepark skatepark ['skeɪtpɑ:k]
Slideshow slide show ['slaɪd ʃəʊ]
SMS text [tekst] **jm. eine SMS schicken** text sb.
Snack snack [snæk]
so like this [laɪk]; so [səʊ]
sodass so that [səʊ ðæt]
Sofa sofa ['səʊfə]
Software software ['sɒftweə]
Sohn son [sʌn]
Sommer summer ['sʌmə]
Sonne sun [sʌn] **Die Sonne scheint.** It's sunny. ['sʌni]
sonnig sunny ['sʌni]
Sonntag Sunday ['sʌndeɪ], ['sʌndi]
sonst or [ɔ:]
Sorte (von) kind (of) [kaɪnd]
Soße sauce [sɔ:s]
Spaghetti spaghetti [spə'geti]
Spaß fun [fʌn] **Spaß haben** have fun [hæv] **Spaß machen** be fun [bi:]
spät: (zu) spät late [leɪt]
später later ['leɪtə]
Spaziergang walk [wɔ:k]
Speisekarte menu ['menju:]
Spiegel mirror ['mɪrə]
Spiel game [geɪm]; match [mætʃ]
spielen play [pleɪ]
Spieler/in player ['pleɪə]
Spielkarte playing card ['pleɪɪŋ kɑ:d]
Spielzeug toy [tɔɪ]
Spitze top [tɒp] **an der Spitze (von)** at the top (of) [æt], [ət]
Sport sport [spɔ:t]; *(Schulsport)* PE (= physical education) [pi: 'i:], [fɪzɪkl edʒu'keɪʃn]
Sportart sport [spɔ:t]
Sporthalle sports hall ['spɔ:ts hɔ:l]
Sprechen speaking ['spi:kɪŋ]
sprechen (mit) speak (to) [spi:k] **deutlich sprechen** speak clearly ['klɪəli] **lauter sprechen** speak more loudly [mɔ:] **sprechen über** speak about [ə'baʊt]
Stadion stadium ['steɪdiəm]
Stadt city ['sɪti]; town [taʊn]
Stadtplan map [mæp]
Stadtzentrum town centre [taʊn 'sentə]
Standuhr clock [klɒk]
Star star [stɑ:]
Starren / der starre Blick stare [steə] **anstarren** stare (at)
Start start [stɑ:t]
stecken: (etwas wohin) stecken put [pʊt]
stehen stand [stænd]
Stell dir / Stellt euch (mal) vor! Guess what! [ges]
stellen: (etwas wohin) stellen put [pʊt]; **sich (hin)stellen** stand [stænd]
Stiefbruder stepbrother ['stepbrʌðə]
Stiefmutter stepmother ['stepmʌðə]; stepmum ['stepmʌm]
Stiefschwester stepsister ['stepsɪstə]
Stiefsohn stepson ['stepsʌn]
Stieftochter stepdaughter ['stepdɔ:tə]
Stiefvater stepdad ['stepdæd]; stepfather ['stepfɑ:ðə]
Stift pen [pen]
still quiet ['kwaɪət]
Stock(werk) floor [flɔ:] **das oberste Stockwerk** top floor [tɒp 'flɔ:]
Strand beach [bi:tʃ] **an den/zum Strand** to the beach [tu], [tə]
Straße *(in Ortschaften)* street [stri:t]
Straßenmusik street music ['stri:t mju:zɪk]
Streetdance *(Tanzstil)* street dance ['stri:t dɑ:ns]
Stück piece [pi:s] **Stück Papier** piece of paper ['peɪpə]
Student/in student ['stju:dnt]
Stufe step [step]
Stuhl chair [tʃeə]
Stunde hour ['aʊə]; *(Unterrichtsstunde)* lesson ['lesn] **pro Stunde** per hour [pɜ:], [pə]
Stundenplan timetable ['taɪmteɪbl]
Superheld/in superhero, *pl* superheroes ['su:pəhɪərəʊ]
Supermarkt supermarket ['su:pəmɑ:kɪt]
Surfing surfing ['sɜ:fɪŋ]
süß cute [kju:t]; sweet [swi:t]
Süßigkeiten sweets *(pl)* [swi:ts]
Sweatshirt sweatshirt ['swetʃɜ:t]

T

Tag day [deɪ]
Tageszeitung newspaper ['nju:speɪpə]; paper ['peɪpə]
Tante aunt [ɑ:nt]
Tanz dance [dɑ:ns]
Tanzen dancing ['dɑ:nsɪŋ]
tanzen dance [dɑ:ns]
Tänzer/in dancer ['dɑ:nsə]
Tasche bag [bæg]
Tätigkeit activity [æk'tɪvəti]
Tausch swap [swɒp]
tauschen swap [swɒp]
Technik technology [tek'nɒlədʒi], *infml auch* tech
Technikunterricht technology [tek'nɒlədʒi], *infml auch* tech
Technologie technology [tek'nɒlədʒi], *infml auch* tech
Tee tea [ti:]
Teelöffel teaspoon ['ti:spu:n]
Teil part (of) [pɑ:t]; piece [pi:s]; share [ʃeə]
teilen share [ʃeə]
Telefon phone [fəʊn] **am Telefon** on the phone [ɒn] **per Telefon / telefonisch** by phone [baɪ]
Telefonanruf (phone) call ['fəʊn kɔ:l]
telefonieren phone [fəʊn]
Telefonnummer phone number ['fəʊn nʌmbə]

Tennis tennis [ˈtenɪs]
Terrarium terrarium [teˈreəriəm]
Test test [test]; quiz, *pl* quizzes [kwɪz], [ˈkwɪzɪz] **Test machen** do a quiz [duː]
testen test [test]
teuer expensive [ɪkˈspensɪv]
Text text [tekst]
Thema topic [ˈtɒpɪk]
Ticket ticket [ˈtɪkɪt]
Tier animal [ˈænɪml]; pet [pet]
Tierarzt/Tierärztin vet [vet]
Tipp tip [tɪp]
Tisch table [ˈteɪbl]
Tischtennis table tennis [ˈteɪbl tenɪs]
Titel title [ˈtaɪtl]
Tochter daughter [ˈdɔːtə]
Toilette toilet [ˈtɔɪlət]
toll great [greɪt]
Tomate tomato, *pl* tomatoes [təˈmɑːtəʊ]
Tomatensauce tomato sauce [təˈmɑːtəʊ sɔːs]
Torte cake [keɪk]
tot dead [ded]
Tour tour [tʊə]
Tourist/in tourist [ˈtʊərɪst]
Touristeninformation tourist information centre [tʊərɪst ɪnfəˈmeɪʃn sentə]
Tradition tradition [trəˈdɪʃn]
traditionell traditional [trəˈdɪʃənl]
tragen wear [weə]
Trainer/in trainer [ˈtreɪnə]
Training training [ˈtreɪnɪŋ]
Trampolin trampoline [ˈtræmpəliːn]
Trampolinspringen/-turnen trampolining [ˈtræmpəliːnɪŋ]
Traum dream [driːm]
träumen (von etwas) dream (of/about sth.) [driːm]
traurig sad [sæd]
treffen: (sich) treffen meet [miːt]
Tretroller scooter [ˈskuːtə]
Trick trick [trɪk]
Trifle *(englischer Nachtisch)* trifle [ˈtraɪfl]
trinken drink [drɪŋk]
trotzdem still [stɪl]
Tschüs. Bye. [baɪ]; See you. [siː]; Speak later. [spiːk ˈleɪtə]
T-Shirt T-shirt [ˈtiː ʃɜːt]
tun do [duː]; **(etwas wohin) tun** put [pʊt] **du hast (viel) zu tun** you're busy [ˈbɪzi] **es genießen, etwas zu tun** enjoy doing sth. [ɪnˈdʒɔɪ] **etwas weiterhin tun** continue to do sth. [kənˈtɪnjuː] **wie man etwas tut / tun kann / tun soll** how to do sth. [haʊ]
Tür door [dɔː]
Turmuhr clock [klɒk]
Tüte: Tüten voller Müll bags of rubbish [bægz]
Tyrann/in bully [ˈbʊli]
tyrannisieren bully [ˈbʊli]

U

üben practice [ˈpræktɪs]
über
1. *(räumlich)* over [ˈəʊvə]
2. *(mehr als)* **über 50** over 50
3. about [əˈbaʊt] **über mich/dich/...** about me/you/...

überall everywhere [ˈevriweə]
überprüfen check [tʃek]
Überprüfung check [tʃek]
überrascht surprised [səˈpraɪzd]
Überschrift heading [ˈhedɪŋ]; title [ˈtaɪtl]
Übung(en) exercise [ˈeksəsaɪz]; practice [ˈpræktɪs]
Übungsheft exercise book [ˈeksəsaɪz bʊk]
Uhr clock [klɒk]
Uhrzeit time [taɪm]
um: um 8 Uhr at 8 o'clock [æt], [ət]
umdrehen turn [tɜːn]
umrühren stir [stɜː]
umweltbewusst green [griːn]
umweltfreundlich werden go green [gəʊ griːn]
und and [ænd], [ənd] **Und du?** What about you? [əˈbaʊt]
unfreundlich unfriendly [ʌnˈfrendli]
unhöflich rude [ruːd]
Uniform uniform [ˈjuːnɪfɔːm]
unordentlich messy [ˈmesi]
Unordnung mess [mes]
Unrecht: Unrecht haben be wrong [rɒŋ]
uns us [ʌs], [əs]
unser/e our [ˈaʊə]
unter under [ˈʌndə]
Unterricht class [klɑːs] **im Unterricht** in class
unterrichten teach [tiːtʃ]
Unterrichtsstunde lesson [ˈlesn]
Unterschied difference [ˈdɪfrəns]
unterstreichen highlight [ˈhaɪlaɪt]
untersuchen research [rɪˈsɜːtʃ]
Urlaub holiday [ˈhɒlədeɪ] **im/in den Urlaub** on holiday

V

Vanille vanilla [vəˈnɪlə]
Vati dad [dæd]
vegan vegan [ˈviːgən]
Veganer/in vegan [ˈviːgən]
Vegetarier/in vegetarian [vedʒəˈteəriən], *infml auch* veggie [ˈvedʒi]
vegetarisch vegetarian [vedʒəˈteəriən], *infml auch* veggie [ˈvedʒi]
verboten no [nəʊ]
Verein club [klʌb]
Vereinigtes Königreich the United Kingdom (the UK) [junaɪtɪd ˈkɪŋdəm], [juː ˈkeɪ]
vergessen: nicht vergessen remember [rɪˈmembə]
verirren: Hast du dich verirrt? Are you lost? [lɒst]
Verkaufsbude kiosk [ˈkiːɒsk]
Verkaufsstand kiosk [ˈkiːɒsk]
verkehrt herum upside down [ʌpsaɪd ˈdaʊn]
verlaufen: Hast du dich verlaufen? Are you lost? [lɒst]
vermischen mix [mɪks]
vermisst missing [ˈmɪsɪŋ]
verschieden different [ˈdɪfrənt]
verschneit snowy [ˈsnəʊi]
verspäten: Ich habe mich verspätet. I'm late. [leɪt] **Verspäte dich nicht.** Don't be late.
verstehen understand [ʌndəˈstænd]
verwenden use [juːz]
Video; Video- video [ˈvɪdiəʊ]
viel/e a lot of [ə ˈlɒt əv], lots of [ˈlɒts əv]; many [ˈmæni]; much [mʌtʃ] **wie viele?** how many? [haʊ]
vielleicht maybe [ˈmeɪbi]
vier four [fɔː]
vierzehn fourteen [fɔːˈtiːn]
vierzig forty [ˈfɔːti]
violett purple [ˈpɜːpl]
Vokabelverzeichnis vocabulary [vəˈkæbjələri], *infml auch* vocab [ˈvəʊkæb]
Vokabular vocabulary [vəˈkæbjələri], *infml auch* vocab [ˈvəʊkæb]
völlig (still) perfectly (still) [ˈpɜːfɪktli]
von from [frɒm]; of [ɒv], [əv]
vor
1. *(zeitlich)* before [bɪˈfɔː] **vor der Schule / der Unterrichtsstunde** before school / the lesson [skuːl], [ˈlesn]
2. *(räumlich)* in front of [ɪn ˈfrʌnt əv]

vormittags: 9 Uhr vormittags 9 a.m. [eɪˈem]
Vorname first name [ˈfɜːst neɪm]
vorsichtig careful [ˈkeəfl]
vorstellen: (jm.) etwas vorstellen present sth. (to sb.) [prɪˈzent]
Vortrag talk [tɔːk]
Vorwahl(nummer) code [kəʊd]

W

Wackelpudding jelly [ˈdʒeli]
wählen choose [tʃuːz]
wahr true [truː]
Wand wall [wɔːl] **an der/die Wand** on the wall [ɒn]
Wandern hiking [ˈhaɪkɪŋ]; walking [ˈwɔːkɪŋ]
wandern hike [haɪk]; walk [wɔːk]
Wanduhr clock [klɒk]
wann when [wen]
warm hot [hɒt]; warm [wɔːm] **warm werden** get warm [get]
warum why [waɪ]
was what [wɒt] **Was ist mit dir?** What about you? [əˈbaʊt]
Wasser water [ˈwɔːtə]
Wassermelone water melon [ˈmelən]
Website website [ˈwebsaɪt]
Weg journey [ˈdʒɜːni]; way [weɪ]
weg away [əˈweɪ]

Weide field [fi:ld] **auf der Weide** in the field
Weihnachten Christmas ['krɪsməs]
Weihnachtstag Christmas Day [krɪsməs 'deɪ]
weil because [bɪ'kɒz]
Weise: Art und Weise way [weɪ]
auf diese Weise (in) this way
auf unterschiedliche Weise in different ways ['dɪfrənt]
weiß white [waɪt]
weitere more [mɔ:] **drei weitere** three more [θri:]
weitermachen continue [kən'tɪnju:]
(mit) etwas weitermachen continue to do sth. [du:]
welche(r, s) which? [wɪtʃ]; what [wɒt] **Welche AGs ...?** Which clubs ...? [klʌb]
Wendung phrase [freɪz]
wenn
1. *(falls)* if [ɪf] **Was wäre, wenn?** What if? [wɒt]
2. *(zeitlich)* when [wen]
wer who [hu:]
werden get [get]
Werken design and technology [dɪzaɪn ən tek'nɒlədʒi]
Werktag weekday ['wi:kdeɪ]
Werkunterricht design and technology [dɪzaɪn ən tek'nɒlədʒi]
Wetter weather ['weðə]
Wettkampf competition [kɒmpə'tɪʃn]; match [mætʃ]
wichtig important [ɪm'pɔ:tnt]
wichtigste(r, s) main [meɪn]
wie *(ähnlich/so wie)* like [laɪk]
wie how [haʊ] **Wie alt bist du?** How old are you? **Wie geht es dir/euch/Ihnen?** How are you? **Wie heißt du?** What's your name? [wɒts] **Wie ist ...? / Wie sieht ... aus?** What's ... like? **wie viele?** how many? **Wie wäre es mit einer/einem ... ?** What about a ... ?
Willkommen in/an ... Welcome to ... ['welkəm]
Wind wind [wɪnd]
windig windy ['wɪndi]
Windsurfen windsurfing [wɪndsɜ:fɪŋ]
winken: (jm. zu-)winken wave (to sb.) [weɪv]
Winken wave [weɪv]
Winter winter ['wɪntə]
wir we [wi:] **Es sind nur wir.** It's just us. [ʌs], [əs] **wir sind** we're (= we are) **wir sind nicht** we aren't
wirklich really ['ri:əli], ['rɪəli]
wissen know [nəʊ]
Witterung weather ['weðə]
witzig funny ['fʌni]
wo where [weə] **Wo kommst du her?** Where are you from?
Woche week [wi:k]
Wochenende weekend [wi:k'end] **am Wochenende** at the weekend
Wochentag weekday ['wi:kdeɪ]
wohnen live [lɪv]
Wohnsiedlung estate [ɪ'steɪt]
Wohnung flat [flæt]
Wohnzimmer living room ['lɪvɪŋ ru:m]
Wok *(chinesischer Kochtopf)* wok [wɒk]
Wolke cloud [klaʊd]
wolkig cloudy ['klaʊdi]
wollen want [wɒnt] **etwas tun wollen** want to do sth. [du:]
Wort word [wɜ:d]
Wörternetz mind map ['maɪnd mæp]
Wortschatz vocabulary [və'kæbjələri], *infml auch* vocab ['vəʊkæb]
Wurst, Würstchen sausage ['sɒsɪdʒ]
würzig spicy ['spaɪsi]
wütend angry ['æŋgri]

Y

Yoga yoga ['jəʊgə]

Z

Zahl number ['nʌmbə]
zahlen: (etwas be-)zahlen pay (for sth.) [peɪ]
Zahn tooth, *pl* teeth [tu:θ], [ti:θ]
Zauberei magic ['mædʒɪk]
Zauberkasten magic set ['mædʒɪk set]
zaubern do magic [du: 'mædʒɪk]
Zaubertrick magic trick ['mædʒɪk trɪk]
zehn ten [ten]
zeichnen draw [drɔ:]
Zeichnen drawing ['drɔ:ɪŋ]
zeigen show [ʃəʊ]
Zeile line [laɪn]
Zeit time [taɪm] **(für) eine lange Zeit** (for) a long time [lɒŋ]
Zeitung newspaper ['nju:speɪpə]; paper ['peɪpə]
Zentrum centre ['sentə]
zerbrechen: etwas zerbrechen break sth. [breɪk]
Zeremonie ceremony ['serəməni]
Zettel piece of paper [pi:s ɒv 'peɪpə]
ziemlich quite [kwaɪt]
Ziffer number ['nʌmbə]
Zimmer room [ru:m]
Zirkus circus ['sɜ:kəs]
Zitrone lemon ['lemən]
Zoo zoo [zu:]
zu; um zu to [tu], [tə]
Zucker sugar ['ʃʊgə]
Zuckerguss icing ['aɪsɪŋ]
zuerst (at) first [fɜ:st]
Zug train [treɪn]
Zuhause home [həʊm]
zuhören listen ['lɪsn]
zumachen close [kləʊz]
zurück back [bæk]
zurzeit at the moment ['məʊmənt]
zusammen together [tə'geðə]
zwanzig twenty ['twenti]
zwei two [tu:]
zweite(r, s) second (2nd) ['sekənd]
Zwiebel onion ['ʌnjən]
zwölf twelve [twelv]
zwölfte(r, s) twelfth (12th) [twelfθ]

English numbers

0 **oh, zero, nil** [əʊ, 'zɪərəʊ, nɪl]
1 **one** [wʌn]
2 **two** [tuː]
3 **three** [θriː]
4 **four** [fɔː]
5 **five** [faɪv]
6 **six** [sɪks]
7 **seven** ['sevn]
8 **eight** [eɪt]
9 **nine** [naɪn]
10 **ten** [ten]

11 **eleven** [ɪ'levn]
12 **twelve** [twelv]
13 **thirteen** [θɜː'tiːn]
14 **fourteen** [fɔː'tiːn]
15 **fifteen** [fɪf'tiːn]
16 **sixteen** [sɪks'tiːn]
17 **seventeen** [sevn'tiːn]
18 **eighteen** [eɪ'tiːn]
19 **nineteen** [naɪn'tiːn]
20 **twenty** ['twenti]

21 **twenty-one** [twenti'wʌn]
22 **twenty-two** [twenti'tuː]
23 **twenty-three** [twenti'θriː]
...

30 **thirty** ['θɜːti]
40 **forty** ['fɔːti]
50 **fifty** ['fɪfti]
60 **sixty** ['sɪksti]
70 **seventy** ['sevnti]
80 **eighty** ['eɪti]
90 **ninety** ['naɪnti]
100 **a / one hundred** [ə/wʌn 'hʌndrəd]

101 **one hundred and one**
102 **one hundred and two**
...

1st **first** [fɜːst]
2nd **second** ['sekənd]
3rd **third** [θɜːd]
4th **fourth** [fɔːθ]
5th **fifth** [fɪfθ]
6th **sixth** [sɪksθ]
7th **seventh** ['sevnθ]
8th **eighth** [eɪtθ]
9th **ninth** [naɪnθ]
10th **tenth** [tenθ]

11th **eleventh** [ɪ'levnθ]
12th **twelfth** [twelfθ]
13th **thirteenth** [θɜː'tiːnθ]
14th **fourteenth** [fɔː'tiːnθ]
15th **fifteenth** [fɪf'tiːnθ]
16th **sixteenth** [sɪks'tiːnθ]
17th **seventeenth** [sevn'tiːnθ]
18th **eighteenth** [eɪ'tiːnθ]
19th **nineteenth** [naɪn'tiːnθ]
20th **twentieth** ['twentiəθ]

21st **twenty-first** [twenti'fɜːst]
22nd **twenty-second** [twenti'sekənd]
23rd **twenty-third** [twenti'θɜːd]
...

30th **thirtieth** ['θɜːtiəθ]
40th **fortieth** ['fɔːtiəθ]
50th **fiftieth** ['fɪftiəθ]
60th **sixtieth** ['sɪkstiəθ]
70th **seventieth** ['sevntiəθ]
80th **eightieth** ['eɪtiəθ]
90th **ninetieth** ['naɪntiəθ]
100th **hundredth** ['hʌndrədθ]

101st **one hundred and first**
102nd **one hundred and second**
...

Titelbild
Cornelsen/Personen: Anja Poehlmann; Brighton Pier: mauritius images/Steve Vidler

Illustrationen
Cornelsen/**Harald Ardeias:** (S. 4 Rucksack; S. 17 A-H; S. 21 ob.; S. 26 1-11; S. 27 mi. re.; S. 29 1-6, ob.re.; S. 31 A-F; S. 32 1-4; S. 33 5-9; S. 35 1-6; S. 38 mi. li.; S. 39; S. 40 A-D; S. 44; S. 45 1-6; S. 48 1-6; S. 49; S. 52 ob.; S. 57; S. 60; S. 61 ob.; S. 62 mi. re.; S. 63 mi. li.; mi. re.; S. 64 1-3; S. 65 4-7; S. 66 ob. re.; ob. li.; S. 67 2; S. 70 ob. li.; mi. re.; S. 71 A-F; S. 72 A-E; S. 73 un. re.; S. 79; S: 80 1-6; S. 81; S. 82; S. 86; S. 88 mi. re.; S. 89 ob. re.; mi. re.; S. 95 1-4; S. 96; S. 98 1-3; S. 99 4-6; S. 101 A+B; S. 105 1-6; S. 110; S. 112 mi. re.; S. 122; S. 123 ob.re.; S. 124; S. 126 mi.; S.130; S. 131; S. 137 a-f; S. 138; S. 142 ob.re.; S. 145; S. 150 un.re.; S. 151 mi.re.; S.152 ob.re.; S. 153 mi.re.; S. 154; S. 155 ob.re.; S. 156 mi.; S. 160 mi.li.; S. 162-164; S. 168 un.re.; S. 169 ob.re.; S. 170 un.li.+un.re.; S. 171 1-6; S. 176 ob.re.; S. 179 1-6; S. 180 un.re.; S. 181 un.re.; S. 182 mi.re.+un.re.; S. 183; S. 184 ob.re.+mi.li.; S. 185 ob.li.+ob.re.; S. 186 ob.li.; S. 188 ob.re.+mi. li.; S. 189 mi.re.; S. 204 Personen; S. 219; S. 220 room). Cornelsen/**Josephine Bienert-Köhler:** (S. 34 ob. re.; S. 75 1-6; S. 107 un.; S. 108 mi. re.; mi. li.; un. re.; un. il.; S. 193 ob.; S. 196 (Alphabet); S. 198 un.re.; S. 199 mi.re. (M) siehe unten; S. 200 ob.re.+un.re.). Cornelsen/**Karen Donnelly:** (un. re. S. 141). Cornelsen/**Klara Luise Frankenberg:** (S. 192; S. 193 mi. re.; un. re.; S. 194; S. 195; S. 199 ob. re.). Cornelsen/**Irina Zinner:** (Umschlagseite vorne + hinten (U2 + U3) Möwe; S. 4-18; S. 23 Möwe; S. 27 Möwen; S. 29 Möwe; S. 30 Möwe; S. 34 Möwe; S. 36 Möwe; S. 37 Möwen; S. 46 Möwe; S. 47; S. 52 Möwe; S. 53 Möwe; S. 55 Möwe; S. 58 Möwe; S. 62 Möwen; S. 63 Möwe; S. 68 Möwen; S. 69 Möwen; S. 88 Möwe; S. 89 Möwe; S. 93 Möwe; S. 94 Möwe; S. 95 Möwe; S. 100 Möwe; S. 102 Möwe; S. 103 Möwe; S. 113 1-6; S. 114 Möwe; S. 116 Möwe; S. 119 Möwe; S. 120 Möwe; S. 121; S. 123 Möwe; S. 125 Möwe; S. 128 Möwen; S. 129 Möwe; S. 132 Möwe; S. 134 ob.re.; S. 135 Möwen; S. 147 Möwe; S. 151 Möwe; S. 152 Möwe; S. 153 Möwen; S. 157 Möwe; S. 160 Möwe; S. 166 Möwe; S. 167 Möwe; S. 178 Möwe; S. 179 Möwe; S. 180 Möwe; S. 190 Möwen;; 196 Möwe; S. 197 Möwe; 201-206 Möwen; 208-210 Möwen; 225-233; 234 ob.re.; 282-283 Illustrationen mit Möwen).

Abbildungen
Umschlagseite vorne (U2): s. S. 18; 20 und 32; **S. 1** s. S. 36; 37; 38; **S. 4-8** Personen: Cornelsen/Anja Poehlmann; **S. 12** un. li.: Shutterstock.com/Pete Pahham; un. mi.: Shutterstock.com/New Africa; un. re.: Shutterstock.com/Djomas; **S. 14** 1: stock.adobe.com/Arija; 2: Panther Media GmbH/Gertrud Böttcher; 3: Shutterstock.com/Dmitrijs Mihejevs; 4: Shutterstock.com/Iakov Filimonov; 5: Shutterstock.com/Eric Isselee; 6: Shutterstock.com/Alex Staroseltsev; 7: Shutterstock.com/bluedog studio; 8: Shutterstock.com/Susan Schmitz; **S. 15-16** Emoticons: Shutterstock.com/Yefym Turkin; **S. 18** 1+2: Cornelsen/Anja Poehlmann; **S. 19** 3+4: Cornelsen/Anja Poehlmann; **S. 20:** Cornelsen/Anja Poehlmann; **S. 21** un.: Shutterstock.com/Monkey Business Images; **S. 22** pencils ob.: Shutterstock.com/Pavlo S; mi.: Cornelsen/Anja Poehlmann; **S. 23** mi.: Cornelsen/Oliver Meibert; **S. 24** Personen: Cornelsen/Anja Poehlmann; 2: Shutterstock.com/zzveillust; 4: Shutterstock.com/JRP Studio; **S. 25** Noah: Cornelsen/Anja Poehlmann; Mum: Shutterstock.com/antoniodiaz; **S. 26** Tintenflecke: mauritius images/alamy stock photo/Daniil Chaban; **S. 28** 1-3, 5: Cornelsen/Anja Poehlmann; 4: mauritius images/alamy stock photo/James Winspear-VIEW; **S. 30** A-F: Cornelsen/Anja Poehlmann; **S. 31** ob: Cornelsen/Anja Poehlmann; **S. 35** ob. re. (Filmstill): Cornelsen/Grasshopper Films; **S. 37** ob. re.: Shutterstock.com/chuyuss; **S. 38** A: Shutterstock.com/file404; B: Shutterstock.com/Quinn Martin; C: Shutterstock.com/Monkey Business Images; D: Shutterstock.com/guig120; **S. 41** Personen: Cornelsen/Anja Poehlmann; A: mauritius images/alamy stock photo/Nigel Cattlin; **S. 42** Fotos li.: Cornelsen/Anja Poehlmann: un.li. Shutterstock.com/Kelley Varisco; ob. re.(logo): Varndean School Brighton; mi. re.: mauritius images/alamy stock photo/Nigel Cattlin; un. re.: stock.adobe.com/susan flashman; Handy-Icons: Shutterstock.com/MARII1; **S. 43** Krawatten: Varndean School Brighton; Jagvir: stock.adobe.com/AJay; Lara: stock.adobe.com/contrastwerkstatt; Holly: stock.adobe.com/denys_kuvaiev; Adam: stock.adobe.com/Stuart Monk; Nia: shutterstock.com/Monkey Business Images; **S. 46** Noah: Cornelsen/Anja Poehlmann; Mum: Shutterstock.com/antoniodiaz; **S. 48** un. re.: Cornelsen/Anja Poehlmann; **S. 50** Sunita&Lily: Cornelsen/Anja Poehlmann; A+B: Cornelsen/li. (Sunita): Cornelsen/Anja Poehlmann; Mitte: Shutterstock.com/insta_photos; re.: Shutterstock.com/V.S.Anandhakrishna; C: Shutterstock.com/Txema Gerardo; D: Shutterstock.com/JacquiMoore; E-J: Shutterstock.com/StockImageFactory.com; **S. 51:** Cornelsen/Anja Poehlmann; **S. 53** un.: Shutterstock.com/all_about_people; **S. 54** A: Shutterstock.com/Cristi Matei; B: Shutterstock.com/Volodymyr Plysiuk; C: mauritius images/alamy stock photo/Maximilian Weinzierl; D: Shutterstock.com/cbpix; un. re.: Shutterstock.com/Bilal Kocabas; **S. 55** ob. re.: Shutterstock.com/Ga_photo; mi. re.: Shutterstock.com/FlavoredPixels; un. re.: Shutterstock.com/D.Bond; un. li.: Cornelsen/Anja Poehlmann; **S. 56** A: mauritius images/alamy stock photo/Natalie Jezzard; B: mauritius images/Novarc Images; C: mauritius images/alamy stock photo/Edward Simons; D: mauritius images/alamy stock photo/Paul Thompson Images; **S. 58** A: Shutterstock.com/Africa Studio; B: Shutterstock.com/alexandre zveiger; C: Shutterstock.com/Breadmaker; D: Shutterstock.com/Gorodenkoff; E: Shutterstock.com/Asya Nurullina; un. re.: Cornelsen/Anja Poehlmann; **S. 59** block of flats: shutterstock/Mr Pics; terraced homes: Shutterstock.com/estherpoon; detached home: Shutterstock.com/Ewelina Wachala; semi-detached homes: Shutterstock.com/Ewelina W; A-C: Shutterstock.com/Peter Turner Photography; D: stock.adobe.com/annamiro;

S. 61 mi. li.: Cornelsen/Anja Poehlmann; **S. 63** un. re.: Shutterstock.com/Aluna1; **S. 64** Emoticon: Shutterstock.com/Yefym Turkin; **S. 65** Emoticon: Shutterstock.com/Yefym Turkin; **S. 67** ob. re.: Cornelsen/Grasshopper Films; 1: hug: Shutterstock.com/AKalenskyi; postbox: stock.adobe.com/lineartestpilot; alarm: stock.adobe.com/SKphotographer; 2 cards: Shutterstock.com/SpicyTruffel; string: Shutterstock.com/Igor Kovalchuk; **S. 70** Lily: Cornelsen/Anja Poehlmann; Mrs. Taylor: Shutterstock.com/Nenad Aksic; **S. 73** 1: Shutterstock.com/Johannes Menge; 2: Shutterstock.com/HRP_Photography; Emoticon: Shutterstock.com/Yefym Turkin; **S. 74** Emoticon: Shutterstock.com/Yefym Turkin; mi. li.: stock.adobe.com/Fly_dragonfly; mi.: Shutterstock.com/WPAINTER-Std; mi. re.: Shutterstock.com/Robles Designery; un. re.: Shutterstock.com/Moravian; **S. 75** doors: Shutterstock.com/Bibadash; paper family (Mitte): stock.adobe.com/Renat; **S. 76** ob. re.: stock.adobe.com/Pixel-Shot; mi.: stock.adobe.com/gertrudda; mi.re.: Shutterstock.com/Vladimir Kruglove; un. re.: stock.adobe.com/Brent Hofacker; mi. li.: Shutterstock.com/hvatkosha; **S. 77** ob. li.: ClipDealer GmbH/szefei; mi. re.: Shutterstock.com/Pichaya Pureesrisak; un. li.: stock.adobe.com/themorningglory; **S. 78** ob. re.: Shutterstock.com/Bilal Kocabas; fehlende Wörter: Cornelsen/SPI Technologies India; mi. re.: Shutterstock.com/T-Vision; **S. 84** A-B: Cornelsen/Anja Poehlmann; Herz: Shutterstock.com/pink.mousy; Emoticon: Shutterstock.com/Yefym Turkin; **S. 85** C-D: Anja Poehlmann; E Cornelsen/Mädchen: Anja Poehlmann, Hintergrund: mauritius images/alamy stock photo/PDMPhotos; **S. 87:** Cornelsen/Mädchen und Hintergrund: Shutterstock.com/Michaelpuche; Junge: Anja Poehlmann; **S. 88** un. re.: Shutterstock.com/Syda Productions; **S. 89** un. re.: Cornelsen/Anja Poehlmann; **S. 90** Shutterstock.com/oneinchpunch; **S. 91** Cornelsen/Anja Poehlmann; **S. 92** ob. re.: Shutterstock.com/Ten03; Mitte: Shutterstock.com/Brian McEntire; un. re.: Shutterstock.com/TunedIn by Westend61; **S. 93** Shutterstock.com/Daisy Daisy; **S. 94** Emoticons: Shutterstock.com/Yefym Turkin; un. re.: Cornelsen/Anja Poehlmann; **S. 97** ob. re.: stock.adobe.com/Chris Van Lennep/ChrisVanLennepPhoto; mi.: Shutterstock.com/Sanit Fuangnakhon; mi. li.: Shutterstock.com/guy42; un. re.: Varndean School Brighton; **S. 101** ob. re. (Filmstill): Cornelsen/Grasshopper Films; **S. 103** mi. li.: Shutterstock.com/Elena Yakusheva; **S. 104:** Daumen(rot+grün) Shutterstock.com/Azizunnahar Sadeq, un.re. (außer Daumen) Shutterstock.com/Panuwach, Daumen(gelb) Shutterstock.com/Cosmic_Design, un.li. Shutterstock.com/Asier Romero, Emoticons Shutterstock.com/Yefym Turkin; **S. 106** Emoticons: Shutterstock.com/Yefym Turkin; **S. 107** ob. re.: Shutterstock.com/Monkey Business Images; **S. 108** ob. re.: Shutterstock.com/Monkey Business Images; **S. 109** ob. li.: stock.adobe.com/Creatista/Scott Griessel; ob. re.: stock.adobe.com/adragan; mi. li.: stock.adobe.com/Prostock-studio; mi. re.: stock.adobe.com/Christin Lola; un. re.: mauritius images/alamy stock photo/Andrew Hasson; un. li.: mauritius images/alamy stock photo/Scott Ramsey; **S. 111** Shutterstock.com/LightField Studios; **S. 112** Würfel: Shutterstock.com/art-sonik; **S. 113** mi. li.: Shutterstock.com/pikepicture; **S. 115** Kalender: Shutterstock.com/Carboxylase; Uhr: Shutterstock.com/Cristian Barrios; Emoticon: Shutterstock.com/Yefym Turkin; Parkbank: Shutterstock.com/Pensiri; Daumen: Shutterstock.com/Lemberg Vector studio; Schirm: Shutterstock.com/Cosmic_Design; Hand: Shutterstock.com/Lemberg Vector studio **S. 116** 1: Shutterstock.com/Gill Copeland; 2 mauritius images/alamy stock photo/Simon Dack News; 3 mauritius images/alamy stock photo/Chris Harris; **S. 117** 4 Cornelsen/Grasshopper Films; 5 mauritius images/alamy stock photo/Peter Moulton; 6 mauritius images/alamy stock photo/Life's Like That; 7 Shutterstock.com/Marius_Comanescu; **S. 118** ob.li. Cornelsen/Mädchen: Anja Poehlmann, Fensterrahmen: Shutterstock.com/Dawid Galecki, Ausblick: mauritius images/alamy stock photo/Nigel Bowles; ob.re. stock.adobe.com/nikolae; **S. 119** ob.re. Cornelsen/Anja Poehlmann; **S. 120** ob.re. stock.adobe.com/Adobe Stock; **S. 125** mi.li. mauritius images/alamy stock photo/Steve Vidler; mi. mauritius images/alamy stock photo/Amongstthemiddlin, Shutterstock.com/CKP1001; mi.re. mauritius images/alamy stock photo/K I Photography; S. 126 ob.re. Cornelsen/Anja Poehlmann; **S. 127** mi.re. mauritius images/alamy stock photo/Eye Ubiquitous; **S. 129** A: stock.adobe.com/Iurii Sokolov; B: Shutterstock.com/smikeymikey1; C: Shutterstock.com/Pawel Piotr; un.re. Shutterstock.com/Gus Design; **S. 133** 1+2+ob.re.(Filmstills): Cornelsen/Grasshopper Films; un.re. stock.adobe.com/gibustudio; **S. 134** mi. Shutterstock.com/Nataliya Dorokhina; **S. 136** un.re. Shutterstock.com/cktravels.com; **S. 137** A: mauritius images/alamy stock photo/Simon Dack; B: mauritius images/alamy stock photo/Nick Hawkes; **S. 139** 1: mauritius images/alamy stock photo/Simon Dack; 2: Shutterstock.com/Gill Copeland; 3: Seil Shutterstock.com/DenisNata, Ball Shutterstock.com/VikiVector; Schirm: Shutterstock.com/Romolo Tavani; Tischtennis: Shutterstock.com/Rawpixel.com; Eishalle: Shutterstock.com/Rawpixel.com; Kino: Shutterstock.com/Mr.Music; Fragezeichen: Shutterstock.com/4zevar; **S. 140** mi.re. Cornelsen/Anja Poehlmann; **S. 141** ob.re. mauritius images/alamy stock photo/Simon Dack; ob.mi. Shutterstock.com/andromina; un.li. stock.adobe.com/carballo; **S. 142** mi.re. Shutterstock.com/shreya sharma01; **S. 143** mi.re. stock.adobe.com/Adobe Stock; **S. 144** mi.li. Cornelsen/Anja Poehlmann; **S. 146** un.mi.+un.re. Shutterstock.com/Laenz; **S. 148** mi. Shutterstock.com/CKP1001; mi.re. Cornelsen/Anja Poehlmann; **S. 149** mi. Shutterstock.com/vm2002; mi.re. Cornelsen/Anja Poehlmann; **S. 150** mi.re. Shutterstock.com/aurielaki; ob.re. Cornelsen/Anja Poehlmann; **S. 155** mi.re. Junge: Cornelsen/Anja Poehlmann; mi.re. Mann: Shutterstock.com/stockfour; **S. 156** A: stock.adobe.com/artinspiring; B: stock.adobe.com/blueringmedia; C+D+E+J+L+M: stock.adobe.com/artinspiring; F: Shutterstock.com/Heitor Barbosa; G: stock.adobe.com/macrovector; H: stock.adobe.com/blueringmedia; I: stock.adobe.com/Gstudio; K: stock.adobe.com/lightgirl; N: Shutterstock.com/kasimasimik; **S. 157** Sonnenbrille: stock.adobe.com/TheFarAwayKingdom; Handschuhe: Shutterstock.com/Salamahin; Würfel: Shutterstock.com/Joannii;

Schokolade: stock.adobe.com/Evgeniy; **S. 158** A-F (Filmstills): Digital Learning Associates Ltd**; S. 159** Scones: Shutterstock.com/Dave Denby Photography; Fish and Chips: Shutterstock.com/Yuriy Golub; Chicken Tikka Masala: Shutterstock.com/Brent Hofacker; **S. 160** Emoticons: Shutterstock.com/Yefym Turkin; mi.re. stock.adobe. com/uckyo; **S. 161** Scones: Shutterstock.com/Dave Denby Photography; Fish and Chips: Shutterstock.com/Yuriy Golub; Chicken Tikka Masala: Shutterstock.com/Brent Hofacker; **S. 165** ob.re. (Filmstill): Cornelsen/Grasshopper Films; mi. Shutterstock.com/Treter; **S. 167** un.re. photoCuisine_StockFood GmbH; **S. 168** 1: Shutterstock.com/ Nattika; 2: Shutterstock.com/Maks Narodenko; 3: Shutterstock.com/PixaHub; 4: Shutterstock. com/V.S.Anandhakrishna; 5: Shutterstock.com/DenisMArt; 6: Shutterstock.com/baibaz; 7: Shutterstock.com/ studiovin; 8: Shutterstock.com/Evgeny Karandaev; **S. 169** Arena: Shutterstock.com/ktsdesign; Torte: Shutterstock. com/Natalia Ruedisueli; **S. 170** mi.li. Shutterstock.com/nelea33; **S. 172** ob.li. stock.adobe.com/grinchh; mi. Shutterstock.com/Africa Studio; ob.re. Shutterstock.com/Monkey Business Images; un.li. Shutterstock.com/ Tetiana Peliustka; un.mi. Shutterstock.com/Yurlick; un.re. Shutterstock.com/jorgen mcleman; **S. 173** ob.li. stock. adobe.com/DenisProduction.com; ob.re. stock.adobe.com/Moving Moment; un. 1-6: Cornelsen/Inhouse/Katrin Heinecke; **S. 174** ob.re. Shutterstock.com/Nevada31; mi.re. Shutterstock.com/SasaStock; un.re. stock.adobe.com/ Grandbrothers; **S. 175** ob.re. stock.adobe.com/Jose Luis Stephens; **S. 176** mi.li. Shutterstock.com/Robert Kneschke; mi.re. Shutterstock.com/Olesia Bilkei; un.li. Shutterstock.com/Monkey Business Images; un.re. Shutterstock.com/ Gulcin Ragiboglu; **S. 182** mi.re. Shutterstock.com/Savinova Yana; **S. 184** un.re. Blatt: Imago Stock & People GmbH/ fStop Images/PatrickxStrattner fStopImages1130014; un.re. Hund: Shutterstock.com/Ian Dyball; **S. 191** mi. Cornelsen/SPI Technologies India; **S. 197** mi.re. Cornelsen/SPI Technologies India; **S. 198** ob.re.+mi.re. Cornelsen/ SPI Technologies India; **S. 199** mi. re.: Cornelsen/Josephine Bienert-Köhler/Möwe: mauritius images/Nature in Stock; Bildschirm: Shutterstock.com/Passatic; **S. 201** ob. re.: Shutterstock.com/chuyuss; **S. 203** Ponys: Shutter-stock.com/YIK2007; Kinder: Shutterstock.com/hisa_nishiya; Bücher: Shutterstock.com/robuart; Hose: Shutter-stock.com/DenisProduction.com; **S. 204** Fahrrad: Shutterstock.com/stockphoto-graf; Bleistift: Shutterstock.com/ OrangeVector; Taschen: Shutterstock.com/dashadima; **S. 211** Käse+Äpfel: Shutterstock.com/owatta; **S. 212** Affen: Shutterstock.com/Laurie Barr; **S. 213**
Affen: Shutterstock.com/Laurie Barr; **S. 214** Zahlen: Shutterstock.com/HitToon; Farben: Shutterstock.com/Africa Studio; **S. 215** bear: stock.adobe.com/perpis; butterfly: ClpDealer GmbH/yuliang11; crocodile: stock.adobe.com/ katrin sauerwein/EyeEm; dolphin: stock.adobe.com/slowmotiongli; duck: Shutterstock.com/Luka Hercigonja; llama: stock.adobe.com/Daniel Prudek; meerkat: Shutterstock.com/Mrinal Pal; owl: stock.adobe.com/martinku-bi; panda: stock.adobe.com/leungchopan; penguin: stock.adobe.com/www.dgwildlife.com/giedriius; rhino: Shutterstock.com/Stu Porter; spider: ClipDealer GmbH/Vitolef; tiger: stock.adobe.com/bertie10; whale: stock. adobe.com/© Seal Photographs/Craig Lambert Photo; **S. 216** baking: stock.adobe.com/DragonImages; climbing: stock.adobe.com/zhukovvvlad; coding: stock.adobe.com/DragonImages; cycling: Shutterstock.com/Jacek Chabraszewski; nail art: Shutterstock.com/Lapina; gaming: mauritius images/Masterfile RM; gymnastics: Shutterstock.com/Aleksey Mnogosmyslov; friends: stock.adobe.com/Jacob Lund; horse riding: Shutterstock.com/ Fotokostic; judo: Shutterstock.com/Kaderov Andrii; kayaking: Shutterstock.com/CroMary; playing the guitar: Shutterstock.com/granata68; reading: Shutterstock.com/LightField Studios; singing: Shutterstock.com/Daisy Daisy; **S. 217** media studies: Shutterstock.com/Draftfolio; RE: Shutterstock.com/Peter Hermes Furian; school club: Shutterstock.com/Lorelyn Medina; business and employement: Shutterstock.com/SpicyTruffel; tutor time: Shutterstock.com/ProStockStudio; study time: Shutterstock.com/Glinskaja Olga; social studies: Shutterstock. com/ekler; science: Shutterstock.com/mentalmind; ethics: Shutterstock.com/Tasha Vector; philosophy: Shutter-stock.com/Olga Krichevtseva; german: Shutterstock.com/buabunya; special needs support: Shutterstock.com/ Merfin; **S. 218** staff room: Shutterstock.com/DGLimages; games room: stock.adobe.com/Ivan; drama room: stock.adobe.com/Daisy Daisy; playground: stock.adobe.com/S ROBIN/OceanProd; office: Shutterstock.com/ goodluz; cinema: stock.adobe.com/Mr. Music/Mr.; library: Shutterstock.com/wavebreakmedia; music room: stock.adobe.com/Monkey Business; swimming pool: Panther Media GmbH/Benis Arapovic; science lab: Shutter-stock.com/Rawpixel.com; sports field: Shutterstock.com/Rawpixel.com; dance room: Shutterstock.com/vipman; running tracks: Shutterstock.com/Sergey Novikov; school garden: stock.adobe.com/Copyright: davidfuentespho-to.com/David Fuentes; auditorium: Cornelsen/Anja Poehlmann; **S. 220** mouse: Shutterstock.com/Ziga Camernik; rat: Shutterstock.com/George Dolgikh; kitten: Shutterstock.com/Nils Jacobi; ferret: Shutterstock.com/Couper-field; budgie: stock.adobe.com/dieter76; chicken: innerShutterstock.com/Moonborne; guinea pig: Shutterstock. com/Tettania; lizard: Shutterstock.com/Michaelpuche; puppy: stock.adobe.com/arezin.com/Aleksey; bearded dragon: Shutterstock.com/Shinedawn; **S. 221** Uhr: Shutterstock.com/Skocko; Hintergrund: Shutterstock.com/ Apple_Mac; **S. 222** bus stop: stock.adobe.com/Kay Ransom; church: Shutterstock.com/Jono Photography; car park: stock.adobe.com/© Sai Chan/Zoe; ice rink: Shutterstock.com/begalphoto; supermarket: Shutterstock.com/ Lizardflms; town hall: stock.adobe.com/Estelle Bowden/Starsphinx; bakery: Shutterstock.com/milanzeremski; mosque: Shutterstock.com/Victor Moussa; temple: mauritius images/alamy stock photo/Edward Herdwick; theme park: Shutterstock.com/SIHASAKPRACHUM; synagogue: mauritius images/alamy stock photo/Peter Llewellyn; bike rack: Shutterstock.com/Aliaksander Karankevich; **S. 223** lettuce: Shutterstock.com/PotaeRin;

cucumber: Shutterstock.com/Maks Narodenko; banana: Shutterstock.com/bergamont; butter: Shutterstock.com/bigacis; cupcake: Shutterstock.com/Wealthylady; tomato: Shutterstock.com/Tim UR; ice cream: Shutterstock.com/stockcreations; potato: Shutterstock.com/Anna Kucherova; peas: Shutterstock.com/WIPHARAT CHAINUPAPHA; cream: Shutterstock.com/grey_and; apple: Shutterstock.com/Roman Samokhin; cabbage: Shutterstock.com/JIANG HONGYAN; eggs: Shutterstock.com/Nattika; sausage: Shutterstock.com/Einsteinstudio; melon: Shutterstock.com/Boonchuay1970; cheese: Shutterstock.com/Tanya Sid; orange: Shutterstock.com/Valentyn Volkov; popcorn: Shutterstock.com/Jiri Hera; beef: Shutterstock.com/MaraZe; carrot: Shutterstock.com/Valentina Razumova; onion: Shutterstock.com/Yeti studio; pepper: Shutterstock.com/DronG; lemon: Shutterstock.com/Maks Narodenko; strawberry: Shutterstock.com/Tim UR; mango: Shutterstock.com/Valentyn Volkov; chicken: Shutterstock.com/JIANG HONGYAN; jelly: Shutterstock.com/cigdem; donuts: Shutterstock.com/Sergey Skleznev; muffin: Shutterstock.com/Binh Thanh Bui; broccoli: Shutterstock.com/smspsy; pork: Shutterstock.com/GSDesign; lamb: Shutterstock.com/TheBusinessMan; milk: Shutterstock.com/New Africa; **S. 224** mix: stock.adobe.com/Africa Studio; boil: Shutterstock.com/Gorlov-KV; pour: Shutterstock.com/Deer worawut; pot: Shutterstock.com/Lipskiy; roll out: Shutterstock.com/Igor Zvencom; cut: Shutterstock.com/husjur02; whisk: Shutterstock.com/nevodka; oven: Shutterstock.com/taist2; frying pan: Shutterstock.com/grey_and; add: Shutterstock.com/Nitr; spoon: Shutterstock.com/Sanit Fuangnakhon; fry: Shutterstock.com/fotopai; baking tray: Shutterstock.com/goh seok thuan; stir: Shutterstock.com/Nebojsa Markovic; bake: Shutterstock.com/IC Production; **S. 234** mi. re.: Shutterstock.com/s_oleg; **S. 235** un. re.: Shutterstock.com/wee dezign; **S. 236** Tim: Shutterstock.com/karelnoppe; Mrs Palmer: Shutterstock.com/Andresr; Elefant+Schlange: Shutterstock.com/Teguh Mujiono;: Fische: Shutterstock.com/Tatyana Vyc;; **S. 237** guitar/bike: Shutterstock.com/OneLineStock.com; chain: Shutterstock.com/Le_Mon; **S. 238** ob. re.: Shutterstock.com/Paket; mi. re.: Shutterstock.com/MicroOne; **S. 239** ob. re.: Shutterstock.com/Adam Gregor; mi. re.: Shutterstock.com/bsd; un. re.: Shutterstock.com/Lapina; **S. 240** alle außer ob.re.+un.re.: Shutterstock.com/jottaonni, ob.re.: Shutterstock.com/miniwide; un. re.: Shutterstock.com/Paleka; **S. 241** Shutterstock.com/jakkapan; **S. 242** ob. re.: Shutterstock.com/EugeneEdge; un. re.: Shutterstock.com/haru; **S. 243** mi. re.: Shutterstock.com/Rawpixel.com; un. re.: Shutterstock.com/Blue.Poppy.Art; **S. 244** maths exercice: Shutterstock.com/Lyudmyla Ishchenko; science lesson: Shutterstock.com/Monkey Business Images; **S. 245** Shutterstock.com/Anna Tyukhmeneva; **S. 246** Opa: Shutterstock.com/Oguz Aral; Schuhe: Shutterstock.com/pikepicture; geben: Shutterstock.com/pjcross; Hunde: Shutterstock.com/Pixel-Shot;; **S. 247** Junge: Shutterstock.com/Standret; Schnecke: Shutterstock.com/Outsider321; **S. 249** Shutterstock.com/4 PM production; **S. 250** Kreis: Shutterstock.com/ChristianChan; Kanninchen: Shutterstock.com/Pavel L Photo and Video; Tierarzt: Shutterstock.com/Noi1990; **S. 251** Haus: Shutterstock.com/Studio Harmony; **S. 252** Eidechse: Shutterstock.com/krolya25; Garten: Shutterstock.com/brgfx; Balkon: Shutterstock.com/dedi57; **S. 253** sonnig: Shutterstock.com/Helga Khorimarko; Haus: Shutterstock.com/PJ photography; Bett: Shutterstock.com/Pavel Adashkevich**;** **S. 254** Roboter: Shutterstock.com/Lecter; Stühle: Shutterstock.com/photka; Küken: Shutterstock.com/Inspiring; Tisch: Shutterstock.com/donatas1205; desk: Panther Media GmbH/Valentyna Chukhlyebova/Vac; **S. 255** Kopfhörer: Shutterstock.com/dantess; **S. 257** Uhr: Shutterstock.com/Gemenacom; **S. 258** Rollstuhl: Shutterstock.com/Nerthuz; Dusche: Shutterstock.com/Sashkin; Reihe: Shutterstock.com/Alastair Wallace; **S. 259** Rad fahren: Shutterstock.com/Ljupco Smokovski; **S. 262** Karte: Shutterstock.com/Michael D Brown**;** **S. 263** Jachthafen: Shutterstock.com/AlyoshinE; **S. 264** Müll: Shutterstock.com/siam.pukkato; **S. 265** ob.mi. Shutterstock.com/Zhiganova Dariaa; ob.re. Shutterstock.com/ONYXprj; **S. 266** Schlange: Shutterstock.com/NextMarsMedia; Regen: Shutterstock.com/Helga Khorimarko; **S. 267** ob.re. Shutterstock.com/Helga Khorimarko; **S. 268** Insel: Shutterstock.com/Peera_stockfoto; **S. 269** Hund: Shutterstock.com/Tienuskin; **S. 270** Maus: Shutterstock.com/Utekhina Anna; **S. 271** Sahne: Shutterstock.com/Tanya Sid; **S. 272** Erbsen: Shutterstock.com/valzan; Tomate: Shutterstock.com/Indigo Photo Club; Brot; Shutterstock.com/Dan Kosmayer; dunkles Brot: Shutterstock.com/de2marco; Gemüse: Shutterstock.com/Anna Shepulova; **S. 273** Wurst: Shutterstock.com/stockcreations; jonglieren: Shutterstock.com/dompr; **S. 274** Geschenk: Shutterstock.com/Rustle; Salat: Shutterstock.com/kochababamba; Packung: Shutterstock.com/JocularityArt; Zitrone: Shutterstock.com/Roman Samokhin; **S. 275** Waage: Shutterstock.com/Ekaterina_Minaeva; Mann: Cornelsen/Michael Fleischmann; Ei: Shutterstock.com/paulista; Teelöffel: Shutterstock.com/PolinaPersikova; **S. 276** Marmelade: Shutterstock.com/Gordon Bell; **S. 277** Zwiebel: Shutterstock.com/Lubava; Kaffee/Tee: Shutterstock.com/igra.design; Teig: Shutterstock.com/Evgeniya Sheydt; **S, 278** Kartoffel: Shutterstock.com/Nataly Studio; Knoblauch: Shutterstock.com/Tim UR; **S. 279** bunt: Shutterstock.com/mffoto**;** **S. 280** Tagebuch: Shutterstock.com/Yurchyks; **S. 281** stark: Shutterstock.com/kristinblack; **S. 307** Zahlen: Shutterstock.com/HitToon; **Umschlagseite hinten (U3):** Karte: stock.adobe.com/lesniewski

Typical tasks	Häufige Arbeitsanweisungen
Act out the conversation / song / story.	Führt das Gespräch / das Lied / die Geschichte vor.
Answer the questions / partner B's questions.	Beantworte die Fragen / Partner Bs Fragen.
Before you read / listen / watch	Bevor du liest / (zu-)hörst / anschaust ...
Check the spelling / your answers / ideas (with a partner).	Überprüfe deine Rechtschreibung / Antworten / Ideen (mit einem/r Partner/in).
Choose the correct answer / word.	Wähle die richtige Antwort / das richtige Wort aus.
Compare the pictures / your answers / ... with a partner.	Vergleiche die Bilder / deine Antworten / ... mit einem/r Partner/in.
Complete the table / list / sentences / ...	Vervollständige die Tabelle / Liste / Sätze / ...
Copy the table / list / notes.	Schreibe die Tabelle / die Liste / Notizen ab.
Correct the false / wrong sentences / answers.	Berichtige die falschen Sätze / Antworten.
Describe the picture / your room / ...	Beschreibe das Bild / dein Zimmer / ...
Draw pictures.	Male / Zeichne Bilder.
Find the answers / the correct / right / wrong words.	Finde die Antworten / die richtigen / falschen Wörter.
Finish the sentences.	Vervollständige die Sätze.
Give feedback.	Gib Feedback / eine Einschätzung.
Interview your partner.	Stelle deinem/r Partner/in Fragen.
Look at the board / at page ...	Schau an die Tafel / auf Seite ...
Look at the photos / pictures /map / title.	Sieh dir die Fotos / Bilder / Karte / die Überschrift an.
Listen and check / practise / repeat / guess.	Höre zu und überprüfe / übe / wiederhole / rate.
Listen again.	Hör nochmals zu.
Listen to the story / conversation / dialogue.	Hör dir die Geschichte / das Gespräch / den Dialog an.
Make groups (of six / ... students).	Bildet Gruppen (zu je sechs / ... Schüler/innen).
Make sentences / notes / lists / a mind map.	Fertige Sätze / Notizen / Listen / eine Mindmap an.
Match the sentence parts / what the friends say.	Verbinde die Satzhälften / das, was die Freunde sagen.
Practise with a partner.	Übe mit einem/r Partner/in.
Put it in you DOSSIER.	Hefte es in deinem DOSSIER ab.
Put the sentences / dialogue in the correct order.	Bringe die Sätze / den Dialog in die richtige Reihenfolge.
Read about ...	Lies über ...
Read the conversation / text / story / article.	Lies den Dialog / Text / die Geschichte / den Artikel.
Stand up when you hear ...	Wenn du ... hörst, steh auf.
Swap (cards) with a partner.	Tausche (die Karten) mit einem/r Partner/in.
Take turns.	Wechselt euch ab.
Talk about ...	Sprich / Sprecht über ...
Talk to a partner.	Sprich mit einem/r Partner/in.
Tell your partner / the class.	Erzähl / Sag es deinem/r Partner/in / der Klasse.
True or false? / True, false or not in the text?	Wahr oder falsch? / Wahr, falsch oder nicht im Text?
Say the four / ... sentences.	Sage die vier / ... Sätze.
Use your notes / the words in a.	Benutze deine Notizen / die Wörter aus Aufgabe a.
Walk around.	Gehe (im Raum) herum.
Watch part / scene 1 / all the film.	Sieh dir Teil / Szene 1 / den ganzen Film an.
Watch again.	Sieh es / sie / ihn nochmals an.
Work alone / with a partner / in groups.	Arbeite allein / mit einem/r Partner/in / in Gruppen.
Write the correct answers / sentences / questions / words.	Schreibe die richtigen Antworten / Sätze / Fragen / Wörter (auf).
Write (more) about ...	Schreibe (mehr) über ...